A New Direction for China's Defense Industry

Evan S. Medeiros

Roger Cliff

Keith Crane

James C. Mulvenon

D1569971

Prepared for the United States Air Force
Approved for public release; distribution unlimited

RAND PROJECT AIR FORCE

The research described in this report was sponsored by the United States Air Force under Contract F49642-01-C-0003. Further information may be obtained from the Strategic Planning Division, Directorate of Plans, Hq USAF.

Library of Congress Cataloging-in-Publication Data

A new direction for China's defense industry / Evan S. Medeiros ... [et al.].
    p. cm.
    "MG-334."
    "RAND Project Air Force."
    Includes bibliographical references.
    ISBN 0-8330-3794-3 (pbk. : alk. paper)
    1. Military readiness—China. 2. Military research—China. 3. Defense industries—China. I. Medeiros, Evan S. II. Project Air Force (U.S.).

UA835.N46 2005
338.4'7355'00951—dc22

2005011668

The RAND Corporation is a nonprofit research organization providing objective analysis and effective solutions that address the challenges facing the public and private sectors around the world. RAND's publications do not necessarily reflect the opinions of its research clients and sponsors.

RAND˚ is a registered trademark.

Cover design by Stephen Bloodsworth.
Photo by Zhu Jianguo/Imaginechina. Aircraft: FC-1 Xiaolong (initially known as Super-7).

Published 2005 by the RAND Corporation
1776 Main Street, P.O. Box 2138, Santa Monica, CA 90407-2138
1200 South Hayes Street, Arlington, VA 22202-5050
201 North Craig Street, Suite 202, Pittsburgh, PA 15213-1516
RAND URL: http://www.rand.org/
To order RAND documents or to obtain additional information, contact
Distribution Services: Telephone: (310) 451-7002;
Fax: (310) 451-6915; Email: order@rand.org

Preface

Since the early 1980s, a prominent and consistent conclusion of Western research on China's defense-industrial complex has been that China's defense R&D and production capabilities are rife with weaknesses and limitations.[1] In this study, we call into question this conventional wisdom. Our research found that certain Chinese defense enterprises are designing and producing a wide range of increasingly advanced weapons that, in the short term, are relevant to the Chinese military's ability to prosecute a possible conflict over Taiwan but also to China's long-term military presence in Asia.[2] This study puts forward an alternative approach to assessing China's defense-industrial capabilities: From the vantage point of 2005, it is time to shift the focus of research to the gradual improvements in and the future potential of China's defense-industrial complex.

This report is intended to help the U.S. Air Force assess the ability of Chinese defense industries to design and produce more-capable weaponry in the coming decades. The study assesses institutional changes in the operations of defense-industry enterprises in

---

[1] Bates Gill, "Chinese Military-Technical Development: The Record for Western Assessments, 1979–1999," in James C. Mulvenon and Andrew N. D. Yang, eds., *Seeking Truth from Facts: A Retrospective on Chinese Military Studies in the Post-Mao Era*, Santa Monica, Calif.: RAND Corporation, CF-160-CAPP, 2001.

[2] To be sure, these new weapon systems are in most cases 1970s- and 1980s-era platforms, which possess updated technologies (e.g., sensors and weapon suites) and are often derived from foreign-influenced designs.

four sectors: missiles, shipbuilding, military aviation, and information technology/defense electronics.

The study, sponsored by the U.S. Air Force's Director for Operational Plans and Joint Matters (AF/XOX) and the Combatant Commander of the Pacific Air Force (PACAF/CC), is part of the RAND Corporation's ongoing research on China and China's military establishment. It is a companion study to

- Keith Crane, Roger Cliff, Evan Medeiros, James C. Mulvenon, and William Overholt, *Modernizing China's Military: Opportunities and Constraints,* MG-260-AF, 2005.

It builds on previous RAND Project AIR FORCE work, including

- Roger Cliff, *The Military Potential of China's Commercial Technology,* MR-1292-AF, 2001
- Zalmay Khalilzad, Abram N. Shulsky, Daniel Byman, Roger Cliff, David T. Orletsky, David A. Shlapak, and Ashley J. Tellis, *The United States and a Rising China: Strategic and Military Implications,* MR-1082-AF, 1999
- James C. Mulvenon and Richard H. Yang, eds., *The People's Liberation Army in the Information Age,* CF-145-CAPP/AF, 1999
- Daniel L. Byman and Roger Cliff, *China's Arms Sales: Motivations and Implications,* MR-1119-AF, 1999
- Erica Strecker Downs, *China's Quest for Energy Security,* MR-1244-AF, 2000
- Richard Sokolsky, Angel Rabasa, and C. R. Neu, *The Role of Southeast Asia in U.S. Strategy Toward China,* MR-1170-AF, 2000
- Mark Burles and Abram Shulsky, *Patterns in China's Use of Force: Evidence from History and Doctrinal Writings,* MR-1160-AF, 2000
- Mark Burles, *Chinese Policy Toward Russia and the Central Asian Republics,* MR-1045-AF, 1999.

The information in this report is current as of January 2005.

RAND Project AIR FORCE

RAND Project AIR FORCE (PAF), a division of the RAND Corporation, is the U.S. Air Force's federally funded research and development center for studies and analyses. PAF provides the Air Force with independent analyses of policy alternatives affecting the development, employment, combat readiness, and support of current and future aerospace forces. Research is performed in four programs: Aerospace Force Development; Manpower, Personnel, and Training; Resource Management; and Strategy and Doctrine.

Additional information about PAF is available on our Web site at http://www.rand.org/paf.

Contents

Preface iii
Figures xi
Tables xiii
Summary xv
Acknowledgments xxv

CHAPTER ONE
Introduction 1
The Changing Shape of China's Defense-Industrial Complex,
    1980–1998 4
Explaining the Defense Industry's Poor Performance 11
    Weaknesses of Past Reforms 14
Understanding "the Soviet Paradox" 18
New Progress in Defense-Industry Reform: The 1998 Reforms
    and Beyond 22
    Beijing's "Grand Strategy" for Improving Defense-Industrial
        Capabilities 24
    The Goals of the 1998–1999 Reforms 28
    Specific Organizational Reforms 31
Systemic Constraints on China's Defense-Industry Reform 47
    Reform Imperatives Versus Social Stability 48
    GAD Versus State COSTIND 48
    Localization Versus Free-Market Practices 49
Organization of This Report 49

CHAPTER TWO

China's Missile Industry 51
Sector Organization and Principal Actors 52
    China Aerospace Science and Technology Corporation 53
    China Aerospace Science and Industry Group Corporation 58
    Non–CASC/CASIC Missile Producers 62
Assessing the Potential for Future Progress 65
    Human and Financial Resources 66
    Access to Foreign Technology 67
    Incentives 69
    Institutions 74
Missile-Industry Production Capabilities and Output 76
    Ballistic Missiles: Strengths and Weaknesses in R&D and
        Production Capabilities 78
    Anti-Ship Cruise Missiles 82
    Surface-to-Air Missiles 86
    Air-to-Air Missiles 90
    Ground-Attack Missiles 94
    Summary 96
Improving the Performance of China's Missile Sector 96
    Perceived Problems and Shortcomings 97
    Strategies for Addressing Weaknesses 99
    Effectiveness of Policy Solutions 104
Conclusions 106

CHAPTER THREE

China's Shipbuilding Industry 109
Key Measures Used to Assess China's Shipbuilding Capabilities 111
Structure and Operation of China's Shipbuilding Industry 112
    Current Composition of China's Entire Shipbuilding Industry 115
    Military Shipbuilding 123
Growth, Expansion, and Modernization of China's
    Shipbuilding Industry 124
    Weaknesses and Limitations of China's Shipbuilding Industry 133
China's Shipbuilding Industry and Naval Modernization 138
Civilian Contributions to Current Naval-Modernization Efforts 140

Improved Production Capabilities 141
Increased Production Capacity 149
Conclusions 152

CHAPTER FOUR
China's Military-Aviation Industry 155
Overview of China's Military-Aviation Sector 156
Current R&D and Production Capabilities 159
Fighters 160
Bombers and Ground-Attack Aircraft 163
Transports 166
Helicopters 168
Engines 170
Efforts to Improve the Performance of China's Military-Aviation
Sector 174
Future Prospects for China's Aviation Industry 181
Manufacturing Technology 182
Human Resources 184
Financial Resources 186
Economic Environment 188
Competition 189
Capital Markets, Technology Markets, Labor Markets 191
Ownership and Funding Sources 193
Institutional Infrastructure 195
Conclusions 200
Future Directions and Challenges 201

CHAPTER FIVE
"The Digital Triangle": A New Defense-Industrial Paradigm? 205
The IT Sector and Chinese Defense Modernization:
The New Paradigm 208
Relationship Between Information Technology and Defense
Modernization 208
The IT Sector as a Defense-Industrial Sector? 211
Dynamics of the IT Industry Structure 213
The Digital Triangle: A New Model of Defense Procurement 215

Strategy and Policy 215
Role of Foreign Companies, Capital, and Technology 241
Overall Implications of the Digital Triangle 246
Implications for Other Defense-Industrial Sectors................... 246
Implications for Chinese Military Modernization 247

CHAPTER SIX
Conclusions: Future Prospects of China's Defense Industry 253
Current R&D and Production Activities Must Be Examined
    Sector by Sector 253
Four Factors Explain Progress in China's Defense Industry 256
There Are Indicators of Future Improvements in Defense-Industry
    Operations.. 258

Bibliography 261

Figures

1.1. Changes in the Organizational Structure of China's Defense
     Industry 15
3.1. Tonnage Delivered by Chinese Shipyards, 1981–2004 125
3.2. Chinese Order-Book Development, 1993–June 2004 126
3.3. China's Market Share of World Order Book, 1993–2003 127
3.4. China's 2003 Shipbuilding Order Book, by Type 133
3.5. China's 2003 Shipbuilding Order Book, by Type as a
     Percentage 134
5.1. The Three Vertices of the Digital Triangle 218
5.2. Partial List of Civilian and Military IT Research Institutes 228

Tables

2.1.   Key Missile-Production Organizations Under CASC/CASIC 64
2.2.   Non–CASC/CASIC Missile-Production Organizations 65
2.3.   Current and Developmental Ballistic-Missile Systems 80
2.4.   China's ASCMs...85
2.5.   Current and Developmental SAM Systems 91
2.6.   Current and Developmental AAMs.............................93
3.1.   Major Chinese Shipyards Involved in Naval Construction 124
4.1.   China's Principal Military-Airframe Manufacturers 158
4.2.   China's Aircraft-Engine Manufacturers 173
5.1.   Foreign Companies Participating in Chinese Military IT
       Alliance 243

Summary

Part of a larger RAND Project AIR FORCE study on Chinese military modernization, this study examines the current and future capabilities of China's defense industry. The goals of this study are to

1. Assess recent trends in China's 25-year-long effort to reform its defense-industrial operations
2. Analyze the individual strengths and weaknesses of four specific defense-industrial sectors: missile, military aircraft, shipbuilding, and information technology/defense electronics
3. Explain variations in performance among different defense-industry sectors, with a focus on differences in institutional arrangements, incentives, and exposure to market forces
4. Evaluate the prospects for China's defense industry and its ability to contribute to military modernization.

Over the past 25 years, a prominent and consistent conclusion of Western research on China's defense-industrial complex has been that it is rife with weaknesses and limitations. This study argues for an alternative approach. From the vantage point of 2005, it is time to shift the focus of research to the gradual improvements in and the future potential of China's defense-industrial complex, rather than concentrating on its past and persistent weaknesses. Certain Chinese defense-industrial enterprises are designing and producing a wide range of increasingly advanced weapons that, in the short term, will enhance China's military capabilities in a possible conflict over the future of Taiwan and, in the long term, China's military position in Asia. More specifically, the following trends underscore the need to focus future research on the gradual improvements in China's defense-industrial capabilities:

- As measured by improvements in the quality of the output of China's defense enterprises, defense-industrial reform has not only taken hold but even accelerated in the past several years (since the late 1990s). These trends suggest a defense industry that is emerging from the doldrums of two and a half decades of systemic neglect, inefficiency, and corruption. The rates of modernization vary by sector, but a modicum of successful reform has been realized across key parts of the defense industry.
- The improvements in China's capabilities for defense research, development, and production have been mixed within sectors and uneven across them. While sweeping conclusions about the backwardness of the defense-industrial complex are no longer accurate, similar claims about systemic reform are equally unwarranted. This study argues that the current research and development (R&D) and production capabilities of China's defense industry must now be evaluated on a sector-by-sector basis.
- China's senior political, industrial, and military leaders have called the next 20 years the "critical stage" (*guanjian jieduan* 关键阶段) in China's modernization of its defense-industrial base. Thus defense-industry reform and renovation will be a gradual, deliberate, and consistent process. It is not likely part of a crash effort requiring a dramatic shift of national priorities from economic development to military modernization.

Explaining the Recent Progress in China's Defense Industry

The recent progress in China's defense-industry modernization can be explained by four mutually reinforcing considerations.

First, the government has consistently devoted more funds to weapon acquisition. From 1990 to 2003, the official defense-budget allocation for military equipment (*zhuangbei* 装备) grew from 5 billion RMB to 64.8 billion RMB. These increases are about twice the rate of growth of the official defense budget. Also, the share of the budget devoted to equipment increased from 16.3 to 34 percent in this time period. For the period 1997–2003, according to official Chinese budget figures, the amount of funding for equipment grew 153 percent, more than for the other two categories in the official defense budget. Such defense spending is bound to positively affect output; these increases likely contributed to the pace at which new systems have come online in recent years. However, the benefits of such increased spending are limited unless defense enterprises actually improve their research, development, and production capabilities.

Second, the gradual development and commercialization of some defense enterprises during the transition in China's economy over the past 25 years have improved their research, development, and production capabilities. The robust and rational commercial business operations of select defense enterprises allowed the accumulation of "spin-on" benefits in some defense sectors. Defense enterprises with the greatest exposure to international markets have been especially effective at improving their R&D and production capabilities, through both partnerships and competition with foreign firms.

Third, the defense industry in the past decade has had consistent access to limited amounts of foreign military equipment and technical assistance, especially from Russia and Israel. This access has assisted the efforts of some defense sectors to copy-produce weapon systems, to integrate advanced technologies into China's production lines, and to raise the technical expertise of Chinese personnel involved in defense production.

Fourth, in past decades, Beijing largely avoided implementing the type of fundamental reforms, such as rationalization and consolidation, which were needed to revitalize the defense industry. However, beginning in spring 1998, China's leadership adopted a new series of policies to revamp the structure and operations of the defense procurement system and to reform the operations of defense enterprises. At a minimum, these reforms importantly signaled recognition of the depth of the problems in China's defense-industrial system. More importantly, these policies initiated institutional changes in the management of China's defense industry in ways that outstripped past efforts in both scope and depth. Specifically, China's leaders aimed to inject into China's defense-industrial system the principles of "competition, evaluation, supervision and encouragement," known as the "Four Mechanisms" (*sige jizhi* 四个机制).

The new reforms were intended to alter both the structure and operation of China's defense industry. Reforms are occurring both at the central-government level and at the enterprise level. In general terms, the reforms aimed to centralize and standardize weapon-procurement decisions at the central-government level of operations while decentralizing defense-enterprise operations in order to increase incentives for efficiency, higher-quality production, and, eventually, innovation (see pages 22–24).

Central Government Reforms

At the level of central government operations, Chinese leaders adopted two major reforms to significantly change the weapon-procurement process to make it more accountable to the military's needs. First, it abolished the military-controlled Commission on Science Technology and Industry for National Defense (COSTIND) and replaced it with a strictly civilian organ under the control of the State Council, but with the same name. Second, the government created a new military-run agency known as the General Armaments Department (GAD), which assumed the responsibilities for military procurement and the life-cycle management of the PLA's weapon systems (from R&D to retirement).

In addition to the "civilianization" of COSTIND and the creation of the GAD, which centralized China's military-procurement system, the 1998 reforms separated the builders (the manufacturers) from the buyers (the military). This separation further rationalized the procurement system to reduce conflicts of interest and corruption. GAD represents the PLA's interests, whereas COSTIND, as a civilian agency, is now supposed to deal with industrial planning and the administrative affairs of defense firms.

To change the weapon-procurement process, the central government adopted policies that included issuing formal procurement regulations and provisions to standardize and unify the procurement process. The new regulations are also meant to accelerate the establishment of a competitive-bidding system for military contracts. Preliminary indications are that various bidding systems are beginning to be used and enforced (see pages 32–39).

Enterprise Reforms

Chinese policymakers adopted several policies to make defense-enterprise operations more efficient and raise R&D and production capabilities. Their main goals were to separate the government administrative units from enterprise operations; make defense enterprises more sensitive to market forces by exposing them to competitive pressures; provide harder budget constraints; introduce new mechanisms for quality assurance and quality control; make enterprises less reliant on state subsidies; lessen the financial burdens on enterprises from the work-group social welfare system.

As part of this reform push, the Chinese government initiated a major enterprise reform in July 1999 to create incentives for competition and efficiency in defense-enterprise operations. The reform involved dividing each of China's five core defense companies into two defense-industrial enterprise groups (*jungong jituan gongsi* 军工集团公司). An eleventh enterprise group, for defense electronics, was established in late 2002. The main goal was to inject competition into defense-enterprise operations. The other goal of the formation of "group corporations" was to establish shareholder arrangements to further remove the government from firm operations, to distribute risk, and to increase enterprise accountability for profits and losses.

Beyond these broad structural reforms, Chinese policymakers have also implemented a variety of specific initiatives to revitalize defense-enterprise operations. These included downsizing and rationalization in certain sectors; a much greater emphasis on quality control; modernization of some production complexes and related facilities; the expansion of partnerships with civilian universities and research institutes to improve educational training relevant to military R&D; the promotion of R&D and production cooperation among defense enterprises located in various provinces and across defense sectors; and reform of the system of military representative offices (MRO) in defense factories (see pages 40–47).

Constraints on Defense-Industry Reform

Beijing has a long and highly blemished history both of adopting weak reforms and of not implementing more radical policy changes. Thus, how quickly and effectively the post-1998 measures can overcome the deep problems that have plagued China's defense-industrial establishment for the last several decades is uncertain.

The government's success at fully implementing defense-industrial reforms will be broadly influenced by several tensions, or contradictions, that persist at both the central-government level and the enterprise level of operations—reform imperatives versus social stability, GAD versus the state COSTIND, and localization versus free-market practices:

- **Reform Imperatives Versus Social Stability:** Efforts to rationalize and downsize China's large, bloated, and inefficient defense enterprises raise concerns about social instability, especially the consequences of increasing unemployment, failing to fulfill pension commitments, and cutting off funding for enterprise-run social welfare programs. These consequences will hinder and, in some cases, halt the pace of enterprise reform, especially in poorer provinces, such as in northeastern and western China. Consideration of these consequences may also influence the government's distribution of large defense-production projects.
- **GAD Versus State COSTIND:** The civilianization of COSTIND and the creation of GAD in the late 1990s injected a variety of new political tensions into defense-industry opera-

tions. These new agencies often compete for influence in the defense-procurement process, and this tension may contribute to delays and inefficient decisionmaking on specific military projects.

- **Localization Versus Free-Market Practices:** Historically, China's defense-industrial enterprises have been highly vertically integrated and have relied on single-source suppliers within their own sector. These economic tendencies have been exacerbated by long-standing political ties within regions and provinces that influence business relations among firms in the same localities.

The success of China's newest round of defense-industry policy adjustments will be influenced by the ability of Chinese officials to balance these tensions in the coming years (see pages 47–49).

Sector-by-Sector Analysis

The changes in the structure, operation, and production capabilities of China's defense-industrial complex are most evident at the level of the individual defense-industrial sectors. This study includes four case-study chapters, which examine in detail the capabilities of China's missile, shipbuilding, military aviation, and information technology/defense electronics sectors. These sectors were chosen because they all contribute to the Chinese military's future power-projection capability.

As indicated in these case studies, reform of the defense industry has been uneven. We find that in each of these sectors the capabilities of manufacturers to design and produce key systems are improving, but weaknesses and limitations persist depending on the sector. Some have been more successful than others: Improvements in information technology and shipbuilding have been extensive, while those in aviation have lagged.

Missile Sector

Partly a legacy of its position as one of China's strategic weapon programs that received preferential treatment, China's missile sector has historically been one of the brightest stars in China's defense industry. While technological progress since the 1980s has been slow, it has accelerated since 2000. Missile-production enterprises continued to develop and produce new and increasingly advanced ballistic and cruise missiles—including serial production of some of these systems, such as the new variants of the DF-11 (CSS-7) and DF-15 (CSS-6) short-range ballistic missiles.

China may soon begin deploying land-attack cruise missiles, fast and highly accurate anti-ship cruise missiles, modern long-range surface-to-air missiles, and anti-radiation missiles. China's ability to produce and deploy increasingly high-quality systems in a timely manner will serve as an indicator of continued reform of the missile sector (see pages 51–108).

Shipbuilding Sector

China's shipbuilding industry has gradually modernized since Deng Xiaopings's reform and openness policies. It rapidly engaged international markets in the 1980s and, as a consequence, gained consistent access to foreign shipbuilding equipment, capital, and know-how. China is now the world's third-largest shipbuilder. As its commercial-shipbuilding business expanded, its naval-production capabilities benefited as well. China's shipbuilding industry now produces a wide range of increasingly sophisticated naval platforms using modern design methods, production techniques, and management practices. China's shipyards are now producing more-advanced naval vessels more quickly and efficiently than in the past. These improvements are best reflected in the serial output of several new classes of military ships in recent years. These innovations and heightened production rates are a first for China's shipbuilding sector and are likely to continue in the coming years (see pages 109–154).

Military-Aviation Sector

For years, China's aviation industry suffered under the weight of a large, bloated, technologically unsophisticated, and highly inefficient collection of R&D institutes and factories that failed to produce modern military aircraft in a timely manner. In the past five years, limited signs of increasing progress in this sector have begun to emerge. China's first indigenously designed and produced combat aircraft (JH-7/FBC-1) has recently entered service, and China is on the verge of producing a domestically developed, fourth-generation aircraft (known as the J-10/F-10), albeit with substantial foreign design assistance. It has also made significant progress toward producing turbofan engines for its newest fighters.

Important gaps in China's aviation design and production capabilities remain, however. China has not yet mastered serial production of such complex aviation platforms as fourth-generation fighters, nor is it able to produce heavy bombers or large transport aircraft. And it has yet to field an indigenously designed helicopter (see pages 155–204).

Information-Technology Sector

China's emerging IT sector is not an officially designated part of China's defense-industrial complex; however, it is probably the most organizationally innovative and economically dynamic producer of equipment for China's military. And it is at the forefront of China's improving defense-production capabilities. Although IT enterprises are primarily (exclusively, in most instances) oriented toward domestic and international commercial markets, the PLA has been able to effectively leverage certain IT products to improve the military's command, control, communications, computers, and intelligence (C4I) capabilities—a critical element of the PLA's modernization efforts (see pages 205–251).

Future Prospects of China's Defense Industry

China's defense industry now has the *potential* to become more competitive with the defense industries of the world's advanced military powers in key sectors within a moderate (10–20 years) amount of time. Indeed, our analysis of their R&D and production capabilities suggests that several defense sectors are already overcoming long-standing weaknesses. To be sure, the prevailing data set related to defense-industrial capabilities is still limited, and current progress has been mixed within defense sectors and uneven across them.

Some of the current weaknesses of China's defense industry could be further ameliorated in the medium term (10–20 years), assuming China does not deviate from its present course of reform of the defense-industrial system and government investment in and, importantly, a continued political commitment to defense procurement. If the government continues to push for open contracting of defense projects and takes a tough line on cost overruns, efficiency gains, the quality of production capabilities, and the degree of innovation should continue to improve. In some sectors, this could occur fairly rapidly.

Even though such reforms are gathering speed, they will not happen overnight. Time is needed to train new employees into skilled defense-industry engineers and technicians. It will also take time to change management behavior and stimulate innovation, even after new management incentive systems are implemented. Such behaviors will be critical indicators of the pace of reform and the future direction of China's defense-industrial capabilities (see pages 253–259).

Acknowledgments

The authors would like to thank Garret Albert, Matt Roberts, and Eric Valko for their assistance with the statistical research; Peter Almquist for his insight and expertise; and Heather Roy and Karen Stewart for their administrative support. We are particularly grateful to Richard Bitzinger, Dennis Blasko, Maggie Marcum, and William Overholt for their careful reading and commentary on earlier drafts of this study.

CHAPTER ONE

Introduction

Since the early 1980s, a prominent and consistent conclusion of Western research on China's defense-industrial complex has been that China's defense R&D and production capabilities are rife with weaknesses and limitations.[1] In this study, we found that China's defense sectors are producing a wide range of increasingly advanced weapons that, in the short term, are relevant to a possible conflict over Taiwan but also to China's long-term military presence in Asia.[2] This core finding argues for an alternative approach: From the vantage point of 2005, it is time to shift the focus of research to the gradual improvements in and the future potential of China's defense-industrial complex.

According to official military budget figures, the Chinese government has been substantially increasing its spending on defense procurement. Based on data in China's 2004 national defense white paper, expenditures on equipment increased by an average of 18 percent per year between 2000 and 2003.[3] These increased expend-

---

[1] Bates Gill, "Chinese Military-Technical Development: The Record for Western Assessments, 1979–1999," in James C. Mulvenon and Andrew N. D. Yang, eds., *Seeking Truth from Facts: A Retrospective on Chinese Military Studies in the Post-Mao Era,* Santa Monica, Calif.: RAND Corporation, CF-160-CAPP, 2001.

[2] To be sure, these new weapon systems are in most cases 1970s- and 1980s-era platforms, which possess updated technologies (e.g., sensors and weapon suites) and are often derived from foreign-influenced designs.

[3] *China's National Defense in 2004,* Beijing, China: Information Office of the State Council, December 27, 2004. Available at http://www.china.org.cn/e-white/20041227/index.htm. The figures on equipment spending are believed to exclude expenditures on military

itures are beginning to manifest themselves as greater-quantity and higher-quality outputs from the defense industry. The technological capabilities of China's defense manufacturing base are improving, and China has a growing pool of technical talent in its civilian sector that Beijing is now attempting to attract to work in the defense industry. The government is also making a concerted effort to reform both the institutional framework and the incentives under which the defense industry operates. Such reforms are taking form slowly, but a number of initial indications detailed later in the volume suggest that progress is occurring, and rapidly in some cases, especially when compared with the previous rounds of rather ineffectual attempts at defense-industry reform in the 1980s and early 1990s. In the words of General Li Jinai, the former head of the General Armaments Department (GAD), the lead defense-procurement agency, "there has been a marked improvement in national defense scientific research and in building of weapons and equipment. The past five years has been the best period of development in the country's history."[4] As we argue in more detail below, these trends bear close watching by U.S. policymakers, analysts, and military planners.

As China's economic and resource base expands in the coming years, Beijing has three broad paths by which to translate these economic achievements into improved military capabilities.[5] The first is to domestically produce all of the weapons needed to equip the country's military. The second is to purchase weapon systems and related components and technologies from the major military equipment producers of the world: the United States, Russia, Britain, France, Israel, and a few other countries. A third path combines these

---

equipment imported from Russia or other countries and may not include expenditures on defense research and development activities.

[4] Wang Wenjie, "Delegate Li Jinai Emphasizes: Grasp Tightly the Important Strategic Opportunity, Accelerate the Development by Leaps of Our Army's Weapons and Equipment," *Jiefangjun bao,* March 8, 2003, p. 1, as translated in *FBIS*, March 8, 2003. As of September 2004, the new head of the GAD is General Chen Bingde.

[5] These three broad pathways are not meant to exclude hybrid pathways that certain sectors have pursued. Thus, up to six or seven different acquisition pathways may be being utilized across China's various defense sectors.

two approaches by attempting to improve design and manufacturing processes so as to produce better-quality weapons domestically while importing key systems to fill short-term needs. After largely pursuing the first path for much of the 1960s, 1970s, and part of the 1980s, China has, since the 1990s, been following the third path— improving domestic production while purchasing from abroad, mostly from Russia and Israel, growing numbers of advanced weapon systems.

China's leaders and strategists do not like being dependent on other countries for their defense-modernization needs and have made it clear that their long-term goal is to return to the first path of "self-reliance" in defense production. However, as the volume of Russian imports in recent years indicates, China's military has been decidedly unsatisfied with the quality of the products from China's defense industry; their needs have become acute in the wake of the People's Liberation Army's (PLA's) accelerated efforts since the late 1990s to develop real military options in the event of a conflict over Taiwan. Yet, over the long term, the ability of the PLA to overcome its self-proclaimed problem of "short arms and slow legs"[6] depends on the ability of China's defense R&D institutes and factories to overcome past inadequacies and produce sophisticated and reliable weapon systems.

This study begins by reviewing the evolution of China's defense-industrial policies since the beginning of Chinese economic reform efforts in the late 1970s. It gives particular attention to China's most recent round of defense-industry reforms initiated in the late 1990s. The study then provides four separate case studies, each of which examines the organization and production capabilities of key sectors in China's defense industry: missiles, military aviation, shipbuilding, and information technology/defense electronics. The study concludes with an estimate of the future production capabilities of China's

---

[6] Since the mid-1990s, China's *PLA Daily* (*Jiefangjun bao*) has been using this phrase to describe the military's limitations.

defense industry over the next two decades and its potential contributions to Chinese military modernization.

Both this overview chapter and each of the case studies focus heavily on changes in two key aspects of China's defense-industrial system: the structure of *institutions* and the nature of *incentives* for increased efficiency, improved R&D and production capabilities and, eventually, innovation. Shifts in both of these aspects in the defense industry have begun to gradually reshape the operations and output of China's defense-industrial sectors. In addition, changes in these two aspects are examined at the levels of *central government* operations (i.e., defense-procurement decisions) and *enterprise* operations (i.e., R&D and production decisions.) By focusing on institutions and incentives at both the central government and enterprise levels of operations, this chapter provides a framework by which to analyze and evaluate progress in China's defense-industrial establishment.

The Changing Shape of China's Defense-Industrial Complex, 1980–1998

From the late 1970s, when Deng Xiaoping initiated reform of China's planned economy, until recently, China's defense industry led a troubled existence.[7] Government procurement of military goods declined dramatically following the adoption of Deng's "Four Modernizations" policy, which placed the military as the last priority.[8] As a result, most defense enterprises were officially

---

[7] In this study, China's "defense enterprises" (*jungong qiye*) are its state-owned industries, which produce weapons and equipment for China's military. They are distinct from "military enterprises" (*jundui qiye*), which produced commercial goods and services and used to be owned and operated by the PLA until the decommercialization of the PLA in the late 1990s. In July 1998, Jiang Zemin called for the PLA to sever its ties to all business enterprises. This process is ongoing. See James C. Mulvenon, "Chinese Military Commerce and U.S. National Security," Santa Monica, Calif.: unpublished RAND Corporation research, 1997.

[8] See John Frankenstein, "China's Defense Industries: A New Course?" in James C. Mulvenon and Richard H. Yang, eds., *The People's Liberation Army in the Information Age*, Santa Monica, Calif.: RAND Corporation, CF-145-CAPP/AF, 1999.

encouraged to diversify into production of non-military/civilian goods (i.e., defense conversion) or engage in arms sales to generate income to replace dwindling government purchases of military equipment. Many firms soon became dependent on these alternate sources of income for their very survival.

Defense conversion (*junzhuanmin* 军转民) was a largely troubled process for most Chinese firms. Despite the Chinese government's claims to the contrary, weapon producers found it difficult to shift to producing goods that could be profitably sold on emerging domestic markets. Military goods producers were hampered by legal constraints and difficulties in attracting foreign partners who could provide new capital, know-how, and technologies. Changing production infrastructure was an additional challenge. They also lacked the managerial flexibility to replicate the successes of the new Chinese companies that emerged during the reform period. These problems were further exacerbated by the general weaknesses of China's state-owned enterprises in absorbing new technologies and management practices, and in developing the technical skills of the labor force. The Chinese government's commitment to self-reliance in military equipment production also hindered the ability of these enterprises to successfully sell to nondefense markets, because factories had to remain capable of producing a full range of components and equipment for military production, forestalling specialization and the accompanying increases in quality and technological sophistication that longer production runs potentially provide. As a result, many civilian goods produced by defense firms have been of low quality and uncompetitive, thus generating few profits.[9]

---

[9] Zhang Yihao and Zhou Zongkui, "China's Science, Technology, and Industry for National Defense Face up to WTO—an Interview with Liu Jibin, Minister in Charge of the Commission of Science, Technology, and Industry for National Defense," *Jiefangjun bao* (Internet version), March 13, 2000, p. 8, in *FBIS* as "WTO Impact on PRC Defense Industry," March 14, 2000; Wang Jianhua, "Thoughts on 'WTO Entry' and Development of Armament," *Jiefangjun bao* (Internet version), March 14, 2000, p. 6, in *FBIS* as "Impact of WTO on PRC Armament Development," March 15, 2000; Ke Wen, "Advantages and Disadvantages of WTO Accession to China's Military Industry, Science and Technology—Interviewing Liu Jibin, Minister in Charge of Commission of Science, Technology, and Industry for National Defense," *Chiao ching,* June 16, 2000, pp. 46–48, in *FBIS* as "Minister

Many of the these problems are becoming more acute as competition in China's domestic market has intensified with the proliferation of new and more market-oriented companies in numerous sectors. In addition, competition from foreign producers has deepened now that China has entered the World Trade Organization (WTO) and China's domestic markets for consumer goods have been opened to foreign manufacturers. Few defense firms were able to use defense conversion to gain access to modern production technologies to upgrade their facilities for producing better military goods—the government's initial rationale for encouraging defense conversion.[10] To be sure, some sectors, such as shipbuilding and electronics, demonstrated an impressive ability to transform themselves into productive firms producing mainly nonmilitary goods. At best, however, defense conversion has had mixed success in China.[11]

By contrast, Chinese weapon sales were a substantial source of income for some defense firms in the 1980s. Chinese arms sales peaked in 1987 at over $1 billion. This source of revenue quickly dried up in the early 1990s, with the cessation of the Iran-Iraq War, which took with it the major source of demand for Chinese weapons. Chinese weapon exporters also lost export markets after the very poor performance of Chinese weapons in Iraq's hands during the 1991 Gulf War. Chinese weapon exporters suffered from the influx of technologically superior and relatively inexpensive Russian weapons

---

Liu Jibin on Pros, Cons of WTO Accession to PRC Defense Industry," June 20, 2000. See also Frankenstein, "China's Defense Industries: A New Course?" 1999.

[10] Liu Jibin, "Implement the Guideline of Military-Civilian Integration, Rejuvenate the National Defense Science and Technology Industry," *Renmin ribao,* February 2, 1999, p. 12, in *FBIS* as "Military-Civilian Integration in Industry," February 2, 1999. See also John Frankenstein, "China's Defense Industries: A New Course?" 1999; Jorn Brömmelhörster and John Frankenstein, eds., *Mixed Motives, Uncertain Outcomes: Defense Conversion in China,* Boulder, Colo.: Lynne Rienner Publishers, 1997; John Frankenstein and Bates Gill, "Current and Future Challenges Facing Chinese Defense Industries," *China Quarterly,* June 1996, pp. 394–427; Bates Gill, "The Impact of Economic Reform on Chinese Defense Production," in C. Dennison Lane, ed., *Chinese Military Modernization,* London, United Kingdom: Paul Kegan International, 1996, pp. 144–167.

[11] Evan S. Medeiros, "Revisiting Chinese Defense Conversion: Some Evidence from China's Shipbuilding Industry," *Issues and Studies,* May 1998.

into international markets following the collapse of the Soviet Union.[12]

China's expanding arms control and nonproliferation commitments gradually prevented Chinese firms from exporting their most competitive and desired military systems, such as surface-to-surface and anti-ship missiles.[13] As a result of these gradually worsening circumstances for weapons exports, China's defense firms, as with many of China's large state-owned enterprises (*guoyou qiye* 国有企业), suffered and staggered along for most of the 1990s by relying on significant government subsidies.[14] As late as 2000, China's defense sectors were described as facing "tremendous challenges."[15]

The difficult circumstances faced by China's defense-industrial enterprises were mirrored in their financial circumstances. Despite the fact that supposedly over 80 percent of the aggregate output of Chinese defense enterprises was civilian goods,[16] few firms were prof-

---

[12] Karl W. Eikenberry, *Explaining and Influencing Chinese Arms Transfers,* Washington, D.C.: National Defense University, McNair Papers 36, February 1995; Bates Gill, *Chinese Arms Transfers: Purposes, Patterns and Prospects in the New World Order,* Westport, Conn.: Praeger Publishers, 1992; Richard Bitzinger, "Arms to Go: Chinese Arms Sales to the Third World," *International Security,* Fall 1992.

[13] Evan S. Medeiros and Bates Gill, *Chinese Arms Exports: Policy, Players, and Process,* Carlisle, Pa.: U.S. Army War College, Strategic Studies Institute, 2000.

[14] *Xinhua,* January 7, 1998, in *FBIS* as "PRC National Ordnance Industry Conference Opens," January 7, 1998; Bie Yixun and Xu Dianlong, *Xinhua Domestic Service,* January 7, 1998, in *FBIS* as "Wu Bangguo Greets Opening of Ordnance Industry Meeting," January 12, 1998. In 2000, the defense sector reportedly received 1.7 billion renminbi (RMB) in direct subsidies, in addition to an uncertain amount of indirect subsidies in the form of government-directed loans from state-owned banks. Fu Jing, "Defense Industry Eyes Foreign Cash," *China Daily,* July 4, 2001, in *FBIS* as "Chinese Defense Industry Eyes More Foreign Investment," July 4, 2001.

[15] Ke Wen, "Advantages and Disadvantages of WTO Accession to China's Military Industry, Science and Technology—Interviewing Liu Jibin, Minister in Charge of Commission of Science, Technology, and Industry for National Defense," 2000.

[16] Liu Jibin, "Implement the Guideline of Military-Civilian Integration, Rejuvenate the National Defense Science and Technology Industry," 1999; Tang Hua, "Science, Technology, and Industry for National Defense Increases Intensity of Innovation," *Liaowang,* July 26, 1999, pp. 16, 17, in *FBIS* as "Report on Innovation in Defense Industry," August 16, 1999; Zhang Yihao and Zhou Zongkui, "China's Science, Technology, and Industry for National Defense Face up to WTO—an Interview with Liu Jibin, Minister in Charge of the

itable. According to the director of the State Commission on Science Technology and Industry for National Defense (COSTIND), for eight consecutive years, from 1993 to 2001, China's entire defense industry, in aggregate terms, ran a net loss.[17]

Aside from the financial problems of China's defense industry, the military systems it produced have also been unimpressive. The weaknesses of China's defense-production capabilities are reflected in the technological backwardness of many of the systems, the historically long R&D and production time lines for most indigenously built weapons, and China's growing reliance on purchases of major weapon systems from foreign countries. The history of China's defense industry is replete with examples of weapon systems with severe technological weaknesses and limitations. While many new

Commission of Science, Technology, and Industry for National Defense"; Ke Wen, "Advantages and Disadvantages of WTO Accession to China's Military Industry, Science and Technology—Interviewing Liu Jibin, Minister in Charge of Commission of Science, Technology, and Industry for National Defense," 2000; Zhao Huanxin, *China Daily* (Internet version), December 19, 2000, in *FBIS* as "China Daily: Military Technology Transfer to Spur Growth in Civilian Sector," December 19, 2000; Fan Rixuan, "The Profound Impact of China's WTO Accession on People's Lives and Thinking, as Well as on National Defense and Military Modernization Drive—Thoughts on China's WTO Admission and National Defense Building," *Jiefangjun bao* (Internet version), April 30, 2002, p. 6, in *FBIS* as "Article Discusses Impact of China's WTO Admission on National Defense Building," May 2, 2002.

[17] "Defense Industry Breaks Even in 2002," *China Daily* (Internet version), January 9, 2002. Prior to 2001, the "aerospace" (i.e., which produces both missiles and satellites) sector was the only "profitable" (Chinese state-owned enterprises have notoriously bad bookkeeping, so profitability is impossible to know) segment of China's defense industry. Zhang Yi, "It Is Estimated That China's Military Industrial Enterprises Covered by the Budget Reduce Losses by More Than 30 Percent," *Xinhua* (Hong Kong Service), January 7, 2002, in *FBIS* as "PRC Military Industry Reports 30 Percent Decrease in Losses for 2001," January 7, 2002. The "ordnance sector" (i.e., ground systems, as well as explosives, artillery, ammunition, aerial bombs, and some missiles) reportedly "suffered serious losses" for over ten years beginning at the end of the 1980s. See Jia Xiping and Xu Dianlong, "China's Ordnance Industry Achieves Marked Successes in Reform and Reorganization to Streamline and Improve Core Business," *Xinhua Domestic Service,* January 19, 2000, in *FBIS* as "PRC Ordnance Industry Reform Results," February 10, 2000; Qian Xiaohu, "Crossing Frontier Passes and Mountains with Golden Spears and Armored Horses—Interviewing Ma Zhigeng, President of China Ordnance Group Corporation," *Jiefangjun bao* (Internet version), April 17, 2000, p. 8, in *FBIS* as "China Ordnance Group Chief Interviewed," April 17, 2000. For additional information and details on the poor economic state of China's defense industry in the 1980s and 1990s, see Frankenstein, "China's Defense Industries: A New Course?" 1999.

types of tanks, artillery, surface-to-air missiles, surface ships, submarines, and air-to-air missiles have entered service since 1980, for the most part the designs of these new systems have been incremental improvements on earlier designs, which in many cases can trace their lineage back to 1950s' Soviet technology.

The limitations of China's defense industry are also reflected in the long production cycles for major defense systems. China's JH-7 (FBC-1) fighter-bombers and J-10 (F-10) multi-role aircraft, its most advanced domestically produced military aircraft, were both under development for two decades. The JH-7 only recently entered into service for the PLA Navy (PLAN), even though it was first designed in the early 1970s. Moreover, despite the very long development times involved, the project is still dependent on jet engines imported from Britain; China has been unable to produce the engine on its own. The J-10 has just entered series production, despite the fact that the program was initiated in the early 1980s and the basic design is largely derived from Israel's canceled Lavi fighter program (which, in turn, was based on U.S. F-16 technology).[18]

Other sectors in China's defense industry have exhibited similar, albeit perhaps not as acute, weaknesses as the aircraft industry. For most of the 1980s or 1990s, China produced no heavy naval cruisers or multi-role destroyers with advanced air-defense or anti-submarine systems. This has changed in recent years, however. Even China's missile sector, which is often heralded as a "pocket of excellence," does not inspire awe. The solid-fuel ballistic missiles and anti-ship cruise missiles on which it has made its reputation are comparable to systems fielded in the West in the 1960s and 1970s. The missile industry has experienced continued problems developing a long-range naval surface-to-air missile (SAM), and the resulting delays have complicated some of the planned upgrades of both current and future platforms. Furthermore, China's long-range ballistic-missile modernization program, which began in the mid-1980s, has so far

---

[18] For a history of the troubled procurement cycles of these aviation programs, see Kenneth W. Allen, Glenn Krumel, Jonathan D. Pollack, *China's Air Force Enters the 21st Century,* Santa Monica, Calif.: RAND Corporation, MR-580-AF, 1995.

resulted in the development of one new long-range, solid-fuel, road-mobile system (known as the DF-31), almost 20 years after its initial conception.[19]

Most critically, China's defense industry has so far been unable to produce the types of radically new technologies, such as low observable systems and precision-guided munitions, that the U.S. military has employed so effectively in recent years. Although the Chinese press is fond of boasting how Chinese weapons have reached "advanced world levels,"[20] numerous sources more soberly acknowledge that China's defense industry has persistently failed to meet the needs of the military and has lagged behind the technological development in the more market-oriented sectors of the Chinese economy.[21]

---

[19] For a useful review of the development cycles of major Chinese weapon systems, see David Shambaugh, *Modernizing China's Military: Progress, Problems, and Prospects,* Berkeley, Calif.: University of California Press, 2003, especially Chapter Six, "Defense Industries and Procurement."

[20] For example, see Wang Fan and Zhang Jie, "A Qualitative Leap in the Overall Strength of National Defense Over Past 50 Years," *Liaowang,* July 26, 1999, pp. 10, 11, 12, in *FBIS* as "Xinhua Journal Reviews PRC Defense Growth," August 4, 1999; Li Xuanqing, Fan Juwei, Su Kuoshan, "Defense Science and Technology Forges Sharp Sword for National Defense—Second Roundup on Achievements of Army Building Over Past 50 Years," *Jiefangjun bao,* September 7, 1999, pp. 1, 2, in *FBIS* as "Overview of PLA Defense S&T Modernization," September 21, 1999; Yu Bin and Hao Dan, "Qualitative Changes in National Defense Modernization Standard, Overall Strength," *Liaowang,* No. 39, September 27, 1999, pp. 52–54, in *FBIS* as "Changes in National Defense, Power," October 18, 1999; Zhongguo Wen She, "China's Military Science and Technology Develop by Leaps and Bounds," *Renmin ribao* (Internet version), July 27, 2000, in *FBIS* as "PRC Claims Military Science, Technology Becoming More 'Dependable,'" July 27, 2000.

[21] Chen Zengjun, "Ordnance Industry Turns into Vital New National Economic Force,"*Jingji ribao,* November 20, 1998, p. 2, in *FBIS* as "Ordnance Industry Becomes 'Vital' Economic Force," December 12, 1998; *Xinhua Domestic Service,* April 27, 1999, in *FBIS* as "Wu Bangguo Speaks at Defense Industry Conference," May 2, 1999; Tang Hua, "Science, Technology, and Industry for National Defense Increases Intensity of Innovation," 1999. An article in *Jiefangjun bao* (*Liberation Army Daily*) characterized China's armaments as suffering from "one low" and "five insufficiencies": a low degree of "informationization"; and insufficient high-power armaments; insufficient strike weapons; insufficient precision-guided weapons; insufficient means of reconnaissance, early warning, and command and control; and insufficient electronic weapons. An Weiping, "Thoughts on Developing Armaments by Leaps and Bounds," *Jiefangjun bao,* April 6, 1999, p. 6, in *FBIS,* April 6, 1999.

Perhaps the strongest indictment of the failures of China's defense industry is the PLA's long-term reliance on purchases of major weapon systems from foreign countries (mainly Russia).[22] Since the mid-1990s, China has sought to fill critical gaps in its force structure, not through indigenous procurement but by purchasing advanced weapon systems and related equipment and technologies from abroad. This foreign procurement has occurred in a broad range of categories of weapon systems. The most significant purchases have included advanced fourth-generation fighter aircraft, modern destroyers with advanced air-defense and anti-surface capabilities, long-range land-based air-defense systems, advanced diesel-electric submarines, jet engines, and advanced defense electronics technologies. The numerous purchases of advanced foreign weapon systems serve as a strong indicator of the PLA's perceived capability gaps as a result of the inability of China's defense-industrial base to meet the PLA's needs.

Explaining the Defense Industry's Poor Performance

The reasons for the slow technological progress in China's defense industry in the 1980s and 1990s are similar to those for the rest of China's state-owned sector[23]—perhaps the most fundamental being a

---

[22] Whether China will continue to purchase weapon systems from Russia in the future is an open question, given the PLA's changing needs and the limitations on what Russia can supply.

[23] See, among others, Erik Baark, "Fragmented Innovation: China's Science and Technology Policy Reforms in Retrospect," in Joint Economic Committee, ed., *China's Economic Dilemmas in the 1990s: The Problems of Reforms, Modernization, and Interdependence,* Washington, D.C.: U.S. Government Printing Office, 1991; Richard P. Suttmeier, "China's High Technology: Programs, Problems, and Prospects," in Joint Economic Committee, ed., *China's Economic Dilemmas in the 1990s: The Problems of Reforms, Modernization, and Interdependence,* Washington, D.C.: U.S. Government Printing Office, 1991; Richard P. Suttmeier, "Emerging Innovation Networks and Changing Strategies for Industrial Technology in China: Some Observations," *Technology in Society,* Vol. 19, Nos. 3 and 4, 1997; and Zhou Yuan, "Reform and Restructuring of China's Science and Technology System," in Denis Fred Simon, ed., *The Emerging Technological Trajectory of the Pacific Rim,* Armonk, New York: M. E. Sharpe, 1995.

lack of incentives for efficiency and innovation. For example, China's defense manufacturers were paid cost-plus-5-percent for equipment they produced. This form of reimbursement provided little incentive for manufacturers to cut costs. Decisions about which company would produce a particular item were made by administrative fiat and ministerial bargaining, rather than through competitive bidding among manufacturers.[24] As a result, military-equipment producers had minimal financial interest in improving the quality of the weapon systems they produced or the efficiency with which they designed, manufactured, or delivered them, because improvements and timeliness had little effect on the orders the company received or their earnings.[25]

In addition to the lack of financial incentives for innovation, China's Soviet-inspired approach to industrial organization inhibited innovation. Under the Soviet model, research and development activities are performed by institutes that are organizationally separate from the actual manufacturers. This situation remained common, although not universal, in China's defense sectors during the 1980s and 1990s. The institutes were funded through annual budgetary allocations from the central government and received minimal input from production enterprises. Not only did this separation result in technology-development projects that were impractical or unrelated to production needs, it meant that research and development institutes were deprived of the valuable technological information generated in the course of routine production.[26]

Another drawback of the Soviet model is its top-down organization. Because technology-development priorities were determined by the central authorities, opportunities that arose serendipitously in the R&D process but did not fit into these predetermined directions

---

[24] Bates Gill and Lonnie Henley, *China and the Revolution in Military Affairs*, Carlisie, Pa.: U.S. Army War College, Strategic Studies Institute, 1996.

[25] Indeed, reductions in the cost of production would actually *reduce* the profits that an enterprise received.

[26] Joseph P. Gallagher, "China's Military Industrial Complex," *Asian Survey*, Vol. XXVII, No. 9, September 1987.

would have been neglected. The hierarchical organizational structure discouraged the horizontal knowledge flows that are critical to technological progress.[27] This knowledge-flow problem was undoubtedly exacerbated by the extreme secrecy associated with defense production in China.

Other problems of the defense industry included excessive production capacity, redundant personnel, inflexibility in hiring and firing, loss of quality personnel to the non-state-owned sector, incorrectly priced inputs, poor management practices, and the inefficient geographic distribution of industry as a result of a 1960s and 1970s policy of relocating defense enterprises to remote interior areas where they would be behind China's "Third Line" (*da san xian* 大三线) of defense from an external invasion.[28]

---

[27] Wendy Frieman, "China's Defence Industries," *Pacific Review,* Vol. 6, No. 1, 1993, p. 54; John Frankenstein and Bates Gill, "Current and Future Challenges Facing Chinese Defense Industries," *China Quarterly,* June 1996; Wendy Frieman, "Arms Procurement in China: Poorly Understood Processes and Unclear Results," in Eric Arnett, ed., *Military Capacity and the Risk of War: China, India, Pakistan and Iran,* Oxford, England: Oxford University Press, 1997, p. 80; Eric Arnett, "Military Technology: The Case of China," *SIPRI Yearbook 1995: Armaments, Disarmament and International Security,* New York: Oxford University Press, 1995, pp. 370–371; Arthur S. Ding, "Economic Reform and Defence Industries in China," in Gerald Segal and Richard S. Yang, eds., *Chinese Economic Reform,* New York: Routledge, 1996, p. 82; Erik Baark, "Military Technology and Absorptive Capacity in China and India: Implications for Modernization," in Eric Arnett, ed*., Military Capacity and the Risk of War: China, India, Pakistan and Iran,* Oxford, England: Oxford University Press, 1997, pp. 92, 106, 108.

[28] Bie Yixun and Xu Dianlong, *Xinhua Domestic Service,* 1998; Hsiao Cheng-chin, "Liu Jibin, Minister in Charge of the State Commission of Science, Technology, and Industry for National Defense and a Veteran Who Has Rejoined His Original Unit," *Hsin pao,* June 3, 1998, in *FBIS* as "Article on New Minister Liu Jibin," June 12, 1998; Peng Kai-lei, "Five Major Military Industry Corporations Formally Reorganized," *Wen wei po,* July 1, 1999, p. A2, in *FBIS* as "Military Industry Reorganization Planned," July 6, 1999; Zhang Yi, "Liu Jibin, Minister of Commission of Science, Technology, and Industry for National Defense, 27 October Says in a Meeting That China's High-Tech Industry for National Defense Will Be Restructured on a Large Scale," *Xinhua Domestic Service,* October 27, 1999, in *FBIS* as "Official Urges Major Defense Industry Shakeup," November 3, 1999; *Xinhua Domestic Service,* "China's Military Industrial Industry Last Year Decreased Losses by a Large Margin," January 5, 2001, in *FBIS* as "PRC Says Military Industry Reduces Losses," January 5, 2001; Richard Conroy, *Technological Change in China,* Paris: Development Centre of the Organization for Economic Co-operation and Development, 1992; John Frankenstein, "The People's Republic of China: Arms Production, Industrial Strategy and Problems of History," in Herbert Wulf, ed., *Arms Industry Limited,* New York: Oxford University Press for SIPRI,

Weaknesses of Past Reforms

The Chinese government recognized the shortcomings of its defense-industrial complex and, during the 1980s and 1990s, made repeated attempts to reform and rehabilitate it. These efforts relied mainly on two strategies: defense conversion, which was discussed above, and institutional reorganization, which involved frequent changing of names and shuffling of organizational responsibilities but few of the systematic consolidation and rationalization measures needed to increase efficiency and bolster innovation. Similar to China's experience with defense conversion, institutional reorganization was largely a cosmetic and ineffective pathway to substantial and sustained reform of China's decaying defense-R&D and production capabilities. A brief recitation of these efforts will help to elucidate their weaknesses. (Figure 1.1.)

Before the early 1980s, China's defense-industrial complex consisted of a series of numbered "machine building industries" (MBIs) representing the major defense sectors, such as nuclear weapons, aviation, electronics, "ordnance" (tanks, artillery, etc.), shipbuilding, and "aerospace" (missiles and space). At that time, these sectors were overseen by numerous organizations with overlapping responsibilities and claims to ownership, including the State Planning Commission, the Ministry of Finance, the PLA's National Defense Science and Technology Commission (NDSTC), the State Council's National Defense Industry Office (NDIO), and the Central Military Commission's Science and Technology Equipment Commission (STECO).

1993; Erik Baark, "Military Technology and Absorptive Capacity in China and India: Implications for Modernization," 1997; Frankenstein, "China's Defense Industries: A New Course?" 1999. On the Third Line (or "Third Front") policy, the seminal work is Barry Naughton, "The Third Front: Defense Industrialization in the Chinese Interior," *China Quarterly,* No. 115, September 1988. See also Richard Conroy, *Technological Change in China,* 1992, pp. 63–64. One additional negative consequence of the Third Line policy on China's defense industries is the difficulty in attracting talented personnel to work in the isolated, backward regions in which China's defense industries are often located. Arthur S. Ding, "Economic Reform and Defence Industries in China," 1996, p. 86.

Figure 1.1
Changes in the Organizational Structure of China's Defense Industry

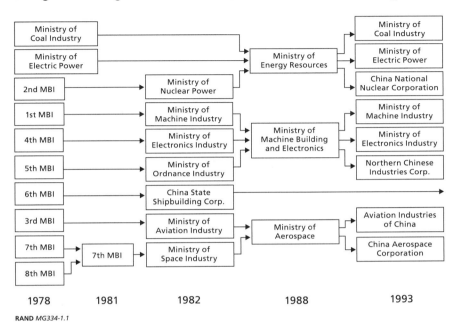

RAND MG334-1.1

In 1981, the 8th MBI (missiles) was merged into the 7th MBI (space), but the first major reorganization of China's defense-industrial complex occurred in 1982. At that time, most of the numbered sectors, formerly belonging to the Ministry of Machine Building Industry, were reorganized into separate and distinct ministries. Five of them were defense-related: the Ministry of Nuclear Energy, the Ministry of Aviation Industry, the Ministry of Electronics Industry, the Ministry of Ordnance Industry, and the Ministry of Space Industry. The 6th MBI was converted into a state-owned company, the China State Shipbuilding Corporation. In addition, 1982 also saw the combination of NDSTC, NDIO, and STECO into a single entity: the Commission on Science, Technology, and Industry for National Defense (COSTIND).

In 1988, a reorganization that involved consolidating ministries took place: The Ministry of Nuclear Energy was combined with the

Ministry of Coal Industry and the Ministry of Electric Power Industry to form the Ministry of Energy Resources; the Ministry of Aviation Industry and the Ministry of Space Industry were combined to form the Ministry of Aerospace; and the Ministry of Electronics Industry and the Ministry of Ordnance Industry were combined to form the Ministry of Machine Building and Electronics.

In 1993, another reorganization took place, this time consisting of redividing the ministries and converting some of the resultant entities into general companies (*zong gongsi* 总公司): The nuclear energy portion of the Ministry of Energy Resources was converted into the China National Nuclear Corporation, and the Ministry of Coal Industry and the Ministry of Electric Power Industry were reestablished; the Ministry of Aerospace was converted into two companies: Aviation Industries of China and China Aerospace Corporation; and the Ministry of Machine Building and Electronics Industry was broken down into the Ministry of Electronics Industry, the Ministry of Machine Industry, and the Northern Chinese Industries Corporation (NORINCO). NORINCO comprised the enterprises formerly under the Ministry of Ordnance Industry. Thereafter, China's defense-industrial sector officially consisted of five corporations: China National Nuclear Corporation, Aviation Industries of China, China Aerospace Corporation, NORINCO, and China State Shipbuilding Corporation.[29]

The goals of these reorganizations were to reduce enterprise's reliance on government support, to spur economic dynamism, and to encourage innovation. These reorganizations (and the goals they

---

[29] The best discussion of these organizational changes is in John Frankenstein and Bates Gill, "Current and Future Challenges Facing Chinese Defense Industries" 1996, pp. 398–400, but see also Joseph Gallagher, "China's Military Industrial Complex," 1987; Wendy Frieman, "China's Military R&D System: Reform and Reorientation," in Denis Fred Simon and Merle Goldman, eds., *Science and Technology in Post-Mao China*, Cambridge, Mass.: Harvard University Press, 1989; Benjamin A. Ostrov, *Conquering Resources: The Growth and Decline of the PLA's Science and Technology Commission for National Defense*, Armonk, N.Y.: M. E. Sharpe, 1991; John Frankenstein, "The People's Republic of China: Arms Production, Industrial Strategy and Problems of History," 1993; Wendy Frieman, "China's Defence Industries," 1993; Arthur S. Ding, "Economic Reform and Defence Industries in China," 1996; Bates Gill and Lonnie Henley, *China and the Revolution in Military Affairs*, 1996.

embodied) were broadly consistent with, although weaker than, government policies toward all of China's state-owned enterprises (SOEs), which aimed to make SOEs less dependent on state funds, more efficient, and, eventually, profitable, and self-sustaining.[30]

As the frequency of the divisions and recombinations described above suggests, in many cases these changes were largely cosmetic. Ministries that nominally were subdivided remained closely bound together; ministries that were officially combined generally remained organizationally distinct; and ministries that were converted into companies continued to be controlled by the government and behave like government ministries.[31]

In the reform of civilian ministries in China, the depth of such reorganizations could typically be seen via the physical effects of reorganizations on the headquarters of the entities in question. The headquarters of entities that were originally in separate locations often remained in separate locations, even after nominal combination. When one entity was split into two, the new headquarters was created by designating one half of the headquarters compound as belonging to one of the new entities and the other half of the compound as belonging to the other new entity. In some instances, the primary physical change was to replace the nameplate on the compound gate. Similarly, when ministries were converted into corporations, ministers were redesignated "general managers"; otherwise, the

---

[30] Barry Naughton, *Growing Out of the Plan,* Cambridge, United Kingdom: Cambridge University Press, 1996; Frankenstein and Gill, "Current and Future Challenges Facing Chinese Defense Industries," 1996; and Brömmelhörster and Frankenstein, eds., *Mixed Motives, Uncertain Outcomes: Defense Industry Conversion in China,* 1997.

[31] Kuan Cha-chia, "Jiang Zemin Sets Up General Equipment Department, Zhu Rongji Advances Military Reform," *Kuang chiao ching,* April 16, 1998, pp. 10–12, in *FBIS* as "Establishment of Military Department Noted," May 6, 1998; Yi Jan (sic), "Jiang-Zhu Relationship As Viewed from Army Structural Adjustment," *Ching pao,* March 1, 1999, pp. 34–35, in *FBIS* as "Jiang-Zhu Relations in Army Reform Viewed," March 9, 1999; Li Xiuwei, "Applying Technology to National Defense," *China Space News,* May 26, 1999, p. 1, in *FBIS* as "Applying Technology to National Defense," June 10, 1999; Peng Kai-lei, "Five Major Military Industry Corporations Formally Reorganized," 1999; Xu Sailu, Gu Xianguang, Xu Xiangmin, *Zhongguo junshi kexue,* June 20, 2000, pp. 66–73, in *FBIS* as "Article on Effects of WTO Membership on PRC Military Economy," July 27, 2000.

personnel and organization often remained unchanged.[32] It is likely that this was the case in the defense sector as well.

Understanding "the Soviet Paradox"[33]

In analyzing the capabilities of China's defense-industrial base, a commonly asked question, which we refer to as "the Soviet paradox," is: During the past 50 years, why were the Soviets able to produce large amounts of relatively sophisticated weapon systems in their planned economy when China largely had the opposite experience? This question is most relevant and curious in view of the fact that when China's defense industry was being rebuilt, following the civil war and the founding of the People's Republic of China (PRC), Chinese planners mainly relied on aid, assistance, organizational structures, and production processes inherited from the Soviet Union during their alliance in the 1950s. China's defense industry was built on the shoulders of the Soviet Union's industrial planning system, yet their experiences with defense production differed drastically. Explaining this paradox helps to elucidate further some of the past problems and present challenges facing China's defense-industrial sector.

Several factors explain the Soviet Union's relative success with serial production of advanced military platforms and, by contrast, China's relative failure on the same front. First, historical considerations play a major role. The Soviet Union's industrial, scientific, and technical base was much broader and more developed than China's in 1949, when the PRC was established. The Soviet Union started from a higher baseline than China in the 1950s. Beginning in the 1920s, the Soviets had made great strides in industrializing their largely

---

[32] For a description of how this occurred in the petroleum sector, see Kenneth Lieberthal and Michel Oksenberg, *Policy Making in China: Leaders, Structures, and Processes,* Princeton, N.J.: Princeton University Press, 1988, pp. 123–127.

[33] This discussion is largely drawn from Peter Almquist, "Chinese and Russian Defense Industries: Problems and Prospects," unpublished manuscript, 2003.

agrarian economy, and World War II (WWII) resulted in a huge expansion of the Soviet defense industry and the bureaucratic structure to support it; massive resources had been spent during WWII to develop technologies and invest in personnel. China, by contrast, had had little in the way of a defense industry (or industry of any kind) at the time of Japan's invasion in 1937. Japan's rapid occupation of China's most economically developed regions precluded significant development of China's defense industry during the war with Japan (as compared with the Soviet Union, which was able to keep much of its industrial capacity out of Germany's hands during WWII). After Japan's defeat in 1945, the Nationalists government's military was largely dependent on U.S. military equipment and little funding was available to stimulate the development of a national defense industry in China.

Chinese and Soviet leaders also did not share the same political commitment to defense-industrial production. There was a sense in the Soviet Union that its defense-industrial power had helped to win the war. Following the end of WWII and its civil war, China's experience could not have been more different. The success of the Chinese Communist Party had little to do with China's limited industrial capabilities; in fact, Mao's military strategies and overall strategic disposition, commonly referred to as the People's War, stressed the primacy of man over machines. Also, following years of Japanese occupation and civil war, by 1949 China's defense infrastructure was devastated and needed to be rebuilt.

Another important historical difference between the Soviet Union and China is the large-scale social and economic upheavals China experienced as a result of the Great Leap Forward and Great Proletarian Cultural Revolution (GPCR). These political movements caused major disruptions to China's economic development from 1958 to 1962 and from 1966 to 1976. These periods of extreme societal and economic tumult devastated China's cadre of designers and technicians with specialized training and skills used in the production of military equipment. The GPCR in particular destroyed the careers of many top scientists. Although certain strategic weapon programs, such as those for nuclear weapons and ballistic missiles, were protected, the effect on the capabilities of China's other defense sectors and programs (such as the aviation industry) was significant. By contrast, the Soviet Union by the mid-1960s had developed an impressive Chief Designer program and had been churning out increasingly advanced weapon platforms.

Moreover, although unrelated to the content of his political campaign, during the GPCR Mao initiated the Third Line policy of relocating and duplicating defense-production facilities to China's interior provinces as a defense against a possible invasion by the United States or Soviet Union. This decision exacerbated, by an order of magnitude, the redundancy and inefficiency in China's defense-industrial complex. Many of these interior locations were far from raw material and component suppliers, had poorly developed transportation links, and, being also far from existing population centers, had no infrastructure to build upon. The result was that hospitals, schools, housing, and other facilities had to be built from scratch. These problems were amplified by the practice of dispersing enterprises across multiple locations, meaning that even communication and movement of materials within individual enterprises were hindered.

Differences in Soviet and Chinese threat perceptions and decisions about resource allocation during the Cold War further affected defense-industrial development in these two countries. When the Cold War began, Soviet leaders perceived themselves as locked in a life-or-death competition with the United States. As a result, they continued to pour resources into the defense industry and to demand much from this system. Chinese leaders did not feel the same urgency and, for several decades, were willing to accept secondary status in defense production to the Soviet Union. In the 1950s, China entered into numerous large defense trade agreements with the Soviets to rebuild its devastated defense infrastructure. In the 1950s, Chinese leaders were initially concerned about consolidating the gains of the Revolution, carrying out Mao's goal of the "communization" of agriculture, and transforming China's industrial sector through the Great Leap Forward campaign. In the 1960s, China was mainly preoccupied with the Cultural Revolution. Beginning in the late 1970s, military modernization and defense-industrial production became the last priority in Deng's Four Modernizations policy .

Another major consideration is the different orientations and preferences of senior State and Party leaders in China and the Soviet Union. The top leaders of the Soviet Union were heavily focused on the capabilities and output of its defense industry; many of them had emerged from that system and, as a result, had a strong orientation toward defense production. Consequently, many of the decisions of the Party and State were geared toward protecting and promoting the defense industry. In China, none of the top leaders in the Politburo Standing Committee had strong personal or political ties to the defense industry. Although certain scientists, such as Nie Rongzhen, Zhu Guangya, and Qian Xuesen, the fathers of China's nuclear weapons and ballistic-missile programs, were widely respected and influential in China, they never became senior leaders with the power to directly make resource-allocation decisions.

However, perhaps the most fundamental reason for the performance of the Chinese defense industry being so much poorer than that of its Soviet counterpart during the Cold War is that the human and material resources available to the Soviet Union were so much greater than those available to China. In the 1950s, the Soviet Union had a large and highly developed industry—civilian and defense—that in some technology areas was among the most advanced in the world. The Soviet Union also had an extensive educational and research system and a highly educated population. China, by contrast, had little in the way of industry and a miniscule cadre of scientists and engineers on which to build a defense-industrial establishment. In 1952, for example, less than one-half of 1 percent of the adult population had received a degree from an institution of higher education.[34] Thus, not only did China never devote as great a

---

[34] State Statistical Bureau, *China Statistical Yearbook 1996,* Beijing, China: Statistical Publishing House, 1996, pp. 72, 632. Graduation rates for the years prior to 1952 are not available but are assumed to be, on average, no higher than in 1952. The graduation rate for 1952 was estimated by dividing the number of graduates by the number of 65-year-olds (i.e., the population cohort that was born in 1930) in China in 1995 as provided in the above

proportion of its human and material resources to its defense industry as the Soviet Union, it also had many fewer resources available for much of the Cold War. Only by the 1980s, when military spending was drastically reduced, did the size of China's industry and educated population begin to approach that of the Soviet Union.

New Progress in Defense-Industry Reform: The 1998 Reforms and Beyond

The situation in China's defense industry became increasingly apparent early this decade as more and better equipment began to emerge from key defense sectors. The specific dimensions of these trends are detailed in the case-study chapters. The accelerating improvements in China's defense-production capabilities are explained by four mutually reinforcing chapters.

First, the government has consistently devoted more funds to weapon acquisition. From 1990 to 2003, the official defense budget allocation for weapon equipment (*zhuangbei* 装备) grew from 5 billion RMB to 64.8 billion RMB. These increases are twice the rate of growth of the official defense budget. Also, the share of the budget devoted to equipment increased from 16.3 to 34 percent during this period.[35] For the 1997–2003 period, according to official Chinese budget figures, the amount of funding for equipment grew 153 percent, more than the other two categories in the official defense budget.[36] Such defense spending is bound to positively affect output; these increases likely contributed to the pace at which some new

---

source. The resulting ratio (0.4 percent) is an upper bound for the graduation rate in 1952, because the size of this cohort was undoubtedly much larger in 1952 than in 1995.

[35] The most recent budget figures are taken from *China's National Defense 2004*, Beijing, China: Information Office of the State Council, December 27, 2004; also see "Chinese Defence Industry: Chinese Puzzle," *Jane's Defence Weekly*, January 21, 2004.

[36] The authors are grateful to Richard Bitzinger for this latter calculation. It is commonly accepted that "off-budget" funds are used for weapons imports. See Richard A. Bitzinger, "Just the Facts, Ma'am: The Challenge of Analysing and Assessing Chinese Military Expenditures," *China Quarterly*, No. 173, 2003, pp. 164–175.

systems have come online in recent years. However, the benefits of such increased spending are limited unless defense enterprises actually improve their capabilities for research, design, and production.

Second, the gradual development and commercialization of some defense enterprises during the reform of China's economy over the past 25 years have improved their research, design, and production capabilities. The "spin-on" benefits of robust and rational commercial business operations (i.e, those that complement the core capabilities of an enterprise) accumulated in some defense enterprises. In particular, defense enterprises with the greatest exposure to international markets have been especially effective at improving their R&D and production capabilities, through both partnerships and competition with foreign firms.

Third, the defense industry in the past decade has had consistent access to limited amounts of foreign military equipment and know-how, especially from Russia and Israel. This access has assisted the efforts of some defense sectors to copy-produce weapon systems and to integrate advanced technologies into China's production lines.

The three preceding factors largely explain the advances in the research, design, and production of the new weapon systems that are currently coming online, because such systems have been in China's procurement pipeline for over a decade. These three factors collectively contributed to raising the R&D and production capabilities of certain defense-industrial sectors as they sought to develop and produce these more-advanced systems to meet PLA needs.

Moreover, a fourth factor—defense-industry policy reforms adopted in 1998 and 1999—also contributed to this process. They did so, in particular, by improving China's ability to more rapidly and efficiently produce the systems that were *already* in the development pipeline. Yet, we assess that this fourth factor will likely have a significant and enduring influence on future defense-industrial modernization in China—and over the entire defense-procurement and -production process in China. The scope of these new reforms is examined below.

Given China's heavy reliance on organizational shuffling and reshuffling, reform measures prior to 1998, unsurprisingly, achieved little, if any, success in improving the performance of China's defense industry. Beijing had avoided implementing the type of fundamental reforms needed to revitalize the moribund defense industry. In particular, little was done to reform the central government's defense-procurement system, which was plagued by inefficiency and corruption. However, beginning in spring 1998, during the 9th Meeting of the National People's Congress, China's leaders initiated a new series of policies to reform the operation of the defense-procurement system at the government level and to restructure the defense industry at the enterprise level.

These policies have set the stage for institutional changes in the management of China's defense industry in ways that outstrip past efforts in both scope and depth. The ensuing reforms indicate an acknowledgment of the depth of the problems of China's defense-industrial system. They seek to genuinely transform the structure and operation of that system by streamlining them, by reducing corruption and inefficiency in the procurement process, and by forcing a degree of rationalization and accountability at the enterprise level. Assessing the current and future potential of China's defense industry, therefore, requires a close examination of these reforms.

Beijing's "Grand Strategy" for Improving Defense-Industrial Capabilities

Beijing's overall "grand strategy" for improving the technological capabilities of China's defense industry has three broad elements.

The first element is selective modernization. China's leaders realize that, given the size of China's economy and the overall technological level of the country, it would be too costly to attempt to acquire the capability to produce advanced weapon systems in every possible category of weapon system. Observing how the Soviet Union's attempt to do so became a drag on the nation's economic development, they are determined to avoid a similar fate. Instead,

China's leaders intend to focus on making breakthroughs in certain key areas of weapons capabilities.[37] One article speaks of exploiting China's strength in aerospace, the manufacturing of missiles, and electronics technology; another article advocates concentrating on "C4ISR [command, control, computers, communications, and intelligence, surveillance, and reconnaissance], accurate strike weapons, and other crucial high-tech equipment."[38] Collectively, these would contribute to the PLA's current effort to acquire capabilities for precision strike, anti-access, and area denial.

The second element of the strategy is civil-military integration. Despite China's past difficulties with defense conversion described above, China's leaders believe that new means of integrating civilian and military production are the key to developing an advanced defense-industrial base. Although in the early 1980s the primary hope was that China's defense manufacturers would be able to use their

---

[37] Xiao Yusheng and Chen Yu, "Historic Leaps in China's Military Scientific Study," *Renmin ribao,* February 25, 1999, p. 9, in *FBIS* as "Military Scientific Studies Take Leap," March 2, 1999; An Weiping, "Thoughts on Developing Armaments by Leaps and Bounds," 1999; *Xinhua Domestic Service,* July 1, 1999, in *FBIS* as "Jiang Congratulates Defense Enterprise Restructuring," July 2, 1999; Gong Fangling, "There Should Be New Ideas in Defense Economic Building," *Jiefangjun bao,* September 14, 1999, p. 6, in *FBIS* as "Article on 'Defense Economic Building'," September 23, 1999; Li Xuanqing, Fan Juwei, and Fu Mingyi, "All-Army Weaponry Work Conference Convened in Beijing," *Jiefangjun bao,* November 4, 1999, p. 1, in *FBIS* as "Army Weaponry Work Conference Opens," November 10, 1999; Wang Congbiao, "Implement the Strategy of Strengthening the Military Through Science and Technology to Improve the Defensive Combat Capabilities of China's Military—Studying Jiang Zemin's 'On Science and Technology'," *Jiefangjun bao* (Internet version), February 13, 2001, p. 1, in *FBIS* as "Review of Jiang Zemin's Views on High-Tech Military," February 13, 2001.

[38] Maj. Gen. Xun Zhenjiang and Captain Geng Haijun, "Exploring the Chinese Way to Develop Military Weaponry," *Zhongguo junshi kexue,* June 20, 2002, pp. 50–55, in *FBIS* as "Chinese General Recommends R&D Strategy for Weapons and Equipment," June 20, 2002; Zhang Zhaozhong, "Master New Development Trends of Military Equipment," *Jiefangjun bao,* April 14, 1998, p. 6. The authors of the first article also express the hope that the ongoing "revolution in military affairs" will enable China to shortcut the process of developing an advanced military by achieving the "informationization" of its military at the same time that it accomplishes the still-incomplete process of mechanizing the PLA. The author of the second article strongly opposes reverse engineering and copy-production ("studied imitation") as a means for advancing China's military technology, because such an approach would leave China in a position of perpetually lagging behind the most advanced military powers.

production capabilities to generate profits in civilian markets, today the principal hope seems to be that, through participation in commercial production, China's defense manufacturers will acquire dual-use equipment and know-how that can be used in the production of weapon systems. In addition, China's leaders continue to count on civilian production by China's defense manufacturers to maintain their financial solvency, reducing the amount of funding the government needs to provide to keep these enterprises afloat.[39]

The third element of Beijing's strategy is acquiring advanced foreign weapons equipment, materials, and technologies.[40] With the aim of not undercutting the long-term goal of self-reliance in defense production, importing foreign technology is seen as essential to enabling China eventually to achieve independence in defense production. Given that China's defense industry is behind those of the advanced nations of the world, the best way to rapidly achieve this goal is seen as involving the importation of technology and technical expertise for the production of state-of-the-art military equipment. As

---

[39] For example, see Liu Jibin, "Implement the Guideline of Military-Civilian Integration, Rejuvenate the National Defense Science and Technology Industry, 1999"; Liu Zhenying and Sun Jie, *Xinhua Domestic Service,* July 1, 1999, in *FBIS* as "More on Zhu at Defense Group Ceremony," July 1, 1999; *Central Television Program One Network,* July 1, 1999, in *FBIS* as "Zhu at Defense Ceremony," July 1, 1999; Peng Kai-lei, "Five Major Military Industry Corporations Formally Reorganized," 1999; *Xinhua,* July 1, 1999, in *FBIS* as "Zhu Rongji Urges Sci-Tech Work for National Defense," July 1, 1999; Ye Weiping, "Challenges and Opportunities for Ordnance Industry Following China's Entry to WTO (Part 2 of 2)," *Ta kung pao* (Internet version), April 26, 2000, in *FBIS* as "Part 2: Ta Kung Pao on WTO Impact on Ordnance Industries," May 3, 2000; Wang Congbiao, "Implement the Strategy of Strengthening the Military Through Science and Technology to Improve the Defensive Combat Capabilities of China's Military—Studying Jiang Zemin's 'On Science and Technology'," 2001.

[40] An Weiping, "Thoughts on Developing Armaments by Leaps and Bounds," 1999; Tang Hua, "Science, Technology, and Industry for National Defense Increases Intensity of Innovation," 1999; Li Xuanqing, Fan Juwei, and Fu Mingyi, "All-Army Weaponry Work Conference Convened in Beijing," 1999; Wang Congbiao, "Implement the Strategy of Strengthening the Military Through Science and Technology to Improve the Defensive Combat Capabilities of China's Military—Studying Jiang Zemin's 'On Science and Technology'," 2001; Liu Jibin, "Implementing Thinking on 'Three Represents,' Reinvigorate National Defense Science, Technology, and Industry," *Renmin ribao* (Internet version), September 29, 2001, p. 5, in *FBIS* as "Renmin Ribao on Implementing 'Three Represents' to Reinvigorate National Defense," September 29, 2001.

two Chinese military officers involved in defense production stated, China should "obtain jade from the rocks of other mountains" (*ta shan zhi shi keyi gong yu* 他山之石可以攻玉), meaning that China should "learn or buy anything we can from foreigners" and "study and buy things by hook and by crook."[41]

Examples of Beijing's use of this strategy abound. For example, Russian experts are currently providing workers at the Shenyang Aircraft Corporation with the know-how to assemble Su-27 fighter aircraft using imported materials and equipment. They are also training Chinese workers and engineers to domestically manufacture many key materials. China has also received weapon-making know-how from Israel Aircraft Industries in the form of assistance in designing and producing its J-10 fighter, and from large numbers of Russian scientists who are said to be employed by other sectors in China's defense industry.[42] In addition to importing know-how, China has also been importing the machinery needed to manufacture sophisticated weapon systems, including illegal imports of nominally civilian machinery and materials that can be used in the manufacture of weapon systems and related components.[43] China has also been active in espionage activities to acquire knowledge needed to supplement indigenous R&D efforts.

Despite these comprehensive efforts to import foreign equipment, materials, and technologies, the determining factor in China's ability to produce advanced weapon systems will be the indigenous

---

[41] Maj. Gen. Xun Zhenjiang and Captain Geng Haijun, "Exploring the Chinese Way to Develop Military Weaponry," 2002. See also General Li Xinliang, "Hi-Tech Local Wars' Basic Requirements for Army Building," *Zhongguo junshi kexue,* November 20, 1998, pp. 15–20, in *FBIS* as "Li Xinliang on High-Tech Local War," May 17, 1999.

[42] For example, see Tung Yi and Sing Tao, *Jih pao,* September 6, 2000, p. A39, in *FBIS* as "Russian Experts Said Helping PRC Make High-Tech Weaponry," September 6, 2000.

[43] For example, from the United States, China has imported machinery that can be used to produce materials that it cannot indigenously produce or legally import. See Government Accountability Office (GAO), *Export Controls: Sensitive Machine Tool Exports to China,* Washington, D.C.: GAO/NSIAD-97-4, November 1996, and GAO, *Export Controls: Sale of Telecommunications Equipment to China,* Washington, D.C.: GAO/NSIAD-97-5, November 1996.

capabilities of its defense sectors. Export controls and the efforts of non-Chinese defense firms to maintain their competitive advantage will prevent China from being able to acquire the complete range of equipment, materials, and technology needed to produce the advanced weapon systems the PLA desires. China will have to rely on the ability of its defense sectors to develop many of these items and to integrate them with imported technology to produce complete weapon systems.

Thus, China's ability to develop and implement a strategy for integrating foreign technologies and developing new ones from its basic and applied research base will be a critical variable in its defense-industrial modernization effort. It is a particularly important consideration in a globalized world in which technology acquisition and assimilation is a prevalent practice among all major defense producers, especially those trying to modernize rapidly.

The Goals of the 1998–1999 Reforms

The reforms adopted in 1998–1999 have a number of goals related to reforming the structure (i.e., institutions) and operations (i.e., incentives) of China's entire defense-industry establishment.[44] An overarching aim is to introduce the "four mechanisms" (*sige jizhi* 四个机制) of competition (*jingzheng* 竞争), evaluation (*pingjie* 评介), supervision (*jiandu* 监督), and encouragement (*guli* 鼓励) into the entire defense-industrial system. These mechanisms are specifically articulated by the Chinese government and are central to

---

[44] Premier Zhu Rongji articulated five goals following the initiation of the 1998 reforms: to separate state and enterprise functions; to establish a mechanism for *moderate* competition; to concentrate science and technology resources on weapon development and production; to promote better military-industry layout and restructuring; and to press enterprises to reduce their losses by helping to create a positive business environment to free enterprises from current difficulties. Tang Hua, "Science, Technology, and Industry for National Defense Increases Intensity of Innovation," 1999; "Chinese Premier Underlines Science, Technology for National Defense," *People's Daily* (English edition), July 2, 1999; Peng Kai-lei, "Five Major Military Industry Corporations Formally Reorganized," 1999.

guiding China's efforts to modernize the operations of its defense industry.[45]

A more specific goal of the reforms is to renovate China's highly ineffective, inefficient, and corrupt defense-procurement system. Chinese analysts have described the past procurement system under a planned economy as simply the "ordering of military products" (*zhuangbei dinghuo* 装备订货); now, the Chinese defense-industry planners are seeking to build a system of "military procurement" (*zhuangbei caigou* 装备采购) that better incorporates market practices. Chinese analysts note that the transition will take time and will likely be problematic.[46]

Moreover, the government sought to separate further the state from defense-enterprise operations in order to inject a greater degree of competition into industry interactions.[47] Although most major defense firms had been converted from ministries into corporations in 1993 (in 1982 in the case of China State Shipbuilding Corporation), China's defense companies in the 1990s continued to behave very

---

[45] *Xinhua Domestic Service,* in *FBIS* as "Wu Bangguo Speaks at Defense Industry Conference," 1999; Liu Zhenying and Sun Jie, in *FBIS* as "More on Zhu at Defense Group Ceremony," 1999; *Central Television Program One Network,* in *FBIS* as "Zhu at Defense Ceremony," 1999; *Xinhua,* in *FBIS* as "Zhu Rongji Urges Sci-Tech Work for National Defense," 1999.

[46] Li Ming and Mao Jingli, eds., *Zhuangbei caigou lilun yu shijian* (*The Theory and Practice of Military Equipment Procurement*), Beijing, China: Guofang Gongye Chubanshe, August 2003, pp. 20–26.

[47] Kuan Cha-chia, "Jiang Zemin Sets Up General Equipment Department, Zhu Rongji Advances Military Reform," 1998; Hsiao Cheng-chin, "Liu Jibin, Minister in Charge of the State Commission of Science, Technology, and Industry for National Defense and a Veteran Who Has Rejoined His Original Unit," 1998; Yi Jan, "Jiang-Zhu Relationship as Viewed from Army Structural Adjustment," 1999; *Xinhua Domestic Service,* in *FBIS* as "Wu Bangguo Speaks at Defense Industry Conference," 1999; Li Xiuwei, "Applying Technology to National Defense," 1999; Peng Kai-lei, "Five Major Military Industry Corporations Formally Reorganized," 1999; *Xinhua,* in *FBIS* as "Zhu Rongji Urges Sci-Tech Work for National Defense," 1999; Tang Hua, "Science, Technology, and Industry for National Defense Increases Intensity of Innovation," 1999; Xu Sailu, Gu Xianguang, Xu Xiangmin, in *FBIS* as "Article on Effects of WTO Membership on PRC Military Economy," 2000; Xiao Yusheng, "Building a Strong People's Army," *Liaowang,* July 29, 2002, pp. 7–9, in *FBIS* as "PRC Article on PLA Military Buildup over Last 10 Years, Preparations for Future," August 8, 2002.

much like the ministries from which they had been created. These companies were involved not only in production but also in regulatory and policymaking issues. The tensions and conflicts of interest resulting from this model created major impediments to making defense-industry firms more efficient and raising their R&D and production capabilities.

A fourth and related aim of the reforms was to provide more autonomy for individual enterprises within each of the large defense-industrial group corporations. The persistence of the ministerial system of organization meant that, although individual enterprises were nominally independent subsidiaries of the large parent companies, in practice the relationship between enterprises resembled that of organizations within a hierarchical bureaucracy. The subordinate enterprises had little autonomy in their decisionmaking and internal management, and they were dependent on the parent entity.[48] This arrangement stifled their initiative and creativity and reduced incentives for greater efficiency.

While providing enterprises with more autonomy, the reforms also sought to make the various defense enterprises and their component factories responsible for their own bottom lines.[49] Like many of China's state-owned enterprises, defense enterprises that suffered excessive losses had not been penalized. Many loss-making enterprises had not been allowed to go bankrupt; they were simply provided with subsidies or bank loans to make up the difference between revenues and expenditures. This lack of financial accountability not only discouraged defense enterprises from taking steps to cut losses but also provided no incentive for efficiency or quality production, since

---

[48] Liu Zhenying and Sun Jie, in *FBIS* as "More on Zhu at Defense Group Ceremony," 1999; *Central Television Program One Network,* in *FBIS* as "Zhu at Defense Ceremony," 1999; Peng Kai-lei, "Five Major Military Industry Corporations Formally Reorganized," 1999; *Xinhua,* in *FBIS* as "Zhu Rongji Urges Sci-Tech Work for National Defense," 1999.

[49] Liu Zhenying and Sun Jie, in *FBIS* as "More on Zhu at Defense Group Ceremony," 1999; *Central Television Program One Network,* in *FBIS* as "Zhu at Defense Ceremony," 1999; Peng Kai-lei, "Five Major Military Industry Corporations Formally Reorganized," 1999; *Xinhua,* in *FBIS* as "Zhu Rongji Urges Sci-Tech Work for National Defense," 1999.

the survival of an enterprise was unrelated to the quality or timeliness of its products.

While providing enterprises with more autonomy, the reforms also sought to increase the degree of horizontal and vertical integration both within each defense sector and across defense sectors. Defense enterprises tended to operate with little coordination or information-sharing among them, which is necessary for developing comparative advantages and real market dynamics.[50] In particular, the reforms sought to combine the functions of research and production, which traditionally had been carried out separately.[51]

Overall, the Chinese leadership's aim was to reshape the entire defense industry into three types of enterprises: "backbone enterprises," which would focus on military production; enterprises that would produce both military and civilian items; and enterprises that would focus on civilian production while using their technological capabilities to raise the overall level of China's science and technology base.[52]

Specific Organizational Reforms
Beginning in 1998, Beijing adopted a series of specific policies to overhaul the organizational structure and operations of China's moribund defense industry. Reforms were initiated both at the cen-

---

[50] Kuan Cha-chia, "Jiang Zemin Sets Up General Equipment Department, Zhu Rongji Advances Military Reform," 1998; Liu Jibin, "Implement the Guideline of Military-Civilian Integration, Rejuvenate the National Defense Science and Technology Industry," 1999; Si Yanwen and Chen Wanjun, *Xinhua Domestic Service,* June 9, 1999, in *FBIS* as "General Armaments Director on Developing Weapons," June 9, 1999; Xu Penghang, "Give Play to the Strength of Military Industries to Participate in Development of China's West," *Renmin Ribao Overseas Edition* (Internet version), March 24, 2000, p. 2, in *FBIS* as "RMRB on Utilizing Military Industries to Develop China's West," March 24, 2000; Xu Sailu, Gu Xianguang, and Xu Xiangmin, in *FBIS* as "Article on Effects of WTO Membership on PRC Military Economy," 2000.

[51] *Xinhua Domestic Service,* in *FBIS* as "Wu Bangguo Speaks at Defense Industry Conference," 1999; Tang Hua, "Science, Technology, and Industry for National Defense Increases Intensity of Innovation," 1999.

[52] Zhu Qinglin, *Zhongguo Caijun yu Guofang Zirenmimbi Peizhi Yanjiu,* Beijing, China: National Defense University Press, 1999, pp. 163–167.

tral government level and at the enterprise level. In general terms, the reforms aimed to centralize and standardize weapon-procurement decisions at the central government level of operations while decentralizing the government's management of defense enterprises.

Central Government Reforms. The government adopted two major reforms that significantly changed the weapon-procurement process. First, during the 9th National People's Congress meeting, the government abolished the military-controlled Commission on Science Technology and Industry for National Defense, which had been created in 1982, and replaced it with a strictly civilian agency of the same name but under the control of the State Council and then-premier Zhu Rongji. The new State COSTIND, which is run by civilian personnel, was formed by combining the defense offices of the Ministry of Finance, the State Planning Commission, and the administrative offices of the five major defense corporations.[53] Previously, COSTIND had reported to both the State Council and the Central Military Commission (CMC) and was staffed by both civilian and military personnel. Responsible for overseeing all aspects of China's defense sectors, it had been involved in the daily management of China's large defense firms. As a quasi-military agency, the old COSTIND had also been very heavily involved in decisions on R&D and the purchase of military equipment. It had acted as a bridge between the PLA and defense enterprises. In that role, COSTIND exerted heavy and, in some cases, preponderant, influence over defense-procurement decisions. COSTIND's leading role contributed to the inefficiency of the procurement process so much so that the PLA was unable to acquire the weapons it needed.

---

[53] *Xinhua,* March 10, 1998, in *FBIS* as "NPC Adopts Institutional Restructuring Plan," March 10, 1998; Tseng Hai-tao, "Jiang Zemin Pushes Forward Restructuring of Military Industry—Developments of State Commission of Science, Technology, and Industry for National Defense and Five Major Ordnance Corporations," *Kuang chiao ching,* July 16, 1998, pp. 18–20, in *FBIS* as "Journal on PRC Military-Industrial Reform," July 28, 1998.

Weapons were frequently delivered late and were often defective or of very poor quality.[54]

In terms of defense procurement and defense production, the restructured COSTIND's responsibilities, resources, and authority were substantially circumscribed. It is no longer heavily involved in government decisions on the acquisition of new military equipment or the direct management of the affairs of defense enterprises.[55] In stark contrast to its previous incarnation, the new COSTIND controls no procurement funds; thus, it possesses minimal influence over procurement decisions.[56]

The new COSTIND is tasked with coordinating procurement negotiations between the CMC/GAD and defense enterprises. In that role, the military uses COSTIND to coordinate when there are multiple bids from several defense enterprises, and COSTIND acts to ensure contract compliance by the enterprises. Some PLA officials have indicated that, because COSTIND is a government agency, they can trust it more than the production enterprises to ensure contract compliance. This role is not fixed, however. COSTIND also controls some R&D funds for basic and applied research, although little of the COSTIND-funded research is directly related to military technologies. PLA institutions now appear to control most defense R&D funds. COSTIND's funds are also not used to directly finance weapon production; rather, COSTIND importantly funds fixed-asset investments in the defense industry, such as facility upgrades and expansions. Such decisions are likely coordinated with other major State Council organs, such as the State Development and Reform Commission.[57]

---

[54] Joseph Gallagher, "China's Military Industrial Complex," 1987. Gallagher was an assistant army attaché in Beijing, and his account is based on his participation in many negotiations with the Chinese in the late 1980s.

[55] Tang Hua, "Science, Technology, and Industry for National Defense Increases Intensity of Innovation," 1999.

[56] Conversations with GAD officials, Beijing, China, October 2002.

[57] Conversations with PLA officials, Beijing, China, May 2003.

The restructured COSTIND is meant to function as the administrative and regulatory agency for China's major defense enterprises. Its principal responsibilities include drafting the annual plans for R&D, investment, and production; formulating laws and regulations relevant to defense-industry operations, and organizing international exchanges, defense cooperation, and arms sales to other countries; and providing export-control administration related to military exports. COSTIND was stripped of responsibility for direct management of the operations of defense enterprises. Thus, COSTIND takes care of the government functions of China's defense companies while leaving them to manage themselves, a process in which COSTIND used to be heavily involved. This separation is intended to allow the enterprises to focus on business decisions regarding production, cost control, and profitability.[58]

Following the "civilianization" of COSTIND, the second major organizational reform, was the creation in April 1998 of a new general department of the PLA, known as the General Armaments Department (GAD 总装备部). GAD assumed the responsibilities for military procurement of the old COSTIND, combined with the roles and missions of the General Equipment Bureau under the General Staff Department, as well as other military equipment- and procurement-related divisions from the General Logistics Depart-

---

[58] "Ten Military Industry Corporations Are Founded," *Zhongguo hangtian* (*China Aerospace*), August 1999, as translated in *FBIS*, August 1, 1999; "Speech of Liu Jibin at COSTIND Working Meeting," *Zhongguo hangkong bao* (*China Aviation News*), April 30, 1999, as translated in *FBIS*, April 20, 1999; "Interview by Central People's Radio Network Reporter Zhao Lianju: Work Earnestly to Usher in the Spring of Science and Industry for National Defense—Interviewing Liu Jibin, Minister in Charge of the Commission of Science, Technology, and Industry for National Defense," March 30, 1998, in *FBIS* as "PRC Minister on Future Projects for Defense Commission," March 30, 1998; Gao Jiquan, "Shoulder Heavy Responsibilities, Accept New Challenges—Interviewing Liu Jibin, Newly Appointed State Commission of Science, Technology, and Industry for National Defense Minister," *Jiefangjun bao,* April 9, 1998, p. 5, in *FBIS* as "New COSTIND Minister Interviewed," April 9, 1998; "National News Hookup," *China Central Television One,* April 21, 1998, in *FBIS* as "Interview with Minister of National Defense Science," April 21, 1998. Also see Tseng Hai-tao, "Jiang Zemin Pushes Forward Restructuring of Military Industry—Developments of State Commission of Science, Technology, and Industry for National Defense and Five Major Ordnance Corporations," 1998.

ment. It was formed largely by appropriating the personnel from these two organizations. The responsibilities of GAD include managing the life cycle of the PLA's weapon systems (from R&D to retirement) and running China's testing, evaluation, and training bases.[59] In addition, GAD, mainly through its Science and Technology Committee, plays a role in broad policy debates about military-modernization, defense-procurement, and arms-control issues.[60]

The significance of the civilianization of COSTIND and the creation of GAD is threefold. First, following the formation of GAD, an additional senior PLA officer was added to the Central Military Commission to promote the critical tasks of management and modernization of PLA equipment.[61] Second, these policy changes centralized China's military-procurement system. Previously, responsibilities for PLA purchases were divided among numerous civilian and military organizations, each with distinct and often-conflicting interests. COSTIND's former predominant influence was a particular problem. The major responsibilities for identifying the PLA's needs and fulfilling them with appropriate equipment are now all located in GAD, with input from the General Staff Department and the service branches. The formation of GAD improved linkages between the R&D and production stages in the procurement cycle. Previously, these steps had been separate in some sectors, which resulted in inefficiencies and disconnects between the design and production of weapons systems. GAD is now directly in charge of setting goals and priorities, and of providing funding for the entire procurement cycle from R&D to testing and evaluation, production, management, and

---

[59] Harlan Jencks, "The General Armaments Department," in James C. Mulvenon and Andrew N.D. Yang, *The People's Liberation Army as Organization: Reference Volume v1.0*, Santa Monica, Calif.: RAND Corporation, CR-182-NSRD, 2002. Available only online at http://www.rand.org/publications/CF/CF182/.

[60] Two of the committee's most-senior members, Zhu Guangya and General Qian Shaojun, afford the S&T Committee a very influential role in Chinese civil and military nuclear affairs. Harlan Jencks, "The General Armaments Department," 2002.

[61] We are grateful to Dennis Blasko for highlighting this point. The first head of GAD was Cao Gangchuan, who is now the Defense Minister.

eventual retirement and replacement.[62] For example, GAD is actively involved in certifying designs and prototypes and in authorizing production start-ups.

Third, the 1998 reforms separated the builders from the buyers—an organizational change that further rationalized the procurement system and aimed to reduce conflicts of interest and possibilities for corruption. GAD now represents the PLA interests, whereas COSTIND, as a civilian agency, now mainly handles the industrial planning and administrative/regulatory affairs of defense firms. Because GAD controls procurement funds, PLA interests now play a decisive role in procurement decisions, whereas, when the former COSTIND had authority over such decisions in the 1980s and 1990s, industry interests dominated in practice (even though COSTIND's staff included representatives of both the PLA and the defense industry). In many cases, PLA purchases were driven more by the production capabilities of certain defense firms (whose interests were promoted by COSTIND) than by the needs of the PLA. The PLA was sometimes forced to purchase weapon systems that it did not need and could not use. Unsurprisingly, the change from past practices has produced conflicts and much bureaucratic competition between GAD and the new COSTIND. Such conflicts complicate ongoing reform of the procurement system.[63]

In addition to these large organizational reforms, the government also adopted specific policies to change the weapon-procurement process.[64] Most of these policies are quite new and their impact

---

[62] Yun Shan, "General Equipment Department—Fourth PLA General Department," *Liaowang,* May 25, 1998, p. 30, in *FBIS* as "China: New PLA General Equipment Department," June 12, 1998; Pai Chuan, "Command System of the Chinese Army," *Ching pao,* December 1, 1998, pp. 40–42, in *FBIS* as "Overview of PLA Structure," December 12, 1998; Xiao Yusheng, "Building a Strong People's Army," 2002.

[63] Conversations with PLA officials, Beijing, China, October 2002.

[64] In addition to focusing on reform of the procurement process, the PLA has devoted equal energy to the reform of the system of life-cycle management for weapon platforms. Since 2000, an entire cottage industry of books and studies on weapon equipment management (*wuqi zhuangbei guanli*) has emerged in China. These polices are aimed at improving the system through which the military utilizes and maintain its weapons throughout their life

on actual production and output is not fully evident; however, their adoption and implementation serve as an indication of the seriousness of the central government's efforts to reform the military procurement system and, ultimately, to improve defense R&D and production capabilities.

According to Chinese officials, these policy reforms are driven by several broad goals, which include standardizing and centralizing the procurement system for military goods, establishing a legally based procurement system to protect both the military's and the enterprises' contractual rights and responsibilities, adopting a system of market competition with open contract bidding and negotiation for defense purchases, and improving the quality and professionalism of the personnel involved in weapon procurement.[65] The Chinese government specifically stated in 2004 it seeks to "establish and improve a mechanism of competition, appraisal, supervision and motivation" in its defense-industrial system.[66]

Procurement-process reforms have taken several forms. First and foremost, the military has sought to create a system that will standardize, unify, and legalize the procurement process for both military equipment (*zhuangbei* 装备) and military materials (*wuzi* 物资). The GAD is in charge of the former, and the General Logistics Department is responsible for the latter. Each process is structured according to distinct regulations and provisions. Since the mid-1980s, when the first procurement regulations were adopted, numerous laws and regulations have proliferated, leading to much confusion in the military purchasing system.

span. Some examples of research work on equipment management include Ci Shihai, *Budui zhuangbei guanli gailun (Army Equipment Management Theory)*, Beijing, China: Junshi Kexue Chubanshe, 2001.

[65] Xie Dajun, "The Procurement and Supervision of the Manufacture of Foreign Armaments," *Xiandai junshi*, August 15, 1999, pp. 52–54, as translated in *FBIS*, August 15, 1999; Liu Cheng, "Creating a New Situation in Weapons and Equipment Modernization Effort," *Jiefangjun bao*, October 14, 2002, as translated in *FBIS*, October 14, 2002.

[66] *China's National Defense in 2004*, Beijing, China: Information Office of the State Council, December 27, 2004; this government-issued white paper can be found at http://www.china.org.cn/e-white/20041227/index.htm.

In October 2002, Jiang Zemin signed an order promulgating and implementing a new set of regulations for military equipment procurement, called "PLA Regulations on Armaments Procurement" (*Zhonghua Renmin Jiefangjun Zhuangbei Caigou Tiaoli* 中华人民解放军装备采购条例).[67] These new regulations are meant to standardize several aspects of the procurement system, including procurement planning, specification of procurement methods, equipment-procurement procedures, procurement contract procedures, executing contracts, and purchasing foreign equipment.[68] In addition, beginning in December 2003, China issued five new "provisions" (*guiding* 规定) to further elucidate various aspects of the above regulations: Provisions on the Management of Armaments Procurement Plans, Provisions on the Management of Armaments Procurement Contracts, Provisions on the Management of Armaments Procurement Modes and Procedures, Provisions on the Management of the Examination of the Qualifications of Armaments Manufacturing Units, and Provisions on the Management of the Centralized Procurement of Armaments of the Same Kind. In 2002, the CMC also issued several new provisions governing procurement of military materials.[69]

These new legal structures are also meant to accelerate the establishment of a competitive-bidding system for PLA contracts, which was first discussed in 1998 when GAD was formed.[70] China's

---

[67] In 1990, the Central Military Commission issued "Work Regulations for the Management of Weapons and Equipment." Since then, additional regulations have proliferated. The Chinese media announced the promulgation of the new rules, but they have not made them publicly available. "Central Military Commission Chairman Jiang Zemin Signs Order Promulgating and Implementing Chinese People's Liberation Army Equipment Procurement Regulations," *Xinhua,* November 1, 2002, as noted in *FBIS*, November 1, 2002.

[68] For research on China's past procurement processes, see Ravinder Pal Singh (Stockholm International Peace Research Institute), *Arms Procurement Decision Making: China, India, Israel, Japan, South Korea and Thailand,* Oxford, United Kingdom: Oxford University Press, 1998.

[69] These provisions are listed in China's 2004 defense white paper, *China's National Defense in 2004,* 2004.

[70] "Government Procurement Again Recommended at NPC," *Xinhua,* March 8, 1999, as translated in *FBIS*, March 8, 1999.

2004 national defense white paper provided details on the nature and functioning of this bidding system:

> The procurement mode has been in an accelerating transition from procurement at designated enterprises to multiple ways of procurement such as open bidding, invited bidding, competitive bargaining and inquiry procurement. This has raised the overall cost-effectiveness of armaments procurement and ensured the procurement at reasonable prices of weapons and equipment advanced in performance, superior in quality and complete as a set. The procurement of military computers and network devices, vehicle chassis, generating sets, shelters, and other types of general-purpose equipment has changed from separate to centralized procurement at the PLA level.

According to Chinese media reports, the government has established a special procurement agency to eventually unify all of the military's purchasing and to use a public bidding process. A *Xinhua* report explained the rationale for this move:

> The main task of the reform is to change the purchasing mode and centralize the purchasing of items, which currently is scattered in various departments to a degree as high as possible in the hands of an institution specializing in doing purchases. Thus gradually setting up a model based mainly on centralized purchasing.[71]

Enterprise-Level Reforms. Beginning in 1998, Beijing adopted far-reaching policies to alter the relationship between the government and defense enterprises. The central government's main goals were to separate the government administrative units from enterprise operations, to make the enterprises more market-oriented by exposing

---

[71] "Standardizing Our Military Armament Procurement Work According to Law," *Jiefang-jun bao,* November 2, 2002, as translated in *FBIS*, November 2, 2002; "PRC Plans Reform of Army Purchasing System," *Xinhua,* January 9, 2002, as translated in *FBIS*, January 9, 2002; "PRC Armed Forces Adopt Government Procurement System to Meet Demands of Economic Reforms," *Xinhua,* January 9, 2002, as translated in *FBIS*, January 9, 2002; "Central Military Commission Chairman Jiang Zemin Signs Order Promulgating and Implementing Chinese People's Liberation Army Equipment and Regulations," 2002.

them to competitive pressures, to provide tighter budget constraints, to make the enterprises less reliant on state subsidies, and to lessen the classic social burdens associated with the *danwei* system. Chinese policymakers adopted several different types of policies to change defense-enterprise operations.

The major organizational reform, which occurred in July 1999, involved the bifurcation of China's five core defense companies into ten defense-industrial enterprise groups (*jungong jituan gongsi* 军工集团公司). An eleventh enterprise group, for defense electronics, was established in late 2002. The Chinese government pursued two goals in undertaking this reorganization. The obvious goal was to inject competition into the defense-industrial sector. China's leaders hope that competition will cause defense enterprises to become more efficient, less of a financial burden on central and local governments, and more capable of technology absorption, assimilation, and independent innovation. The then–new head of COSTIND, Liu Jibin, explained in July 1999 the core rationale for this organizational change, noting that each of the general companies is divided into two roughly equivalent groups in terms of capability. It is expected that through "proper competition each of the new companies['] efficiency can be improved and management mechanisms can be transformed."[72]

The extent to which real competition has emerged between the enterprise groups in each sector is mixed. As addressed in the case studies, in some sectors limited competition over defense systems, key subsystems, and parts has emerged. In others, the defense products of the two group companies are different enough that there is little to no direct competition between the two companies. Some Chinese writings indicate that the real goal of the 1998–1999 reforms was not to promote competition in terms of products but rather in terms of "systems of organization" and "operational mechanisms."[73] That is, splitting each defense sector into two enterprise groups is apparently

---

[72] "Ten Military Industry Corporations Are Founded," 1999.

[73] Li Xiuwei, "Applying Technology to National Defense," 1999.

supposed to allow them to separately explore different approaches to organization and management so that they can learn from each other's successes and failures. This is an approach that might be adopted for increasing the efficiency of government organizations, not an effort to allow the defense-enterprise groups to behave as true competitors operating in a free market. It again suggests that China's defense sectors are still to some degree treated as though they are government agencies, not as truly independent economic entities.[74]

The other goal of the 1999 bifurcation policy was the formation of "group corporations" (*jituan gongsi* 集团公司). This new category of company was an element of the government's broader effort to reform ownership structures in SOEs, including defense enterprises.[75] These group corporations were part of an effort to establish shareholder relationships within a company to further remove the government from firm operations, to distribute risk, and to increase accountability for profits and losses.[76] Many of China's major firms under the large group corporations have a long list of shareholders that own a (noncontrolling) stake in enterprise operations. This effort at ownership reform is one of the newest policies aimed at marketizing enterprise operations.

Beyond these broad structural reforms, Chinese policymakers have also implemented a variety of specific policy initiatives to revitalize defense-enterprise operations. First, one trend is the growing use of nongovernment funds for military-related production projects. Enterprises manufacturing military equipment may use capital from other firms, internal monies, or investment from foreign countries to fund projects that produce weapons that are then marketed to the

---

[74] The fact that the headquarters of the new enterprise groups were apparently formed simply by subdividing the headquarters compounds of the old defense corporations reinforces this impression. See Peng Kai-lei, "Five Major Military Industry Corporations to Be Reorganized," 1999.

[75] Yi-min Lin and Tian Zhi, "Ownership Restructuring in Chinese State Industry: An Analysis of Evidence on Initial Organizational Changes," *China Quarterly,* September 2001, pp. 305–341.

[76] Peng Kai-lei, "Five Major Military Industry Corporations Formally Reorganized," 1999.

PLA or abroad. The Chengdu Aircraft Corporation (AVIC I) is using its own and Pakistani funds to subsidize the development of the FC-1/Super-7 light fighter program. This platform is in the final stages of development and was test-flown for the first time in August 2003. It is not clear whether the PLA Air Force is going to buy it, however. The FC-1 is intended primarily for the Pakistani and other Third World militaries, but it is possible that the PLA Air Force will acquire some. While the FC-1 does not represent a major technological leap for the Chinese aviation industry, its financing mechanism is innovative for the Chinese defense industry. Now that PLA procurement is no longer guaranteed to defense enterprises, defense firms, such as the Guizhou Aviation Corporation, which is developing an advanced jet trainer, have begun marketing designs of future systems in an effort to find investors to support the development of new weapon systems.[77]

Second, some defense firms have created subsidiary organizations listed on domestic Chinese stock exchanges in Shanghai or Shenzhen. These joint stock companies potentially provide the controlling enterprise with an additional source of capital for possible reinvestment in enterprise operations. Listing on Chinese capital markets has the additional advantage of carrying with it minimal transparency requirements, an issue of particular concern to defense companies. To date, over 40 defense enterprises have been listed on the Shanghai and Shenzhen exchanges. While some of these companies have been fully converted to nonmilitary production—but are still considered defense enterprises by dint of their origins—some of the defense firms listed may continue to be involved in military projects, as well as in production of civilian goods.[78]

A third emerging change in the defense industry is the expansion and pluralization of partnerships with civilian universities and research institutes to improve educational training relevant to the

---

[77] Data are from Guizhou Aviation Corporation brochure, 2002.

[78] "Jungong Shangshi Qiye 2001 Nian Pandian," *Zhongguo junzhuanmin* (*China Defense Conversion*), July 2002, p. 4.

development of new military technologies. The growing number of partnerships between the defense industry and national educational institutions is notable. GAD and COSTIND have begun to partner with universities in various parts of the country to improve the PLA's access to individuals with technical training. In 2002, COSTIND gave several million renminbi to at least two aerospace and shipbuilding academies in Jiangsu Province to develop their defense-related course offerings, to recruit students interested in defense research, and to provide additional training on defense technology issues to the current staff of these academies.[79] These partnerships are in addition to the numerous universities that have traditionally been linked to China's defense-industry establishment.[80] This government-industry-university cooperation is most notable in the information technology (IT) industry, but it is rapidly growing in other sectors involved in defense R&D and production.

Fourth, a limited amount of rationalization has occurred in recent years in the defense industry, although much more is needed in light of the continuing inefficiencies and redundancy still prevalent in several sectors. Some shipbuilding and "ordnance" (ground systems) industrial groups, for example, have transferred large enterprises to provincial authorities. Such transfers represent a major trend in the shipbuilding industry, in which roughly 60 percent of China's shipyards are now controlled by the CSSC and CSIC (China's top two state-owned shipbuilding group corporations; see Chapter Three); the remainder is run by provincial and local authorities. Another aspect of rationalization has been layoffs and downsizing, which have been occurring in fits and starts. According to one report, 61,000 ordnance industry workers were laid off in

---

[79] See *Guangming ribao,* August 27, 2002; *Guangming ribao,* June 6, 2002.

[80] COSTIND directly administers seven higher education institutions: Harbin Institute of Technology; Beijing University of Aeronautics and Astronautics; Beijing Institute of Technology; Nanjing University of Aeronautics and Astronautics; Northwestern Polytechnical University; Nanjing University of Science and Technology; Harbin Engineering University. In addition, the provincial branches of COSTIND, together with provincial governments, jointly administer a number of institutes and schools. For example, see http://www.jxgfgb.gov.cn/jgzy/index.htm.

2001 and 100 other enterprises were earmarked for bankruptcy or takeover the following year.[81] The General Manager of NORINCO, Ma Zhigeng, noted in a 2004 interview that since 1999 he had downsized NORINCO's staff from 476,000 to some 360,000.[82]

A fifth reform initiated by COSTIND and GAD is the promotion of R&D and production cooperation among defense enterprises located in multiple provinces. In the past, one of the organizational deficiencies within China's defense industry was the extensive reliance on single-source suppliers to produce defense platforms. This problem has been particularly acute in China's aviation sector. Such practices have contributed to the inefficiency, redundancy, and high degree of insularity in China's defense industry. GAD and COSTIND are trying to address this problem by promoting greater integration and information-sharing among defense enterprises and R&D institutes in various provinces. During 2000, for example, the Beijing Military Representative Bureau reportedly began to cooperate with its counterparts in the national defense departments of universities, colleges, and scientific research institutes of five cities in northern China. The aim of this initiative was to facilitate better cross-province information-sharing about technical innovations and potential markets for new products—both military and civilian.[83] While it is far from clear how successful this effort has been in overcoming deeply ingrained localization in defense production, the adoption of this plan to boost cross-province defense-industry cooperation indicates that the government recognizes the problem and is making initial efforts to overcome it.

---

[81] "Defense Commission Minister Sets Targets for 2002," *Zhongguo xinwen she,* January 7, 2002, as translated in *FBIS,* January 7, 2002.

[82] Ai Min, "China Ordnance Moves Toward High-Tech Internationalization," *Liaowang,* April 12, 2004, pp. 32–33, as translated in *FBIS,* April 12, 2004.

[83] Jiang Huai and Fu Cheng, "Beijing Military Representatives Bureau Cooperates with Five Provinces and Cities in North China in Building Regional Cooperation with Various Layers and Professions," *Jiefangjun bao,* September 18, 2000, p. 8, as translated in *FBIS,* September 18, 2000.

A sixth change from past practices has been the growing emphasis on quality assurance and quality control in defense production—a lack of which has long plagued military production in China. There appears to be a gradual change in incentives structures for personnel and organizations directly involved with quality-control functions; this structure includes punishing (through financial penalties/fines) quality-control personnel for quality-control failures and rewarding them for exceptional work. In July 2003, three aerospace-sector units were punished relatively severely for a lack of knowledge about their products and for producing and procuring poor-quality products. They were also punished for submitting deceptive quality-control reports. The quality-control managers at theses units were fired, subordinate personnel were fined, and the subsidies for the military personnel involved (e.g., the military representatives) were suspended for a prolonged period. The quality-control personnel were also criticized in a circular and sent for additional training. Three other research institutes in the aerospace sector were warned about their quality control as well.[84]

Seventh, the reform of the system of military representative offices (MRO) has become a recent priority for senior leaders in the GAD system. For 20 years, the PLA has used a system of military representative offices at the city, enterprise, and factory levels to assure quality control and contract compliance at factories and research institutes.[85] In light of the high degree of diversification of defense factories into civilian production since the 1980s, most MROs are based in factories and institutes involved in both civilian work and defense research, development, and production. Yet, the MRO system has been troubled and ineffective for many years. MRO offices are understaffed, and military personnel are reportedly overworked.

---

[84] *China Space News,* July 16, 2003.

[85] Chinese media reports have identified military representative offices in Beijing, Wuhan, Shenyang, Changsha, Shanghai, and Wuhan. According to one report, seven military representatives were in a factory. See *Jiefangjun bao,* November 14, 2001, as translated in *FBIS* as "PRC: Article on PLA Plant Manufacturing Special Military Vehicles," November 14, 2001.

Many MRO personnel lack the technical expertise to effectively carry out their contract-compliance and quality-assurance roles, a problem that in some cases is exacerbated by a high turnover in MRO staff. Overall, staffers have done a poor job of monitoring and evaluating ongoing equipment production. In addition, the objectivity and reliability of many MROs are problematic because representatives who reside at factories for a long time tend to shift their loyalties from the military to protecting the interests of local factories and townships.[86]

These weaknesses in the MRO system are significant, because many manufacturers show a disregard for ensuring the quality and reliability of their finished products and often miss production deadlines. Factories often give a higher priority to the production of civilian products than to military products, because civilian products often have higher profit margins. As a result, in recent years the government has initiated a major effort to overhaul the MRO system to improve contract compliance and quality-control monitoring. Both the State Council and COSTIND issued a series of new policies on improving the quality of military production, including an entire system for improving monitoring and boosting education of military representatives. The effectiveness of these measures, however, is far from clear.[87]

These efforts to improve the MRO system and to boost quality control are being adopted in parallel with new standards within GAD for training and utilizing staff with technical skills. GAD has adopted new measures to recruit, train, and retain personnel with science and

---

[86] The authors are grateful to Tai Ming Cheung for his insights on the MRO system; also see Wu Ruihu, "Navy Military Representative Hard at Work in Supervising Armament Development," *Jiefangjun bao,* April 10, 2002, as translated in *FBIS,* April 10, 2004; "Military Representatives of Engineering Corps Work Hard to Ensure Assault Boats['] Quality," *Jiefangjun bao,* July 17, 2002, p. 10, as translated in *FBIS,* 2004.

[87] Zhang Yi, "The State Adopts Effective Measures for Improving Quality of National Defense-Related Products," *Xinhua,* March 23, 2000, as translated in *FBIS,* March 23, 2000; Fan Juwei, "Quality of Our Large-Sized Complicated Armaments Is Steadily Improving," *Jiefangjun bao,* July 19, 2001, p. 1, as translated in *FBIS,* July 19, 2001.

technology training.[88] A report from China's *Science and Technology Daily* indicates that the specific GAD policies include

> to actively recruit and replenish high quality talents, provide the talent with positions compatible with their skills, establish special positions in high priority disciplines, gather outstanding experts to serve armament development and research, and build up post doctoral mobile stations into the frontline for recruiting high level staff. . . .[89]

Systemic Constraints on China's Defense-Industry Reform

Since 1998, China has adopted numerous institutional and incentive-based reforms to improve the structure and operations of its defense industry. However, Beijing has a long and highly blemished history of adopting weak reforms and of not implementing more-radical policy changes. Thus, it is not clear how quickly and effectively the post-1998 measures can overcome the inertia and extensive problems that have plagued China's defense-industrial establishment for the past several decades. Many of these difficulties are deeply entrenched in the central government bureaucracy, provincial-level agencies, and enterprise-level business operations. The government's ability to reform the management of defense procurement and to change the incentive structures in and among defense enterprises will have a direct impact on the future production capabilities of China's defense-industrial complex.

---

[88] *Xinhua*, April 11, 2000, in *FBIS* as "PRC's PLA 'Speeds Up' Training for Armament Officers," April 11, 2000; Zou Fanggen and Fan Juwei, "Chinese Army's Armament, Scientific Research, and Procurement System Insists on Simultaneously Promoting Development of Scientific Research and Cultivation of Skilled Personnel," *Jiefangjun bao* (Internet version), February 19, 2002, p. 1, in *FBIS* as "PRC: PLA Implements Measures to Simultaneously Train Personnel, Develop New Weaponry," February 19, 2002.

[89] Liu Cheng, Jiang Hongyan, and Liu Xiaojun, "Talented Personnel to Support Leapfrog Developments of Weaponry," *Keji ribao* (Internet version [http://www.stdaily.com.cn]), October 31, 2001, as translated in *FBIS*, October 31, 2001.

The government's success at fully implementing defense-industrial reforms will be broadly influenced by several tensions, or "contradictions," that persist at both the central government level and the enterprise level of operations. These tensions constitute the broad, systemic constraints on China's newest, post-1998 effort to reform the defense-industry system. The major tensions include reform imperatives versus social stability, GAD versus State COSTIND, and localization versus free-market practices.

Reform Imperatives Versus Social Stability

Efforts to rationalize and downsize China's large, bloated, and inefficient defense enterprises raise concerns about social instability; specific concerns include increasing unemployment, inability to fulfill pension commitments, and cutting off funding for enterprise-run social welfare programs. The 1998 reforms eliminated many of the social welfare obligations, such as housing and health care, of many state-owned defense enterprises, but leaders of some defense enterprises are reluctant to swiftly implement these reforms for fear of their effect on social stability. Riots and social unrest related to rationalization at defense factories have occurred in China. Such concerns will likely limit the pace and scale of defense-enterprise reform. These concerns are especially acute in China's northeastern "rustbelt" region and in its poorest provinces in the westernmost part of the country. Chinese policymakers have also identified specific plans to facilitate defense-industrial reform in these specific regions.[90]

GAD Versus State COSTIND

The civilianization of COSTIND and the creation of GAD injected a variety of new tensions into the 1998 round of defense-industry reforms. GAD gained influence over central government procurement-related decisions at the expense of COSTIND. These new agencies often compete for influence in the defense-procurement

---

[90] See "Guofang Keji Gongye Jinyibu Canyu Xibu Dakaifa he Dongbei Zhenxing de Zhidao Yijian," *Kegongwei Tongzhi* (*COSTIND Notification*), No. 815, July 17, 2004. Available online at www.costind.gov.cn; accessed January 2005.

process, and this tension contributes to delays and inefficient decisionmaking on specific military projects. The competition between these agencies will continue to complicate the government's ability to streamline the procurement process and to reform defense-enterprise operations.

Localization Versus Free-Market Practices

Historically, China's defense-industrial enterprises have been highly vertically integrated and relied on single-source suppliers. These economic tendencies have been exacerbated by long-standing political ties within regions and provinces that influence business relations among firms in the same localities. As a consequence, many defense enterprises are reluctant to seek cooperation with firms in other regions, even though such firms may offer higher-quality and lower-cost products. This reluctance constitutes a significant barrier to improving the quality of weapon systems and reducing the costs of defense production in all of China.

Organization of This Report

The success of China's newest round of defense-industry policy adjustments will be influenced by the ability of Chinese officials to balance these tensions in the coming years. Within the context of the dynamics between these tensions and the pace of reform, an evaluation of the impact of the post-1998 series of reforms is further constrained by the limited amount of data on the actual operations of China's defense enterprises. The production capabilities of China's defense industry are most often assessed by examining its output; data on how the government actually chooses suppliers and factories produce military items have been limited.

In an attempt to shed further light on these issues, the following chapters of this study are specific case studies of four key defense-industry sectors: missile (Chapter Two), shipbuilding (Chapter Three), military aviation (Chapter Four), and information technology/defense electronics (Chapter Five). These case studies seek to illuminate how specific reforms have been implemented and what their effects on the operations and output of China's defense-industrial complex have been. These four sectors were chosen as the focus of our analysis because the apparent changes in their operations and the quality of their output in recent years have been significant, and these sectors are particularly relevant to assessing the PLA's future power-projection capabilities.

CHAPTER TWO

China's Missile Industry[1]

Analyzing China's missile industry is critical to evaluating the changing nature of China's defense-industrial capabilities as well as the PLA's overall prospects for modernization. Ballistic and cruise missiles have assumed a central role in Chinese military doctrine and operational planning in the past decade. The Chinese military increasingly relies on all types of missiles for strategic deterrence, coercion, and warfighting. In addition, China's missile industry has always been considered a leading sector in the defense industry, and its research and production capabilities serve as an important benchmark for the defense industry as a whole. To examine the missile sector's capabilities, in this chapter we outline the structure and components of China's defense industry that are involved in the research, development, and production of missiles, and assess the missile industry's current and future research, development, and production capabilities.

The missile sector has long been described as a "pocket of excellence" within China's long-troubled defense-industrial establishment—a characterization that results not only from the missile sector's proven record of capability but also from its having consistently been a priority for the political leadership and the military. It has, over the past several decades, consistently produced a wide range

---

[1] In this chapter, "missile industry" refers to any organizations involved in the research, design, and production of guided missiles, not just those entities that are part of China's two state-owned "aerospace" conglomerates.

of missile systems, some of which are currently comparable to those deployed in modern Western militaries.

China's steady improvement of its missile technology over the past 50 years and, in particular, over the past two decades, stands in contrast to the defense industry's relative inability to produce indigenously developed modern aviation or naval platforms. The missile sector's moderately successful record owes largely to its organization, as well as to its access to resources and to technology transfers from foreign countries.

At the same time, China's missile sector suffers some of the same problems as China's other defense-industrial sectors. In this sense, this sector might better be characterized as a "pocket of adequacy" (rather than a "pocket of excellence") within a historically mediocre and inefficient defense-industrial establishment. Thus, although it has historically performed better than many other defense-industrial sectors, certain weaknesses and inefficiencies of the missile sector persist and are a barrier to China becoming a state-of-the-art developer and producer of weapon systems.

Sector Organization and Principal Actors

China's missile sector differs from its other defense sectors in that not all missiles are produced by the subsidiaries of just two state-owned corporations. Most missiles are indeed produced by the subordinate enterprises of two large holding companies, the China Aerospace Science and Technology Corporation (CASC; *Zhongguo Hangtian Keji Jituan Gongsi* 中国航天科技集团公司) and the China Aerospace Science and Industry Corporation (CASIC; *Zhongguo Hangtian Kegong Jituan Gongsi* 中国航天科工集团公司).[2] However, enterprises controlled by China Aviation Industries Corporation I (AVIC

---

[2] Missiles produced by CASC and CASIC are marketed by the China Precision Machinery Import and Export Corporation (CPMIEC), a company jointly owned by CASC and CASIC. CASC and CASIC also own China Great Wall Industry Corporation, which markets China's space launch services.

I), China Aviation Industries Corporation II (AVIC II), and China North Industries Group Corporation (CNGC; *Zhongguo Binggong Gongye Jituan Gongsi* 中国兵器工业集团公司), one of China's two principal producers of ground weapon systems) are also involved in missile research, development, and production. These organizations produce almost all air-to-air missiles (AAMs), as well as some anti-ship cruise missiles (ASCMs), surface-to-air missiles (SAMs), and ground-attack missiles.

CASC and CASIC were created in July 1999 by dividing into two parts a single state-owned corporation, the China Aerospace Corporation (which also used the acronym CASC), which was created in 1993 when the former Ministry of Aerospace Industry (MAS) was corporatized.

China Aerospace Science and Technology Corporation

The China Aerospace Science and Technology Corporation is a large holding company. As of 2002, CASC and its subordinate enterprises employed roughly a total of 103,000 people.[3] CASC comprises eight major research academies and production "bases" (some of these academies and bases are now more corporate entities called "group corporations"). These academies and bases, in turn, encompass multiple research institutes, production facilities, and companies. CASC also directly controls over 100 research institutes, production facilities, and companies that are subordinate to it. CASC's business areas include ballistic missiles, space launch vehicles, satellites, manned spacecraft, and civilian products.

As with other defense conglomerates in China, the principal actors in CASC are its subordinate enterprises, rather than the holding company itself. CASC's primary subsidiaries are

---

[3] Wang Ti, *Xinhua,* July 3, 2000, in *FBIS* as "PRC Aerospace Technology Achievements Viewed," July 3, 2000; Zhang Yi and Zhang Yusheng, "Continue to Maintain PRC Aerospace Industry's Leading Position—An Interview with Wang Liheng, President of the China Aerospace Science and Technology Corporation," *Xinhua,* November 11, 2000, in *FBIS,* November 11, 2000; "China Aerospace Science and Technology Corporation," *Zhongguo hangtian* (*China Aerospace*), October 1, 2002, pp. 3–6, in *FBIS,* October 2002.

- China Academy of Launch Vehicle Technology (also referred to as the 1st Academy)
- Academy of Aerospace Solid Propulsion Technology (also referred to as the 4th Academy)
- China Academy of Space Technology (also referred to as the 5th Academy)
- Academy of Aerospace Liquid Propulsion Technology (also referred to as Base 067 [4])
- Shanghai Academy of Space Flight Technology (also referred to as the 8th Academy)
- China Academy of Space Electronics Technology (also referred to as the 9th Academy [5])
- Aerospace Time Instrument Corporation (also referred to as the 10th Academy [6])

---

[4] No statement was found explicitly identifying the Academy of Aerospace Liquid Propulsion Technology (AALPT) as Base 067, but in 1996, prior to its division into CASC and CASIC, China Aerospace Corporation was said to consist of seven academies and four "industrial groups" (bases). See Christian Lardier, "Chinese Space Industry's Ambition," *Air & Cosmos/Aviation International,* October 25, 1996, pp. 36–37, in *FBIS* as "Ambitions of Nation's Space Industry Outlined at IAF 96 World Space Congress," October 25, 1996. The seven academies—indicated as the 1st, 2nd, 3rd, 4th, and 5th Academies, the Shanghai Academy of Space Technology, and the China Academy of Space Electronics Technology—all still exist (see remainder of this section). The AALPT was not identified as one of the academies at that time but is said to have been established in 1965 (see "China Aerospace Science and Technology Corporation," 2002); therefore, it is likely that one of the industrial groups (bases) was subsequently renamed AALPT. Of the four industrial groups mentioned in 1996, only one—the Shaanxi Lingan Machinery Company (SLMC)—appears to have been based in Shaanxi, where AALPT is headquartered (Xi'an is the capital of Shaanxi Province); therefore, it is likely that SLMC is the organization that was renamed AALPT. Base 067 is also known to be in Shaanxi Province (see Su Hui, "The Development of Scientific and Technological Industry for National Defense in Shaanxi," *Shaanxi ribao,* March 28, 2001, in *FBIS* as "Report on Development of Shaanxi's Military Industry," March 28, 2001); therefore, it is likely that SLMC, Base 067, and AALPT are all names for the same organization.

[5] "China Aerospace Science and Technology Corporation," 2002, lists all other academies in numerical order, with CASET falling between the Shanghai Academy of Space Flight Technology (8th Academy) and Aerospace Time Instrument Corporation (10th Academy).

[6] No statement was found explicitly identifying the Aerospace Time Instrument Corporation (ATIC) as the 10th Academy, but the founding date for ATIC is the same as that of the 10th Academy and its stated areas of specialization appear to be identical. See Sun Zifa, "China Forms Aerospace Instrument Company," *Zhongguo xinwen she,* July 28,

- Sichuan Aerospace Industry Corporation[7] (also referred to as Base 062 [8]).

The China Academy of Launch Vehicle Technology (CALT; *Zhongguo Yunzai Huojian Jishu Yanjiu Yuan* 中国运载火箭技术研究院) is China's primary developer and producer of ballistic missiles and space launch vehicles. Headquartered in Beijing's southern suburbs, CALT employs 20,000 people, including 10,000 "intermediate to senior technicians, engineers, and scientists." Subordinate to CALT are 12 research institutes, four factories, and various other companies. Its products include liquid- and solid-fuel ballistic missiles and liquid-fuel space launch vehicles.[9]

The Academy of Aerospace Solid Propulsion Technology (AASPT; *Hangtian Dongli Jishu Yanjiu Yuan* 航天动力技术研究院) is China's primary producer of solid propellant rocket motors. Headquartered in Xi'an, AASPT employs 10,000 people, including 4,000 "intermediate to senior" technicians and engineers. Subordinate to AASPT are six research institutes, four factories, and various other companies. Its primary products are solid rocket motors for ballistic missiles and SAMs.[10]

2001, in *FBIS*, July 28, 2001; "China Aerospace Science and Technology Corporation," 2002.

[7] "China Aerospace Science and Technology Corporation," 2002.

[8] No statement was found explicitly identifying the Sichuan Aerospace Industry Corporation (SAIC) as Base 062, but Base 062 appears to be the only aerospace industry "base" in Sichuan Province, where SAIC is headquartered. See Chen Lan, "Xie Shijie, Zhang Zhongwei Address, Huang Yinki Presides, at Seminar Held by Provincial Party Committee and Provincial Government for Some of the War Industry Enterprises and Institutions: Have a Clear Understanding of the Situation, Change Concept, and Seize Opportunity to Speed Up Development," *Sichuan ribao,* December 4, 1999, in *FBIS* as "Provincial Party Holds Seminar for War Industry Firms," December 4, 1999.

[9] Christian Lardier, "Chinese Space Industry's Ambition," 1996; Tseng Shu-wan, "Special Dispatch," *Wen wei po*, October 31, 2000, in *FBIS*, October 31, 2000; "China Aerospace Science and Technology Corporation," 2002*;* Cao Zhi, Tian Zhaoyun, and Xu Zhuangzhi, "Launch of 'Shenzhou' Spacecraft," *Xinhua,* December 29, 2002, in *FBIS*, December 29, 2002.

[10] Huang Jianding and Zhang Fenglin, *Hangtian*, May 1995, pp. 6–7, in *FBIS* as "Solid Rocket Motors for Launch Vehicles, Tactical Missiles Detailed," May 1, 1995; Christian

The China Academy of Space Technology (CAST; *Zhongguo Kongjian Jishu Yanjiu Yuan* 中国空间技术研究院) develops and produces satellites and manned spacecraft. It plays a central role in China's manned space program (including the launch of China's first manned space vessel, the *Shenzhou-5*, in October 2003). CAST is headquartered in Beijing's Zhongguancun district and employs about 10,000 people, including 1,700 senior technicians, engineers, and scientists. Underneath CAST are ten research institutes, two "other enterprises" (presumably factories), and various subsidiary companies. Its products include satellites for communications, weather, earth resources, reconnaissance, navigation, and scientific research, and manned spacecraft.[11]

The Academy of Aerospace Liquid Propulsion Technology (AALPT; *Hangtian Tuijin Jishu Yanjiu Yuan* 航天推进技术研究院) appears to be China's sole producer of liquid-propellant rocket motors. AALPT is headquartered in Xi'an and produces a variety of different types of motors for ballistic missiles and space launch vehicles.[12]

The Shanghai Academy of Space Flight Technology (SAST; *Shanghai Hangtian Jishu Yanjiu Yuan* 上海航天技术研究院) develops and produces ballistic missiles, space launch vehicles, satellites,

---

Lardier, "Chinese Space Industry's Ambition," *Air & Cosmos/Aviation International,* October 25, 1996, pp. 36–37, in *FBIS* as "Ambitions of Nation's Space Industry Outlined at IAF 96 World Space Congress," October 25, 1996; "China Aerospace Science and Technology Corporation," 2002; Ye Dingyou and Zhang Dexiong, *Zhongguo hangtian,* December 1, 2002, pp. 24–27, in *FBIS*, December 1, 2002.

[11] Christian Lardier, "Chinese Space Industry's Ambition," 1996; *Zhongguo hangtian (Aerospace China),* No. 7, July 1997, pp. 3–4, in *FBIS* as "Additional Details on Launch of FY-II Geostationary Meteorological Satellite," July 1, 1997; Tseng Shu-wan, "Special Dispatch," 2000; Xi Qixin and Liu Siyang, "Jiang Zemin Watches the Launch of a Spacecraft from the Manned Spacecraft Launch Center," March 25, 2002, in *FBIS* as "PRC President Jiang Zemin Observes Launch of Shenzhou-3 Spacecraft," March 25, 2002; "China Aerospace Science and Technology Corporation," 2002; Xi Qixin, "PRC Successfully Launches 'China Resources-II' Satellite," *Xinhua,* October 27, 2002, in *FBIS*, October 27, 2002; Liao Wengen and Xi Qixin, "Our Country's Third Beidou Navigation and Positioning Satellite Launched into Space," *Xinhua,* May 24, 2003, in *FBIS*, May 24, 2003.

[12] Christian Lardier, "Chinese Space Industry's Ambition," 1996; "China Aerospace Science and Technology Corporation," 2002.

manned spacecraft, SAMs, and AAMs. It is headquartered in Shanghai and employs 20,000 people, including 6,000 engineering and technical personnel. Underneath SAST are 40 "military product research institutes and civilian product manufacturing companies," and one publicly traded company. SAST has participated (with CALT) in the production of liquid-fuel ballistic missiles and space launch vehicles and (with CAST) in the production of weather satellites and manned spacecraft. It has also developed and produced infrared (IR)-guided man-portable air-defense systems (MANPADS), semi-active radar (SAR)-guided short-range SAMs, and SAR-guided AAMs.[13]

The China Academy of Space Electronics Technology (CASET; *Zhongguo Hangtian Dianzi Jichu Jishu Yanjiu Yuan* 中国航天电子基础技术研究院) produces electronics for the missile and space industry. It is headquartered in Beijing and employs over 5,000

---

[13] Christian Lardier, "Chinese Space Industry's Ambition," 1996; *Zhongguo hangtian,* July 1997; Zhang Huiting, *Hangtian,* May/June 1997, pp. 34–35, in *FBIS* as "HQ-61 SAM Weapon System Described," September 29, 1997; Shi Hua, *China Daily,* September 1, 1999, in *FBIS* as "PRC Challenges U.S. Satellite Design," September 1, 1999; Zheng Wei and Zhang Jie, "Long March Rockets, Developed by Shanghai Aerospace Bureau, Achieve 20 Successful Consecutive Launches; 'Long March' Rockets Never Miss Target," *Wen hui bao,* October 21, 1999, in *FBIS* as "Shanghai Space Unit Sets Record in Long March Launches," October 21, 1999; Zeng Min, *China Daily,* February 3, 2001, in *FBIS* as "China to Launch More Meteorological Satellites in 'Fengyun' Series," February 3, 2001; Jiang Zemin et al., in *FBIS* as "Report on PRC Central Leaders' Activities 26 Aug–6 Sep," September 7, 2001; Xi Qixin and Liu Siyang, "Jiang Zemin Watches the Launch of a Spacecraft from the Manned Spacecraft Launch Center," 2002; Liu Cheng and Tian Zhaoyun, "China Launches First Marine Satellite," *Xinhua,* May 15, 2002, in *FBIS* as "Xinhua: China Launches Weather, Marine Satellites 15 May," May 15, 2002; "Fourteen Pilots with Right Stuff Ready for Liftoff," *South China Morning Post,* May 22, 2002, p. 8, in *FBIS* as "China Prepares Fourteen Pilots as Astronauts," May 22, 2002; Zheng Wei, "Fengyun-4: Gaze Upon the Earth After 10 Years," *Wen hui bao,* September 6, 2002, in *FBIS* as "PRC S&T: Fengyun-4 Meteorological Satellite to Launch in 10 Years," September 6, 2002; "China Aerospace Science and Technology Corporation," 2002; Xi Qixin, "PRC Successfully Launches 'China Resources-II' Satellite," 2002; James C. O'Halloran, "CNPMIEC Hong Nu-5 Series Man-Portable Anti-Aircraft Missile System," *Jane's Land-Based Air Defence,* November 11, 2003 (available online at http://online.janes.com; accessed November 25, 2003); Robert Hewson, "PL-11 (PL-10) and FD-60, AMR-1," *Jane's Air-Launched Weapon Systems,* Vol. 43, November 26, 2004 (available online at http://online.janes.com; accessed January 21, 2005).

people, including 2,600 engineering and technical personnel. It controls two research institutes and three factories.[14]

The China Aerospace Time Instrument Corporation (ATIC; *Hangtian Shidai Yiqi Gongsi* 航天时代仪器公司), a subsidiary of CASC, develops navigation and guidance systems. Headquartered in Beijing, it employees 5,200 people and has assets of 1.6 billion RMB ($140 million). Underneath it are three manufacturing factories and numerous other subsidiaries. Its products include inertial navigation systems, electro-optical products, electrical and electronic components, precision instruments, and computer hardware and software.[15]

Sichuan Aerospace Industry Corporation (SAIC; *Sichuan Hangtian Gongye Zong Gongsi* 四川航天工业总公司) is headquartered in Chengdu and employees 20,000 people. Underneath it are 30 "research and design institutes and production enterprises." SAIC's known products include multiple rocket systems; given the scale of the enterprise, it undoubtedly produces other missile systems as well.[16]

China Aerospace Science and Industry Group Corporation

China Aerospace Science and Industry Group Corporation comprises six major research academies and bases, as well as a number of smaller, directly subordinate enterprises, for a total of nearly 200 enterprises and institutes under CASIC. CASIC's business areas include ballistic missiles, ASCMs, SAMs, space launch vehicles, satellites, satellite applications, electronics, communications systems, information technologies, energy resources, and environmental protection. As of November 2002, a total of 100,000 people worked for CASIC

---

[14] Christian Lardier, "Chinese Space Industry's Ambition," 1996; and "China Aerospace Science and Technology Corporation," 2002.

[15] Sun Zifa, "China Forms Aerospace Instrument Company," 2001; "China Aerospace Science and Technology Corporation," 2002; Aerospace Times Instrument Corporation, company brochure, 2002.

[16] "China Aerospace Science and Technology Corporation," 2002.

and its subordinate enterprises.[17] CASIC's main subsidiaries are

- Changfeng Electromechanical Technology Design Institute (also referred to as the 2nd Academy)
- China Haiying Electromechanical Technology Academy (also referred to as the 3rd Academy)
- China Hexi Chemical and Machinery Company (also referred to as the 6th Academy)
- China Aerospace Architectural Academy
- China Jiangnan Space Industries (also referred to as Base 061)
- China Sanjiang Space Group (also referred to as Base 066).

The China Changfeng Electromechanical Technology Design Institute (*Zhongguo Changfeng Jidian Jishu Shiji Yuan* 中国长峰机电技术设计院) produces SAMs, ballistic missiles, sensors, and electronics. Its SAM products include command-guided medium-range and short-range systems. So far, Changfeng has unveiled only one type of ballistic missile, a 150-km-range conventionally armed model that may be based on one of its SAM designs.[18] Other products include IR detectors, satellite tracking and receiving systems, microelectronics, and photo-electronics. The 2nd Academy "has total assets of 5 billion renminbi (US$600 million); employs 13,000 people, including about 8,000 engineers and "ordinary technical personnel" (*yiban jishu renyuan* 一般技术人员); and has ten specialized research institutes,

[17] Zhang Yi and Zhang Yusheng, "Speed Up Marketing of High-Tech Aerospace Products—Interview with General Manager Xia Guohong of China Aerospace Machinery and Electric Equipment Group," *Xinhua,* November 12, 2000, in *FBIS,* November 12, 2000; *Zhongguo hangtian,* October 1, 2002, pp. 7–9, in *FBIS* as "PRC S&T: CASIC Displays New Aerospace Products," October 1, 2002; "Company Introduction," CASIC website (www.casic.com.cn/docc/jieshao/jianjie.asp; accessed December 31, 2003); *Xinhua,* September 3, 1999, in *FBIS* as "Missile Experts Refute Li's Splittist Remarks," September 3, 1999; Yang Jian, "Li Peng Sends Letter to the China Aerospace Science and Industry Corporation on Its Important Progress," *Zhongguo hangtian bao,* January 15, 2000, pp. 1–2, in *FBIS* as "PRC CAMEC Development Strategies 2000–2010," January 15, 2000.

[18] Robert Karniol, "Beijing Displays New Tactical Surface-to-Surface System," *Jane's Defence Weekly,* November 10, 2004; Duncan Lennox, "CSS-8 (M-7/Project 8610)," *Jane's Strategic Weapon Systems,* June 4, 2004 (available online at http://online.janes.com/; accessed January 4, 2004).

three factories, nine integrated technology, manufacturing, and trading companies, a simulation center, a school, and a hospital.[19]

China Haiying Electromechanical Technology Academy (CHETA; *Zhongguo Haiying Jidian Jishu Yanjiu Yuan* 中国海鹰机电技术研究院) researches, designs, and produces ASCMs and ASCM-based TV-guided land-attack cruise missiles (LACMs). Other products include power systems, automatic control equipment, radar electronic equipment, computer applications, and infrared laser equipment. CHETA has total assets of 4.5 billion RMB ($550 million) and employs 13,000 people, including 2,000 researchers and senior engineers, and 6,000 technicians. In 1996, it had ten institutes and two manufacturing plants.[20]

China Hexi Chemical and Machinery Company (*Zhongguo Hexi Huagong Jixie Gongsi* 中国河西化工机械公司) develops, produces, and tests solid rocket motors. Prior to August 1999, it was part of CASC's 4th Academy, which is also involved in producing solid rocket motors. Its products include solid-fuel motors for strategic and tactical missiles, upper stages of space launch vehicles, braking motors for recoverable satellites, and earth perigee kick motors (EPKMs) for

---

[19] Data were taken from CASIC website (www.casic.com.cn/docc/qiye/content.asp?id=59; accessed December 29, 2003); Christian Lardier, "Chinese Space Industry's Ambition," 1996; Zhang Xinyu et al., "Infrared Detector Array with Quartz Microlens," *Hongwai yu haomibo xuebao,* April 1998, pp. 147–152, in *FBIS* as "IR Detector Array with Quartz Microlens," April 1, 1998; Xu Yunxin, "Shipborne Meteorological Satellite Tracking System Displays Invincible Might," *Keji ribao,* April 27, 1998, p. 7, in *FBIS* as "Shipborne Weather Satellite Tracking System," April 27, 1998; Wen Yangyang, "Beijing Changfeng Shiji Satellite Science and Technology Corporation Pushes Forward the Field of Satellite Application," October 11, 2002, in *FBIS* as "PRC S&T: Changfeng Century Develops Mobile Communications System," October 11, 2002; Sun Zhifan, *Zhongguo xinwen she,* November 28, 2002, in *FBIS* as "ZXS: China Aerospace Second Academy Strives to Become First-Class Institution," November 28, 2002; Huang Tung, "China's 'New Flying Leopard' Short-Range Air Defense Missile System," *Kuang chiao ching,* No. 365, February 16, 2003, p. 61, in *FBIS* as "China's New 'Flying Leopard' Short-Range Air-Defense Missile System," February 16, 2003.

[20] Data were taken from CASIC website (www.casic.com.cn/docc/qiye/content.asp?id=60; accessed December 29, 2003); Wang Jianmin and Zhang Zuocheng, "Speed Up the Progress of Basic Model, Then Serialization, and Work Hard to Develop China's Cruise Missile Industry," *Zhongguo hangtian,* September 1996, pp. 12–17, in *FBIS* as "President of CASC's Third Academy Details Contribution of HY-2, C601, C801 Cruise Missile Series," September 1, 1996; Christian Lardier, "Chinese Space Industry's Ambition," 1996.

geosynchronous satellites. Hexi is headquartered in Hohhot, Inner Mongolia, and has more than 5,000 employees, including 2,000 specialized technical personnel and 400 senior technical personal. It has three research institutes, two manufacturing facilities, and a measurement station.[21]

Employing about 800 people, the China Aerospace Architectural Academy (*Zhongguo Hangtian Jianzhu Sheji Yanjiu Yuan* 中国航天建筑设计研究院) is a relatively small organization that designs research facilities, factories, and campuses for China's missile and space sector.[22]

China Jiangnan Space Group (*Zhongguo Jiangnan Hangtian Jituan* 中国江南航天集团) is headquartered in Zunyi, Guizhou. This study was unable to identify any military systems produced by this entity, but its nonmilitary products include light automobiles, agricultural vehicles, motorcycle parts, refrigerators, injection-molding equipment, metal-drawing equipment, hydraulic transmissions, satellite receivers, oil-well measuring equipment, and medical equipment. Jiangnan has total assets of 3.86 billion RMB (US$470 million) and employs 27,000 people, including 8,300 technical personnel and 860 senior engineers. It has 23 factories, two research institutes, three technology centers, and three schools.[23]

---

[21] Data were taken from CASIC website (www.casic.com.cn/docc/qiye/content.asp?id=113; accessed December 29, 2003); data were also taken from the CASIC 6th Academy website (www.zghx.com.cn.gaikuang.htm; accessed December 31, 2003); Shi Lei et al., "Tingzhi de Jiliang—Zhongguo Hangtian Kegong Jituan Gongsi Liu Yuan Fazhan Jishi," *Guofang keji gongye*, No. 10, 2001, pp. 8–12; *Hangtian*, June 28, 1996, p. 8, in *FBIS* as "Chinese Perigee Kick Motor Developed, Used for AsiaSat, Echostar Satellite Launches," June 28, 1996; Ye Dingyou and Zhang Dexiong, *Zhongguo hangtian*, December 1, 2002, pp. 24–27, in *FBIS* as "PRC S&T: Progress in Solid Rocket Propellant Technology," December 1, 2002.

[22] See CASIC website (www.casic.com.cn/docc/qiye/content.asp?id=114; accessed December 29, 2003).

[23] Data were taken from Jiangnan Space Group website (www.cjspace.com.cn; accessed December 31, 2003); Christian Lardier, "Chinese Space Industry's Ambitions," 1996; Ma Xiaojun, "While Inspecting Guizhou Province, Zeng Qinghong Stresses That a Modern Distance Education Project Should Be Built to Let Cadres Be Educated Regularly and Let Peasants Get Real Benefits for a Long Time," *Guizhou ribao*, April 16, 2003, in *FBIS* as "PRC Vice President Zeng Qinghong Inspects Guizhou, Promotes Distance Education," April 16, 2003; Zhou Jiahe, "Zeng Qinghong Inspects No. 061 Base, Encouraging the Base

China Sanjiang Space Industry Group Company (*Zhongguo Sanjiang Hangtian Gongye Jituan Gongsi*, 中国三江航天工业集团公司), which is headquartered in Wuhan, is believed to produce the DF-11 solid-fuel short-range ballistic missile (see below). Other, known products include "large-tonnage cross-country vehicles," which appears to be a description of the transporter-erector-launcher (TEL) vehicles used for carrying mobile missiles, chassis for "specialized vehicles" (*tezhong zhuanyong che* 特种专用车), encryption equipment, pulverizers, and luggage carts.[24]

Non–CASC/CASIC Missile Producers

As noted above, not all of China's missiles are produced by CASC and CASIC entities. Subsidiaries of AVIC I and AVIC II produce all of China's AAMs and some ASCMs and SAMs. In addition, CNGC produces wire-guided ground-attack missiles and markets a SAM system based on the PL-9 AAM.[25]

The AVIC I/AVIC II subsidiaries involved in missile development and production include the Hongdu Aviation Industry Group (formerly known as the Nanchang Aircraft Manufacturing Company), the China Air-to-Air Missile Research Institute (AAMRI), the Luoy-

---

to Make Greater Contributions to the Modernization of National Defense," *Zhongguo hangtian bao,* April 18, 2003, in *FBIS* as "PRC S&T: Zeng Qinghong Inspects 061 Aerospace Plant," April 18, 2003.

[24] Duncan Lennox, "CSS-7 (DF-11/M-11)," *Jane's Strategic Weapon Systems,* Vol. 40, June 3, 2003 (available online at http://online.janes.com; accessed November 25, 2003); China Sanjiang Space Industry Group website (http://www.cssg.com.cn; accessed December 29, 2003); *Xinhua,* October 16, 1995, in *FBIS* as "Hubei Becomes French Market Foothold," October 16, 1995; *Xinhua,* April 26, 1998, in *FBIS* as "Belarus to Cooperate with China to Build Trucks," April 26, 1998; Glenn Schloss, "Arms Dealer Norinco Out in Open in Hong Kong," *South China Morning Post,* June 14, 1998, p. 1, in *FBIS* as "Mainland's Military Links Run Deep," June 14, 1998; *Xinhua,* July 18, 2001, in *FBIS* as "PRC: MOFTEC Says PRC-Belarus Economic Cooperation Increased by 366.7% in '00," July 18, 2001; *FBIS,* "Highlights: PRC Central Leaders' Activities 3 Jun–1 Jul 03," July 1, 2003.

[25] James C. O'Halloran, "NORINCO PL-9C Low-Altitude Surface-to-Air Missile System," *Jane's Land-Based Air Defence,* January 27, 2003 (available online at http://online.janes .com; accessed November 25, 2003); Robert Hewson, "HJ-8 (HONGJIAN 8)," *Jane's Air-Launched Weapons,* Vol. 41, September 12, 2002 (available online at http://online .janes.com; accessed November 25, 2003).

ang Institute of Electro-Optical Equipment (LIEOE), China National South Aeroengine Company (formerly known as the Zhuzhou Aeroengine Factory), the No. 607 Institute in Wuxi, an entity called the "Hanzhou Nanfeng Machine Factory," and possibly other organizations as well.[26]

The Hongdu Aviation Industry Group produces the Feilong ("Flying Dragon" *fei long* 飞龙) series of ASCMs. AAMRI appears to be China's primary overall developer of AAMs; LIEOE develops and produces the seekers for IR-guided AAMs. The No. 607 Institute may develop active radar seekers for AAMs.[27] South Aeroengine was the primary manufacturer for AAMs in the past, but it is not clear if it is still involved in missile production.[28] South Aeroengine also manufactures the turbojet engines for ASCMs produced by both CASIC's CHETA and AVIC II's Hongdu Group. "Hanzhou Nanfeng" reportedly manufactures the PL-5 AAM and may produce other missiles as well.[29]

The principal known enterprises involved in production for China's missile sector are listed in Tables 2.1 and 2.2.

---

[26] Duncan Lennox, "CSS-N-1 'Scrubbrush Mod 2' (FL-1), CSS-NX-5 'Sabbot' (FL-2), FL-7, and FL-10," *Jane's Strategic Weapon Systems*, Vol. 40, July 31, 2003 (available online at http://online.janes.com; accessed November 25, 2003). The Hai Ying series of ASCMs now produced by CHETA was apparently originally developed and produced by Hongdu as well, but at some point production was transferred to CHETA. See E. R. Hooten, "CSS-N-1 'Scrubbrush' (SY-1/HY-1); CSS-N-2 'Silkworm'; CSS-N-3 'Seersucker' (HY-2/FL-1/FL-3A)," *Jane's Naval Weapon Systems*, Vol. 39, September 11, 2003 (available online at http://online.janes.com; accessed November 25, 2003).

[27] Duncan Lennox, "AMR-1," *Jane's Air-Launched Weapons*, Vol. 37, January 16, 2001 (available online at http://online.janes.com; accessed November 25, 2003).

[28] Duncan Lennox, "PL-1," *Jane's Air-Launched Weapons*, Vol. 37, January 16, 2001 (available online at http://online.janes.com; accessed November 25, 2003); Robert Hewson, "PL-7," *Janes Air-Launched Weapons*, Vol. 42, April 30, 2003 (available online at http://online.janes.com; accessed November 25, 2003). South Aeroengine's brochure from the 2002 "Airshow China" in Zhuhai does not list missiles among its products, but neither does that of Hongdu, which is believed to produce the Feilong series of ASCMs.

[29] The NORINCO subsidiaries that produce wire-guided missiles and the DK-9C self-propelled SAM system (which employs the PL-9 AAM) were not identified by this study. Robert Hewson, "PL-5," *Jane's Air-Launched Weapons*, Vol. 43, September 19, 2003 (available online at http://online.janes.com; accessed November 25, 2003).

Table 2.1
Key Missile-Production Organizations Under CASC/CASIC

Name	Affiliation	Location	Missile-Related Products
China Academy of Launch Technology (1st Academy)	CASC	Beijing	Ballistic missiles, space launch vehicles
Changfeng Electromechanical Technology Design Institute (2nd Academy)	CASIC	Uncertain	SAMs, ballistic missiles, sensors, electronics
China Haiying Electromechanical Technology Academy (3rd Academy)	CASIC	Uncertain	ASCMs, LACMs
Academy of Aerospace Solid Propulsion Technology (4th Academy)	CASC	Xi'an, Shaanxi	Solid rocket motors
China Hexi Chemical and Machinery Company (6th Academy)	CASIC	Hohhot, Inner Mongolia	Solid rocket motors
Shanghai Academy of Space Flight Technology (8th Academy)	CASC	Shanghai	Launch vehicles, satellites, manned spacecraft, SAMs
China Academy of Space Electronics Technology (9th Academy)	CASC	Beijing	Electronics for the missile and space industry
Aerospace Time Instrument Corporation (10th Academy)	CASC	Beijing	Inertial navigation systems, electro-optical products, electrical and electronic components, precision instruments, computer hardware and software
Jiangnan Aerospace Group (Base 061)	CASIC	Zunyi, Guizhou	None identified
Sichuan Aerospace Industry Corporation (Base 062)	CASC	Chengdu, Sichuan	Multiple rocket systems
Sanjiang Aerospace Industrial Group (Base 066)	CASIC	Wuhan, Hubei	Ballistic missiles, TELs
Academy of Aerospace Liquid Propulsion Technology (Base 067)	CASC	Xi'an, Shaanxi	Liquid rocket motors

Table 2.2
Non–CASC/CASIC Missile-Production Organizations

Name	Affiliation	Location	Missile-Related Products
Hongdu Aviation Industry Group	AVIC II	Nanchang, Jiangxi	ASCMs
China Air-to-Air Missile Research Institute	AVIC I	Luoyang, Henan	AAMs, SAMs
Luoyang Institute of Electro-Optical Equipment	AVIC I	Luoyang, Henan	IR seekers for AAMs
No. 607 Institute	AVIC	Wuxi, Jiangsu	Active radar seekers for AAMs
China National South Aeroengine Company	AVIC II	Zhuzhou, Hunan	AAMs, turbojets for ASCMs
"Hanzhou Nanfeng Machine Factory"	AVIC I?	Uncertain	AAMs
Unidentified enterprises	CNGC	Beijing	Ground-attack missiles

Assessing the Potential for Future Progress

Four variables have a direct bearing on the missile industry's research and production capabilities:

- human and financial resources
- access to advanced technology
- incentives for innovation and efficiency
- the institutional environment.

By examining these four variables, this section assesses the potential for future technological progress of China's missile industry. It finds a mixed but improving picture of R&D and production capabilities.

Perhaps the greatest strength of China's missile industry is a solid institutional foundation. The industry's human and financial resources are also substantial and improving, although the latter will require continued increases in government funding in the coming years. Potential sources of access to advanced technology are the manned space program, expanding cooperation with foreign aerospace firms, and direct transfers of missile technology from foreign countries. Unlike some of China's other defense sectors, significant competition (although still managed) exists within the missile sector, and this competition generates positive pressures for more efficient and innovative R&D and production.

Human and Financial Resources

In terms of sheer numbers, China's missile sector is relatively well endowed with human resources. CASC and CASIC have over 200,000 employees between them, including about 80,000 technical personnel.[30] Moreover, a significant number of employees within AVIC I, AVIC II, and CNGC are also involved in the development and production of missiles. By comparison, Lockheed Martin and Raytheon, the two largest missile producers in the United States, collectively employ about 200,000 people, including roughly 60,000 scientists and engineers.[31] It is not clear, however, whether China's "technical personnel" are comparable to the "scientists and engineers" employed by Lockheed Martin and Raytheon. Chinese publications describe such personnel as "specialized technicians" or "technical professionals," which probably include less highly trained personnel than those who would be identified as scientists and engineers.

The scientists and engineers in China's missile sector may also be less capable than their U.S. counterparts. Although some earn considerable sums by Chinese standards—US$10,000/year—scientists and engineers can earn several times this amount working for foreign-invested or domestic firms in China's export-oriented industries.

---

[30] Zhang Yi and Zhang Yusheng, "Continue to Maintain PRC Aerospace Industry's Leading Position—An Interview with Wang Liheng, President of the China Aerospace Science and Technology Corporation," 2000; also see *Zhongguo hangtian,* October 1, 2002, pp. 7–9.

[31] Telephone interview with Ms. Megan Merriman of the Lockheed Martin Corporation and Raytheon's website, http://www.raytheon.com/about/ (accessed December 29, 2003). Lockheed Martin employs 40,000 scientists and engineers, but no comparable number was available for Raytheon. We estimated the total number of scientists and engineers employed by the two firms by assuming that they represented roughly the same proportion of Raytheon employees as they do of Lockheed Martin employees—30 percent.

Moreover, the quality of higher educational training in China, although improving, still falls short of that in the West, while those Chinese scientists and engineers who go abroad for graduate study (and these are generally the most capable) have tended to stay abroad or seek employment in China's export-oriented industries.

Thus, the talent pool available to China's missile sector has likely been diminishing for the past two decades, although the impact on CASC and CASIC may be less than that on other defense firms, given the relatively high prestige associated with working for China's missile and space industry.

The financial resources available to China's missile sector are difficult to estimate. Chinese statistics suggest that they are increasing rapidly; yet, the picture is incomplete. CASIC's total revenues in 1999 were said to be 8.4 billion RMB (US$1.0 billion), a 25-percent increase over those of the preceding year.[32] By 2002, CASIC was ranked 57th out of China's 100 top firms, with revenues of 22.67 billion RMB (US$2.74 billion), an increase of 170 percent in just three years.[33] By comparison, however, U.S. missile-maker Raytheon had revenues of US$16.8 billion in 2002.[34]

Access to Foreign Technology

China's missile industry has long benefited from having access to the missile systems and related equipment, and the materials and technologies, of other countries. Foreign technical assistance to China's missile programs has assisted R&D and production as well. Most of China's current missile systems are based on foreign systems or incor-

---

[32] Yang Jian, "Li Peng Sends Letter to the China Aerospace Science and Industry Corporation on Its Important Progress," January 15, 2000; Zhang Yi, "Li Peng Sends Letter to Congratulate the China Aerospace Science and Industry Corporation on Its Important Progress in Developing New and High Technology, Weapons and Equipment," *Xinhua*, January 23, 2003, in *FBIS* as "Li Peng Congratulates China Aerospace Industry Corporation on Its Achievements," January 23, 2003.

[33] The authors are grateful to Dennis Blasko for pointing out these data. The entire list can be found at http://www.cec-ceda.org.cn/news/?id=288.

[34] Available online at http://www.raytheon.com/about/ (accessed December 29, 2003).

porate foreign missile technologies. During the 1950s and 1960s, China's missiles were based largely on Soviet designs. By the 1980s, China began to design its own systems, but even these incorporated substantial amounts of French and Israeli missile technology. France's missile technology transfers ended after the European Union's imposition of a ban on the sale of "lethal" military systems following the Tiananmen incident in 1989, but Israel's transfers have continued.

Beginning in the early 1990s, Russia reemerged as a major supplier of missiles, related goods and technologies, and technical assistance. It has provided both complete SAM, AAM, and ASCM systems and assistance in developing and producing China's own AAM, SAM, anti-radar, and cruise missile systems, among others. Russian missile sales to China will likely continue, and China's access to foreign missile technology may increase. Ukrainian aerospace firms are reportedly interested in expanding their business interactions with Chinese companies, building on a space-cooperation deal signed in 2000.[35] In addition, a number of European governments have recently indicated their desire to resume weapon sales to China. Thus, China will likely continue to enjoy a steady stream of at least partial access to advanced missile technology for the foreseeable future.

The ability of Chinese firms to translate foreign technology imports into improved missile capabilities is limited by three considerations:

- First, absorbing foreign technology is not a trivial process, and there is inevitably a lag between the time when China acquires a missile-related technology and when Chinese systems based on that technology become operational.[36] Thus, by the time that

---

[35] "Ukraine Highly Optimistic About Prospects for Defense Ties with China," *Moscow Interfax*, November 18, 2002. In 2000, China and Ukraine signed a space-cooperation deal that includes joint work on satellites and launch vehicles.

[36] Christopher Yung estimated that, historically, it took China about 15 years to reverse engineer a weapon system, from the time samples of a system were acquired to the time-series production of that system was initiated. See Christopher D. Yung, *People's War at Sea: Chinese Naval Power in the Twenty-First Century*, Alexandria, Va.: CNA Corporation (CNAC), CRM 95-214, March 1996.

China absorbs these technologies, if it does so at all, they could be out of date.

- Second, countries and companies may not be willing to transfer their most advanced technologies to China. For example, although Israel provided China with the technology for its Python-3 AAM (see below), it has apparently not been willing to transfer its most advanced AAM, the Python-4. China currently enjoys the follower's advantage of benefiting from technological advances of other countries. Although significant now, this advantage will diminish over time as China begins to catch up to the most advanced countries. This constraint may become increasingly acute because the pace at which China's main supplier of missile technology, Russia, is developing new systems has slowed dramatically since the end of the Cold War and the breakup of the Soviet Union.
- Third, the United States will likely continue to press other Western countries to limit their military trade with China.

Incentives

There are a growing number of incentives for innovation in China's missile industry. They emanate from the rapid expansion of the Chinese government's demand for missiles, the missile manufacturers' exposure to domestic competition for military and civilian goods, and the missile manufacturers' exposure to and interactions with global markets for commercial aerospace-related products and services.[37] The second of these stands in contrast to that of other defense sectors, such as aviation, which lack competition-based incentives for greater innovation and efficiency.

As noted above, China's internal "market" for missiles (i.e., government purchases) appears to have expanded rapidly in recent years

---

[37] China's missile nonproliferation commitments mean that Chinese firms are no longer legally permitted to engage in foreign sales of missiles and related technologies. Exceptions are SAMs and AAMs, which are not restricted under China's existing nonproliferation pledges.

as the PLA has sought to use missiles to coerce Taiwan. Such a situation stimulates greater efficiency and perhaps innovation, because the potential return on investment in R&D is much greater in an expanding market than in a static or contracting market.[38] Moreover, there appears to be some competition within China for the development, production, and sales of various missile systems.

The DF-15 and DF-11 conventionally armed short-range ballistic missiles (SRBMs), for example, were developed by different organizations in competition with one another. The DF-15 was developed by CALT, a subsidiary of CASC, and the DF-11 was developed by Sanjiang Aerospace Industrial Group (also known as Base 066), a subsidiary of CASIC.[39] The subsequent improvements in the operational capabilities of these systems suggest continued competition between CALT and Sanjiang. The range, payload, and accuracies of both of these SRBMs have improved since the first models were introduced. Moreover, with the appearance at the November 2004 Airshow China in Zhuhai of the B611 SRBM developed by the Changfeng Electromechanical Technology Design Institute, a third producer of conventional SRBMs has now emerged.[40] Similarly, both CASIC's CHETA and AVIC II's Hongdu Aviation Industry Group produce ASCMs; CASC's SAST, CASIC's 2nd Academy, and AVIC I/AVIC II/CNGC all produce vehicle-mounted short-range SAMs[41]; both CASC's SAST and CASIC's Liuzhou Changhong Machinery

---

[38] The degree to which market growth actually stimulates innovation, of course, depends on the amount of competition that exists in the market. If firms are guaranteed that their goods will be purchased regardless of performance, then there is no incentive to innovate, even in an expanding market.

[39] Duncan Lennox, "CSS-7 (DF-11/M-11)," *Jane's Strategic Weapon Systems,* Vol. 40, June 3, 2003 (available online at http://online.janes.com; accessed November 25, 2003); Duncan Lennox, "CSS-6 (DF-15/M-9)," *Jane's Strategic Weapon Systems,* Vol. 40, June 3, 2003 (available online at http://online.janes.com; accessed November 25, 2003).

[40] Robert Karniol, "Beijing Displays New Tactical Surface-to-Surface System," *Jane's Defence Weekly,* November 10, 2004.

[41] SAST's SAMs are SAR-guided, CASIC's are command-guided, and AVIC I/AVIC II/CNGC's are IR-guided.

Manufacturing produce MANPADS; and both CASC's SAST and AVIC I/II's AAMRI produce AAMs.

Aside from competition among domestic missile builders, another source of competitive pressure stems from China's missile imports. Since the 1990s, China has imported advanced Russian ASCMs, SAMs, AAMs, and anti-radiation missiles. However, as with other types of weapons that China has imported, these imports have occurred primarily in areas in which Russian capabilities are clearly a generation ahead of Chinese capabilities—representing competition for Chinese firms only insofar as orders for existing Chinese systems may be reduced in favor of the imported systems. Moreover, imports of Russian systems have been limited and appear intended to serve as stopgaps until comparable Chinese systems become available. Thus, foreign imports may represent only limited competition to China's missile producers (as well as serving as a critical source of technology for reverse-engineering projects for future Chinese missile systems).

Another area in which competition occurs is CASC and CASIC's commercial space launch vehicle (SLV) business. CASC and CASIC actively market their SLVs throughout the world on the basis of their low cost and decent reliability. The exposure to the international SLV market serves as an incentive for Chinese rocket builders to improve the reliability and quality of their products, as well as to improve their management practices and the financial efficiency of the company. The benefits to China's missile programs are manifold. Although Chinese missiles were not originally developed with the space launch market in mind, technological advances to improve the SLVs have likely been incorporated into ballistic-missile design and production as well. All China's SLVs are based on its ballistic-missile designs. The Long March (*Chang Zheng* 长征) 1 (LM-1) launch vehicle, for example, is based on the DF-4 missile, and the LM-2C, LM-2D, LM-2E, LM-3, and LM-4 are all based on the DF-5.[42] More recently,

---

[42] Christian Lardier, "Chinese Space Industry's Ambition," 1996; Duncan Lennox, "CSS-3 (DF-4)," *Jane's Strategic Weapon Systems*, Vol. 40, June 3, 2003 (available online at http://online.janes.com; accessed November 25, 2003); Lennox, "CSS-4 (DF-5)," *Jane's*

CASIC entities have begun marketing the *Kaituozhe* ("Pioneer" 开拓者) mobile solid-fuel launch vehicle, which is based on the DF-21 missile.[43]

The high priority and visibility accorded China's manned space program provides strong incentives for innovation and improved quality in the development of space launch vehicles and related technologies. Many of the technological improvements resulting from this program will have applicability to China's missile programs. Moreover, there appears to be domestic competition for SLV production as well—offering a further incentive for innovation and efficiency. SAST reportedly once developed a liquid-fuel launch vehicle, designated FB-1, which was intended to be a follow-on to the LM-1. There was thus apparently competition in the design of the follow-on to the LM-1.[44] Similarly, there appears to have been competition for the assignment to produce the earth perigee kick motor for placing satellites in geosynchronous orbit.[45]

In addition to competition in the production of major systems, competition in the supply of military components and services is another source of incentives within the missile industry. CASC and CASIC subsidiaries that supply components or provide services for the civilian market are allowed to also participate in the military systems market. Such participation for these enterprises suggests the possibility of competition between them and enterprises that are dedicated solely to military production in the provision of

---

Strategic Weapon Systems, Vol. 40, June 3, 2003 (available online at http://online.janes.com; accessed November 25, 2003).

[43] Gu Ti, *Zhongguo hangtian bao*, November 20, 2002, p. 3, in *FBIS* as "PRC S&T: Kaituozhe New Choice for Small Satellite Launches," November 20, 2002, states that the KT-1 was developed "based on a certain type of missile" and notes that the "maximum diameter" of the rocket is 1.4 meters. China's only ballistic missile with this diameter is the DF-21. See Duncan Lennox, "CSS-5 (DF-21)," *Jane's Strategic Weapon Systems*, Vol. 40, June 3, 2003 (available online at http://online.janes.com; accessed November 25, 2003).

[44] Christian Lardier, "Chinese Space Industry's Ambition," 1996. The FB-1 design reportedly lost out to CALT's LM-2 and was abandoned.

[45] Shi Lei et al., "Tingzhi de Jiliang—Zhongguo Hangtian Kegong Jituan Gongsi Liu Yuan Fazhan Jishi," 2001, pp. 8–12.

components and services to the military. Thus, in addition to competition at the *prime-contractor* level, there appears to be competition at the *subcontractor* level.

To be sure, it is unclear how much Western-style market competition exists in China's missile sector. While some clearly exists, most competition likely falls short of true free-market competition, which is not dissimilar from defense industries in other countries. The simultaneous existence of related, but not identical, missile systems in the military's inventory (e.g., the DF-11 and DF-15) suggests that, instead of the best design being chosen for production, both organizations offering designs have been awarded production contracts. It is also possible that missile-producing enterprises are explicitly or implicitly guaranteed a certain level of revenues, regardless of the success of their products. As in other procurement decisions in China, multiple factors play a role, including personal and political relationships between the leaders of the enterprises in question and government ministries. There are indications, however, that such past practices are changing in the missile industry, as well as in other sectors (i.e., shipbuilding and IT) addressed in this volume.

Chinese missile industry executives have been explicit about how they view competition in light of the defense-industrial reforms initiated in 1998 and 1999. In 1999, Chinese officials stated that "the competition between [CASC and CASIC will not be] competition in terms of their products, rather it [will be] *competition in terms of their systems of organization and their operational mechanisms.*"[46] Thus, the government's goal appears to be a situation of "managed competition" between the two large enterprise groups. The other case studies in this volume reflect similar practices in other defense sectors. Another factor lessening competition and incentives for innovation is that, at present, there appears to be no intention to make producers of military systems within CASC and CASIC solely responsible for their finances. In other words, some government subsidization will be continued in order to ensure that producers of military systems

---

[46] Li Xiuwei, "Applying Technology to National Defense," 1999. Emphasis added.

continue to focus on military technology development and that production lines stay open.[47]

Institutions

The institutional infrastructure of China's missile sector appears to be more robust than that in China's other defense-industrial sectors. This robust infrastructure may be the greatest strength for China's missile industry as it seeks to modernize. As noted earlier, CASC and CASIC differ from AVIC I and AVIC II in the closer integration between research institutes and production enterprises. The system of academies and bases provides an institutional framework that can facilitate communication between production enterprises and research institutes and, at least in theory, provide a mechanism for ensuring that designs are consistent with actual production capabilities and converting the desire for increased production orders into pressure for timely and capable designs.

CASC and CASIC also appear to have a growing infrastructure of technology-services companies that are financially self-supporting and thus have an incentive to aggressively market their services to enterprises. The existence of these specialized organizations increases the level of available technical expertise and facilitates the flow of knowledge within the industry. This practice contrasts with the traditional situation in China, in which each defense enterprise simply provided such services for itself, contributing to redundant capabilities and inhibiting the flow of knowledge among enterprises.

CASC and CASIC themselves, the overarching holding companies, play an important institutional role by facilitating cooperation among organizations on projects that are beyond the capabilities of a

---

[47] Zhu Zhaowu, "Pushing Forward Reform of Administrative Logistics, Promoting Development of Aerospace Industry," *Jingji ribao,* February 1999, p. A3, in *FBIS* as "Aerospace Administrative Logistics Reform," February 19, 1999; Zhou Jiahe and Zhu Shide, "Jiangnan Aerospace Group Revived Through Great Efforts," *Guizhou ribao,* September 14, 2000, p. 1, in *FBIS* as "PRC: Article Says Jiangnan Aerospace Group Revived Through Reform," September 14, 2000; Xia Guohong, You Zheng, Meng Bo, and Xin Peihua, *Zhongguo hangtian,* August 1, 2002, in *FBIS* as "PRC S&T: Aerospace Qinghua Satellite Technology Company," August 1, 2002.

single entity. For example, SAST and CALT cooperated in the development and production of intercontinental ballistic missiles (ICBMs) and space launch vehicles, and SAST and CAST have cooperated in the production of manned spacecraft and satellites.[48] CASC and CASIC are no longer involved in the day-to-day management and financial affairs of their component enterprises, but they do manage the capital flows among their various entities. In that role, they can also facilitate and manage the competition among their subordinate entities.

Another important institutional function that CASC and CASIC provide is a range of information services that promote the dissemination of information and ideas, critical for technological progress across a large and geographically dispersed industry. CASC and CASIC jointly publish *Zhongguo hangtian bao* (中国航天报 *China Aerospace News*), the official newspaper of China's missile and space industry. CASC sponsors the National Aerospace Information Center of China (*Zhongguo Hangtian Xinxi Zhongxin* 中国航天信息中心), which publishes the trade journals *Zhongguo hangtian* (中国航天 *China Aerospace*), *Hangtian gongye guanli* (航天工业管理 *Aerospace Industry Management*), *Junmin liangyong* (军民两用 *Dual Use*), *Hangtian zhishi chanquan* (航天知识产权 *Aerospace Intellectual Property Rights*), and *Shijie hangkong hangtian bolan* (世界航空航天博览 *World Aviation*

---

[48] Christian Lardier, "Chinese Space Industry's Ambition," 1996; *Zhongguo hangtian,* July 1997; Shi Hua, *China Daily,* September 1, 1999; Zheng Wei and Zhang Jie, "Long March Rockets, Developed by Shanghai Aerospace Bureau, Achieve 20 Successful Consecutive Launches; 'Long March' Rockets Never Miss Target," 1999; Zeng Min, *China Daily,* February 3, 2001, in *FBIS* as "China to Launch More Meteorological Satellites in 'Fengyun' Series," February 3, 2001; *FBIS,* "Report on PRC Central Leaders' Activities 26 Aug–6 Sep," September 7, 2001; Xi Qixin and Liu Siyang, "Jiang Zemin Watches the Launch of a Spacecraft from the Manned Spacecraft Launch Center," March 25, 2002; Liu Cheng and Tian Zhaoyun, "China Launches First Marine Satellite," May 15, 2002; "Fourteen Pilots with Right Stuff Ready for Liftoff," 2002; Zheng Wei, "Fengyun-4: Gaze Upon the Earth After 10 Years," *Wen hui bao,* September 6, 2002, in *FBIS* as "PRC S&T: Fengyun-4 Meteorological Satellite to Launch in 10 Years," September 6, 2002; "China Aerospace Science and Technology Corporation," 2002; Xi Qixin, "PRC Successfully Launches 'China Resources-II' Satellite," 2002.

and Aerospace Survey).[49] There is also a Chinese Society of Astronautics, which publishes the journal *Yuhang xuebao* (宇航学报 *Astronautics Journal*), and over 100 other technical journals focused on aviation and aerospace technology.[50] These organizations and journals are important mechanisms for the diffusion of information within the industry, which is vital to technological progress.

A final set of institutions affecting the future capabilities of China's missile sector is research and educational institutions. In addition to the research institutes within CASC, CASIC, and the other defense conglomerates that are involved in missile production, considerable applied research of relevance to missile R&D and production is conducted by the Chinese Academy of Sciences (CAS) and by China's institutes of higher education, including the Beijing University of Aviation and Aerospace, Tsinghua University, Northwestern Polytechnic University, and the East China University of Science and Technology.[51] These universities, particularly those with specialized aerospace programs, and CAS also represent important institutions for training scientists and engineers for the missile sector.

Missile-Industry Production Capabilities and Output

Compared with other developing nations, China's missile-production capabilities are impressive and, in some areas, even approach those of

---

[49] For example, see http://www.spacechina.com/index.asp?modelname=htzz_gd; accessed December 30, 2003.

[50] Wang Zhigang, Li Qing, Chen Shilu, and Li Renhou, *Yuhang xuebao,* November 1, 2001, pp. 35–39, in *FBIS* as "PRC S&T: Orbit Transfer of Three-Satellite Constellation," November 1, 2001; Dai Longji, Zhang Qisu, Cai Ronghua, eds., *Index of Core Chinese Journals,* Beijing: Peking University Press, 2000, pp. 626–629.

[51] For example, see *Xinhua,* April 9, 1998, in *FBIS* as "Beijing Plans to Develop 500-Meter Radio Telescope," April 9, 1998; Zhang Jinfu, "CAS Reveals Past Role in China WMD Programs," *Kexue shibao,* May 6, 1999, pp. 1–3, in *FBIS,* May 6, 1999; Ye Dingyou and Zhang Dexiong, 2002, pp. 24–27; *Xinhua,* February 3, 2003, in *FBIS* as "Xinhua Cites Chinese Scientists on Columbia Tragedy, PRC Space Flight," February 3, 2003.

modern Western militaries. Nonetheless, key weaknesses remain in important areas. As in other defense sectors in China, some of these weaknesses have been recognized and are being remedied, whereas others persist. In this section, we evaluate the current R&D and production capabilities of China's missile industry. The trends described above will facilitate a continued improvement in the R&D and production capabilities in the missile sector in the coming years. This improvement will be most evident in both the new platforms coming online and the increasing speed by which the platforms are produced.

The most notable and impressive characteristic of China's missile sector is the sheer breadth of the products it produces. Companies in CASC, CASIC, AVIC I, AVIC II, and CNGC turn out numerous types of ballistic missiles, ASCMs, SAMs, AAMs, LACMs, and precision ground-attack missiles. Many of the currently deployed systems are quite modern and comparable to those currently used by the United States and other militaries. China's SRBM arsenal is perhaps most significant in this regard. These missiles provide China with a capability that other militaries do not possess and are particularly useful in addressing the perceived needs of deterrence, coercion, and warfighting with regard to Taiwan.

Nonetheless, China's missile industry over the past several decades has experienced numerous weaknesses, and the legacies of these weaknesses persist. The development time lines for most missile systems have been long, China's missile industry has heavily relied on imported designs and technologies, and, in many areas, the industry has failed consistently to meet the needs of the PLA. China's substantial imports of modern SAMs, ASCMs, AAMs, and related technologies from Israel and Russia in the last decade clearly indicate the industry's shortcomings. The greatest weaknesses are in the areas of medium- and long-range SAR-guided SAMs, fire-and-forget AAMs, and LACMs.

Moreover, even the Chinese missile systems that are comparable to those in use in modern militaries did not enter service until a decade or longer after their foreign counterparts had. Many of these foreign systems are now soon to be replaced by more-advanced systems, although it is not clear whether China's missile producers will soon be replacing their versions of these systems or whether they will continue to lag a decade or more behind their foreign counterparts.

Ballistic Missiles: Strengths and Weaknesses in R&D and Production Capabilities

China's defense industry is perhaps best known for its ballistic missiles. In past decades, China has been one of very few nations to produce a full range of indigenously designed ballistic missiles, including ICBMs. Currently, Beijing's growing numbers of conventional SRBMs deployed across Taiwan's coastline have generated much international attention. Yet close examination of China's ballistic-missile production capabilities reveals that they lag well behind those of the advanced military powers. In many cases, China is just now reaching a level that the United States and Soviet Union achieved in the late 1960s and early 1970s.

China's first ballistic missiles were license-produced versions of the Soviet SS-2 liquid-oxygen/alcohol-powered missile (itself a development of the World War II German V-2) and given the designator *Dong Feng* (东风 "East Wind") 1 (DF-1), which first test-flew in 1960. Soviet technical assistance to China in all areas, including defense industries, ended that same year and did not resume until the 1990s. In the meantime, China developed successive models of DF-1–based liquid-fuel missiles of increasing range and accuracy. Today, China fields liquid-fueled ballistic missiles with ranges of up to 13,000 km and circular error probable (CEP) accuracies as low as 500 meters.[52]

In addition, beginning in the 1960s, China also began to develop solid-fuel ballistic missiles. The original impetus for this effort was to produce a submarine-launched ballistic missile (SLBM), the *Ju Lang*

---

[52] Duncan Lennox, "CSS-1 (DF-2)," *Jane's Strategic Weapon Systems,* Vol. 40, June 3, 2003 (available online at http://online.janes.com; accessed November 25, 2003); Duncan Lennox, "CSS-2 (DF-3)," *Jane's Strategic Weapon Systems,* Vol. 40, June 3, 2003 (available online at http://online.janes.com; accessed November 25, 2003); Duncan Lennox, "CSS-3 (DF-4)," 2003; Duncan Lennox, "CSS-4 (DF-5)," 2003.

(巨浪 "Giant Wave") 1 (JL-1), but a land-based version of the missile, the DF-21 was subsequently developed as well. Unlike China's liquid-fuel ballistic missiles, the DF-21 was designed to be fired from a road-mobile TEL, increasing its survivability.[53]

The DF-21 and all of China's liquid-fuel ballistic missiles carry nuclear warheads. However, following the development of the DF-21, shorter-range solid-fuel missiles were developed and designed to carry conventional warheads. These SRBMs may have originally been developed for export, but they were subsequently acquired by the PLA. Today, the PLA fields solid-fuel ballistic missiles with ranges from 350 to 2,150 km and CEPs as low as 50 m, and efforts are ongoing to improve the accuracy of these missiles and extend their range.[54] In addition, nuclear-armed, solid-fuel, road-mobile ICBMs are under development.

China's current and developmental ballistic-missile systems are described in Table 2.3.

China has possessed the capability to independently design and produce ballistic missiles since the 1960s, and in 1981 China became the first developing country to field an ICBM. Yet, compared with the United States, the performance of China's ballistic-missile sector is unremarkable, and significant limitations are evident. The United States fielded its first ICBM in 1960, 21 years earlier than China. Since 1963, all newly developed U.S. ICBMs have been solid-fueled, whereas China's first solid-fueled ICBM, the 8,000-km-range DF-31,

---

[53] Duncan Lennox, "CSS-5 (DF-21)," 2003; Duncan Lennox, "CSS-N-3 (JL-1/-21)," *Jane's Strategic Weapon Systems*, Vol. 40, June 3, 2003 (available online at http://online.janes.com; accessed November 25, 2003). The DF-3 and DF-4 intermediate-range missiles are believed to be road- and/or rail-transportable, but can only be fired from prepared sites and take 2 to 3 hours to be readied for launch. See Duncan Lennox, "CSS-2 (DF-3)," 2003, and "CSS-3 (DF-4)," 2003.

[54] Duncan Lennox, "CSS-7 (DF-11/M-11)," 2003; Duncan Lennox, "CSS-6 (DF-15/ M-9)," 2003; Duncan Lennox, "CSS-5 (DF-21)," 2003.

Table 2.3
Current and Developmental Ballistic-Missile Systems

Designator	Fuel	Entered Service	Payload (kg)	Range (km)	CEP (m)
DF-3A	Liquid	1987	2,150	2,800	1,000
DF-4	Liquid	1980	2,200	5,500+	1,500
DF-5	Liquid	1981	3,000	12,000	800
DF-5A	Liquid	1986	3,200	13,000	500
DF-11 (M-11)	Solid	1992	800	350	600
DF-11A	Solid	1998	500	500+	200
DF-15 (M-9)	Solid	1990	500	600	300
DF-15A	Solid	Unknown	500	600+	30–45
DF-21	Solid	1987	600	2,150	700
DF-21A	Solid	Unknown	500	2,500	50
DF-31	Solid	By 2010	1,050–1,750	8,000	300
DF-31A	Solid	By 2010?	1,050–1,750	10,000	300
B611	Solid	Unknown	480	150	150
JL-1	Solid	2003	600	2,150	700
JL-2	Solid	By 2010	1,050–2,800	8,000	300

SOURCES: *Jane's Strategic Weapon Systems,* Vol. 40, June 3, 2003; Office of the Secretary of Defense, *Proliferation: Threat and Response,* Washington D.C.: U.S. Government Printing Office, January 2001; U.S. Department of Defense, *Annual Report on the Military Power of the People's Republic of China,* Washington DC: July 28, 2003; U.S. Department of Defense, *Annual Report on the Military Power of the People's Republic of China,* Washington D.C.: May 28, 2004; Robert Karniol, "Beijing Displays New Tactical Surface-to-Surface System," *Jane's Defence Weekly,* November 10, 2004.
NOTE: Data are based on unclassified sources and may contain some inaccuracies.

is not expected to be deployed until the later part of this decade.[55] Moreover, the DF-31 is expected to have a CEP of 300 m, whereas the otherwise-comparable U.S. Minuteman II, which entered service in 1965, had a published CEP of 200 m.[56]

---

[55] Duncan Lennox, "CSS-4 (DF-5)," 2003. David Miller, *The Cold War: A Military History,* New York: St. Martin's Press, 1999; Timothy M. Laur and Steven L. Llanso, *Encyclopedia of Modern U.S. Military Weapons,* New York: Berkley Books, 1995; Office of the Secretary of Defense, *Proliferation: Threat and Response,* 2001, p. 16; U.S. Department of Defense, *Annual Report on the Military Power of the People's Republic of China,* Washington D.C., July 28, 2003, p. 31.

[56] Duncan Lennox, "LGM-30F Minuteman II," *Jane's Strategic Weapon Systems,* Vol. 40, October 27, 2003 (available online at http://online.janes.com/; accessed November 30, 2003).

Similarly, the United States fielded the Pershing I, a road-mobile solid-fuel SRBM with a range of 740 km and a CEP of 150 m, in the late 1960s, whereas China's first SRBM, the DF-15, with a range of 600 km and a CEP of 300 m, did not enter service until around 1990.[57] The DF-15A SRBM and DF-21A MRBM are expected to have CEPs of less than 50 m when they become operational in the next few years, but the U.S.'s Pershing II MRBM, which entered service in 1984, also had a CEP of 50 m.[58]

Finally, the United States has had an operational SLBM capability since 1960. China appears to be just achieving this capability.[59] The U.S. 7,400 km-range, 450-m-CEP Trident C-4 entered service in 1979; the comparable JL-2 is not expected to enter service until the end of this decade.[60] Thus, China's SLBM capabilities appear to be comparable to those of the United States 30 years ago, its ICBM capabilities appear to be comparable to those of the United States 40 years ago, and its SRBM/MRBM capabilities appear to be comparable to those of the United States 20 years ago. Moreover, there is no evidence that China's rate of progress in this area has accelerated.

Although unimpressive in a relative sense, China's SRBMs and MRBMs nonetheless provide a significant strike capability for the PLA. The only U.S. conventional ballistic missile, for example, is the Army Tactical Missile System (ATACMS), with a maximum range of

---

[57] Duncan Lennox, "MGM-31A Pershing I," *Jane's Strategic Weapon Systems,* Vol. 40, June 3, 2003 (available online at http://online.janes.com/; accessed November 29, 2003); Duncan Lennox, "CSS-6 (DF-15/M-9)," 2003.

[58] Duncan Lennox, "CSS-6 (DF-15/M-9)," 2003; Duncan Lennox, "CSS-5 (DF-21)," 2003; Duncan Lennox, "MGM-31B Pershing II," *Jane's Strategic Weapon Systems,* Vol. 40, June 3, 2003 (available online at http://online.janes.com/; accessed November 29, 2003).

[59] Duncan Lennox, "UGM-27 Polaris (A-1/-2/-3)," *Jane's Strategic Weapon Systems,* Vol. 40, June 3, 2003 (available online at http://online.janes.com/; accessed November 30, 2003); U.S. Department of Defense, *Annual Report on the Military Power of the People's Republic of China,* 2003, p. 31.

[60] Duncan Lennox, "UGM-96 Trident C-4," *Jane's Strategic Weapon Systems,* Vol. 40, October 27, 2003 (available online at http://online.janes.com/; accessed November 30, 2003); U.S. Department of Defense, *Annual Report on the Military Power of the People's Republic of China,* 2003, p. 31.

300 km.[61] (The U.S. Pershing and comparable Russian systems have been eliminated as a result of the 1987 Intermediate Nuclear Forces Treaty, which prohibits the United States or Russia from fielding ground-launched ballistic or cruise missiles with ranges between 500 and 5,500 km.) While the United States relies on aircraft or air- or sea-launched cruise missiles to attack targets at ranges greater than 300 km, China's SRBMs have the advantages of being extremely difficult for modern air-defense systems to intercept, being independent from vulnerable fixed airbases, and being virtually impossible to locate and attack prior to launch. Conversely, even the newly developed DF-15A and DF-21A will lack the accuracies of cruise missiles or precision-guided munitions delivered by aircraft.

Anti-Ship Cruise Missiles
China's ASCMs have also attracted attention, largely because of their alleged sales to Iran in the 1980s and again in the 1990s. Although, as with China's ballistic missiles, China's ASCM production capabilities are advanced compared with the rest of China's defense sectors, they still lag behind those of the most advanced militaries.

As with its ballistic missiles, the first ASCMs produced in China were license-produced versions of a Soviet system (the liquid-fuel P-15—called the SS-N-2A "Styx" in the West). This missile, designated SY-1 in China, entered service in the late 1960s. An indigenously improved version, designated *Hai Ying 1* (海鹰 "Sea Eagle") (HY-1), entered service in 1974. Subsequent models based on the underlying design (including the *Fei Long 1*, HY-2, HY-3, HY-4, YJ-6, YJ-16, and YJ-62), but with improved range, speed, and propulsion systems, was introduced in subsequent years.[62]

---

[61] Duncan Lennox, "MGM-140 ATACMS (M39) Pershing I," *Jane's Strategic Weapon Systems,* Vol. 40, October 27, 2003 (available online at http://online.janes.com/; accessed December 31, 2003).

[62] E. R. Hooton, "CSS-N-1 'Scrubbrush' (SY-1/HY-1); CSS-N-2 'Silkworm'; CSS-N-3 'Seersucker' (HY-2/FL-1/FL-3A)," 2003; Duncan Lennox, "CSS-N-1 'Scrubbrush' (SY-1), CSS-N-2 'Safflower' (HY-1), CSSC-2 'Silkworm' (HY-1), CSSC-3 'Seersucker' (HY-2/C-201)," *Jane's Strategic Weapon Systems,* Vol. 40, July 31, 2003 (available online at http://online.janes.com/; accessed November 25, 2003); Duncan Lennox, "CSS-N-1

In 1984, China introduced a completely new type of ASCM, the *Ying Ji-1* (YJ-1, 鹰击 "Eagle Strike") (often referred to by its export designator, C-801). This missile is solid-fueled and much smaller and lighter than any of the P-15–based missiles listed above, making it more reliable, significantly more difficult for radar to detect, and more suitable for airborne carriage. Around 1994, a longer-range, turbojet-powered version of the missile, designated YJ-2 (often referred to by its export designator, C-802), entered service. The YJ-1 is comparable in capability (and appearance) to the French Exocet ASCM, which entered service in 1975, and the YJ-2 is comparable to early versions of the U.S. Harpoon ASCM, which entered service in 1977.[63]

China also has a number of other ASCMs in development. One may be called the Fei Long 10 (FL-10) and is designed for launch from

'Scrubbrush Mod 2' (FL-1), CSS-NX-5 'Sabbot' (FL-2), FL-7 and FL-10," 2003; Robert Hewson, "HY-4 (C-201)," *Jane's Air-Launched Weapons*, Vol. 40, July 9, 2002 (available online at http://online.janes.com/; accessed November 25, 2003); Duncan Lennox, "CAS-1 'Kraken' (YJ-6/YJ-62/YJ-63/C-601/C-611)," *Jane's Strategic Weapon Systems*, Vol. 40, July 31, 2003 (available online at http://online.janes.com/; accessed November 25, 2003); Robert Hewson, "YJ-6/C-601 (CAS-1 'Kraken')," *Jane's Air-Launched Weapons*, Vol. 40, July 9, 2002, (available online at http://online.janes.com/; accessed November 25, 2003); Duncan Lennox, "CSSC-5 'Saples' (YJ-16/C-101)," *Jane's Strategic Weapon Systems*, Vol. 40, July 31, 2003 (available online at http://online.janes.com/; accessed November 25, 2003); Duncan Lennox, "YJ-16/C-101," *Jane's Air-Launched Weapons*, Vol. 38, November 9, 2001 (available online at http://online.janes.com/; accessed November 25, 2003); Duncan Lennox, "CSSC-6 'Sawhorse' (HY-3/C-301)," *Jane's Strategic Weapon Systems*, Vol. 40, July 31, 2003 (available online at http://online.janes.com/; accessed November 25, 2003); Lu Yi, "China's Antiship Missile Draws Attention of World's Military Circles," *Kuang chiao ching*, August 16, 2001, pp. 32–35, in *FBIS* as "Article on China's Development of Antiship Missiles," August 16, 2001.

[63] E. R. Hooton, "CSS-N-4 'Sardine' (YJ-1/C-801); CSS-N-8 'Saccade' (YJ-2/C-802); CY-1/C-803)," *Jane's Naval Weapon Systems*, Vol. 39, August 28, 2003 (available online at http://online.janes.com/; accessed November 25, 2003); Duncan Lennox, "CSS-N-4 'Sardine' (YJ-1/-12/-82 and C-801) and CSSC-8 'Saccade' (YJ-2/-21/-22/-83 and C-802/803)," *Jane's Strategic Weapon Systems*, Vol. 40, July 31, 2003 (available online at http://online.janes.com/; accessed November 25, 2003); Duncan Lennox, "YJ-1 (C-801) and YJ-2 (C-802)," *Jane's Air-Launched Weapons*, Vol. 38, November 9, 2001 (available online at http://online.janes.com/; accessed November 25, 2003); Duncan Lennox, "MM 38/40, AM 39 and SM 39 Exocet," *Jane's Strategic Weapon Systems*, Vol. 40, July 31, 2003 (available online at http://online.janes.com/; accessed November 30, 2003); Duncan Lennox, "AGM/RGM/UGM-84 Harpoon/SLAM/SLAM-ER," *Jane's Strategic Weapon Systems*, Vol. 40, October 27, 2003 (available online at http://online.janes.com/; accessed November 30, 2003).

helicopters and fast attack craft. At the November 2004 Zhuhai Airshow China, the Hongdu Aviation Industry Group, maker of the Fei Long series, displayed models of ASCMs designated JJ/TL-10A and JJ/TL-10B, which may be the same missile as the FL-10. (The JJ/TL-10A is an optically guided version, and the JJ/TL-10B is microwave radar–guided.) Another model displayed by Hongdu was of a larger, radar-guided missile designated JJ/TL-6B, which may also be known as the FL-6.

All of the missiles described in the preceding paragraph are nominally being codeveloped and coproduced with Iran and may not enter service with the PLA. CHETA has developed a small ASCM, comparable to the French AS 15TT (or the anti-ship versions of the U.S. AGM-65 Maverick), with the designator C-701. As with the FL-10, this missile is designed for launch from helicopters and fast attack craft and is apparently being codeveloped with Iran. Test firings of this missile have been carried out, but, as with the FL series, it is not clear whether this missile will enter service with the PLA.[64]

The characteristics of China's known ASCMs are shown in Table 2.4.

Compared with that of the advanced military powers, the performance of China's missile industry in developing ASCMs has been respectable. In particular, the YJ-1 entered service nine years after the comparable Exocet, and the more-advanced YJ-2 entered service 17 years after the comparable Harpoon. However, unlike its ballistic

---

[64] Duncan Lennox, "CSS-N-1 'Scrubbrush Mod 2' (FL-1), CSS-NX-5 'Sabbot' (FL-2), FL-7 and FL-10," 2003; Robert Hewson, "C-701 (YJ-7)," *Jane's Air-Launched Weapons,* Vol. 42, July 16, 2003 (available online at http://online.janes.com/; accessed November 25, 2003); Richard Fisher, "Report on the 5th Airshow China," December 13, 2004; Robert Hewson, "China, Iran Share Missile Know-How," *Jane's Defence Weekly,* December 4, 2002; Xu Tong, "China's C701 Small-Scale Multifunctional Missile," *Bingqi zhishi,* March 2000, pp. 2–3, in *FBIS* as "PRC Missile C701 Able 'To Target Patrol Boat Threats'"; Duncan Lennox, "C-701," *Jane's Air-Launched Weapons,* Vol. 36, May 13, 2000 (available online at http://online.janes.com/; accessed November 25, 2003); E. R. Hooton, "C-701," *Jane's Naval Weapon Systems,* Vol. 38, December 20, 2002 (available online at http://online.janes.com/; accessed November 25, 2003); Douglas Barrie, "Chinese Fireworks," *Aviation Week and Space Technology,* November 8, 2004.

Table 2.4
China's ASCMs

Designator	Launch Platforms	Entered Service	Propulsion	Range (km)	Speed (mach)
SY-1	Ship, shore	~1967	Liquid-fuel rocket	40	0.9
HY-1	Ship, shore	1974	Liquid-fuel rocket	85	0.9
HY-2 (C-201)	Ship, shore	1978	Liquid-fuel rocket	95	0.9
HY-3 (C-301)	Shore	1995	Ramjet	140	2.0
HY-4	Ship, shore, air	1985	Turbojet	135	0.8
FL-1	Ship	1980	Liquid-fuel rocket	45	0.9
JJ/TL-6/FL-6	Unknown	Unknown	Unknown	35	Unknown
JJ/TL-10/FL-10	Ship, air	Unknown	Unknown	18	Unknown
YJ-16 (C-101)	Ship, shore	1988	Ramjet	45	2.0
YJ-6 (C-601)	Air	1985	Liquid-fuel rocket	110	0.9
YJ-62 (C-611)	Air	1989	Liquid-fuel rocket	200	0.9
YJ-1/YJ-81 (C-801)	Ship, shore, submarine, air	1984	Solid-fuel rocket	40–50	0.85
YJ-2/YJ-82 (C-802)	Ship, shore, air	1994	Turbojet	120–130	0.85
C-701	Ship, air	Unknown	Solid-fuel rocket	15	0.8

SOURCES: *Jane's Strategic Weapon Systems,* Vol. 40, 2003; *Jane's Naval Weapon Systems,* Vol. 39; *Jane's Air-Launched Weapons,* Vols. 38, 40, 2000, 2001; Richard Fisher, "Report on the 5th Airshow China," 2004; Xu Tong, "China's C701 Small-Scale Multifunctional Missile," 2000; Douglas Barrie, "Chinese Fireworks," 2004.

NOTE: Data are based on unclassified sources and may contain inaccuracies.

missiles, China's ASCMs apparently do not fully meet the needs of the Chinese military, as evidenced by the PLA Navy (PLAN) acquisitions of Sovremenny-class destroyers from Russia. These ships incorporate SS-N-22 "Sunburn" supersonic, sea-skimming ASCMs, missiles that have a low-level cruise speed of Mach 2.1 and were reportedly specifically designed to defeat the U.S. Aegis naval air- defense system.[65] This acquisition likely reflects concerns about the ability of

---

[65] Duncan Lennox, "SS-N-22 'Sunburn' (P-80/-270/3M-80/3M82 Zubr/Moskit)," *Jane's Strategic Weapon Systems,* Vol. 40, September 25, 2003 (online at http://online.janes.com/; accessed November 30, 2003).

Chinese-built ASCMs to penetrate capable air-defense systems, such as those employed by U.S. Navy ships.[66]

Surface-to-Air Missiles

As with China's ballistic missiles and ASCMs, the SAMs manufactured by China's defense industry initially were license-produced Soviet designs. The first one was the S-75 (SA-2, "Guideline") command-guided low-to-high-altitude SAM, designated *Hong Qi-1* (HQ-1, 红旗 "Red Flag") by the PLA. It entered service in 1966. The 2nd Academy of the 7th Ministry of Machine Building (now the Changfeng Electromechanical Technology Design Institute under CASIC) was assigned responsibility for developing an improved version with anti-jamming capabilities. This improved system, the HQ-2, entered service in 1967. Successive incremental improvements on the HQ-2 remained in production at least into the 1990s.[67]

The first primarily indigenously designed Chinese SAM was the HQ-61, a low-to-medium altitude, short-range, SAR-guided system developed by SAST. The HQ-61 reportedly entered service with the PLA in 1991, and a shipboard version entered service in 1992. This design was apparently unsuccessful, however. The HQ-61 is currently in limited service with the PLA ground forces and only mounted on the Jiangwei I–class frigates in the PLAN.[68]

---

[66] Although the Chinese YJ-16 and HY-3 are also capable of Mach 2, neither apparently has ever been mounted on a major surface combatant.

[67] "CPMIEC Hongqi-1 Medium- to High-Altitude Surface-to-Air Missile System," *Jane's Land-Based Air Defence 1996–1997*, April 12, 1996 (available online at http://online.janes.com/; accessed November 25, 2003); James C. O'Halloran, "CNPMIEC Hongqi-2 Low- to High-Altitude Surface-to-Air Missile System," *Jane's Land-Based Air Defence*, September 4, 2003 (available online at http://online.janes.com/; accessed November 25, 2003); Duncan Lennox, "CSA-1/HQ-2," *Jane's Strategic Weapon Systems*, Vol. 39, January 6, 2003 (available online at http://online.janes.com/; accessed November 25, 2003).

[68] James C. O'Halloran, "CNPMIEC Hongqi-61A Low- to Medium-Altitude Surface-to-Air Missile System," 2003; Duncan Lennox, "CSA-N-2 (HQ-61/RF-61/SD-1)," *Jane's Strategic Weapon Systems*, Vol. 39, January 6, 2003 (available online at http://online.janes.com/; accessed November 25, 2003); E. R. Hooton, "SD-1 (CSA-N-2)," *Jane's Naval Weapon Systems*, Vol. 39, May 6, 2003 (available online at http://online.janes.com/; accessed November 25, 2003).

SAST's experience in developing the HQ-61 was not a total failure, however. Another low-to-medium-altitude, short-range SAR-guided SAM developed by SAST, the *Lieying-60* (LY-60, 猎鹰 "Falcon"), entered service around 1995. (This system may have benefited from SAST's earlier contacts with Italy's Alenia regarding possible license-production of the Aspide AAM. The LY-60 missile is similar in size and shape to the Aspide.) The LY-60 system is capable of simultaneously engaging three separate targets and is viewed by the Chinese military as far more successful than the HQ-61. It is currently in service with the PLA ground forces, is reportedly replacing the HQ-61 on the PLAN's Jiangwei I–class frigates, and may be fitted onto China's destroyers in the future.[69]

China's missile industry also produces a command-guided, low-altitude, short-range SAM, the HQ-7 (export designator FM-80), which entered service around 1991. This system, developed by Changfeng Electromechanical Technology Design Institute, closely resembles the French Thomson-CSF R-440 Crotale, which suggests that the HQ-7 benefited either from licensing of the Crotale technology or from reverse engineering it. The HQ-7 is currently in service with the PLA ground forces and on PLAN destroyers. An enhanced version, the HQ-7A (export designator FM-90), has reportedly been developed.[70] Given the HQ-7's short range, however, it can provide only terminal point-defense for Chinese naval vessels. In

---

[69] James C. O'Halloran, "CNPMIEC Lieying-60 (LY-60) Low- to Medium-Altitude Surface-to-Air Missile System," *Jane's Land-Based Air Defence*, September 4, 2003 (available online at http://online.janes.com/; accessed November 25, 2003); Duncan Lennox, "LY-60/HQ-11/RF-11," *Jane's Strategic Weapon Systems*, Vol. 39, January 6, 2003 (available online at http://online.janes.com/; accessed November 25, 2003).

[70] James C. O'Halloran, "CNPMIEC HQ-7 (FM-80) Shelter-Mounted Surface-to-Air Missile System," *Jane's Land-Based Air Defence*, September 4, 2003 (available online at http://online.janes.com/; accessed November 25, 2003); James C. O'Halloran, "CNPMIEC FM-90 Surface-to-Air Missile System," *Jane's Land-Based Air Defence*, January 27, 2003 (available online at http://online.janes.com/; accessed November 25, 2003); Duncan Lennox, "CSA-4/-5, HQ-7/RF-7, FM-80/-90," *Jane's Strategic Weapon Systems*, Vol. 39, January 6, 2003 (available online at http://online.janes.com/, accessed November 25, 2003).

recent years, the PLAN has sought far more capable systems to meet the demands of area defense for its naval vessels.

Changfeng has also apparently developed a follow-on to the HQ-2 series, known as the KS-1, which is a command-guided, low-to-high-altitude SAM. Unlike the HQ-2, this system incorporates a phased-array radar and is capable of multiple simultaneous engagements. It is said to now be in production for the PLA. A more advanced phased-array-radar SAM also is under development, the 150-km-range HQ-9, which is based on the highly capable Russian S-300 PMU (SA-20). A navalized version of this missile is expected to be deployed on China's new classes of destroyers.[71]

China's missile industry also has developed and produced a variety of MANPADS. The HN-5, developed by SAST and based on the Russian Strela-2 (SA-7), entered service in 1985; SAST has subsequently developed the more-capable, all-aspect, IR-guided FN-6. The Liuzhou Changhong Machinery Manufacturing Corporation (*Liuzhou Changhong Jiqi Zhizao Gongsi* 柳州长虹机器制造公司), a manufacturing enterprise directly controlled by CASIC, produces the *Qian Wei* (前卫 "Vanguard") series of MANPADS, which is said to be similar to the Russian Kolomna KBM Igla-1 (SA-16). The latest version of this missile, the QW-3, is capable of laser semi-active homing guidance, in addition to IR guidance.[72]

---

[71] James C. O'Halloran, "CNPMIEC KS-1/KS-1A Low- to High-Altitude Surface-to-Air Missile System," *Jane's Land-Based Air Defence,* May 28, 2003 (available online at http://online.janes.com/; accessed November 25, 2003); Duncan Lennox, "KS-1/-2/HQ-8/FT-2100," *Jane's Strategic Weapon Systems,* Vol. 39, January 6, 2003 (online at http://online.janes.com/; accessed November 25, 2003); Richard Fisher, "Report on the 5th Airshow China," 2004; James C. O'Halloran, "Chinese Self-Propelled Surface-to-Air Missile System Programmes," *Jane's Land-Based Air Defence,* January 27, 2003 (available online at http://online.janes.com/; accessed November 25, 2003); Duncan Lennox, "HQ-9/-15, HHQ-9A, RF-9," *Jane's Strategic Weapon Systems,* Vol. 39, January 6, 2003 (available online at http://online.janes.com/; accessed November 25, 2003). It is unclear what organization in China is developing the HQ-9, although according to the last of these sources the developer is AASPT (the 4th Academy). If true, this would be the first time AASPT was the primary developer for a SAM system.

[72] James C. O'Halloran, "CNPMIEC Hong Nu-5 Series Man-Portable Anti-Aircraft Missile System," 2003; James C. O'Halloran, "CNPMIEC FN-6 Low-Altitude Surface-to-Air Missile System," *Jane's Land-Based Air Defence,* November 11, 2003 (available online at

In addition, CNGC markets the DK-9C self-propelled SAM system, which employs the PL-9 all-aspect, IR-guided missile originally developed for an air-to-air role by AAMRI.[73] This system, which is comparable to the U.S. Chaparral system employing the AIM-9 Sidewinder AAM, provides a more capable low-altitude air- defense capability than China's MANPADS. Similarly, at the 2004 Airshow China, AAMRI was marketing a vehicle-mounted SAM version of its *Tian Yan-90* (TY-90, 天燕 "Heavenly Swallow") helicopter-borne AAM.[74]

Finally, China is believed to be developing two anti-radiation SAMs for use against early-warning and jamming aircraft. One, the FT-2000, appears to be based on the S-300 PMU. The other, the FT-2000A, appears to be based on the HQ-2. Which organizations are developing these systems is not clear, and neither system has entered service.[75]

---

http://online.janes.com/; accessed November 25, 2003); James C. O'Halloran, "CNPMIEC QW-1 Vanguard Low-Altitude Surface-to-Air Missile System," *Jane's Land-Based Air Defence,* November 11, 2003 (available online at http://online.janes.com/; accessed November 25, 2003); James C. O'Halloran, "Liuzhou Changhong Machinery Manufacturing's QW-2—Low-Altitude Surface-to-Air Missile System," *Jane's Land-Based Air Defence,* November 11, 2003 (available online at http://online.janes.com/; accessed November 25, 2003); Robert Karniol, "Air Defence Systems Unveiled," *Jane's Defence Weekly,* November 17, 2004.

[73] James C. O'Halloran, "NORINCO PL-9C Low-Altitude Surface-to-Air Missile System," *Jane's Land-Based Air Defence,* January 27, 2003 (available online at http://online.janes.com/; accessed November 25, 2003); Robert Hewson, "PL-9," *Jane's Air-Launched Weapons,* Vol. 42, July 23, 2003 (available online at http://online.janes.com/; accessed November 25, 2003); Zhong Aihua, "New Weapons Compete for Attention at International Defense Electronics Exhibition," *Xinhua,* April 1, 2002, in *FBIS* as "Defense Electronics Exhibition Presents New PRC Air Defense Equipment," April 3, 2002.

[74] Richard Fisher, "Report on the 5th Airshow China," 2004.

[75] James C. O'Halloran, "FT-2000 Missile System," *Jane's Land-Based Air Defence,* February 20, 2003 (available online at http://online.janes.com/; accessed November 25, 2003); James C. O'Halloran, "CNPMIEC FT-2000 Surface-to-Air Anti-Radiation Missile System," *Jane's Land-Based Air Defence,* January 27, 2003 (available online at http://online.janes. com/; accessed November 25, 2003; Duncan Lennox, "HQ-12, FT-2000," *Jane's Strategic Weapon Systems,* Vol. 39, January 6, 2003 (available online at http://online.janes.com/; accessed November 25, 2003).

The characteristics of China's current and developmental SAM systems are shown in Table 2.5.

China's missile industry has clearly demonstrated the capability to design and produce short-range SAM systems, whether command-guided (such as the HQ-7/7A), SAR-guided (such as the LY-60), or IR/laser-guided (such as the HN-5, FN-6, QW-1/2/3, TY-90, and PL-9). These systems entered service 15 to 20 years after their counterparts abroad, however, and China's missile industry has not demonstrated a capability to produce modern, long-range SAR-guided SAM systems comparable to the U.S. MIM 104 Patriot or Russian S-300 (SA-10/20)[76]—a major weakness and limitation of the indus try. However, if the HQ-9, which reportedly possesses better capabilities than the Russian S-300 PMU, enters service in the next few years, this shortcoming will be rectified.[77]

Air-to-Air Missiles

As with China's other types of missile systems, its first AAM was a license-produced version of a Soviet system, the RS-2 (AA-1) radar beam–riding AAM. This missile, designated *Pi Li-1* (PL-1, 霹雳 "Thunderbolt"), entered service in 1964. The Soviet R-3 (AA-2) IR-guided AAM, a copy of the U.S. AIM-9B Sidewinder, was also licensed to China; it entered service as the PL-2 in 1967. AAMRI and

---

[76] For example, the Russian Strela-2M entered series production in 1970, as opposed to 1985 for the comparable HN-5, and the French Crotale entered service in 1971, as opposed to 1991 for the comparable HQ-7. James C. O'Halloran, "Kolomna KBM Strela-2/Strela-2M—Low-Altitude Surface-to-Air Missile System," *Jane's Land-Based Air Defence,* September 4, 2003 (available online at http://online.janes.com; accessed December 1, 2003); James C. O'Halloran, "Thales Defence Systems Crotale Low-Altitude Surface-to-Air Missile System," *Jane's Land-Based Air Defence,* January 27, 2003 (available online at http://online.janes.com; accessed January 2, 2004).

[77]Duncan Lennox, "SA-10/20 'Grumble' (S-300, S-300 PMU, Buk/Favorit/5V55/48N6)," *Jane's Strategic Weapon Systems,* February 21, 2003 (available online at http://online.janes.com; accessed December 1, 2003).

Table 2.5
Current and Developmental SAM Systems

Designator	Entered Service	Guidance	Maximum Range (km)	Maximum Altitude (m)
DK-9C	1991	IR	10	4,500
FT-2000	Not yet in service	Anti-radiation	100	20,000
FT-2000A	Not yet in service	Anti-radiation	60	18,000
FN-6	Unknown	IR	5	3,000
HN-5	1985	IR	4.2	2,300
HQ-2	1967	Command	35	27,000
HQ-61	1991	SAR	12	10,000
HQ-7 (FM-80)	1991	Command	12	5,000
HQ-7A (FM-90)	1998	Command	15	6,000
HQ-9	Not yet in service	SAR	150	27,000
KS-1	Unknown	Command	50	25,000
LY-60	1995	SAR	18	12,000
QW-1	~1994	IR	5	4,000
QW-2	~2002	IR	6	3,500
QW-3	Unknown	IR/Laser	6	4,000

SOURCES: *Jane's Strategic Weapon Systems,* Vol. 39, 2003; *Jane's Land-Based Air Defence,* 2003; Richard Fisher, "Report on the 5th Airshow China," 2004; Robert Karniol, "Air Defence Systems Unveiled," *Jane's Defence Weekly,* 2004.
NOTE: Data are based on unclassified sources and may contain inaccuracies.

Zhuzhou Aeroengine Factory (now South Aeroengine) subsequently developed an improved version of the PL-2, designated PL-3, which entered service in 1980.[78]

China's first AAM with significant domestic technology content was the PL-5, developed by AAMRI, which appears to also have incorporated elements from the U.S. AIM-9G. The PL-5 was certified for military service in 1986 and has a greater off-boresight capability than the PL-2, although initial versions were still limited to tail-aspect engagements. Improved models have subsequently been developed, and the PL-5 remains in service with China's military.[79]

[78] Duncan Lennox, "PL-1," 2001; Robert Hewson, "PL-2/PL-3," *Jane's Air-Launched Weapons,* Vol. 40, May 30, 2002 (available online at http://online.janes.com/; accessed November 25, 2003).

[79] Robert Hewson, "PL-5," 2003.

Unidentified AVIC I/AVIC II subsidiaries (most likely led by AAMRI) have also developed and produced more-advanced IR-guided AAMs. These AAMs include a version of Israel's Rafael Python 3, which entered service in China in 1997 with the designator PL-8. Another AAM, the PL-9, is a new missile design that appears to be based on the French Matra "Magic" airframe but likely incorporates technologies acquired or developed during the development of the PL-8/Python 3 and other programs. AAMRI has also developed a small IR-guided AAM, the TY-90, for use on helicopters.[80]

China's first radar-homing AAM, the PL-11, apparently did not enter service until at least 2000. As with the LY-60, the PL-11 is apparently based on Alenia's SAR-homing Aspide AAM (which, in turn, is based on the U.S. AIM-7E Sparrow), but it entered service several years after the LY-60.[81] In addition, with assistance from Russia's Vympel and Agat research institutes, AVIC I/AVIC II subsidiaries (most likely led by AAMRI) are developing a more advanced active-radar missile known as the SD-10/PL-12. Four successful test firings of this missile were reportedly carried out in 2004, and it is expected to enter service by 2006–2007. The PL-12 is expected to be roughly comparable in capability to the Russian R-77 (AA-12) and U.S. AIM-120 AMRAAM.[82]

The characteristics of China's current and developmental AAMs are shown in Table 2.6.

---

[80] Robert Hewson, "PL-7," *Jane's Air-Launched Weapons,* Vol. 42, April 30, 2003 (available online at http://online.janes.com/; accessed November 25, 2003); Robert Hewson, "PL-8," *Jane's Air-Launched Weapons,* Vol. 42, April 30, 2003 (available online at http://online.janes.com/; accessed November 25, 2003); Robert Hewson, "PL-9," 2003; Douglas Barrie, "Chinese Fireworks," 2004; Chen Song, *Bingqi zhishi,* November 2003; Robert Hewson, "TY-90," *Jane's Air-Launched Weapons,* Vol. 41, January 17, 2003 (available online at http://online.janes.com/; accessed November 25, 2003).

[81] Robert Hewson, "PL-11 (PL-10) and FD-60, AMR-1," 2004.

[82] Robert Hewson, "SD-10 (PL-12)," *Jane's Air-Launched Weapons,* Vol. 42, July 16, 2003 (available online at http://online.janes.com/; accessed November 25, 2003); Robert Hewson, "China's New Air-to-Air Missile Operational This Year," *Jane's Defence Weekly,* January 7, 2004; Douglas Barrie, "Chinese Fireworks," 2004.

Table 2.6
Current and Developmental AAMs

Designator	Entered Service	Guidance	Range (km)
PL-5E	Late 1990s	IR	14
PL-8	By 1997	IR	15
PL-9	Unknown	IR	15–22
PL-11	2000	SAR	25
SD-10/PL-12	2006–2007	Active Radar	~70
TY-90	Unknown	IR	6

SOURCES: *Jane's Air-Launched Weapons,* Vols. 37, 38, 40, 41, 42, 43, 2001–2003.
NOTE: Data is based on unclassified sources and may contain inaccuracies.

The overall capability of China's missile sector to develop and produce short-range, IR-guided AAMs is respectable, largely due to technology transfers from France and Israel. The PL-8 entered service only 15 or so years after the comparable U.S. AIM-9M. The PL-9, which will enter service soon, if it has not already, is expected to be superior to the Python 3 and the U.S. AIM-9M. Nonetheless, the PL-8 and PL-9 are not comparable in capability to super-agile IR-guided missiles such as the Russian R-73 (AA-11), which entered service in 1987, the Israeli Python 4, which entered service around 1993, or the U.S. AIM-9X, which is now entering service.

The major weakness of China's missile sector has been in the area of advanced beyond-visual-range AAMs with fire-and-forget capabilities. The PL-11 SAR-guided AAM did not enter service until 2000, and the SD-10/PL-12 has yet to enter service. The SAR version of the U.S. AIM-7 Sparrow, by contrast, entered service in 1958, and the active-radar-guided AIM-120 Advanced Medium-Range, Air-to-Air Missile (AMRAAM) entered service in 1991.[83] If the SD-10/PL-12 enters service in 2006–2007, it will represent a qualitative leap in China's AAM capability, although this leap will have occurred over 15 years after the U.S. equivelent entered service.

[83] Timothy M. Laur and Stephen L. Llanso, *Encyclopedia of Modern U.S. Military Weapons,* 1995, pp. 238, 239.

Ground-Attack Missiles

Chinese companies produce only a few types of precision ground-attack missiles (other than ballistic missiles). One type is anti-tank guided missiles (ATGMs). In the 1970s, "ordnance industry" companies (i.e., those involved in producing such ground systems as tanks and artillery) developed a version of the Soviet AT-3 "Sagger" wire-guided ATGM, designated *Hong Jian-73* (HJ-73, 红箭 "Red Arrow").

An improved version, designated HJ-8, entered service in the military in 1988. The HJ-8 was originally designed as a man-portable system, but vehicle-mounted and helicopter-launched versions have also been produced. A recent model (HJ-8F, revealed in 2002) is designed for use against both buildings and armored vehicles. A longer-range derivative of the HJ-8, the HJ-9, has also reportedly been developed and deployed on Chinese army vehicles. The latest version of the HJ-9 (the HJ-9A) uses a millimeter-wave command link, and the pedestal-mounted tracking system has infrared capability for use during poor weather or at night.[84]

China is also developing two types of land-attack cruise missile (LACM). One, the YJ-63, is based on the YJ-6 (C-601) air-launched ASCM developed in the 1970s. The YJ-63 appears to be designed for launch from an H-6 bomber and can carry a 500-kg warhead to a range of 400 to 500 km. The missile is believed to use inertial and global positioning system (GPS) mid-course guidance and some form of electro-optical system, possibly a TV seeker, for terminal guidance, providing a CEP of 10 to 15 m. The second type of LACM is apparently designated the *Dong Hai-10* (DH-10, 东海 "East Sea") and is said to be a more advanced, "second-generation" LACM. It has a range of more than 1,500 km and is considered likely to use inertial navigation and GPS, supplemented with a terrain-contour-mapping

---

[84] Robert Hewson, "HJ-8 (HONGJIAN 8)," 2002; Christopher F. Foss, "China Markets Upgraded Anti-Tank Weapon, *Jane's Defence Weekly,* July 23, 2003; *Bingqi zhishi,* March 2004, in *FBIS* as "PRC Anti-Tank Missile HJ-9A Features Advanced Guidance System"; Christopher F. Foss, "China Markets Improved Red Arrow 9 Missile," *Jane's Defence Weekly*, November 10, 2004.

system, for mid-course guidance, and a digital scene-matching terminal-homing system with a CEP of 10 m.[85]

China is also developing shorter-range air-to-surface missiles (ASMs). One is reportedly a version of the Russian Kh-31P (AS-17) anti-radiation missile, with the Chinese designator YJ-91. This missile reaches a speed as high as Mach 3.0 and could be launched from aircraft such as the Su-30 or JH-7.[86] In addition, the C-701, although designed as an ASCM, has a TV seeker and therefore could be used in a ground-attack role comparable to the U.S. Maverick. Chinese sources recognize this possibility, although, as of 2000, the missile was being tested only in an anti-ship mode.[87]

Ground-attack missiles are clearly a current weakness of China's missile sector. The only known anti-tank missile is the wire-guided HJ-8/HJ-9. China does not produce missiles comparable to the U.S. IR-guided Javelin, laser-guided AGM-114 Hellfire, and TV- or IR-guided Maverick. China's first-generation LACM is a relatively short-range TV-guided system based on the vulnerable 1950s-era Soviet P-15 "Styx" airframe. The YJ-91 will provide a formidable anti-radiation capability, however, and more-advanced LACMs (and other precision-guided munitions, such as laser-guided bombs) are believed to be in development. [88]

---

[85] Robert Hewson, "YJ-6/C-601 (CAS-1 'Kraken')," *Jane's Air-Launched Weapons,* Vol. 40, July 9, 2002 (online at http://online.janes.com/; accessed November 25, 2003); "China Tests New Land-Attack Cruise Missile," *Jane's Missiles and Rockets,* October 1, 2004; Douglas Barrie, "Chinese Fireworks," 2004.

[86] Robert Hewson, "YJ-91, KR-1 (Kh-31P)," *Jane's Air-Launched Weapons,* Vol. 43, September 19, 2003 (available online at http://online.janes.com/; accessed November 25, 2003); Robert Hewson, "AS-17 'Krypton' (Kh-31A, Kh-31P), YJ-91/KR-1," *Jane's Air-Launched Weapons,* Vol. 43, September 19, 2003 (online at http://online.janes.com/; accessed November 25, 2003); Douglas Barrie, "Chinese Fireworks," 2004.

[87] Xu Tong, "China's C701 Small-Scale Multifunctional Missile," 2000.

[88] U.S. Department of Defense, *Annual Report on the Military Power of the People's Republic of China,* 2004; Robert Hewson, "500 kg Laser-Guided Bomb (LGB)," *Jane's Air-Launched Weapon Systems,* Vol. 43, October 7, 2003 (online at http://online.janes.com/; accessed November 25, 2003).

Summary

China's missile R&D and production capabilities are improving but are mixed, at best. The record of China's missile industry over the past several decades is more one of adequacy and limited success than one of excellence. While the industry has produced an impressive array of missiles in all categories, the capabilities of these systems are limited (e.g., many are short-range systems) and lag well behind those of the most advanced militaries. Notable gaps exist in the capabilities of current SAMs, AAMs, and ground-attack missiles. In the 1990s, the Chinese military looked to Russia to fill many of these gaps, especially with the provision of technical assistance.

Gradual improvements are occurring, however, and the fruits of the missile sector's efforts are accumulating. China has made important advances in boosting the range and accuracy of its SRBMs, and is in the process of deploying its first road-mobile ICBM. China may also soon deploy a modern, long-range SAM, an advanced BVR AAM with fire-and-forget capabilities, and land-attack cruise missiles. These trends suggest that some of the missile industry's past limitations are finally being surmounted in order to meet the needs of the PLA.

Improving the Performance of China's Missile Sector[89]

The preceding analysis of China's missile industry shows that, while missile development and production has historically been one of the better-performing sectors in China's defense industry, it nonetheless suffers from numerous shortcomings. In the late 1990s, missile industry leaders admitted the need to improve the quality and reliability of products and acknowledged that the missile industry was not internationally competitive. They further recognized their low output rates,

---

[89] The descriptions in this section of the assessments of the problems of the missile industry and strategies for improving its performance refer primarily to the CASC/CASIC complex. References to "the leadership of China's missile industry" should be understood as references to the leadership of CASC and CASIC, not to leaders of enterprises outside of the CASC/CASIC complex who are also involved in producing missiles. For information on strategies affecting the performance of missile producers in the AVIC I/AVIC II complex, see Chapter Four, "China's Military-Aviation Industry."

the general financial difficulties of companies, delays in development and production, the inability to innovate, and inefficiencies in turning research results into products.[90]

This section examines the recent efforts by missile industry leaders to solve these problems and improve the industry's future prospects.

Perceived Problems and Shortcomings

Chinese sources identify a variety of reasons for the unsatisfactory performance of the missile industry. The bureaucratic organization of the industry has not easily adapted to the challenges posed by today's fast-changing foreign and domestic markets. The geographic dispersion, redundancy, and lack of economies of scale in the missile industry are major sources of problems as well. Some personnel in the missile industry have, at least until early in this decade, endured poor living conditions and low pay, with resulting low morale and high attrition rates. The enterprises are also burdened with redundant and unproductive workers, whom they are unable to lay off because of concerns about social stability. In addition, these enterprises have traditionally been required to operate schools, hospitals, and other

---

[90] Li Xiuwei, "Applying Technology to National Defense," 1999; Yang Jian, "Li Peng Sends Letter to the China Aerospace Science and Industry Corporation on Its Important Progress," 2000; Zhang Zhiqian and Wang Shibin, "Creating the World's Top-Class Aerospace Corporation—Interview with Wang Liheng, President of China Aerospace Science and Technology Group," *Jiefangjun bao,* May 1, 2000, p. 3, in *FBIS,* May 1, 2000; Wang Li, *Xinhua,* 2000; Zhang Yi and Zhang Yusheng, "Speed Up Marketing of High-Tech Aerospace Products—Interview with General Manager Xia Guohong of China Aerospace Machinery and Electric Equipment Group," *Xinhua,* November 11, 2000, in *FBIS,* November 11, 2000; Sun Hongjin and Sun Zifa, "Research and Manufacturing System of China's Space Technology Has Realized a Major Change," *Zhongguo xinwen she,* December 28, 2001, in *FBIS,* December 28, 2001; Jian Yun, " 'Hongqi' Dares to Compare Itself with 'Sidewinder'—Interview with Zhong Shan, Academician at Chinese Academy of Engineering and Chief Designer of Hongqi Low-Altitude Missile Series," *Qingnian cankao,* February 20, 2002, in *FBIS,* February 20, 2002; Zhang Yi and Zhang Xiaosong, "Wu Bangguo Calls on China Aerospace Science and Technology Corporation to Make New Contributions to China's Aerospace Undertaking," *Xinhua,* August 13, 2002, in *FBIS* as "Wu Bangguo Sends Letter to China Aerospace Science, Technology Corp. on Occasion of Its 2nd Work Meeting," August 13, 2002; Zhang Yi, "Li Peng Sends Letter to Congratulate the China Aerospace Science and Industry Corporation on Its Important Progress in Developing New and High Technology, Weapons and Equipment," 2003.

money-losing (for the enterprises) services, although this burden has been diminishing since 1999.[91]

In an unusually candid January 2000 article about CASIC's first working conference (after its establishment in July 1999), *Zhongguo hangtian bao* acknowledged that CASIC's poor performance was also due to numerous "policy problems" in its enterprises. This report indicates that missile-industry leaders clearly recognize their challenges. The "economical operation and management" of the enterprises was said to be backward. It was noted that enterprises were expected to provide and receive resources without compensation; the personnel system was said to be in need of a complete overhaul; an overall lack of accountability and responsibility was referred to; a lack of incentives for learning and innovation was recognized; the internal auditing system was said to be in need of improvement; a lack of regulations, standards, or procedures for production and business activities was noted; and insufficient emphasis on team building and training was (tacitly) acknowledged. In particular: resources were apparently still allocated by administrative fiat; enterprises under CASIC did not have policies for attracting talent, retaining personnel, promoting excellence, or rewarding performance; managers were never brought in from outside of CASIC; and managers were not held responsible for the performance of their organizations. Criticism was specifically directed at the leadership of enterprises, with "some leaders" said to lack an understanding of the market economy. Business management was said to be unimaginative, passive,

---

[91] Yan Yan, "Paradigm for Small Satellite Development," *Keji ribao,* June 17, 1999, p. 5, in *FBIS* as "Paradigm for Small Satellite Development," June 17, 1999; Yang Jian, "Li Peng Sends Letter to the China Aerospace Science and Industry Corporation on Its Important Progress," 2000; Sun Zifa, "China Forms Aerospace Instrument Company," 2001. At one point, the "general designing department" at CALT reportedly had an annual turnover rate of 50 percent among its university graduates. "Living Condition and Wage of China's Aerospace Scientists Are Much Improved and Sci-Tech Talents Are Returning to Their Original Units," *Zhongguo xinwen wang,* December 2, 2002, in *FBIS,* December 2, 2002.

unresourceful, unmotivated, and afraid to innovate. A poor work ethic and corruption among the enterprise leadership were also implied.[92]

Strategies for Addressing Weaknesses

As the *Zhongguo hangtian bao* article cited above indicates, the leaders of China's missile industry are certainly aware not only that industry performance has not been satisfactory but also of the causes of this unsatisfactory performance. They are aware of the need to increase the rate of technological progress, to accelerate the process of turning research results into weapons, and to develop a new generation of significantly more capable weapons.[93] Their stated goal is to transform China's missile sector into a highly efficient, "lean and mean" industry that is internationally competitive and possesses state-of-the-art technology by the 2018–2023 time frame.[94]

As is common in China, however, much of the discussion on how to achieve these goals is vague and abstract. Frequent reference is made to intentions to "deepen the reforms," "adopt market principles," "implement the modern enterprise system" (never defined), "emancipate minds," "raise consciousness," "change mentality," and "improve thought politics." All of these ideas suggest that, while the

---

[92] Yang Jian, "Li Peng Sends Letter to the China Aerospace Science and Industry Corporation on Its Important Progress," 2000, pp. 1–2. Note that CASIC was at the time called China Aerospace Mechanical and Electrical Company (CAMEC).

[93] Li Xiuwei, "Applying Technology to National Defense," 1999, p. 1; Zhang Zhiqian and Wang Shibin, "Creating the World's Top-Class Aerospace Corporation—Interview with Wang Liheng, President of China Aerospace Science and Technology Group," 2000; Wang Li, "Applying Technology to National Defense," 2000; Zhang Yi and Zhang Yusheng, "Speed Up Marketing of High-Tech Aerospace Products—Interview with General Manager Xia Guohong of China Aerospace Machinery and Electric Equipment Group," 2000.

[94] Yang Jian, "Li Peng Sends Letter to the China Aerospace Science and Industry Corporation on Its Important Progress," 2000; Zhang Yi, "Li Peng Sends Letter to Congratulate the China Aerospace Science and Industry Corporation on Its Important Progress in Developing New and High Technology, Weapons and Equipment," 2003. (In January 2000, the goal was to be internationally competitive within 10 years; by January 2003, this target had been revised to 15–20 years.)

need for reforms is acknowledged, the leaders have had difficulty coming to agreement on many of the specifics.[95]

Nonetheless, there is clearly agreement on certain core principles. One is to separate the management and production of military products from those of civilian products.[96] Whereas representatives of other defense sectors in China express the belief that participating in commercial markets will improve the technology and production efficiency of military goods, leaders of China's missile sector have reached the opposite conclusion. The precise reasons for this decision are unclear, but they are probably related to a second goal, which is to turn service providers and producers of civilian goods into autonomous companies responsible for their own finances and management.[97] The leaders of China's missile industry appear to be unwilling to provide the same independence for producers of military systems, possibly out of fear that such independence will undercut their incentives for military work.

Although enterprises under CASC and CASIC that are designated as "military producers" are not allowed to produce non-aerospace goods for commercial markets goods (e.g., buses, motorcycles), those enterprises that are "mainly civilian" are increasingly being allowed to produce for the military. This situation suggests a desire to

---

[95] For example, see Yang Jian, "Li Peng Sends Letter to the China Aerospace Science and Industry Corporation on Its Important Progress," 2000, pp. 1–2; Xia Guohong, You Zheng, Meng Bo, and Xin Peihua, *Zhongguo hangtian,* 2002, pp. 11–13.

[96] CASIC website (www.casic.com.cn/docc/qiye/content.asp?id=59; accessed December 29, 2003); Zhu Zhaowu, "Pushing Forward Reform of Administrative Logistics, Promoting Development of Aerospace Industry," 1999; Yang Jian, "Li Peng Sends Letter to the China Aerospace Science and Industry Corporation on Its Important Progress," 2000; "CASC's Solid Rocket Motor Research Institute Celebrates 40 Years," *Shaanxi ribao,* July 1, 2002, in *FBIS,* July 1, 2002.

[97] Zhu Zhaowu, "Pushing Forward Reform of Administrative Logistics, Promoting Development of Aerospace Industry," 1999; Zhou Jiahe and Zhu Shide, "Jiangnan Aerospace Group Revived Through Great Efforts," 2000; Xia Guohong, You Zheng, Meng Bo, and Xin Peihua, *Zhongguo hangtian,* 2002, pp. 11–13. It could also stem from a belief that, if producers of military systems are allowed to participate in commercial markets, they will focus their energies and resources on potentially far more lucrative civilian production and marketing, to the detriment of their responsibilities for production of military equipment. The experience of China's other defense industries would certainly provide little evidence to contradict such a belief.

allow some of the dynamism of China's commercial sector to infuse the aerospace industry.[98] Moreover, there is clearly a desire to increase the volume of CASC and CASIC civilian production and services,[99] a desire that may be based on the assumption that civilian business activities will be profitable for the large holding corporations[100] or that may reflect a belief that technology and management experience acquired through civilian activities will improve military production as well.

Another element of the missile industry leaders' strategy for improving its performance is to strengthen certain channels of control and responsibility. China's missile industry is highly decentralized. CASC and CASIC have a total of about 300 enterprises under them, and the major academies and bases each contain a dozen or so subordinate enterprises. Traditionally, the academies and bases have been merely administrative units, with little ability to exercise detailed control. Actual design, assembly, testing, and experimentation of missiles have been controlled by the individual enterprises.

Now, some academies and bases are making efforts to increase control over their subordinate enterprises so that design, assembly, testing, and experimentation activities can become more closely integrated.[101] Exactly how this integration will be accomplished is unclear, but, as in other defense industries, one mechanism paradoxically appears to be "corporatization." *Corporatization* involves converting

---

[98] Yang Jian, "Li Peng Sends Letter to the China Aerospace Science and Industry Corporation on Its Important Progress," 2000.

[99] Compared to China's other defense conglomerates, civilian sales represent a relatively small proportion of CASIC's revenues. See Yang Jian, "Li Peng Sends Letter to the China Aerospace Science and Industry Corporation on Its Important Progress," 2000.

[100] The leaders of CASC and CASIC and their subordinate academies, bases, and corporations are held responsible for the overall financial success of their organizations, not just for military production.

[101] Yang Jian, "Li Peng Sends Letter to the China Aerospace Science and Industry Corporation on Its Important Progress," 2000; Sun Hongjin and Sun Zifa, "Research and Manufacturing System of China's Space Technology Has Realized a Major Change," 2001; Sun Zhifan, *Zhongguo xinwen she,* 2002. For reasons that are unclear, this is referred to as a "dumbbell-type" system of organization. As noted above, design and production are more closely integrated in CASC and CASIC than in AVIC I/AVIC II, but, at least through 2000, this degree of integration was still considered inadequate.

the institutes and factories into independent companies and emphasizing the parent-subsidiary relationship between them and the academies/bases, as opposed to the institutes and factories behaving essentially as subdepartments of a ministry. As such, the academies and bases may have the power to appoint the directors and senior managers of their subordinate enterprises and to hold them accountable for the performance of their enterprises.[102]

This corporatization of academies' and bases' subsidiaries may also enable the leaders of China's missile industry to achieve another goal: focusing efforts on a smaller number of projects.[103] In the past, the system tended not to reward or punish enterprises according to their performance, resulting in a distribution of resources across too many disparate efforts. Corporatization, by replacing a bureaucratic relationship between the academies/bases and their subordinate enterprises with a contractual relationship, will in theory allow resources to be concentrated on a smaller number of high-priority efforts. In practice, however, there will undoubtedly continue to be pressures to ensure the continuing viability of all enterprises, even if doing so means channeling funding to enterprises that are not significantly contributing to those high-priority efforts.

Related to the effort to increase control over enterprises has been a limited degree of consolidation along the lines of functional expertise. The aim of such consolidation is to eliminate redundancy in the missile sector. This principle was reflected in the creation in 2001 of the Aerospace Time Instrument Company, which gathered CASC enterprises involved in the research, development, and production of inertial navigation systems that were scattered across the country (including the Beijing Institute of Aerospace Control Devices, the Beijing Xinghua Machinery Company, the Shaanxi Cangsong

---

[102] Yang Jian, "Li Peng Sends Letter to the China Aerospace Science and Industry Corporation on Its Important Progress," 2000; Sun Hongjin and Sun Zifa, "Research and Manufacturing System of China's Space Technology Has Realized a Major Change," 2001.

[103] Zhang Zhiqian and Wang Shibin, "Creating the World's Top-Class Aerospace Corporation—Interview with Wang Liheng, President of China Aerospace Science and Technology Group," *Jiefangjun bao*, May 1, 2000, in *FBIS*, May 1, 2000; Wang Li, "Applying Technology to National Defense," 2000.

Machinery Factory, the Shaanxi Dengta Motor Factory, and the fiber-optic gyroscope division of Shanghai Xinyue Instrument Factory), and grouped them under a single entity, with the goal of reducing repetition, increasing coordination, and encouraging economies of scale.[104] This consolidation appears to be related to a broader effort to limit duplicate facilities and reduce the geographic dispersion of the missile industry.[105]

CASIC has also decided to partially privatize some firms by selling ownership shares on Chinese capital markets. The goal of this effort is to raise funds that these enterprises could use for business development, thus lessening their reliance on the parent organizations. Steps in this direction have been tentative. CASIC's plan in 2000 was to list six companies (out of a total of nearly 200 subordinate enterprises) on Chinese capital markets by 2005. The companies that issue stock, moreover, will not be enterprises that are designated producers of military goods; rather, they will be enterprises involved primarily in civilian production.

The missile industry hopes to develop new sources of financing and technology by further integrating with the rest of China's economy, as well as with the outside world. Companies are urged to engage in technical cooperation and exchanges with foreign companies, particularly Russian and European companies (but also companies from the United States, to the extent possible, given U.S. technology export controls). They are similarly encouraged to engage with domestic partners outside of the CASC/CASIC system. They are also called on to export their products and services, and to attract foreign investment.[106]

---

[104] Sun Zifa, "China Forms Aerospace Instrument Company," 2001; *Aerospace Times Instrument Corporation,* company brochure, 2002.

[105] Yang Jian, "Li Peng Sends Letter to the China Aerospace Science and Industry Corporation on Its Important Progress," 2000.

[106] Yang Jian, "Li Peng Sends Letter to the China Aerospace Science and Industry Corporation on Its Important Progress," 2000; Zhang Yi and Zhang Yusheng, "Speed Up Marketing of High-Tech Aerospace Products—Interview with General Manager Xia Guohong of China Aerospace Machinery and Electric Equipment Group," 2000; Ma Dongpo, "China's Twinstar Positioning System and Its Uses," *Xiandai bingqi,* January 1, 2002, pp. 4–5, in *FBIS,* January 1, 2002; Zhang Qingwei, "China Explores Path for

Missile-industry leaders have suggested a variety of measures to address problems with the quality of personnel and to reverse the outflow of human capital. These measures include improving the pay and working conditions of employees, particularly those involved in production of military systems; rewarding performance; emphasizing team-building and training; and hiring managers from outside the system. At the same time, missile-industry leaders are seeking ways to provide reemployment and otherwise protect the livelihood of laid-off workers so that they can eliminate redundant and unproductive employees.[107]

Other measures to improve the performance of China's missile industry include the following: requiring enterprises to pay for the goods and services they are provided; divesting the enterprises of their "social burdens" (schools, hospitals, etc.); implementing a "position responsibility system" and "project responsibility system" (i.e., making managers and project leaders responsible for the financial performance of their organizations); creating a science and technology (S&T) innovation fund and generally increasing technology investment; strengthening financial controls; establishing regulations, standards, and procedures; emphasizing the development of dual-use products, such as information systems; implementing computer-integrated manufacturing systems (CIMS); and otherwise making use of information technology.[108]

Effectiveness of Policy Solutions

In China, there is usually a significant gap between proclaimed policy and actual practice. It is difficult to assess the precise extent to which

Diversified Space Development," *Liaowang*, June 2, 2003, pp. 13–15, in *FBIS*, June 2, 2003.

[107] Yang Jian, "Li Peng Sends Letter to the China Aerospace Science and Industry Corporation on Its Important Progress," 2000; "Living Condition and Wage of China's Aerospace Scientists Are Much Improved and Sci-Tech Talents Are Returning to Their Original Units," 2002.

[108] Yang Jian, "Li Peng Sends Letter to the China Aerospace Science and Industry Corporation on Its Important Progress," 2000; Zhou Jiahe and Zhu Shide, "Jiangnan Aerospace Group Revived Through Great Efforts," 2000.

the strategy described in the previous subsection has been implemented. By 2002, however, reports from China were already claiming success in achieving at least some of the elements of the strategy. The pay and living conditions of scientists in the missile industry were said to be much improved, with enterprises having built recreational facilities and "garden-like" living areas for their employees. (Apparently, therefore, some enterprises have not divested themselves of the "social burden" of providing housing for their workers.) The average income of staff members of CASC reportedly increased by 57 percent from 1999 to 2001. The annual income of a new college graduate at CASC was said to exceed $3,000, three times the per-capita annual income in China, and the annual income of some "mainstay" (*gugan* 骨干) scientists was said to exceed $10,000.[109] Some staff members who had left the missile industry were said to have returned to their original units, and nearly 5,000 graduates of institutes of higher education reportedly joined CASC over this period. The turnover rate at CALT's general design department, which was previously over 50 percent, fell to about 15 percent, which was said to represent "a normal flow of personnel."[110]

The financial performance of China's missile industry appears to have improved as well. CASIC reported profits of 689 million RMB in 2002, as compared with 50 million RMB in 1999 and losses of 50 million RMB in 1998. By 2002, it was claiming to be the most profitable of China's 11 major defense-industry conglomerates.[111] Profitability is, however, not necessarily a measure of efficiency in China,

---

[109] Although these incomes do not seem impressive by U.S. standards, it should be noted that, in purchasing-power parity, $10,000 in China is equivalent to about $50,000 in the United States and that items such as housing may be provided at subsidized prices.

[110] "Living Condition and Wage of China's Aerospace Scientists Are Much Improved and Sci-Tech Talents Are Returning to Their Original Units," *Zhongguo xinwen wang,* 2002.

[111] Yang Jian, "Li Peng Sends Letter to the China Aerospace Science and Industry Corporation on Its Important Progress," 2000; "CASIC Displays New Aerospace Products," *Zhongguo hangtian,* October 1, 2002, pp. 7–9, in *FBIS,* October 1, 2002; Zhang Yi, "Li Peng Sends Letter to Congratulate the China Aerospace Science and Industry Corporation on Its Important Progress in Developing New and High Technology, Weapons and Equipment," 2003.

because inputs are not always acquired nor are products always sold at market prices. In addition, capital costs are generally not correctly accounted for. Moreover, sales of military equipment have likely increased dramatically in recent years. According to official Chinese statistics, expenditures on military equipment increased by 66 percent between 2000 and 2003 alone.[112] Finally, as in past years, it is highly likely that China's missile producers still receive direct subsidies.[113]

Conclusions

China's missile sector clearly possesses numerous strengths relative to its other defense sectors. Its financial resource base has improved in recent years, government funding to key civilian and military programs in the industry will continue, missile industry entities possess strong institutional capabilities for facilitating further modernization, and a limited degree of competition exists at various levels of industry. Moreover, missile industry leaders are aware of the problems in their industry and are implementing policies to resolve them. Nonetheless, important weaknesses remain.

This mixture of strengths and weaknesses is reflected in China's currently deployed missile capabilities. China's short-range, solid-fuel, conventional ballistic missiles provide it with a unique and difficult-to-counter capability, but China's ICBM systems are not particularly impressive or modern. Similarly, China's most capable ASCM, the YJ-2, is comparable to early versions of the U.S. Harpoon, which remains the U.S. Navy's mainstay ASCM, but falls far short of the capability represented by the Russian SS-N-22. China's short-range SAM sys-

---

[112] China's National Defense in 2002, December 9, 2002, in FBIS as "Xinhua: 'Full Text' of White Paper on China's National Defense in 2002," December 9, 2002; "White Paper on National Defense Published," China Internet Information Center (online at http://www.china.org.cn/english/2004/Dec/116032.htm; accessed December 30, 2004).

[113] As late as 2002, CASIC's general manager acknowledged that, unlike CASIC's producers of civilian goods, its producers of military goods were still dependent on state "investment." See Xia Guohong, You Zheng, Meng Bo, and Xin Peihua, *Zhongguo hangtian*, August 1, 2002, pp. 11–13.

tems are also quite capable, but China lacks a modern, high-altitude SAM capability comparable to early versions of the U.S. Patriot or Russian S-300 system. China's most capable short-range IR-guided AAMs, the PL-8 and PL-9, compare well with the AIM-9M, which remains in service with the U.S. military, but are a generation behind the Russian R-73, Israeli Python 4, and U.S. AIM-9X. China still lacks a fire-and-forget AAM, a capability that the United States has possessed for 15 years. Finally, the TV-guided YJ-63 LACM provides China with a basic land-attack cruise missile capability and the YJ-91 will represent a formidable anti-radiation missile, but China's missile industry has otherwise failed to produce an array of precision ground-attack missiles similar to the ones the United States used in the 1991 Gulf War.

Thus, in some areas (ASCMs and short-range SAMs and AAMs), China's current missile capabilities are comparable to those of the United States but these are generally areas in which the United States is not the world leader. More importantly, there are major gaps in China's missile capabilities, such as in ICBMs, medium- and long-range SAMs and AAMs, and precision ground-attack missiles.

The critical question for the immediate future is, Will China's missile industry be able to fill in these gaps in order to meet the needs of the PLA? A number of obstacles are likely to impede the technological progress of the Chinese missile industry. Although China can take advantage of technology transfers and technical assistance from countries such as Russia and Israel, continuing to rely on such an approach would consign China's missile systems to being perpetually out of date, because there would inevitably be lags between the time a technology was developed abroad and transferred to China, and when China's missile industry acquired the capability to produce such systems.

Moreover, the successful implementation of such a "follower" strategy depends on the willingness and ability of foreign suppliers to provide China with state-of-the-art missile technology. At present, Israel and France appear to be unwilling to allow China to acquire their best technology, and, although Russia appears to have fewer such qualms, whether Russia's defense industries will be able to continue to develop advanced missile technologies in the future is unclear. For China's missile industry to join those of other countries in independently developing leading-edge technologies, on the other hand, would require a dramatic increase in the amount of resources being channeled into the sector.

A final major obstacle to rapid technological progress is, as in China's other defense sectors, state ownership of the missile producers. As long as these firms remain state-owned, they are likely to lack exposure to intense, market-based incentives for innovation and efficiency. Overall, CASC and CASIC seem to be moving much more slowly than some of China's other defense enterprises in implementing public stock offerings and other means of allowing private-ownership shares in their subsidiary companies. In any case, the Chinese government appears unwilling to allow private-ownership shares in any of its principal producers of military systems. Thus, for the foreseeable future, the influence of private ownership for China's missile industry will be confined, at best, to service providers and suppliers of components.

Barring a massive increase in the amount of financial resources being channeled to the missile industry or privatization of China's missile manufacturers, it is unlikely that China will emerge as a world leader in missile technology in the near future. China's missile industry is attempting to address the gaps in its current capabilities, however, and there is no reason to believe that it will fail in these efforts. As China tackles these challenges, the missile sector will increasingly produce a wider range of systems comparable in capability to many in use today in the world's most modern militaries, although China will not be a world leader. Therefore, unless the world's leading military powers field a new generation of missile systems, China could, by the end of this decade, reach a point at which the systems produced by its defense industry are comparable to many of those in service in the world's most advanced militaries.

CHAPTER THREE

China's Shipbuilding Industry

China's shipbuilding industry (SBI) is a large, geographically dispersed, and increasingly modern sector that sits at the nexus of China's burgeoning civilian economy and its defense-industrial complex. The SBI is responsible for supplying China's navy with warships, submarines, and related combatants as China strives to develop a more advanced naval force. In contrast to some of the moribund and perennially troubled parts of China's defense-industrial establishment, the SBI is unique in many ways. In the early 1980s, as China was first exploring defense conversion, the SBI's relatively rapid diversification into commercial shipbuilding, especially into international sales, and its sustained access to foreign equipment, materials, and technical expertise have allowed it to prosper and modernize in the past 25 years. China's SBI provides an illuminating example of the complex and evolving relationship between China's civilian economy and its defense-industrial complex.[1] Thus, examining China's shipbuilding is key to assessing the present and future ability of China to indigenously research, develop, and construct quality naval platforms and related equipment for China's modernizing navy.

This chapter evaluates the present and future capabilities of China's shipbuilding industry and assesses the implications of these capabilities for Chinese naval modernization. The central organizing

---

[1] One of the most useful and detailed assessments of the evolution of the shipbuilding industry can be found in Thomas G. Moore, *China in the World Market,* Cambridge, UK: Cambridge University Press, 2002.

question for this chapter is, Will China's shipbuilding industry be able to meet the needs of China's People's Liberation Army Navy (PLAN) as it strives to build a modern naval fighting force, potentially with power-projection capabilities?

This chapter maintains that the SBI's growing commercial business activities, especially its interactions with foreign shipbuilders, have allowed China's shipbuilding industry to improve the quality and efficiency of its research and development techniques, production processes, and management practices. These developments, in turn, have allowed Chinese shipyards gradually to improve their shipbuilding *capabilities* and expand their *capacity*. Numerous shipyards have modernized and expanded in the past 25 years, and further efforts are afoot in key parts of the country. These trends are also reflected in the improvements in Chinese warships commissioned in the late 1990s and in many of the new naval projects currently coming online. The newest vessels are more durable, are more capable of surviving damage, have longer ranges, are stealthier, and are capable of carrying a variety of modern weapon systems. China's serial production of a variety of new naval platforms in the past five years is notable in this regard. The current degree of simultaneous production of several new classes of naval platforms has not been seen in China for decades. To be sure, the extent to which the SBI has progressed and improved in its R&D and production of naval vessels has been due largely to the very low technological base from which the SBI started in the early 1980s.

As of 2005, China's SBI still exhibits some technological and production weaknesses: a still-limited ability to develop and/or absorb advanced production equipment and technologies; limited project-management skills; and frequently inefficient production methods. These weaknesses are manifest in SBI's inability to develop and produce highly advanced, state-of-the-art types of civilian ships and its inability to produce critical subsystems needed to outfit large commercial ships. Many such systems still need to be imported.

These weaknesses are more problematic for naval projects. Although China is designing and building increasingly sophisticated warships, Chinese naval shipbuilders still need to import key components or modules, such as propulsion systems, navigation and sensor suites, and major weapon systems, to outfit these vessels. Such a reliance on imported subsystems creates systems-integration challenges, as well as security concerns stemming from dependence on foreign suppliers. China appears to be improving its ability to absorb imported equipment and technologies, but it will take time before these and other problems are overcome. To be sure, there is a momentum in the shipbuilding sector that suggests that these problems are being addressed and will eventually be overcome as the government devotes more resources to making China the world's top shipbuilder in the next 10 to 20 years.

This chapter begins with an outline of the structure of China's shipbuilding industry, emphasizing particularly the growth, expansion, and modernization in the past decade. It then assesses the current and future capabilities of China's SBI, with specific emphasis on naval production capabilities. In making this assessment, this case study examines the structure and institutions of China's SBI and the overall capabilities of Chinese shipbuilders, including facilities, equipment, and personnel. These factors are key to evaluating the current and future ability of the SBI to improve its R&D and production capabilities and to innovate.[2]

Key Measures Used to Assess China's Shipbuilding Capabilities

In assessing the capabilities of China's shipbuilding industry, we relied in this chapter on a series of measures of the degree of modernization in China's SBI. These various measures, of both organizational and technological capabilities, are referenced throughout this study in order to assess improvements and continued weaknesses in the SBI's R&D and production capabilities.

---

[2] These factors are drawn from the methodology used in Roger Cliff, *The Military Potential of China's Commercial Technology,* Santa Monica, Calif.: RAND Corporation, MR-1292-AF, 2001.

First, this chapter examines overall SBI capabilities by looking at progress in three broad areas: (1) research and development capabilities; (2) production processes; and (3) management practices used in large shipbuilding projects.

Second, in assessing the ability of China's SBI to develop and produce quality commercial and military vessels, the chapter references the four general areas relevant to modern shipbuilding: hull design and production; vessel superstructure; propulsion; and navigation technologies. The ability of China's shipyards to improve R&D and production capabilities in these four areas will determine its level of advancement in the global shipbuilding industry.

Third, in addition to the four capabilities noted above, others aspects of shipbuilding are unique and particular to naval shipbuilding, including the ability to build and outfit naval vessels with (1) radars and sensors; (2) weapons systems such as anti-ship missiles, anti-submarine torpedoes, and air-defense assets (both short- and long-range); (3) integration of these various systems; and (4) special design attributes that are unique to naval vessels, including damage-control capabilities; seaworthiness for long trips; special habitations requirements for the crew; and enhanced durability for warfighting.

Structure and Operation of China's Shipbuilding Industry

For the past 50 years, China's SBI has been state-owned and -operated; it has been organized along the lines of a classic planned economy, with a large central ministry-like agency at the top of a hierarchy with many production enterprises (shipyards and marine-product factories) below it. The top-level ministry functions as an administrative agent, allocating production projects and funding to various shipyards and factories located throughout China. As shipyards and factories gained increasing autonomy during the reform era, this model changed; however, the hierarchical structure persists today, albeit in a looser form.

China's numerous shipyards and factories are the SBI's core production units and, thus, are the focus of this case study. Yet, their placement in the SBI's overall hierarchy and their interactions with the ministry-level units above them continue to have a strong influence on their activities; they are the political and financial contexts in which shipyards and marine-product factories operate. The interactions with and relationships between the ministry-level organs and the shipyards both constrain and enable the SBI's production activities. Given this context, in this section we outline the past and current relationship between the various entities in China's SBI as a baseline for assessing the SBI's current and future development and production capabilities.

During the pre-reform period, China's Sixth Ministry of Machine Building (MMB) was in charge of all shipbuilding enterprises. At that time, military shipbuilding orders accounted for most industrial activities. Only a few shipyards were involved in constructing small civilian vessels for coastal transport.[3] In 1982, when China began to restructure its defense industry and Deng Xiaoping pushed all of China's defense enterprises toward "defense conversion," the Sixth MMB was transformed into the China State Shipbuilding Corporation (CSSC). The CSSC, the first defense-industry entity to be "corporatized," was in charge of administering the vast majority of China's commercial and military shipbuilding activities (including marine-engine production). The Ministry of Communication (MoC) and the PLA also operated a few shipyards involved in shipbuilding and ship-repair projects.

The formation of the CSSC began China's gradual and impressive move into the global shipbuilding industry. An enormous industrial entity, the CSSC at its peak had authority over 27 large shipyards (and an unknown number of smaller shipyards that each employed 1,000 to 3,000 workers), 67 marine-equipment factories, and 37 R&D institutes involved in the research, development,

---

[3] David Muller, *China as a Maritime Power,* Boulder, Colo.: Westview Press, 1983.

production, testing, marketing, and sales of ships and a wide range of maritime products.[4]

The CSSC existed *as a single entity* until July 1999, when it was divided into two distinct entities: the China State Shipbuilding Corporation (CSSC) and the China Shipbuilding Industry Corporation (CSIC). Both successor entities are state-owned enterprises that ultimately report to the State Council.[5] Yet, the new CSSC and CSIC have also taken on the form of "group corporations" (*jituan gongsi* 集团公司), which can act similarly to holding companies: They hold shares in multiple subsidiary enterprises (i.e., shipyard groups) but are not expected to be involved in running the daily affairs of the subsidiaries. Rather, CSSC and CSIC are mainly responsible for choosing the leaders of the major shipyards and for reviewing major capital expenditures, such as shipyard expansion and relocation.

The bifurcation of the old CSSC into group corporations was part of the government's broader effort to inject a degree of competition into defense-industrial enterprises by breaking up the large, monopolistic companies that had dominated the defense sector for the past 25 years. In the late 1990s, Chinese leaders sought to change the incentive structure to make defense firms more autonomous and to create pressures to improve the quality of the output.

The division of the CSSC resulted in both a geographic and a functional division of labor in China's SBI. Both the CSSC and CSIC produce multiple types of civilian and military vessels. As a result, there is some competition between CSSC's and CSIC's entities, as well as among the mutitple enterprises under each group corporation. They compete for domestic and international customers and for access to domestic and international capital. While they may also compete for military projects, that system is more managed than

---

[4] This information was taken from a translation of a 1996 CSSC brochure. The translation was done by Office of Naval Research, U.S. Navy, Asia Office, Tokyo, Japan, March 21, 1996.

[5] Two of the most important State Council entities involved in managing large SOEs are the National Development and Reform Commission (*Guojia Fazhan yu Gaige Weiyuanhui*) and the National Large Industry Commission (*Guojia Da Qiye Weiyuanhui*).

civilian shipbuilding (i.e., there is a higher degree of government management in the allocation of military shipbuilding contracts).

Current Composition of China's Entire Shipbuilding Industry

China's entire shipbuilding industry—including newbuilding, repair, and conversion shipyards—comprises an enormous number of shipyards and related marine-production facilities capable of building the largest classes of merchant vessels to the smallest river boats. Recent studies on China's shipbuilding industry have identified over 1,200 shipyards that produce a wide range of vessel sizes and types. For the purposes of this chapter, a small number of large shipyards, major research and development (R&D) institutes, and marine-equipment production facilities are relevant.

The CSSC and CSIC currently constitute about 60 to 70 percent of China's overall shipbuilding output. Several other shipbuilding entities produce the remaining 30 to 40 percent of national output, although few of them are involved in military shipbuilding.[6] These other shipbuilding entities are scattered throughout China, both in coastal and inland areas.[7] According to Chinese statistics, in 2004 the output of China's entire shipbuilding sector was 8.5 million tons; however, non-Chinese estimates put national output closer to 4 million tons.[8] The non-CSSC and -CSIC entities in the shipbuilding sector are as follows:

- **Provincially owned shipyards, which are at least partially owned and operated by the governments of Fujian, Guangzhou, and Jiangsu**

---

[6] These activities include not only newbuilding but also ship repair and conversion.

[7] See *China's Shipyards: Capacity, Competition and Challenges,* London, UK: Drewery Shipping Consultants Ltd., July 2003.

[8] "China's Shipbuilding Capacity Remains Third in World," *Xinhua,* January 24, 2005. The non-Chinese estimates that are noted in Figure 3.1 are from Lloyds' Register, *World Shipbuilding Statistics,* London, UK, 2004. It is not clear what accounts for the wide discrepancy in figures.

—The largest provincial shipbuilding company is the Fujian Shipbuilding Industry Group Corporation (FSGIC)
- **Shipyards owned by Chinese shipping conglomerates**
  —COSCO Shipyard Group
  —China's Shipping Industry Company (CIC)
- **Joint-venture shipyards**
  —Two Nantong-Kawasaki-COSCO shipyards (Japan)
  —Shanghai Edward Shipyard (Germany)
  —Yantai Raffles shipyard (Singapore)
  —Samsung-Ningbo shipyard (Japan)[9]
- **PLA Navy factories/shipyards**
  —PLA Factories 4804, 4805, 4806, 4807, 4810
- **There are also a number of smaller shipyards that are owned and operated by municipalities in various provinces.**

One of the key trading arms of China's SBI is known as the China Shipbuilding Trading Corporation (CSTC). Some, although not all, shipyards use the CSTC to sell ships and ship components on the international market and to purchase key items from foreign suppliers. In the past three to five years, a growing number of other Chinese trading companies have been involved in brokering exports of merchant ships. In this regard, CSTC faces far more competition than in the past. CSIC stood up its own trading arm in 2003, known as the China Shipbuilding and Offshore International Co., Ltd. However, all exports of *military-related* vessels must go through the CSTC, because it is the only entity authorized by the State Council to conduct trade in military vessels.[10] Now that China has joined the WTO and Chinese shipbuilders have the right to conduct their own foreign commercial activities, the role of the CSTC will likely diminish. Particularly for large shipyards, which already possess extensive

---

[9] See Commission of the European Communities, *Second Report from the Commission to the Council on the Situation in World Shipbuilding,* Brussels, May 2000, p. 31. Available at http://europa.eu.int/comm/enterprise/maritime/shipbuilding_market/doc/com2000263_en.pdf.

[10] The official CSTC website is http://www.cstc.com.cn.

international contacts and prefer to negotiate their own export deals, CSTC's role is likely to be negligible.[11]

Drawing on this broad overview of China's entire shipbuilding industry, the following sections explore in detail the structure and capabilities of the CSSC and CSIC. This sets the empirical basis for the subsequent analysis in this chapter.

China State Shipbuilding Corporation[12] (CSSC; *Zhongguo Chuanbo Gongye Jituan Gongsi* 中国船舶工业集团公司)

The new CSSC was given authority for shipbuilding and related facilities in *eastern* and *southern* China—principally, facilities located in Shanghai and the provinces of Guangdong and Jiangxi. Most of its shipbuilding activities are centered in Shanghai. The CSSC states that it controls 58 enterprises and organizations, including shipyards, R&D institutes, factories, and various shareholding companies. The CSSC employs approximately 95,000 people and is capitalized at 6.4 billion RMB (US$771 million). According to Chinese media reports, CSSC yards in 2004 produced over 3.5 million tons of ships, although its shipbuilding capacity is expanding each year. In 2003, it was rated as China's 71st-largest company, with a business income estimated at US$3.08 billion.[13]

The CSSC's core units are five shipbuilding "bases," or divisions, which were formed as the result of consolidation activities in recent years. The five bases are

- **Jiangnan Shipbuilding Group (Shanghai)**
  —Jiangnan Shipyard
  —Qiuxin Shipyard

---

[11] To be sure, foreign shipbuyers will still likely use government-backed trading companies until shipyards have the capabilities to offer both refund guarantees and financing for major shipbuilding projects.

[12] Much of these data are drawn from CSSC publications and its official website at www.cssc.net.cn/.

[13] This figure was taken from the list of top-500 Chinese firms in 2003; see http://www.cq.xinhuanet.com/subject/2004/500qiang/.

- **Zhonghua-Hudong Shipbuilding Group (Shanghai)**
  —Hudong Shipyard
  —Zhonghua Shipyard
  —Shanghai Edward Shipyard (joint venture with Hudong and Germany's Hansa)
  —Huarun Dadong Shipyard (joint venture with Hudong and Hong Kong's China Resources)
- **Shanghai Waiqaoqiao Group (Shanghai)**
- **Shanghai Shipbuilding Group (Shanghai)**
  —Shanghai Puxi Shipyard
  —Shanghai Pudong Shipyard
  —Chengxi Ship-Repair Yard (Jiangsu Province)
- **Guangzhou Shipbuilding Group (Guangdong Province)**
  —Guangzhou International Shipyard
  —Huangpu Shipyard
  —Wenchong Shipyard.

CSSC also controls a combination of smaller yards in Shanghai, Jiangxi, Anhui, and Guangxi provinces, including Chengxi Shipyard in Jiangsu; Donghai Shipyard in Shanghai; Guijiang Shipyard in Guangxi; Jiangxin and Jiangzhou Shipyards in Jiangxi; Wuhu Shipyard in Anhui; and Xijiang Shipyard in Guangxi.[14]

Each of the CSSC's five shipyard groups noted above operates as a conglomerate engaged in building ships and in conducting numerous other marine- and nonmarine-related industrial construction services (e.g., bridge building). Most of the groups control subsidiary companies with one or two shipyards (each with multiple berths, slipways, and docks), ship repair/conversion facilities, metalworking facilities, companies that produce marine engines and work on non-marine projects, and entities that invest in real estate and capital-

---

[14] "China's Shipbuilding Giant Consolidates Bases," *Xinhua,* November 26, 2002. In addition to these five core shipbuilding bases, the CSSC also has authority over numerous other smaller yards in southern and eastern China. A full listing of CSSC-controlled yards can be found at www.cssc.net.cn.

intensive construction projects. The smaller yards mainly focus on building ships and producing marine products.

The CSSC also controls the Marine Design & Research Institute of China (MARIC), China's oldest and largest shipbuilding R&D institute. Its staff of about 1,700 engineers and technicians has created over 550 designs for commercial ships, including tankers, bulk carriers, containerships, timber carriers, and liquefied petroleum gas (LPG) carriers; and it has designed large research ships, vessels to assist China's space program, supply ships, amphibious assault ships capable of landing tanks, training ships, and minesweepers. MARIC is on the cutting edge of all of China's merchant ship design. It designed China's first liquefied natural gas (LNG) carriers; a new-generation, larger LPG tanker; and large container vessels up to 6,000 TEU (twenty-foot equivalent units).

Many MARIC designs have been sold to foreign clients in Germany, Norway, Hong Kong, Greece, the United States, and other nations. According to reports from shipbuilding experts who conducted on-site interviews in China, MARIC interacts with shipyards on a contract basis to produce designs. Sometimes, MARIC works with shipowners on precontract designs. In other cases, a foreign shipowner asks MARIC to purchase a basic design package from an overseas architectural group. MARIC then creates the detailed production design for the Chinese shipyard based on the foreign owner's request. As a testament to MARIC's capabilities, its design facilities are supported by various testing facilities, including a towing tank, an ocean engineering basin, a cavitation tunnel, and a wind tunnel.[15]

In addition to MARIC, CSSC controls a second professional ship-design institute, known as the Shanghai Ship Design and Research Institute, or SDARI. It is smaller than MARIC and is viewed as the second best design institute in China. SDARI specializes in developing cargo vessels, engineering ships, harbor boats, and

---

[15] Philip C. Koenig, *Report on SNAME's Technical Delegation to China,* December 29, 2000; available at http://www.onrglobal.navy.mil/reports/2000/sname.htm. Interviews with foreign shipbuilders involved in projects with Chinese shipyards, October 2004.

offshore and military support vessels. In recent years, it has designed several classes of offshore supply and support ships.[16]

CSSC also controls a variety of factories involved in the production of marine equipment. For example, CSSC's Shanghai-based Hudong Heavy Machinery is a large diesel-engine manufacturer in China. It is part of the Hudong-Zhonghua shipbuilding group that was formed out of the merger of the main engines divisions of the Hudong and Shanghai Shipyards.

CSSC shipyards can produce a wide variety of ships from basic tankers and bulk cargo vessels. They have also constructed offshore rigs and platforms. CSSC yards have consistently produced China's most complex merchant ships, such as chemical carriers and LPG carriers. CSSC yards are currently involved in building one or two LNG carriers for an Australian client, although the project has had mixed success (i.e., it has experienced delays and cost overruns). Some CSSC yards are involved in producing naval vessels, such as destroyers, frigates, supply ships, and survey ships. Most of China's newest classes of destroyers and frigates are being built in CSSC yards. CSSC naval and commercial ships have been exported to countries all over the world, including the United States, the United Kingdom, Thailand, Norway, Greece, and Singapore.

China Shipbuilding Industry Corporation (CSIC; *Zhongguo Chuanbo Zhonggong Jituan Gongsi* 中国船舶重工集团公司)[17]

When the CSIC was formed in July 1999, it assumed responsibility for shipbuilding and related facilities in northeastern China (Tianjin, Hebei, and Liaoning Provinces), inland China (Sichuan and Shannxi Provinces), and Shandong Province. The CSIC is a far larger industrial entity than the CSSC.

The CSIC consists of 48 industrial enterprises (including ten large shipyards), 28 research and design institutes, and 15 shareholding companies, spread over 20 provinces in China. It employs

---

[16] The official website is located at www.sdari.com.cn.

[17] These data are drawn from CSIC publications, as well as from its official website at www.csic.com.cn/.

approximately 170,000 people, almost *twice* as many as the CSSC. According to Chinese data, in 2004, CSIC shipyards built 2.14 million tons of ships, a 30-percent increase from the previous year. In 2003, CSIC was ranked as China's 56th-largest company, with a business income of US$3.53 billion; in 2002, it was ranked as China's 70th-largest enterprise, with an income of US$2.24 billion.[18]

According to CSIC official information, its main business activities are

> management of all the state owned assets of the corporation and its subsidiaries; domestic and overseas investment and financing; undertaking scientific research and production of military products (mainly of warships); design, production and repair of domestic and overseas civil vessels, marine equipment and other non-ship products; various forms of economic and technological co-operation; overseas turnkey project contracting; labor export; engineering project contracting; engineering construction; building construction and installation; and other business authorized, required by the government and allowed by the law.[19]

The ten large shipyards CSIC controls in China are as follows:

- Dalian New Shipyard Heavy Industries Ltd. (Liaoning)
- Dalian Shipyard (Liaoning)
- Bohai Shipyard Heavy Industry Company Ltd. (Liaoning)
- Wuchang Shipyard (Hubei)
- Shanghaiguan Shipyard (Hebei)
- Qingdao Beihai Heavy Industries Company Ltd. (Shandong)
- Chongqing Shipyard (Chongqing)
- Chuandong Shipyard (Chongqing)
- Xingang and Xinhe Shipyards (Tianjin).[20]

---

[18] This information was taken from a list of China's top-500 largest firms; see http://www.cq.xinhuanet.com/subject/2004/500qiang/.

[19] These data were taken from the CSIC website.

[20] A full listing of all the shipyards controlled by CSIC can be found at www.csic.com.cn/.

As to the structure of the group corporation, the CSIC's backbone components are six regional shipbuilding companies (*diqu gongsi* 地区公司); the CSIC is a shareholder in each. Each of these groups comprises numerous shipyards, factories, and related engineering facilities.

- Dalian Shipbuilding Industry Group
- Xian Marine Industry Company
- Kunming Shipbuilding Industry Corporation
- Wuhan Shipbuilding Industry Company
- Chongqing Shipbuilding Industry Company
- Tianjin Shipbuilding Industry Company.[21]

In addition to these six regional companies, CSIC also controls 15 shareholding companies and 28 R&D institutes. The CSIC maintains that it is the largest producer of marine equipment in China, with close to 40 factories producing diesel and turbine engines, as well as numerous other types of marine equipment. The Dalian and Yichang marine diesel works are notable in this regard.

The CSIC also controls the China Ship Research and Development Academy, one of the premier organizations involved in commercial and military ship R&D. CSIC materials states that it is "the country's main force in research and design of military ships." As with the CSSC, some CSIC shipyards and facilities are also involved in naval construction. CSIC shipyards in Dalian, Wuhan, and Bohai (Huludao) have historically been centers for production of destroyers and submarines (both conventional and nuclear).

The CSIC's nonmilitary business is highly diversified in both marine and nonmarine activities, including shipbuilding, marine engineering, and production of diesel engines, storage batteries, large steel structure fabrications, port machinery, turbochargers, tobacco machinery, gas meters, and automation distribution systems. The CSIC describes its business scope as

---

[21] This entity appears to have largely dissolved in recent years as its yards have become independent.

management of all the state owned assets of the corporation and its subsidiaries; domestic and overseas investment and financing; undertaking scientific research and production of military products (mainly of warships); design, production and repair of domestic and overseas civil vessels, marine equipment and other non-ship products; various forms of economic and technological co-operation; overseas turnkey project contracting; labor export; engineering project contracting; engineering construction; building construction and installation; and other business authorized, required by the government and allowed by the law.[22]

Military Shipbuilding

Since its inception, China's shipbuilding industry has always been involved in constructing ships for the PLA Navy (PLAN). As noted above, the initial rationale for the SBI was to build naval vessels, and this rationale persisted until the late 1970s. During China's reform era, the SBI quickly began to leverage its extensive industrial infrastructure to shift toward civilian shipbuilding for domestic and international clients. Yet, several Chinese yards retained a core military production capability to meet the needs of the PLAN. In light of the relative slowdown in naval production in the 1980s and 1990s, a limited number of yards and factories remained involved in naval production. Yet, in recent years, as construction of naval vessels has increased, more yards have become involved in naval construction projects. Also, a limited degree of specialization by certain yards in building specific, advanced naval platforms—such as new classes of destroyers, frigates, and submarines—may be emerging—a claim that needs to be tested by future developments. Table 3.1 shows the major Chinese yards currently involved in the construction of naval vessels and naval weaponry.

---

[22] These data on CSIC are taken from its official website at www.csic.com.cn/.

Table 3.1
Major Chinese Shipyards Involved in Naval Construction

Shipyards	Affiliation	Military Product
Jiangnan-Qiuxin Shipyards (Shanghai)	CSSC	Luyang I and II destroyers
Hudong-Zhonghua Shipyards (Shanghai)	CSSC	New 054-class frigate; Jiangwei and Jianghu frigate upgrades; auxiliary vessels; new Type 072-III amphibious landing vessels
Xijiang Shipyard (Guangxi)	CSSC	Fast attack crafts
Huangpu Shipyard (Guangdong)	CSSC	New 054-class frigate; fast attack craft; replenishment vessels
Guangzhou Shipyards (Guangdong)	CSSC	Replenishment vessels
Huludao Shipyard (Liaoning)	CSIC	Nuclear submarines: 093 and 094 classes
Wuchang Shipyard (Wuhan/Hubei)	CSIC	Conventional-powered submarines: new classes and existing ones
Dalian Old Shipyard (Liaoning)	CSIC	Luhai destroyer and Luda destroyer upgrades; new Type 072-III amphibious landing vessels

Growth, Expansion, and Modernization of China's Shipbuilding Industry

The shipbuilding industry has grown enormously in the past 20 years. In the late 1970s, at the beginning of the reform period, Chinese shipyards built very few commercial ships, with estimates ranging from 30,000 to 100,000 tons built from 1978 to 1980. By 1996, China had become the third-largest shipbuilder in the world (after Japan and South Korea). The growth of China's shipbuilding industry and its penetration of the world shipbuilding market are extensive and serve as an indicator of the future direction of that industry. Indeed, much of this growth occurred despite several downturns in the global shipbuilding market in the early 1990s and again in the late 1990s, following the Asian financial crisis. In addition, among China's defense-industrial sectors, the SBI has by far the greatest interactions with the global market. Beginning in 1981, the output of China's SBI increased from 135,000 gross tons annually to 3.7 million gross tons by 2003 (Figure 3.1).

The growth of the SBI's order book is even more impressive, because it serves as an indication of the growing demand for Chinese-built vessels. From 1993 to 2004, the total order book of China's shipbuilding industry has expanded from 1.9 million tons to over 17 million gross tons (Figure 3.2), breaking China's own national goal for 2005. China's share of the world shipbuilding market has grown accordingly. China's market share expanded from 3 percent in 1993 to 13.8 percent in 2003 (Figure 3.3). Chinese shipyards have begun to break into markets for more-sophisticated ship types, as well. Some Chinese yards have begun to produce more-advanced ship types, such as LPG tankers, cruise ships, and Roll-on–Roll-off (Ro-Ro) ships.

Figure 3.1
Tonnage Delivered by Chinese Shipyards, 1981–2004

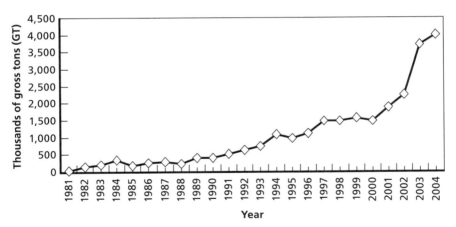

SOURCE: The information in this figure is based on data from Lloyd's Register, *World Shipbuilding Statistics*, London, UK, 2004.

NOTE: The above figure for 2004 shipyard output is an estimate based on past growth trends. As of June 2004, output was over 2 million gross tons for the year.

RAND MG334-3.1

Figure 3.2
Chinese Order-Book Development, 1993–June 2004

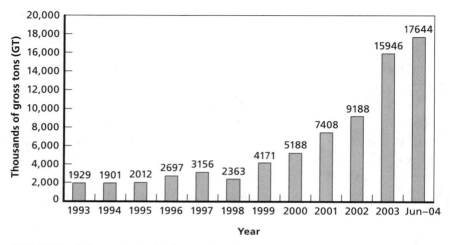

SOURCE: The information in this figure is based on data from Lloyd's Register, *World Shipbuilding Statistics*, London, UK, 2004.
RAND MG334-3.2

Chinese statistics tell a more optimistic story of the industry's expanding output. According to Chinese data, 2004 was a banner year for China's shipbuilding industry, as well as for the entire global shipbuilding market. Chinese shipyards completed an estimated 8.5 million deadweight tons (DWT) of ships, about 70 percent of which were constructed by CSSC and CSIC shipyards.[23] In 2004, the CSSC constructed 3.57 million DWT (a 64.5-percent increase from 2003), and the CSIC produced 2.13 million DWT (a 30-percent increase from 2003). For both the CSSC and CSIC, the number of new-building deals concluded in 2004 increased by over 200 percent.[24]

[23] Non-state-owned Chinese shipyards account for the some 30 to 40 percent of annual production, depending on the year.

[24] Non-Chinese estimates put output at about 4 million tons for 2004. See "China's Largest Shipbuilding Company Receives 6 Million Tons of New Orders in 2004," *Xinhua*, January 24, 2005.

Figure 3.3
China's Market Share of World Order Book, 1993–2003

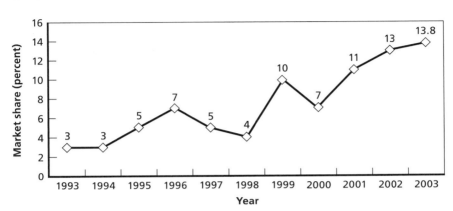

SOURCE: The information in this figure is based on data from Lloyd's Register, *World Shipbuilding Statistics*, London, UK, 2004; Commission of the European Communities, *Second Report from the Commission to the Council on the Situation in World Shipbuilding*, Brussels, May 2000.
RAND MG334-3.3

Regardless of the statistics used to evaluate the SBI's growth, Chinese shipyards clearly benefited from the historic increase in demand in the world shipbuilding market. Given these market conditions, Chinese order books are full until 2007 or 2008.[25] As of 2004, 14 Chinese shipyards from the CSSC, CSIC, and joint-venture companies were among the world's top-50 largest shipyards (as measured by order-book gross tonnage).

This massive growth in China's SBI has been due to several factors, including China's low labor costs and, hence, its cost-competitiveness; the SBI's experience with civilian shipbuilding during the pre-reform era; the early corporatization of the shipbuilding ministry into the CSSC; the immediate focus on international market demand; the implementation of a decentralized organizational structure, which provided autonomy to shipyards; an initial focus on simple ship designs; and the SBI's concentration in prosperous coastal

---

[25] These statistics were taken from Chinese reports on www.shipbuilding.com.cn. Also see "China Sets New Record in Shipbuilding in 2003," *People's Daily Online*, January 6, 2004.

regions, such as Shanghai, Guangdong, Jiangsu, Zhejiang, and Dalian, where there were generally greater opportunities to gain access to foreign capital.[26]

The growth in domestic and international orders has made it possible for many Chinese shipbuilding enterprises to expand and modernize their facilities. Chinese shipbuilders are building new, modern yards, as well as expanding capacity at existing ones—a considered and deliberate plan by the Chinese government, as reflected in both the 9th and 10th Five Year Plans. For example, in China's 9th Five Year Plan (1996–2000), the central government approved the construction of a new, very large, and highly modern shipbuilding enterprise in Shanghai known as the Shanghai Waigaoqiao Shipbuilding Co., Ltd. The first phase was completed in early 2003. Offering some of the most advanced shipbuilding production facilities in all of China, the enterprise includes two large drydocks, Goliath cranes, flat-panel production lines, and the use of computer-aided design and management systems. The yard will also eventually operate four production centers for steel cutting and fabrication, flat-panel assembling, curved-panel assembling, and blasting and painting. The yard now has a maximum annual production of 1.05 million DWT and, when the second phase is complete, will increase to 1.8 million DWT. The Waigaoqiao facility is expected to produce numerous large and advanced commercial ships, such as 300,000-DWT very large crude carriers (VLCCs), 170,000-DWT Capsize bulk carriers, and 160,000-DWT Suezmax and 100,000-DWT Aframax tankers.[27] It is not yet known whether this new facility will produce military vessels; however, its size and

---

[26] For a more comprehensive assessment of conversion in China's shipbuilding industry, see Evan S. Medeiros, "Revisiting Chinese Defense Conversion: Some Evidence from the PRC's Shipbuilding Industry," 1998; Huang Pingtao, "Strengthen International Cooperation to Promote the Conversion to Civilian Shipbuilding Production," paper presented at the International Conference on the Conversion of China's Military Industries, Beijing, June 1995. For a comprehensive overview of the structure and operation of China's entire shipbuilding industry see *China's Shipyards: Capacity, Competition and Challenges,* 2003.

[27] Current data on the Waigaoqiao facility can be found on its official website at www.chinasws.com.

capabilities are such that it could conceivably be used to construct an aircraft carrier *if* China should ever decide to build one in the future.[28]

In addition to new yard construction, China's SBI is also seeking to modernize and expand its capabilities through major yard relocations and facility upgrades. Several of China's oldest and largest shipyards around Shanghai, such as the Jiangnan Shipyard, the Shanghai Shipyard, and the Hudong Shipyard, are all going to be moved to new, massive facilities being built on Changxing and Chongming Islands, supposedly by 2010, in time for the World's Fair in Shanghai. The Qingdao Beihai Yard is developing a new shipbuilding and repair facility at Haixiwan. The following yards have also expanded their facilities: Zhoushan, Xiamen, Yichang, Xigang, Yangzijiang, Biinjiang, and Zhejiang.[29]

The increases in China's shipbuilding capacity are further reflected in the growing number of yards in China that can construct VLCC vessels (over 300,000 DWT). The New Century Shipyard (formerly Jingjing Shipyard) in Shanghai recently inaugurated a new VLCC yard; the Hudong-Zhonghua Shipyards opened a new VLCC dock in 2002; both Dalian and Dalian New Shipyards have plans to convert or expand existing facilities into VLCC docks; and a VLCC dock is being planned at Qingdao's new Haixiwan Bay shipbuilding base. In total, China's SBI currently operates eight VLCC construction facilities (six are for newbuilding) and another four may come online by 2006 or 2007. (By comparison, Japan has 12 VLCC facilities and Korea operates 17 for newbuilding.[30])

The modernization of China's shipyards and the emergence of "shipbuilding centers" is not a recent phenomenon, although their

---

[28] Current data indicate that China is highly unlikely to build an aircraft carrier in the foreseeable future because of the costs and logistical problems associated with defending and supplying such a vessel, including the provision of carrier aircraft.

[29] *China's Shipyards: Capacity, Competition and Challenges,* 2003.

[30] The data in this paragraph are drawn from company data on the respective shipyards, as well as from *China's Shipyards: Capacity, Competition and Challenges,* 2003, and *The Shipbuilding Market in 2001,* consultant report, Paris, France: Barry Rogliano Salles Shipbrokers, 2002 (available at http://www.brs-paris.com/research/index.html).

pace has accelerated in recent years. The industry has shown a steady, consistent pattern of technological modernization and capacity expansion since the early 1980s. This does not mean that China now has a state-of-the art commercial or naval shipbuilding capability, however. In light of the low technological base from which China's SBI started in the early 1980s, its current technological and production levels are impressive—although, technologically, most Chinese yards are still inferior to modern yards in Korea, Japan, and Europe. (Some estimates put the majority of Chinese shipyards at the level of early-1980s technologies.[31]) Moreover, a large number of indicators reflect the steady, consistent improvement of the technological level of Chinese shipyards over the past two decades, such as the entirely new and modern shipyards for newbuilding, repair, and conversion projects being built at Waigaoqiao, and in areas around Shanghai, as noted above, and the new shipyard being constructed on the south side of the Haixiwan Bay, opposite Qingdao. Similar to Waigaoqiao, these new facilities are expected to be outfitted with advanced design and production equipment.

Another indicator of the modernization of China's SBI is the improvements in China's ship-design capabilities. According to several foreign shipbuilding experts who have interacted with Chinese shipbuilders for years, Chinese ship-design capabilities are now in line with global state-of-the-art ship-design standards. China's major ship-design houses, SDARI and MARIC, as well as the large Chinese yards, all use computer-aided design and manufacturing (CAD/CAM) systems. As of 1990, few if any Chinese yards utilized CAD/CAM software. Currently, all of China's major shipyards have replaced manual template copy techniques with "science and technology centers," which utilize CAD/CAM software to design ships and manage production. Thirteen of the world's largest shipyards are Chinese and users of Swedish TRIBON ship-design software; over 40

---

[31] See Commission of the European Communities, *Second Report from the Commission to the Council on the Situation in World Shipbuilding*, 2000.

yards in China use TRIBON.[32] This growing use of CAD/CAM methods has resulted in improved ship design, materials, and structure tolerance control, and pre-outfitting and welding efficiency in ship construction.[33] Moreover, China's SBI operates a wide variety of R&D institutes devoted to shipbuilding. Many of these institutes are in the process of forging linkages with Chinese universities and improving their cooperation with shipyards in their R&D and production processes. China's SBI operates a robust set of institutions focused on shipbuilding R&D.

Some of this modernization has resulted from technical cooperation between Chinese yards and foreign shipbuilders from Japan, Korea, and European nations. These interactions provided Chinese shipbuilders with access to R&D techniques, production technologies, and management practices, which have helped to raise the design and production capabilities at various Chinese shipyards. Cooperation has ranged from design training, provision of CAD/CAM software, technology acquisition, and cooperation in various stages of ship production. Major Japanese partners include Mitsubishi Heavy Industries, Kawasaki Heavy Industries, IHI Heavy Industries, Sumitomo Heavy Industries, and Hitachi Zosen. For example, the Jiangnan Shipyard has concluded three five-year technology-transfer agreements with Mitsubishi.[34]

Interactions with foreign shipbuilders have been extensive. Many large Chinese commercial vessels are based on joint designs between domestic designers and foreign firms. The CSSC has organized study-abroad visits for its designers, has invited foreign experts to lecture in China, and has established partnerships with foreign design firms. In 1994, the CSSC hosted a meeting with several for-

---

[32] The extent to which Chinese yards are able to fully exploit TRIBON design technologies is not clear, nor is whether such technologies substantially contribute to the yards' shipbuilding capabilities. The data on the use of TRIBON in China are taken from an official TRIBON website: http://www.tribon.com/corporate/pressRelease020418.asp.

[33] "TRIBON Dominant in Asia," *Japan Maritime Daily*, October 9–23, 1998.

[34] See website of Jiangnan Shipyard at www.jnshipyard.com.cn; Thomas G. Moore, *China in the World Market*, 2002; and Commission of the European Communities, *Second Report from the Commission to the Council on the Situation in World Shipbuilding*, 2000.

eign technical experts to inspect several shipyards and vessels in China, including a new aerial-survey ship and a missile frigate. One Chinese source noted that, since the commercialization of China's SBI, Chinese ship-design institutes have "developed and optimized" over 500 new designs.[35] For example, the Number 702 Research Institute of the former CSSC claimed to have developed a "deep-V-shaped" hull to facilitate the easy modernization of onboard naval equipment and to improve performance in "heavy seas."[36] Such interactions have also exposed Chinese shipbuilders to international practices. The CSSC in the late 1990s began to emphasize the study of international design standards, practices, and classification requirements.[37]

Beyond actual shipbuilding, Chinese institutes and factories have coproduced numerous models of marine engines and other marine equipment based on original designs by firms from Germany, Denmark, Switzerland, Austria, Norway, and other countries.[38] For Chinese firms, the aim of such agreements is to absorb or reverse engineer these technologies and then produce copies under a Chinese label. This approach has had some successes. China can produce marine diesel engines of all sizes, and they are known for their reliability.

This modernization within China's SBI has begun to be reflected in shipyard output. In recent years, some of China's modern shipyards have begun to produce more-advanced vessels, such as LNG and chemical carriers, and Ro-Ro–type vessels, which require

---

[35] Huang Pingtao, "Strengthen International Cooperation to Promote the Conversion to Civilian Shipbuilding Production," 1995, pp. 19–21.

[36] *China Ship News,* December 1995.

[37] The CSSC has also collected, translated, and published the shipping standards of seven nations in a 48-volume set. Huang Pingtao, "Strengthen International Cooperation to Promote the Conversion to Civilian Shipbuilding Production," 1995, pp. 19–21.

[38] For a list of coproduction agreements, see www.chinaships.com/co/xuke.htm; accessed June 2003. This website of the China Shipbuilding Trading Corporation listed in 2003 that Chinese shipyards had undertaken 29 licensed-production and 10 coproduction agreements with foreign companies for products such as diesel engines, propellers, gas turbine engines, and other goods.

more-sophisticated designs and more-advanced production tech-niques. However, as indicated above, the vast majority of CSSC- and CSIC-produced vessels are simpler ship types, such as bulk tankers, general cargo vessels, and bulk carriers. China has come to dominate the low end of the international shipbuilding market for some time, given its low labor costs and its large production capacity. (Figures 3.4 and 3.5.)

Weaknesses and Limitations of China's Shipbuilding Industry

Despite the consistent improvements in design and production capa-bilities over the past 25 years, Chinese shipyards still suffer from three separate but related categories of problems: financial, technological, and managerial. There is poor cost control; production still uses out-dated and inefficient equipment and technologies, and there is poor

Figure 3.4
China's 2003 Shipbuilding Order Book, by Type

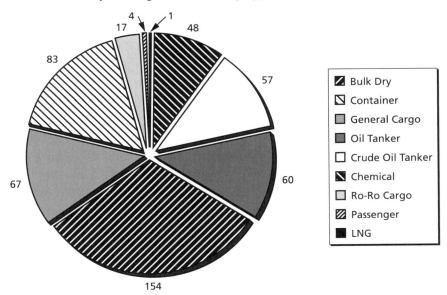

SOURCE: The information in this figure is based on data from Lloyd's Register, *World Shipbuilding Statistics*, London, UK, 2004.
RAND *MG334-3.4*

Figure 3.5
China's 2003 Shipbuilding Order Book, by Type as a Percentage

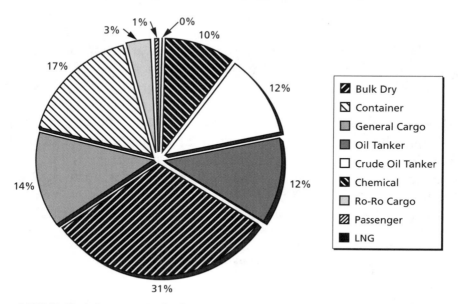

SOURCE: The information in this figure is based on data from Lloyd's Register, *World Shipbuilding Statistics*, London, UK, 2004.
RAND *MG334-3.5*

management of large shipbuilding projects. Many of these problems are of long standing and are gradually being addressed—in particular, in the large state-owned shipyards. These persistent weaknesses constitute a barrier to bridging the quality gap between Chinese yards and the SBI's major competitors in Japan, Korea, and Europe.

A Chinese industry analyst was frank about the SBI's weaknesses:

> At the present time, China's shipbuilding industry has the following problems: obsolete production modes, yet-to-be formed effective technological innovation systems, lack of experienced

scientific research personnel, and lack of administrative and management personnel, etc.[39]

A European Commission (EC) study on China's shipbuilding industry characterized the main problems in China's SBI as poor productivity due to the centralized system of group management, poor project management, inefficient planning procedures, lack of knowledge about international practices in shipbuilding, and corruption.[40] Poor financial accounting is a problem that pervades all stages of the construction process. Because most major yards are still state-owned enterprises, they do not engage in detailed financial accounting. Consequently, they have difficulty in tracking costs and taking steps to reduce unnecessary expenditures. The EC report notes that it is not clear that Chinese shipyards actually know their true costs.

This particular deficiency may not have been important to the shipyards' operations in the past, but at a time when wages and material costs in China are rising and enterprises are less able to rely on government assistance, the financial survival of Chinese shipyards will depend on greater attention to project management and cost controls. In the past, these issues contributed to a degree of inefficiency in Chinese shipyards. Yet they may become more consequential because the costs of steel and personnel are rising in China. In addition, overmanning (i.e., too many workers for one project) and poor management have contributed to delivery delays and quality-control problems, for which Chinese shipyards have become fairly well known. Most foreign ship buyers send eight to ten advisors to China to supervise construction of their vessels to ensure that they meet the buyers' standards and are completed in a timely manner.

Some Chinese yards have sought to resolve these and other problems through technology transfers rather than through changes in management practices—a policy choice that has had mixed results.

---

[39] Liu Xiaoxing et al., "The Development Strategy of China's Shipbuilding Industry," *Chuanbo gongcheng (Ship Engineering)*, Vol. 25, No. 4, August 2003.

[40] Commission of the European Communities, *Second Report from the Commission to the Council on the Situation in World Shipbuilding*, 2000.

Technological upgrades in recent years have not directly translated into better-quality and more-efficient production capabilities. Some shipyards have acquired advanced equipment, such as automated panel lines, but they lack qualified personnel to exploit fully such equipment. Similar problems have occurred with modern design software. Some Chinese R&D centers at shipyards have not been able to fully utilize these design tools due to lack of training in and experience with them.[41]

Chinese shipbuilding managers apparently recognize these problems. China's top leaders such as Hu Jintao and Wen Jiabao, during recent trips to Shanghai shipyards, specifically noted that Chinese yards need to improve the level of their technological capabilities and their management practices.[42] China's shipbuilding industry press is equally frank about the financial and management challenges that shipyards face. One Chinese analyst detailed the scale of the challenges that China's SBI faces in the future:

> For many years, China's shipbuilding industry has overlooked improving the quality of its own enterprises while experiencing rapid development. As a result, its industrial structures were upgraded slowly; the degree of its conventional ships' standardization and serialization was not satisfactorily high; the percentage of the high-tech and high value-added ship products was low; and the development of the corresponding complementary and auxiliary ship equipment capability lagged behind that of the shipbuilding capability. The low cost advantage has been the lifeline in competitions for China's ship industries. However, for a long time, the management fees of both materials and equipment as well as the operation costs have climbed increasingly without effective control effective. Furthermore, its production efficiency has been improved very slowly. For instance, China's

---

[41] Commission of the European Communities, *Second Report from the Commission to the Council on the Situation in World Shipbuilding,* 2000, p. 31.

[42] Ji Xiang, "China's Shipbuilding Industry Moving to World's Top Ranks," *Ta kung pao,* October 27, 2004.

unit shipbuilding cost was increased by 12.5% annually in the 1980s. This figure was even higher for the 1990s.[43]

Huang Pingtao, the former head of the CSSC, specifically noted in 2000 the technological shortcomings of CSSC yards. While all of these problems may not be as acute today, many of them persist, especially in medium- and small-sized shipyards. He noted:

> Nevertheless, we must notice that China's shipbuilding industry is facing a grim situation in which its competitiveness has been declining in the last few years. Price competitiveness has always been the major strong point with which China's shipping-related products have managed to acquire a "deserved place" in the international shipping market. . . . More seriously, a new effective technological innovation system has not yet taken place in China's shipbuilding industry. Therefore the industry lacks the capability to make technological innovations, so its technology develops slowly. Moreover, the industry's technological gap with its counterparts in advanced countries is expanding.[44]

Chinese shipbuilding-industry analysts have put forward a variety of suggestions to improve these weaknesses, including consolidating China's state-owned and local shipyards into three or four large shipbuilding groups, as in Japan and Korea; raise the technical capabilities of Chinese shipyards; and improve financing of large ship-construction projects. Given the current boom in the global shipbuilding industry and the fact that Chinese shipyard order books are filled to 2008, it is not clear that the leaders of China's SBI will rapidly implement such changes in this bullish business climate. The pace and scope of the efforts of various shipbuilding enterprises to address these lingering problems will serve as a strong indicator of the future of the SBI, as China seeks within the next ten years to become the world's top shipbuilding nation.

---

[43] Liu Xiaoxing et al., "The Development Strategy of China's Shipbuilding Industry," 2003.

[44] Zhou Chengqiang, "Hoisting the Sails While the Wind Is Fair—Interviewing Huang Pingtao, President of the CSIC," *Jiefangjun bao*, April 3, 2000, p. 8, as translated in *FBIS*, April 3, 2000.

The contrasting trends of the expansion and modernization in China's SBI on the one hand and the persistent weaknesses in shipyard operations on the other hand raise numerous questions about the SBI's past and current contribution to naval modernization and its future capability to produce advanced ships for the navy. This chapter now turns to these questions.

China's Shipbuilding Industry and Naval Modernization

This section explores the relationship between the expansion and modernization of China's commercial shipbuilding capabilities and naval modernization. On one level, since China's SBI has moved into commercial shipbuilding, naval construction does not appear to have suffered or impinged on commercial shipbuilding. At the same time that the SBI has aggressively moved into building commercial ships over the past two decades, it has been able to continue to expand and improve its naval design and production capabilities.

As the SBI expanded into commercial production in the 1980s and 1990s, the PLA Navy also continued to grow quantitatively and qualitatively—albeit at a fairly slow pace. Since the early 1980s, the PLAN has followed a two-track approach to naval modernization: It has modified first-generation, Soviet-designed vessels using newer naval technologies, and it has built second- and third-generation ships based on indigenous designs and incorporating mainly foreign weapon systems. During the 1980s, the CSSC built the Jianghu-class II/III frigates at the Huangpu Shipyard by modifying previous designs, upgraded Wuhan-class conventional submarines at the Wuchang Shipyard, and modified several Luda III–class destroyers at Guangzhou and Dalian to augment their capabilities. In terms of smaller vessels, the Guangzhou International and Dalian Shipyards produced new classes of minesweepers and minelayers in 1987 and 1988, respectively.

In the early 1990s, China produced its second-generation ships like the Jiangwei-class frigates and Luhu-class destroyers at the Hudong and Jiangnan Shipyards, respectively. In the late 1990s,

Jiangwei-class frigates were upgraded to Jiangwei II–class frigates at the Hudong Shipyard; the Dalian Old Shipyard produced China's Luhai-class destroyer—on a curious, one-time basis. China also commissioned several new Song-class submarines to be built at the Wuchang Shipyard in Wuhan. China also began developing a new class of nuclear-powered attack submarines (SSN), designated Type 093 and a second-generation ballistic-missile nuclear-powered submarine (SSBN), designated Type 094. Both are being constructed at the Bohai Shipyard near Huludao.[45] In the 1990s, other shipyards constructed several different types of military ships, including the Yuting-, Yulu-, Yukan-, and Yudeng-class vessels used for amphibious landing, training, salvage, survey and research, and replenishment. The Huangpu yard continued to produce small, guided-missile patrol craft.

Outside of China's shipbuilding industry, factories and R&D institutes in the aerospace and electronics industry contributed to naval development by producing naval variants of surface-to-surface-missile and surface-to-air-missile systems; these included the C-801 and C-802 sea-skimming cruise missiles and the HQ-61, HQ-7, and the LY-60N SAM systems for air defense. Chinese electronics enterprises also developed radars, hydro-acoustic equipment, and other naval electronic systems. However, the capabilities of most of China's current naval SAM and SSM systems and much of its naval electronics are limited and not equivalent to U.S. capabilities or those of other Asian militaries. The limited range and accuracy of Chinese SSMs and SAMs create serious problems for air-defense and anti-submarine warfare. Many of these systems also do not operate with over-the-horizon targeting, further degrading their already-limited capabilities.[46]

---

[45] "Maritime Ambition: China's Naval Modernization," *Jane's Navy International,* April 1998, p. 15; Office of Naval Intelligence, *Worldwide Submarine Challenges,* Suitland, Md.: U.S. Navy, 1996, p. 27; Richard Sharpe, *Jane's Fighting Ships, 1996-1997,* Surrey, UK: Jane's Information Group, 1995, pp. 113–115.

[46] U.S. Department of Defense, *Annual Report on the Military Power of the People's Republic of China,* Washington, D.C.: annual report to Congress pursuant to FY2000 National Defense Authorization Act, 2002.

Furthermore, few—if any—advances were made in the development and production of naval propulsion or navigation equipment in the 1980s or 1990s. This lack continues to be a major weakness in China's domestic naval production efforts, and one that the PLAN's heavy reliance on foreign subsystems for its second-generation vessels testifies to. China was forced to cancel its production of the Luhu class of destroyers because the U.S.-made gas turbine engines were no longer available after the United States imposed export restrictions on military-related goods following the Tiananmen Square incident in 1989. China's newest operational destroyers use Ukrainian, not Chinese, engines.

Civilian Contributions to Current Naval-Modernization Efforts

The expansion and modernization of China's shipbuilding industry contributed to the PLAN's efforts to design and build better naval vessels. Beginning in the early 1980s, the gradual influx of modern production equipment, foreign technical assistance, foreign investment in Chinese shipyards, the adoption of foreign management techniques, and the incorporation of modern ship-design methods coincided with improvements in the SBI's R&D and production *capabilities* and its expanding production *capacity*. These improvements have benefited commercial and military shipbuilding projects alike. Imported equipment, R&D expertise, improved management skills, and modern design methods have raised the level of capabilities of many of China's major shipyards. These developments have enabled Chinese shipbuilders to build more-seaworthy and more-reliable naval ships with better habitability, damage control facilities, engines, and electronics. In short, Chinese shipbuilders have become more efficient, better skilled, and more sophisticated in designing and building ships for the PLAN.

Improved Production Capabilities

The ability of Chinese shipyards and R&D institutes to build better-designed and better-constructed ships has resulted from several factors. First, a great number of Chinese shipyards have acquired foreign production equipment and technologies. China's main shipyards such as Dalian, Jiangnan, Hudong, Guangzhou, Shanghai, and Bohai, signed major technical-cooperation agreements with foreign shipbuilding firms in Japan, Germany, and South Korea. These agreements allowed China's shipyards to acquire advanced production technologies, including computer-aided manufacturing and management systems, hull construction integration systems, processing and testing equipment, high-efficiency processing facilities, and other technologies through purchase, licensing, and consignment.

These inputs have also allowed Chinese shipyards to expand and improve their ship R&D facilities, metalworking operations, fitting-out areas, hull-welding and assembly workshops, slipways, dockyards, and floating drydocks. In particular, China's SBI is becoming more efficient in designing, pre-outfitting, and building ships in sections, which reduces labor costs and increases the efficiency of construction.[47] These techniques have been applied readily to recent naval production projects.

CSSC and CSIC factories that produce components and marine systems have benefited from imports of foreign technology, as well. The Wuhan Special Machinery Plant and the Dalian Marine Diesel Engine Plant have been modernized and renovated with technology imports for diesel engine production. Specifically, SBI factories are acquiring technology to design and manufacture various types of marine diesel engines, gas turbines, and gearboxes through joint production arrangements with German, Japanese, French, Swiss, and

---

[47] China is integrating imported modular construction, section production, and assembly technology to build ships. It is acquiring modern engineering methods, such as optimal placing of joints between ribs and crossbeams for the construction of hull blocks. These methods reduce the use of material and improve the efficiency of construction. Philip C. Koenig, *Report on SNAME's Technical Delegation to China*, December 29, 2000. Available online at http://www.onrglobal.navy.mil/reports/2000/sname.htm.

Danish companies.[48] These developments have even spurred some SBI factories and institutes to cooperate with their counterparts from other parts of China's defense-industrial complex to develop better shipboard equipment.[49]

Furthermore, China's shipyards have also begun to utilize Western management techniques, such as a greater reliance on decentralized decisionmaking, to improve overall shipyard efficiency. Many shipyards now allow managers to foster international contacts, give them greater "shop floor" authority, and encourage them to utilize modern accounting techniques to improve construction quality and resource allocation. These more-efficient management practices, combined with technology acquisitions, have improved the SBI's production capabilities, allowing more-sophisticated and better-quality ships to be built faster and more efficiently.

For example, some of China's shipyards have already begun to move beyond building basic bulk carriers and tankers to building more-sophisticated types of ships, such as chemical tankers, shuttle oil tankers, container ships, and refrigerator tankers, requiring modern production techniques and advanced expertise.[50] The average building period for vessels of over 10,000 DWT has been reduced to

---

[48] The former CSSC has manufactured marine diesel engines developed on the basis of imported technology from such companies as Howaldtswerke-Deutsch Werft AG (Germany), Sulzer (Switzerland), Wartsila (Finland), SEMT France, and Kawasaki Heavy Industries Co. Ltd. (Japan). See the homepage of the China Shipbuilding Trading Co., Ltd., for a list of license and coproduction agreements: http://www.chinaships.com/co/xuke.html.

[49] Huang Pingtao, "Strengthen International Cooperation to Promote the Conversion to Civilian Shipbuilding Production, 1995. Also see *Shipbuilding in the PRC,* Hong Kong: Asian Strategies Limited, 1995, unpublished consultant's report (see www.asiaonline.net.hk/asl/s_ship.htm for a summary); Edward Ion, "Guangzhou Provides Beacon for Mainland," *Shipbuilding and Shiprepair,* Winter 1995, p. 20; Edward Ion, "China Mounts Renewed Challenge," *Shipbuilding and Shiprepair,* Summer 1992, p.12.

[50] China's shipyards have made great strides in production quality and efficiency, but they still take longer than South Korea's yards to construct the same ship and much longer than Japanese yards, its two largest competitors. Quality control remains a concern for many owners. China's advantage over Japan and South Korea is that it is price-competitive and has available berth space in many (but not all) of its yards. The CSSC also produces almost all types of commercial ships. See *Shipbuilding in the PRC,* 1995.

16 to 18 months, three months less than previously needed. In some yards, the average time needed to construct ships in the 35,000-ton class has been cut from 120 to 90 days.[51]

These improvements in the quality of design and shipbuilding have benefited the PLAN, because they have been transferred to the construction of more-seaworthy and combat-capable naval ships. One of the long-standing problems with many of its first-generation destroyers and frigates is poor design and construction quality. Neither the Luda-class destroyers nor the Jianghu-class frigates—which currently constitute the majority of China's ocean-going fleet—are well built. Both suffer from poor welding with signs of premature failure, inoperable machinery, and overall poor hull workmanship. These deficiencies, in turn, seriously degraded their war-fighting ability. Research has indicated that both the Luda and Jianghu are vulnerable to sinking from just one torpedo or missile hit.[52] Considering that most shipyards conduct both civilian and military projects, a "spin-on" effect of improving the construction of military vessels because of advances in civilian shipbuilding techniques is highly likely.

In addition to poor construction, weak ship designs were a major shortcoming of the PLAN's first- and second-generation Chinese-built naval vessels. The majority of the PLAN's older frigates and destroyers exhibit basic design deficiencies that degrade anti-submarine capabilities (due to their noisiness), limit their operational life span, and increase their vulnerability to torpedo and missile strikes. China's Jianghu-class frigates and Luda-class destroyers lack both damage-control facilities and basic safety features (such as fire-retardant systems, automatic firefighting systems, or watertight

---

[51] See Yong S. Park," China's Shipbuilding Leaping Forward, Improvement in Repair Technology and Increased Export Volume," 1996.

[52] Gordon Jacobs, "PLAN's ASW Frigate Siping," *Navy International,* March/April 1993, pp. 69–70; Gordon Jacobs, "Chinese Navy Destroyer Dalian," *Navy International,* September/October 1992, pp. 263–264.

doors), and these ships still use voice-tube intercom systems.[53] Even China's Luhu-class destroyers possess damage-control facilities with very limited capabilities, exhibit basic design flaws in their weapon-control room that seriously degrade the vessel's warfighting capabilities, and use basic anti-contamination systems.[54] Many of these design flaws were further exacerbated by the poor construction techniques used by China's shipyards in past years.

Improvements in design and production capabilities in recent years have enabled Chinese shipyards to produce faster, safer, more-seaworthy naval ships with better warfighting capabilities. In particular, the naval ships built in the past five years clearly indicate that China's SBI has recovered from past design and production deficiencies and is rapidly improving its ability to build modern naval vessels. The speed and efficiency of naval production appear to be improving, as well.

The PLAN's newest warships provide solid evidence of the SBI's gradual improvement in the design, construction, and management of naval projects. The Luhai-class destroyer, which was launched in October 1997 and commissioned into the PLAN in late 1998, represented a significant design advance over China's second-generation Luhu-class destroyer. In terms of overall size, the Luhai is 20 percent larger. It has a widened hull beam to enhance stability, armament-carrying capacity, and crew living space. In particular, the Luhai's larger size permits four quad launchers for C801/C802 anti-ship missiles, which is double the number, deployed on the Luhu. The Luhai also uses a gas turbine engine, which is more powerful than the

---

[53] Brad Kaplan (USN), "China's Navy Today: Storm Clouds on the Horizon . . . or Paper Tiger?" *Seapower,* December 1999; Gordon Jacobs, "PLAN's ASW Frigate Siping," 1993, p. 70; Gordon Jacobs, "Chinese Naval Developments Post Gulf War," *Jane's Intelligence Review,* February 1993, p. 84.

[54] The Luhu's damage-control capabilities are limited to a room with an illuminated display board of the entire ship, but no actions can be taken from the room to address emergencies when they occur. In the weapon-control room, none of the operator's seats was bolted to the floor; during combat, operators would be thrown around. Discussions with private experts that toured China's destroyer *Harbin* (DDG 112) during its visit to San Diego, California, March 21–25, 1997. See also Brad Kaplan, "China's Navy Today: Storm Clouds on the Horizon . . . or Paper Tiger?" 1999.

Luhu's diesel gas turbine system. In addition, the design of the Luhai's bridge and superstructure exhibits a number of stealthy characteristics (particularly in comparison to the Luhu's structure). These design features include a streamlined superstructure with inclined angles and two solid masts with fewer protruding electronic sensor arrays. The stepped superstructure may have been designed with the intention to equip the Luhai with vertical launch systems, possibly for SAMs for an enhanced area-defense capability. The absence of such a system on the Luhai suggests that that option was deferred for a time.[55]

These improvements in naval design and production have continued with the next generation of destroyers. Around 2000, China began building two new classes of destroyers, skipping over the Luhai—of which only one was built.[56] (This is the first time in PRC naval history that only one of a new class of destroyer class was built.)

The follow-on classes to the Luhai represent important advances in the shipbuilding industry's overall design and production techniques. The first new class of guided-missile destroyer is known as the Luyang I 052B-class; two were built at the Jiangnan Shipyard and are currently being outfitted with weapon systems, sensors, and electronics. An additional two vessels, known as Luyang II 052C-class guided-missile destroyers, are also currently being built at Jiangnan. The latter have a similar design as the former, but they appear to be optimized for air-defense missions. Both new classes have reportedly

---

[55] Yihong Zhang, "Beijing Develops New Radar-Absorbing Materials," *Jane's Defence Weekly*, February 24, 1999, p. 3; "China Launches A Powerful Super Warship," *Jane's Defence Weekly*, February 3, 1999; and authors' assessment of personal photographs of models of the Luhai class destroyer and Song class submarines taken at a PLA exhibition in Beijing, September 1999. Also, for a useful assessment of some of the key features of the Luhai and Song class vessels, see the *Chinese Defense Today* website at http://www.sinodefence.com/.

[56] The data on these platforms are drawn from two websites: www.sinodefence.com and Chinese Military Aviation, http://www.concentric.net/~Jetfight/index.htm.

undergone "builder's trials," but it is not known how many of each will eventually be constructed.[57]

These four new destroyers represent an important evolution in shipbuilding design capabilities, production techniques, and management practices. The hulls are larger than the Luhai's, which increases their weapons capacity, versatility, and stability on the high seas. The designs of these vessels are even stealthier, with sloped sides and a superstructure with a reduced profile—attributes that, collectively, reduce the vessel's radar signature. Also, these hulls were built using modular shipbuilding, a technique increasingly widespread in China's most modern shipyards. Modular construction (as opposed to keel-up) allows for work to be done on different sections at the same time, increasing the efficiency and speed of the production process. One of the most significant aspects of the new destroyers is the fact that China constructed these four new destroyers at the same time and quite quickly as well, at least compared with past experiences. This serial production of an indigenously designed vessel is a first in the PRC's naval history and a testament to improved project management. The four new 052B- and 052C-class vessels have been built or have been under construction within the past four years. By comparison, in the entire decade of the 1990s China only built a second Luhu (1993) and one Luhai (1997) destroyer.[58]

The 052C-class destroyer, in particular, possesses several important attributes. First, according to Goldstein and Murray, it uses a phased array or planar radar on the four corners of the bridges' vertical superstructure, which would be used with a SAM vertical launch system (VLS) for air-defense missiles—a second important innovation. Both of these attributes are a first for a Chinese combatant and help the PLAN resolve its long-standing weakness

[57] Lyle Goldstein and William Murray, "China Emerges as a Maritime Power," *Jane's Intelligence Review*, October 2004.

[58] As of late 2004, both of the 052B-class vessels are in the water, and one of the 052C-class vessels is in the water, being outfitted. The fourth 052C-class destroyer is still being constructed.

with air defense.[59] In the past, Chinese combatants relied on short-range SAMs for air defense. A medium-range VLS SAM system would provide the Chinese navy with its first, real area-defense vessel, and a collection of such ships could allow the PLA Navy to operate surface action groups. If China is able to successfully reverse engineer Russian-purchased SAMs, then it may deploy them on the 052C destroyer. Some reports indicate that China may deploy its HQ-9 system (a Chinese version of a Russian SAM with a range of about 120 km) on the new destroyers. Such a system on the front of the new platform, combined with older Chinese SAMs in the stern, would give the Chinese their first fleet air-defense vessels.[60]

In addition to new destroyers, China's Hudong Shipyard in Shanghai and Huangpu Shipyard in Guangzhou are currently building new "Type 054 class" frigates.[61] Two have already been launched since 2003, and both of those have undergone sea trials. The design of the new frigate is larger and more modern than that of China's Jiangwei II–class frigates. Like China's new destroyers, the new frigate has a more streamlined design and has a larger displacement. These changes augment the new vessel's warfighting capabilities and its seaworthiness. Some sources note that the 054 frigate resembles the French Layfayette-class guided-missile frigate because of the minimalist design of the Type 054's superstructure. The design of the new frigate also offers greater options for outfitting the vessel with various weapon suites. Some estimates indicate that the new frigate will have a significantly enhanced set of weapon capabilities over the Jiangwei-class frigates, possibly including VLS capabilities.

A final major trend in surface ship construction is the notable increase in China's development and production of new classes of amphibious vessels[62]—a testament to the SBI's improved production

---

[59] Lyle Goldstein and William Murray, "China Emerges as a Maritime Power," 2004.

[60] Lyle Goldstein and William Murray, "China Emerges as a Maritime Power," 2004.

[61] Information on this platform is drawn from Lyle Goldstein and William Murray, "China Emerges as a Maritime Power," 2004; also see www.sinodefence.com.

[62] The information in this section is drawn mainly from Lyle Goldstein and William Murray, "China Emerges as a Maritime Power," 2004.

capacity, as well as to advances in ship-design and project-management skills. In the past few years, China has designed a new class of landing ships/tanks (LSTs) and has built at least seven of them. This new follow-on to the Yuting-class vessels is enlarged and has a greater carrying capacity. With these new ships, China's inventory of LSTs has grown from 16 to 23. China also designed and built several new medium-landing ships (LSMs), which appear to be a follow-on to China's Yuedeng-class vessels. In addition, Goldstein and Murray note that the PLA Navy aspires to building a 12,300-ton amphibious transport dock (LDP) capable of transporting several helicopters and air-cushion landing crafts.

These trends are not limited to surface warfare vessels. The design and production rates of China's new Song-class diesel submarine represent a significant advance over its predecessor, the Ming-class submarine. The Song class has a hydrodynamically sleek (teardrop) profile, possesses new cylindrical environmental sensors, and relies on German engines for propulsion. Most significantly, the Song is much quieter because it is fitted with an asymmetrical seven-blade skew propeller, and the Song uses anechoic rubber dampening tiles on the hull and shock absorbency for the engine to reduce its acoustic signature. The Song may also be able to launch cruise missiles when submerged, another design advance for China's conventional submarines. Seven Song-class vessels have reportedly been launched already, and additional ones have entered serial production at the Wuchang Shipyard in Wuhan. The rate of Song production has clearly increased in recent years.[63]

China has also reportedly absorbed some key submarine technologies from the Kilo-class vessels purchased from Russia. Evidence of China's advances in submarine design and construction emerged in July 2004, when Western media reports suddenly revealed China's production of the new Yuan class of conventional submarine. While much is still unknown about the Yuan, it appears to possess attributes of both the Song- and Kilo-class vessels, suggesting that China may

---

[63] Lyle Goldstein and William Murray, "China Emerges as a Maritime Power," 2004; also see "Maritime Ambition: China's Naval Modernization," 1998, p. 14.

have optimized features from each vessel class to meet its specific requirements for underwater warfare.

Increased Production Capacity

In addition to the advances in China's shipbuilding capabilities, the commercialization of China's SBI in the past two decades has brought with it a dramatic increase in China's shipbuilding capacity. Adding production capacity and improving existing shipyard infrastructure have contributed to PLAN modernization. On one level, this expansion will allow China's shipyards to build greater numbers of large warships, such as modern cruisers and battleships, simultaneously if a political decision is made to increase naval procurement significantly.

This increased capacity also has direct implications for China's ability to build an aircraft carrier. For the past decade, rumors have circulated that China is interested in buying or building a carrier. A Chinese military delegation is known to have considered buying Ukraine's Varyag, and the Spanish shipbuilder Bazan is reported to have submitted to China a design for a basic carrier.[64] As noted earlier in this chapter, China now has eight yards capable of VLCC and ULCC construction, and it will add more such yards in the coming years. Many of these yards would be suitable for the construction of a large carrier. Another option for China would be to build a medium-sized carrier (30,–50,000 tons) for launching and retrieving helicopters or vertical short take-off/landing (VSTOL) fixed-wing aircraft. Such a ship could be built from a relatively basic design based on LHD-type platforms (i.e., multipurpose amphibious assault ships) similar to the ones used by the United Kingdom, Japan, and Thailand. Such a vessel could also be completed at a number of modern yards in China, even ones without VLCC capacity—although with substantial naval shipbuilding experience.

---

[64] Bruce Gilley, "Flying Start: Europeans Offer China Aircraft-Carrier Systems," *Far Eastern Economic Review,* March 11, 1999, p. 24. Joris Janssen Lok and Robert Karnoil, "Spain Offers Carrier Designs to Chinese," *Jane's Defence Weekly,* February 18, 1995, p. 8.

Although Chinese shipbuilders are quite capable of building the hull, other parts of China's defense industry would have to develop the equipment necessary to outfit an aircraft carrier with the necessary propulsion systems, navigational electronics, or weapon suites for self-defense or long-range operations. In addition, China lacks the capability to build either large-capacity aircraft-lift elevators or steam catapults for the movement and launching of aircraft; so a Chinese carrier would have to rely on a ski-jump design. Thus, a Chinese carrier would not resemble in any way, shape, or form a U.S. "big-deck" carrier, which serves as the operational hub for an entire carrier battle group. If China chooses to build an aircraft carrier, the need for more ships will become especially pressing in order to regularly protect and replenish the carrier. The PLAN currently lacks enough modern, multipurpose warships to adequately meet the needs of defending and replenishing a carrier. It is to this end that an expanding and improving shipbuilding infrastructure is a necessary condition for the development of modern, long-range naval capabilities.

The expansion of the SBI's production capacity will also benefit the PLAN by increasing the number and types of ships produced in China. Military officials have shown a growing interest in using commercial or merchant ships for such potential military contingencies as an invasion of Taiwan.[65] To compensate for the deficiencies in China's existing amphibious lift capabilities, Chinese naval officials have begun to draft plans to refit merchant ships to transport military troops and supplies, carry out maintenance, provide medical care, and assist with shore-bombardment, anti-submarine and air-defense operations. According to one report,

> Merchant ships have a strong carrying capacity and spacious decks and can carry out military missions during wartime under the escort of warships and fighters. Container ships can be equipped with container-type guided missile vertical launching systems or area air defense guided missiles . . . merchant ships can accomplish much in sealing off the sea, fighting submarines,

---

[65] Wu Jinning and Wang Guoxin, "Introduction to Deploying Civilian Vessels in Landing Operations," *Guofang,* October 2004, p. 28.

controlling the airspace, minelaying and minesweeping, and monitoring missions.[66]

China has already demonstrated its ability to convert some of its commercial ships into military vessels. In 1996, the Navy and the former CSSC jointly converted a Ro-Ro cargo ship into China's first "defense mobilization vessel" to perform such functions as navigation and helicopter training and defense-mobilization drills. The ship's large size also permits it to function as a "floating hospital" and to carry resupply containers in support of long-range naval operations.[67] This converted vessel could also be used to assist long-range amphibious missions and, possibly, as a platform for VSTOL aircraft, both of which are needed for effective power projection.[68] The United States is known to have conducted similar conversions for logistics pur-poses during the 1991 Gulf War. In other areas, China's air-cushion/hydrofoil boats, which are commonly used as passenger ferries on the Yellow River, have also been utilized by the PLAN as troop-transport vessels, such as during the large military exercises held in March 1996.[69] The conversion of these commercial ships rep-resents yet another example of China's use of its expanding civilian industrial base to benefit military modernization.

---

[66] "PLA Refits Merchant Ships in Reserve," *Ming pao,* November 2, 1999, p. 14, as trans-lated in *FBIS,* November 2, 1999; Su Hongyu, "How to Cross the Taiwan Strait," *Jianchuan Zhishi (Naval and Merchant Ships),* July 19, 1999, as translated in *FBIS,* July 24, 1999.

[67] The CSSC and the PLA Navy jointly modified the vessels with a naval inspector on-site at the Quixin Shipyard during construction. Chen Wanjun and Chen Guofang, "Birth of China's First Defense Mobilization Vessel," *Jianchuan zhishi (Naval & Merchant Ships),* February 6, 1997, p. 2, as translated in *FBIS,* FBIS-CHI-97-089, February 6, 1997.

[68] Richard Sharpe, *Jane's Fighting Ships 1995–1996,* Surrey, UK: Jane's Information Group, 1995, p. 131.

[69] Private conversation with former Taiwanese military official, June 30, 1997.

Conclusions

China's shipbuilding industry has made numerous advances since Beijing embarked on its economic reform and openness policies in 1978. Over the past 25 years, China has become the third-largest builder of merchant ships in the world. Similarly to other industries in China, shipyards have leveraged the cheap costs of labor and materials in China to enter and occupy a large segment at the low end of the global shipbuilding market. Chinese yards are known for cheaply producing the inexpensive, simpler ships, although poor quality and frequent delays have been chronic problems. China's SBI has achieved this increase in output despite a number of downturns in the global shipbuilding market.

Throughout the past two decades, China's shipbuilding sector has successfully expanded its share of the global market. Progress, growth, and modernization in China's shipbuilding industry are almost certain to continue. In recent years, major Chinese yards have consistently sought to upgrade their R&D, production capabilities, and output capacity through technical modernization and expansion. Technology-sharing agreements with foreign shipbuilders and adoption of foreign project-management techniques have facilitated these processes, and such cooperation continues. The SBI was reorganized in a way that was meant to stimulate competition and accelerate the development of specialization in the larger shipyards. Over time, these changes are likely to improve further the efficiency, quality, and profitability of Chinese shipbuilding firms, and there are strong signs that such improvements have already begun. SBI R&D institutes have also made great strides in assimilating modern ship-design techniques, and most such institutes are linked to the actual shipyards, which improves the overall ship-production process. In other parts of China's defense industry, the links between R&D and production have not been strong. Yet, the new and expanding interactions between R&D institutes and academic organizations in China should further accelerate the improvement in the SBI's research, development, and design capabilities.

The advances in design and construction capabilities have provided consistent benefits for Chinese naval construction projects—
especially given the high degree of collocation of merchant and naval
shipbuilding. For many of the basic problems exhibited by China's
first- and second-generation naval combatants—poorly designed and
fabricated ships—improvements in civilian shipbuilding capabilities
have helped provide remedies. Chinese destroyers and submarines
built in the late 1990s and early 2000s have exhibited significant
design and construction advances over the previous generation. The
newest vessels are more seaworthy and battle-ready, and the newest
designs permit the inclusion of advanced weapons and sensor suites.
They were built far more quickly and efficiently than in the past, as
well.

The expanding capacity of many large Chinese shipyards may
further assist the PLA Navy as its needs for more and larger ships
grows or if its seeks to use merchant vessels for some military operations. At the same time, China's SBI exhibits a number of limitations
and weaknesses that will constrain naval modernization. Although the
design and construction of vessels have improved, the SBI has
experienced numerous problems producing quality subsystems for
both merchant and naval vessels. Chinese shipbuilders have had to
rely heavily on foreign imports for the power plants, navigation and
sensor suites, and key weapon systems for its newest naval platforms.
For example, Chinese marine-engine factories have had difficulties
producing gas turbine engines powerful enough for large destroyers
and related combatants. The last two classes of Chinese destroyers
have relied on imported gas turbine engines, for example. This high
degree of reliance on foreign goods creates major challenges for
systems integration and, given the inconsistent availability of certain
weapon systems, complicates serial production of some platforms.

In particular, Chinese combatants lack long-range air-defense
systems, modern anti–submarine warfare (ASW) weapons, and
advanced electronic warfare capabilities needed to outfit its new ships.
China's other defense sectors have been slow to produce modern
versions of these crucial technologies beyond copies or modifications
of Soviet or Western systems. For example, Chinese firms have

experienced several delays in the indigenous production of a medium- and long-range SAM system for naval area defense, which has complicated the completion of some naval projects. As indicated in other chapters in this volume, this situation is changing as China's defense-industrial complex modernizes. But, some past weaknesses persist and, over the medium term, they will continue to constrain China's ability to project and sustain naval power for extended periods in the coming decade.

CHAPTER FOUR
China's Military-Aviation Industry

China's military-aviation industry is in the midst of a transformation
that appears to be resulting, finally, in significant improvements in
military-aviation production capabilities. Although some manufacturers continue to produce airframes and engines that are obsolete by
Western standards, many aviation firms are also beginning to produce
military systems that are comparable to aircraft in service with the
world's advanced militaries. China's aviation sector is finally realizing
the fruits of a decade of civilian production, license-production of
military platforms, and foreign assistance.

Aviation industry leaders are making efforts to improve further
the operations of the aviation sector by making individual enterprises
responsible for their own finances and management, engaging military-aircraft producers in production for civilian aircraft, acquiring
Russian and Israeli military aircraft technology, and listing aviation
firms on China's capital markets. China's aviation industry has considerable human resources and a strong institutional foundation, is
upgrading its design and manufacturing capabilities, is receiving
increasing financial inputs, and enjoys the "follower's advantage" of
being able to acquire mature technologies at a lesser cost than the
original developer. In addition, the modicum of competition that
occurs at different levels in the aviation sector has created some
incentives for greater efficiency and innovation in military production. Such competition is limited, however, because labor, capital,
and technology markets are underdeveloped and all military aviation
firms are still state-owned. Thus, while the technological gap

between China's military-aviation industry and the world's advanced producers will narrow in coming years, China will continue to lag behind the most advanced producers unless fundamental reforms are undertaken.

This chapter begins with a brief overview of the structure of China's military-aviation industry; it then assesses the sector's current R&D and production capabilities with reference to specific military platforms; a third section assesses recent efforts to improve the performance of this sector; and a fourth section assesses the future prospects of China's military-aviation capabilities.

Overview of China's Military-Aviation Sector

Over 100 small, medium, and large enterprises are involved in manufacturing components for China's aviation industry, but only a handful manufacture military airframes. The most important of these are the Shenyang Aircraft Corporation (twin-engine fighters), Chengdu Aircraft Industry Group (single-engine fighters), Xi'an Aircraft Company (bombers and medium transports), Hongdu Aviation Industry Group (attack aircraft and fighter trainers), Shaanxi Aircraft Company (medium transports), the Harbin Aircraft Industry Group (helicopters and light transports), and the Changhe Aircraft Industries Group (helicopters). In addition, the Guizhou Aviation Industry Group produces fighter trainers.

Although functionally specialized insofar as each one essentially produces a narrow class of military aircraft, these enterprises are also involved in producing civilian goods for sale on domestic and international markets. In some instances, such goods are aviation-related products; in others, they are cars, motorbikes, and other, non-aviation-related products.

Each of China's aviation manufacturers belongs to one of two large holding companies that make up China's aviation industry: China Aviation Industry Corporation I (AVIC I; *Zhongguo Hangkong Gongye Diyi Jituan Gongsi* 中国航空工业第一集团公司) and China Aviation Industry Corporation II (AVIC II; *Zhongguo Hangkong*

Gongye Dier Jituan Gongsi 中国航空工业第二集团公司). Between them, these two companies control over 100 industrial enterprises, 33 research institutes, 42 other subsidiary companies and institutes, and 450,000 employees. In 2003, they had combined revenues of about US$10 billion.[1] As shown in Table 4.1, of the military airframe manufacturers, Shenyang, Chengdu, Xi'an, and Guizhou belong to AVIC I; Shaanxi, Harbin, Changhe, and Hongdu belong to AVIC II.

AVIC I and AVIC II were created in 1999, when the Chinese government bifurcated the former China Aviation Industry Corporation (AVIC), which was established in 1993 when the former Ministry of Aerospace Industry was corporatized. At that time, the Ministry was split into two companies: AVIC, to handle aircraft production, and the China Aerospace Corporation (CASC), to handle rocket and missile production. Today, AVIC I companies produce fighters, bombers, and transports; AVIC II companies produce attack aircraft, helicopters, and transports. Both conglomerates produce aircraft for military and civilian use.

In addition to aviation, both AVIC I and AVIC II companies produce for a wide variety of other markets. Neither derives the majority of its revenues from aircraft production; most of their revenues come from sales of nonaviation products. In 1997, for example (prior to AVIC's division), 80 percent of AVIC's total revenue came from the sale of nonaviation products.[2] AVIC II, in particular, derives most of its revenues from the production of cars and trucks; aircraft manufacture is much less important in terms of revenue: Within AVIC II's output value, 75 percent consists of automotive products,

---

[1] *China Aviation Industry Corporation I* and *China Aviation Industry Corporation II,* company brochures, November 2002; *Guoji hangkong,* February 2004, pp. 10–15, in *FBIS* as "PRC S&T: Focusing on China's Aviation Industry in 2004."

[2] See Ye Weiping, "Challenges and Opportunities for Ordnance Industry Following China's Entry to WTO (Part 2 of 2)," 2000.

Table 4.1
China's Principal Military-Airframe Manufacturers

Name	Affiliation	Location	Principal Military Products
Shenyang Aircraft Corporation	AVIC I	Shenyang, Liaoning	Heavy fighters
Chengdu Aircraft Industry Group	AVIC I	Chengdu, Sichuan	Light fighters
Xi'an Aircraft Company	AVIC I	Xi'an, Shaanxi	Bombers, medium transports
Shaanxi Aircraft Company	AVIC II	Chenggu, Shaanxi	Medium transports
Harbin Aircraft Industry Group, Ltd.	AVIC II	Harbin, Heilongjiang	Helicopters, light transports
Changhe Aircraft Industries (Group) Co. Ltd.	AVIC II	Jingdezhen, Jiangxi	Helicopters
China National Guizhou Aviation Industry (Group) Co. Ltd.	AVIC I	Guiyang, Guizhou	Fighter trainers
Hongdu Aviation Industry Group	AVIC II	Nanchang, Jiangxi	Attack aircraft, fighter trainers

and only 10 percent is aviation-related.[3] In 1999, for example, AVIC II sold 184,000 automobiles and motorcycles, including more than half of the minicars sold in China.[4]

This diversification applies not just to the two holding companies, AVIC I and AVIC II, but also to the individual enterprises within them. All of China's principal military aircraft manufacturers are engaged in substantial nonaviation production and sales. Chengdu Aircraft Industry Group, for example, in addition to producing jet fighters and components for airliners, also manufactures washing machines and equipment for making cardboard boxes.[5] Such division

---

[3] Xu Dashan, "Military Firm Eyes Rosy Market Future," *China Daily* (Internet version), January 11, 2001, in *FBIS*, January 11, 2001; Michael Mecham, "Staking a Claim in Civil Production," *Aviation Week and Space Technology*, November 4, 2002, p. 60.

[4] "China Company to Export 200 Planes in Next 5 Years," *Xinhua*, January 10, 2000, in *FBIS*, January 10, 2000.

[5] Xu Zeliang, "Chengji: Yi "Yalingxing" Moshi Zouxiang Shichang," (CAIG: Using the 'Dumbell-Shaped' Model to Enter the Market"); *Guofang keji gongye* (Defense Science and Technology Industry), No. 1, 2002.

of focus runs counter to current Western management practices, which hold that firms should concentrate on their "core competencies" and outsource or create subsidiaries to run secondary business areas.[6] Involvement in nonaviation business activities, which are potentially more profitable than military production, may divert attention and resources away from improving military-production capabilities, depending on the relationship between these civilian and military activities in a given aviation enterprise.

Current R&D and Production Capabilities

Many—although not all—of the military products of China's aviation sector are obsolete by Western standards. Some fighters and attack aircraft still produced in China are based on 1950s-era Soviet designs. Although inexpensive to maintain and relatively fast and agile, the performance of these aircraft falls well short of those being produced in the United States, Russia, Europe, and Japan in terms of acceleration, rate of climb, and weapon load. Most importantly, some of these aircraft lack the sophisticated avionics and weapon systems that make modern fighters formidable.

The bombers that China produces are medium bombers that are also based on a 1950s-era Soviet design. Although these aircraft are still serviceable in certain roles (e.g., delivery of cruise missiles), China does not produce long-range heavy bombers or any type of stealthy aircraft. Similarly, while China is able to produce turboprop medium transports, it is unable to produce large jet transports. Finally, the only helicopters currently produced in China are licensed versions of foreign light utility and multi-role craft.

There are signs of improvement in China's military-aviation industry, however. Importantly, China is now producing more-modern aviation platforms. China has begun constructing an indigenously designed fighter-bomber, the JH-7, that is comparable in

---

[6] For example, see Michael Porter, *Competitive Strategy: Techniques for Analyzing Industries and Competitors,* New York: Free Press, 1980.

performance to Western and Russian aircraft that are still in service, and China is producing a modern light fighter, the J-10, that is expected to be comparable in performance to the U.S. F-16. With Russian firms, China is coproducing the Su-27, a modern heavy fighter. In addition, work is under way on an indigenously designed multi-role medium-lift helicopter.

Fighters

As of 2005, most of China's fighter forces still consist of aircraft based on 1950s-era Soviet designs. The most numerous of these are the J-6, a license-produced version of the Soviet MiG-19, which first flew in 1952 or 1953. Production of the J-6 ended in the early 1980s, but production of the second-most-numerous aircraft in China's air forces, the Chengdu J-7, which is based on the Soviet MiG-21, continues to this day, and new variants with improved operational capabilities are still being developed.[7] The MiG-21 entered service with the Soviet air forces in 1958 and was copy-produced in China beginning in the 1960s.[8] The engine, avionics, fuel capacity, and weapons of the J-7 have been considerably improved since that time. The latest versions, for example, are equipped with the Liyang Machinery Corporation WP-13 turbojet engine, which produces 15 percent more power than the original Soviet-designed engine, and they have all-weather day/night combat capability, have nearly twice the range of the original model, and can carry the capable PL-8 and PL-9 short-range air-to-air missiles (see Chapter Two). The basic airframe is little changed, however, and, while highly agile for a "second-generation" fighter, the J-7 is not as agile as such "fourth-generation" aircraft as the U.S. F-16. It cannot carry nearly the

---

[7] See Richard Fisher, "Report on the 5th Airshow China," 2004.

[8] See Kenneth W. Allen, Glenn Krumel, and Jonathan D. Pollack, *China's Air Force Enters the 21st Century*, 1995, p. 222.

weapon load of the F-16 or air-to-ground beyond-visual-range air-to-air munitions.[9]

The Shenyang J-8 is a domestic design, but it is essentially a twin-engine "stretched" version of the MiG-21 intended as a high-altitude interceptor. The two engines give the J-8 a higher top speed and greater rate of climb than the J-7, but the J-8 is not nearly as maneuverable (maximum sustained turn rate of less than 5 g, as opposed to 7–8 g for the J-7). The much larger airframe of the J-8 (31,500 lb normal take-off weight vs. 16,600 lb for the J-7), however, does enable it to carry more weapons (seven external stores stations as opposed to five for the J-7), more-capable avionics, and beyond-visual-range air-to-air missiles, such as the PL-11 and SD-10/PL-12 (see Chapter Two).[10] The J-8 entered service in 1982 and is still in production, even though Shenyang Aircraft Corporation is now also producing the Su-27. The latest version, the J-8 III, is believed to have fly-by-wire flight controls and an Israeli Aircraft Industries–supplied fire-control radar, but its capabilities still fall short of fourth-generation heavy fighters such as the Su-27 or U.S. F-15, which combine greater speed and rates of climb with maneuverability superior to that of the J-7 and more-capable avionics and weapon systems.[11]

Currently under development in China is the Chengdu J-10, an F-16–class light fighter. Photos of the J-10 show strong similarities to

[9] Bill Gunston and Mike Spick, *Modern Air Combat: The Aircraft, Tactics, and Weapons Employed in Aerial Warfare Today,* New York: Crescent Books, 1983, pp. 106, 128–129; Kenneth Munson, "CAC J-7," *Jane's All the World's Aircraft,* April 22, 2004 (available online at http://online.janes.com; accessed May 18, 2004).

[10] Robert Hewson, "PL-11 (PL-10) and FD-60, AMR-1," 2004; Douglas Barrie, "Great Leap Forward . . . in Small Steps," *Aviation Week and Space Technology,* November 8, 2004, pp. 51–54.

[11] Kenneth W. Allen, Glenn Krumel, and Jonathan D. Pollack, *China's Air Force Enters the 21st Century,* 1995, pp. 225–226; Kenneth Munson, "SAC J-8 II," *Jane's All the World's Aircraft,* November 24, 2003 (available online at http://online.janes.com; accessed May 18, 2004); Paul Jackson, "Sukhoi Su-27," *Jane's All the World's Aircraft,* October 16, 2003 (available online at http://online.janes.com; accessed May 18, 2004); Bill Gunston and Mike Spick, *Modern Air Combat: The Aircraft, Tactics, and Weapons Employed in Aerial Warfare Today,* 1983, p. 124.

the Israel Aircraft Industries (IAI) Lavi and the Eurofighter Typhoon, but the J-10 is significantly larger than the Lavi and significantly smaller than the Typhoon, which is a twin-engine aircraft. The performance of the J-10 is expected to be comparable to that of the F-16 and other fourth-generation light fighters.

The J-10 program reportedly began in 1988, and first flight by a prototype was in 1996. At least eight prototype aircraft have been produced to date, and, as of November 2004, more than a dozen production-standard aircraft had reportedly been delivered.[12] The J-10 will be China's first fourth-generation aircraft when it enters service sometime around 2005. It is expected to be capable of 9-g turns, employ a fly-by-wire flight control system and advanced fire-control radar, and carry up to 4,500 lb of weapons on 11 external stores points. Initial production aircraft are expected to be powered by Saturn/Lyulka turbofans imported from Russia, but subsequent versions may use the domestic WS10 turbofan being developed by the Shenyang Liming Engine Manufacturing Corporation (see below).[13]

Another aircraft under development is the Chengdu Xiao Long (枭龙 "Brave Dragon," formerly known as the Super-7), generally known by its export designator FC-1. The FC-1, which is based on the J-7 (i.e., is derived from the 1950s-era MiG-21 airframe), is being developed jointly with Pakistan. It is a low-cost light fighter designed to replace the J-7s, MiG-21s, F-5s, Mirage-IIIs, J-6s, and similar aircraft in the inventories of China, Pakistan, and other developing countries, such as Iran, some African states, and countries in the Western Hemisphere.[14] The design of the FC-1 reportedly began in

---

[12] Douglas Barrie, "Great Leap Forward . . . in Small Steps," 2004.

[13] Kenneth Munson, "CAC J-10," *Jane's All the World's Aircraft,* 2004; "Chinese Puzzle," *Jane's Defence Weekly,* January 21, 2004.

[14] Su Yen, "Undercover the Mysterious Veil of China's New-Type Fighter Plane," *Zhongguo tongxun she,* September 20, 2002, in *FBIS* as "HK ZTS Describes PRC-Made Super-7 Combat Plane for Export Market," September 20, 2002; Cassie Biggs, "China Looks Abroad to Tap Potential of Aviation Market," *AFP in English,* November 6, 2000, in

1994, and the debut flight of the first prototype occurred in August 2003, with at least three prototypes assembled by November 2004. Deliveries to the People's Liberation Army Air Force (PLAAF) and Pakistan Air Force are expected to begin in 2006.[15] The official Chinese media state that the FC-1 will be comparable in capability to a MiG-27 or Mirage-III, which are late "third-generation" fighters.[16]

Given that the J-10 is expected to be more capable than the FC-1 and that the J-10 program is further along than the FC-1, it is unclear why the PLAAF would add to its already-diverse and complicated inventory by purchasing a platform that would play a similar role but with less capability. One reason may be to convince foreign purchasers of its quality. Pakistan's order of 150 FC-1s is said to be contingent on the PLA also committing to its acquisition.[17] This possible explanation would be consistent with a Chinese media report stating that the FC-1 is to become one of the "main fighters" of the PLA in the early part of the 21st century while noting that the PLA has ordered only 100 aircraft.[18]

Bombers and Ground-Attack Aircraft

The mainstay bomber of China's air forces is the Xi'an H-6, which is based on the Soviet Tu-16 "Badger" medium bomber, for which a

---

FBIS as "AFP: China Hoping Foreign Alliances Will Boost Aviation Industry," November 6, 2000.

[15] Su Yen, "Undercover the Mysterious Veil of China's New-Type Fighter Plane," 2002; Yihong Chang, "China Launches FC-1 Fighter Production," *Jane's Defence Weekly,* January 22, 2003, p. 13; Kenneth Munson, "CAC FC-1 Xiaolong," *Jane's All the World's Aircraft,* January 15, 2003 (available online at http://online.janes.com; accessed March 8, 2004); Douglas Barrie, "Great Leap Forward . . . in Small Steps," 2004; Ayesha Siddiqa, "Sino-Pakistani Fighter Deliveries to Start in 2006," *Jane's Defence Weekly,* April 28, 2004.

[16] Su Yen, "Undercover the Mysterious Veil of China's New-Type Fighter Plane," 2002.

[17] Kenneth Munson, "CAC FC-1 Xiaolong," 2004.

[18] Su Yen, "Undercover the Mysterious Veil of China's New-Type Fighter Plane," 2002. Some foreign press reports suggest that, attracted by the FC-1's low cost, the PLAAF will acquire as many as 1,000, but the PLAAF is said to be evaluating the aircraft still. See Douglas Barrie, "Great Leap Forward . . . in Small Steps," 2004; Ayesha Siddiqa, "Sino-Pakistani Fighter Deliveries to Start in 2006," 2004; Richard Fisher, "Report on the 5th Airshow China," 2004.

production license was granted to China in 1957. This aircraft is a subsonic medium bomber with a combat radius of 1,800 km and maximum bomb load of 20,000 lb. The H-6's low speed and lack of stealth render it vulnerable to interception. As the USAF's continued use of the equally old B-52 demonstrates, however, subsonic non-stealthy bombers continue to have utility in certain roles. In particular, the primary role of the H-6 now appears to be as a carrier platform for cruise missiles (naval and land-attack). Meanwhile, Chinese aviation enterprises may be working with Russian companies to develop a new, stealthy bomber.[19]

The Hongdu Aviation Industry Group produces the Q-5, a supersonic attack aircraft based on the MiG-19, whose production technology the Soviet Union transferred to China in 1958. Design work on the Q-5 began in 1958 and the aircraft entered series production at the end of 1969. The Q-5 is moderately agile, being capable of turns of up to 7.5 g when carrying no external stores and having a maximum rate of climb of 29,000 feet per minute at sea level. But it compares poorly with modern multi-role aircraft, such as the F-16, which is capable of turns of up to 9 g, has a rate of climb of 50,000 feet per minute, and has nearly twice the maximum speed. Most important, although the latest versions of the Q-5 reportedly have laser rangefinder/designators for use with laser-guided bombs, the Q-5 otherwise has none of the sophisticated targeting sensors that make Western attack aircraft so effective.[20]

China's newest bomber is the Xi'an JH-7 fighter-bomber (also referred to as the "Flying Leopard" [fei bao 飞豹]), which the official Chinese press states is the first combat aircraft to have been designed

---

[19] Richard Fisher, "Report on the 5th Airshow China," 2004.

[20] Jamie Hunter, "Nanchang Q-5," *Jane's All the World's Aircraft*, February 10, 2004 (available online at http://online.janes.com; accessed May 18, 2004); Bill Gunston and Mike Spick, *Modern Air Combat*, 1983, pp. 106, 138; Lindsay Peacock, "Lockheed Martin F-16 Fighting Falcon," *Jane's All the World's Aircraft*, February 27, 2004 (available online at http://online.janes.com; accessed May 17, 2004).

and produced without external assistance.[21] The JH-7 program began in 1981; the aircraft was first test-flown in 1988; and it reportedly participated in a joint exercise in the East China Sea in 1995. It made public appearances at the 1998 Zhuhai Aerospace Show and 1999 October 1 military parade in Beijing. It is now in service with the PLA Navy Air Force (PLANAF).[22]

According to the Chinese media, some of the JH-7's performance "surpasses that of aircraft such as the 'American Tiger' [presumably the Northrop F-5 Tiger], 'Gale' [presumably the Panavia Tornado], F4, and Russian Su-24." The 25,000-lb maximum take-off weight (MTW) of the F-5 is not really comparable to a 63,000-lb MTW aircraft like the JH-7, but the 62,000-lb-MTW F-4, 88,000-lb-MTW Su-24, and 62,000-lb-MTW Tornado are comparable, and some dimensions of the JH-7's performance are indeed superior to those of some of these aircraft. In particular, the JH-7's maximum level speed of Mach 1.7 (at 36,000 feet) and estimated 7-g turn capability are better than those of the Su-24, and its range of 3,650 km is better than that of the F-4. Thus, the JH-7 may be regarded as comparable in capability to these third-generation fighter-bombers. But, unlike these fighter-bombers, it is only now entering service, whereas the F-4 entered service in the early 1960s, the Su-24 entered service in 1975, and the Tornado, which, although broadly comparable, is clearly superior in performance, entered service in the

---

[21] "China's Flying Leopard Will Be Shown at the Great Celebration," *Ta kung pao,* September 21, 1999, p. A2, in *FBIS* as "New Generation of Jets To Appear at National Day," September 21, 1999. This statement apparently does not include the engines, which were provided by Rolls-Royce. See Kenneth Munson, "XAC JH-7," *Jane's All the World's Aircraft,* June 17, 2003 (available online at http://online.janes.com; accessed March 8, 2004).

[22] Guo Yuanfa, "The Painstaking Development of an Ace Aircraft—Report on the Birth of China's All Weather Supersonic Fighter-Bomber 'Flying Leopard'," *Liaowang,* October 4, 1999, pp. 32–33, in *FBIS* as "Development of 'Flying Leopard' Recounted," October 4, 1999; Fu Zhenguo, "Go, Go, Flying Leopard, Flying Leopard," *Renmin ribao* (Overseas Edition), October 4, 1999, p. 5, in *FBIS* as "PLA Air Force Displays 'Flying Leopard,' Aerial Refueling," October 8, 1999; Wang Yawei, "New Military Aircraft Displayed at the National-Day Grand Military Parade," *Liaowang,* November 8, 1999, pp. 30–31, in *FBIS* as "Article on New Fighters Displayed on 1 Oct," December 20, 1999.

early 1980s. And while the F-4, Su-24, and Tornado remain in service in many air forces, production of these aircraft has ended in favor of more-advanced fighter-bombers, such as the F-15E and Su-30. Thus, although the JH-7 represents a significant advance in China's capabilities to design and produce fighter-bombers, it is still a generation behind the most advanced U.S. and Russian designs.[23] An improved version of the JH-7, the JH-7A, with upgraded avionics and radar, is now under development.[24]

Transports

Transport aircraft are the underlying platforms for aircraft dedicated to a variety of missions. In addition to cargo aircraft and troop carriers, transports are the basis for refueling aircraft, airborne early warning aircraft, and electronic warfare aircraft. China's principal military transports, aside from those purchased from abroad, are the Xi'an Y-7 and Shaanxi Y-8 turboprop-powered medium transports. These aircraft are based on the Soviet An-24 and An-12.[25] Although these designs are not modern, they remain more than adequate in many roles: The U.S. military, for example, continues to employ the Lockheed C-130, an aircraft comparable to the Y-8/An-12. Shaanxi

---

[23] "China's Flying Leopard Will Be Shown at the Great Celebration," 1999; Wang Yawei, "New Military Aircraft Displayed at the National-Day Grand Military Parade," 1999; Kenneth Munson, "XAC JH-7," 2004; Jamie Hunter, "Boeing (McDonnell Douglas) F-4 Phantom II," *Jane's All the World's Aircraft,* January 26, 2004 (available online at http://online.janes.com; accessed May 18, 2004); Jamie Hunter, "Sukhoi Su-24," *Jane's All the World's Aircraft,* April 28, 2004 (available online at http://online.janes.com; accessed May 18, 2004); Jamie Hunter, "Panavia Tornado IDS," *Jane's All the World's Aircraft,* April 15, 2004 (available online at http://online.janes.com; accessed May 18, 2004).

[24] Douglas Barrie, "Great Leap Forward . . . in Small Steps"; Richard Fisher, "Report on the 5th Airshow China," 2004.

[25] Jamie Hunter, "Xian (Antonov) Y-7," *Jane's Aircraft Upgrades 2004–2005,* February 10, 2004 (available online at http://online.janes.com; accessed March 8, 2004); Kenneth Munson, "SAC Y-8," *Jane's All the World's Aircraft,* June 17, 2003 (available online at http://online.janes.com; accessed March 8, 2004).

is developing an improved model of the Y-8 with assistance from Pratt & Whitney Canada and Rockwell Collins.[26]

To date, China has been unable to produce an indigenously designed and developed jet transport. Harbin Aircraft Industry Group, however, has recently begun coproducing Embraer's ERJ-145 50-seat regional jet.[27] In addition, Chinese military-aviation enterprises produce a wide range of components and subassemblies for other Western aircraft manufacturers, including manufacturers of large jetliners. At least 15 Chinese aviation manufacturers, including the Xi'an Aircraft Company, Chengdu Aircraft Industry Group, Shenyang Aircraft Corporation, and Guizhou Aviation Industry Group, have produced tailpieces, horizontal stabilizers, wing ribs, cabin doors, access doors, flaps, outer-wing casings, fuselages, noses, composite material components, and other aircraft parts and maintenance tools for Boeing, Airbus, McDonnell Douglas, Bombardier, French Aerospace, Dassault, and Italian Aerospace aircraft.[28] Many of these companies have plans to increase their involvement in China.

---

[26] "ARJ-21 Will Be the Centerpiece of Airshow China 2004," *Aviation Week and Space Technology,* September 13, 2004, p. S9.

[27] "ARJ-21 Will Be the Centerpiece of Airshow China 2004," *Aviation Week and Space Technology,* 2004.

[28] *Xinhua,* January 23, 1998, in *FBIS* as "Chengdu Plant Delivers Aircraft to Boeing," January 23, 1998; *Xinhua* (Hong Kong), April 23, 1998, in *FBIS* as "Xian Aircraft Company Wins Europe Subcontract Market," April 23, 1998; Wang Hanlin, "Chengdu Aircraft [Corp] Uses High Technology to Grab New Vitality," *Keji ribao (Science and Technology Daily*), May 28, 1998, p. 1, in *FBIS* as "Chengdu Aircraft Industry Corp Profiled," June 15, 1998; Xue Cheng, *China Daily* (Internet version), June 25, 1999, in *FBIS* as "Further on AVIC-Airbus Agreements," June 25, 1999; Wang Xiaoqiang, "Whither China's Aviation Industry?" *Ta kung pao,* August 25, 1999, in *FBIS* as "Article Views Civil Aviation Industry," September 21, 1999; *Xinhua,* October 8, 1999, in *FBIS* as "Airbus Expands Partnership with Chinese Aviation Industry," October 8, 1999; *Xinhua,* December 21, 1999, in *FBIS* as "Xian Aircraft Group Produces Boeing 737 Vertical Tails," December 21, 1999; Ye Weiping, "Challenges and Opportunities for Ordnance Industry Following China's Entry to WTO (Part 2 of 2)," 2000; Cassie Biggs, "China Looks Abroad to Tap Potential of Aviation Market," 2001, p. 2; *Xinhua,* March 19, 2002, in *FBIS* as "Chinese, French Firms Sign Aircraft Fuselage Subcontract," March 19, 2002; Bertrand Marotte, "Bombardier Rival Strikes Regional Jet Deal in China," *The Globe and Mail* (Internet version), September 13, 2002, in *FBIS* as "Canada's Bombardier, Brazil's Embraer Compete for PRC Regional Jet Market," September 13, 2002; "Regional

Helicopters

China's current capabilities to design and produce helicopters are modest but improving. This part of the aviation sector has benefited from consistent interactions and joint-production projects with foreign enterprises. Production volume to date has been limited, and the models that are produced are primarily foreign designs. China has shown the ability to modify existing designs and, through collaboration with foreign helicopter manufacturers, is likely acquiring the capability to develop indigenous designs.

The Harbin Aircraft Industry Group (AVIC II) produces various versions of the Z-9, a light utility helicopter based on the Eurocopter AS 365N Dauphin 2. Between 1982 and 1990, Harbin built 50 Z-9s under a license agreement signed in 1980. Since that time, Harbin has increased the level of local content and has produced upgraded versions, including a shipborne version and a gunship version armed with air-to-air missiles.[29]

The Changhe Aircraft Industry Group (AVIC II) produces the Z-11 light utility helicopter, which appears to be based on the Eurocopter AS 350B Ecureuil, although Changhe claims that China owns independent intellectual property rights for the Z-11.[30] Changhe also has produced the Z-8, a version of the Aerospatiale Super Frelon multi-role transport helicopter. Seventeen Z-8s were reportedly

---

Overviews: China," Airbus website (available at http://www.airbus.com/media/china.asp; accessed January 18, 2005).

[29] Kenneth Munson, "HAI (Eurocopter) Z-9 Haitun," *Jane's All the World's Aircraft*, November 24, 2003 (available online at http://online.janes.com; accessed March 8, 2004); Wang Yawei, "New Military Aircraft Displayed at the National-Day Grand Military Parade," 1999; Xu Dashan, *China Daily* (Internet version), September 13, 2001, in *FBIS* as "China Daily: Helicopter Sector to Be Promoted," September 13, 2001; Xu Dashan, *China Daily* (Internet version), July 11, 2002, in *FBIS* as "PRC's New H410A Helicopter Model Receives Certification; CAAC Says 'Huge Achievement'," July 11, 2002; Robert Sae-Liu, "China Advances Helicopter Projects," *Jane's Defence Weekly*, May 3, 2002.

[30] Kenneth Munson, "CHAIG Z-11," *Jane's All the World's Aircraft*, June 17, 2003 (available online at http://online.janes.com; accessed March 8, 2004).

manufactured between 1994 and 1997, and there have been indications that production could be restarted.[31]

Chinese aircraft manufacturers, led by the Harbin Aircraft Industry Group, are participating in development and production of the EC-120 B Colibri helicopter, a joint venture between AVIC II, Eurocopter, and Singapore's Technologies Aerospace. Harbin is responsible for designing and producing the fuselage, fuel system, and operating system for this aircraft. More recently, Eurocopter and AVIC II have signed an agreement to develop a new 7-ton-class helicopter: a joint venture involving United Technology's Sikorsky subsidiary, which assembled ten piston-engine-powered light helicopters, and Bell Helicopter, which plans to manufacture fuselages for its Model 430 in China.[32]

An indigenously designed medium-lift multi-role helicopter, the Z-10, is believed to be under development in China. Eurocopter is said to be assisting in the development of the rotor system, and AgustaWestland is reportedly responsible for performing vibration analysis and designing the transmission system. Test flights of prototypes reportedly began in 2003, and production is expected sometime after 2006.[33]

---

[31] Kenneth Munson, "CHAIG Z-8," *Jane's All the World's Aircraft,* June 17, 2003 (available online at http://online.janes.com; accessed March 8, 2004); Robert Sae-Liu, "China Advances Helicopter Projects," 2002; *Guoji hangkong,* 2004.

[32] Xu Dashan, *China Daily* (Internet version), August 19, 2000, in *FBIS* as "PRC: Prospects for Joint EC120 Helicopter Project Noted," August 19, 2000; Xu Dashan, *China Daily* (Internet version), August 16, 2001, in *FBIS* as "Experts Say Helicopter Sector 'Important' for Increasing PRC's Military Hardware," August 16, 2001; Paul Beaver, "Business Focus: China Focuses on Core Aerospace Production," *Jane's Defence Weekly,* March 11, 1998, p. 27; Michael A. Taverna and Pierre Sparaco, "Courting China," *Aviation Week and Space Technology,* October 18, 2004, p. 35; "ARJ-21 Will Be the Centerpiece of Airshow China 2004," 2004.

[33] Kenneth Munson, "CHRDI Z-10," *Jane's All the World's Aircraft,* April 22, 2004 (available online at http://online.janes.com; accessed May 19, 2004).

Engines

The most glaring weakness of China's aviation industry has been in the area of jet engines. Although China is capable of producing turbojet engines (used in older combat aircraft), turboprop engines (for transport aircraft), and turboshaft engines (for helicopters), no Chinese-produced turbo*fan* engine (used in modern combat aircraft and jet transports) has yet been accepted for installation in a Chinese aircraft.[34] This is undoubtedly a major reason why China does not produce heavy bombers or jet transports, because turbojets lack the power and fuel efficiency needed to propel large aircraft over long distances.

Over the past decade, Chinese engine research institutes have developed several models of turbofans. For example, in the 1970s, the Xi'an Aeroengine Group received a license from Rolls-Royce to manufacture the Spey Mk 202 turbofan engine. However, until very recently, Chinese manufacturers were unable to produce satisfactory examples of this type of engine. Older Chinese combat aircraft designs still in production in China, such as the J-7, J-8, Q-5, and H-6, all use domestically produced turbo*jet* engines; China's more-modern combat aircraft, the JH-7, J-10, and FC-1, use imported turbofan engines (the Rolls-Royce Spey Mk 202, the Russian Lyulka AL-31, and the Klimov RD-93, respectively).[35] Moreover, until

---

[34] In a turbofan engine, in addition to directly producing thrust as in a turbojet, the engine core is also used to drive a low-pressure compressor, known as a *fan,* attached to the front of the engine. Some of the air compressed by this fan enters the engine core, but the rest is ducted around the engine, combined with the discharge of the engine core, and accelerated through a nozzle to produce thrust. The combination of the high-pressure thrust and the low-pressure thrust is more efficient than high-pressure thrust alone, and it makes possible the greatly increased power output of the engines used on modern fighter aircraft and jet transports. For details, see Obaid Younossi, Mark V. Arena, Richard M. Moore, Mark A. Lorell, Joanna Mason, and John C. Graser, *Military Jet Engine Acquisition: Technology Basics and Cost-Estimating Methodology,* Santa Monica, Calif.: RAND Corporation, MR-1596-AF, 2002, pp. 9–14.

[35] Kenneth Munson, "XAC JH-7," 2004; Kenneth Munson, "CAC J-10," 2004; "Country Briefing—People's Republic of China, Air Force Frontliners to See New Fighter Breed," *Jane's Defence Weekly,* December 16, 1998; Douglas Barrie and Jason Sherman, "China Seeks British Engine," *Defense News,* July 2–8, 2001; Ayesha Siddiqa, "Sino-Pakistani Fighter Deliveries to Start in 2006," 2004. Hongdu Aviation Industry Group's

recently, even China's turbojets were merely derivatives of foreign (primarily Soviet) designs. The Kunlun-series power plant proudly displayed during the Airshow China 2002 in Zhuhai is reportedly the first completely indigenously designed turbojet to have been accepted for production by the PLA (after 21 years in development).[36]

There are signs of improvement, however, in China's aircraft engine manufacturing capabilities. After 30 years of efforts, Xi'an Aeroengine early this decade reportedly started producing the Spey engines licensed to it by Rolls-Royce in the 1970s.[37] Reportedly, these engines will be installed in the JH-7A. The China Gas Turbine Establishment (*Zhongguo Ranqiwolun Yanjiu Yuan* 中国燃气涡轮 研究院), a research institute in Chengdu, Sichuan, claims to have developed a small turbofan engine, designated WS-500, for use in unmanned aerial vehicles or light business jets.[38] Another turbofan engine, the WS-10, designed to power fighter aircraft, is in development at the Shenyang Liming Engine Manufacturing Corporation. The WS-10 is expected to eventually be installed on the J-10 and, possibly, the Su-27s that China is coproducing at Shenyang.[39] According to the 2004 U.S. Defense Department report on Chinese military capabilities, "Recent testing reportedly has

---

K-8 basic jet trainer, which is widely exported, uses turbofans made by the United States' Honeywell or Ukraine's Motor Sich. See Robert Sae-Liu, "Beijing Seeks More Engines from Ukraine," *Jane's Defence Weekly,* October 6, 2004.

[36] Robert Karniol, "Airshow China 2002–China's New Turbojet Engine," *Jane's Defence Weekly,* November 13, 2002; *China Daily* (Internet version), June 1, 2002, in *FBIS* as "China's 'Kunlun' Engine Ready Soon to Power Nation's Military Planes," June 1, 2002. The Kunlun's power output is claimed to be comparable to 1980s' state of the art, but it is unclear what the reference point for 1980s' turbojet aviation engine technology is. By the 1980s, turbofan engines were the industry standard.

[37] Conversations with senior manager of Western aircraft engine manufacturer's China operations; Richard Fisher, "Report on the 5th Airshow China," 2004.

[38] Robert Karniol, "Turbofan Engine Boasts Greater Thrust Capability," *Jane's Defence Weekly,* November 17, 2004.

[39] Yihong Chang, "China Launches New Stealth Fighter Project," *Jane's Defence Weekly,* December 11, 2002.

attained the standard of the Russian AL-31F."[40] In December 2004, however, a contract was finalized for Russia's Salyut to supply 250 AL-31FN engines for the J-10 (in addition to 54 previously supplied), suggesting that development of the WS-10 has not been satisfactory.[41]

China's engine manufacturers are apparently able to produce satisfactory turboprop engines, including the 4,192-shaft-horsepower China National South Aeroengine Company WJ6A used in the Y-8 medium transport. However, the Y-12 light transport and the new MA60 airliner (based on the Y-7) use engines manufactured by Pratt & Whitney Canada (P&WC), presumably because these engines are more efficient or reliable than Chinese-made turboprops. P&WC engines are also reportedly being considered for an upgraded version of the Y-8.[42]

The turboshaft engines for the Z-8 helicopter were produced by the Changzhou Lanxiang Machinery Works. The Z-9 and Z-11 use license-produced Turbomeca Arriel engines produced by South Aeroengine, and P&WC engines have been selected to power the developmental Z-10.[43] In addition, Chinese enterprises produce components for all three major Western engine manufacturers: General Electric, Rolls-Royce, and Pratt & Whitney.[44]

Table 4.2 lists China's eight aircraft engine manufacturers and the types of aircraft engines they have produced. The most important manufacturers are Liming, which made turbojets for the J-5, J-6, J-7,

---

[40] U.S. Department of Defense, *Annual Report on the Military Power of the People's Republic of China,* Washington, D.C.: FY04 Report to Congress on PRC Military Power Pursuant to the FY2000 National Defense Authorization Act, May 2004.

[41] Nikolai Novichkov, "China Buys Fighter Aircraft Engines from Russia," *Jane's Defence Weekly,* January 12, 2005.

[42] Kenneth Munson, "SAC Y-8," 2003; Robert Hewson, "China Unveils Future Y-8 Airlifter," *Jane's Defence Weekly,* December 4, 2002.

[43] Kenneth Munson, "CHRDI Z-10," 2003.

[44] For example, see *Xinhua,* April 16, 1999, in *FBIS* as "China Aviation, Rolls-Royce Agree on Compensation Trade"; *Guoji hangkong,* February 2004.

Table 4.2
China's Aircraft-Engine Manufacturers

Name	Affiliation	Location	Products
Liming Engine Manufacturing Corporation	AVIC I	Shenyang, Liaoning	Turbojets, turbofans
Xi'an Aeroengine Group	AVIC I	Xi'an, Shaanxi	Turbojets
China National South Aeroengine Co.	AVIC II	Zhuzhou, Hunan	Turboprops, turboshafts, small turbojets
Liyang Machinery Corporation	AVIC I	Pingba, Guizhou	Turbojets
Chengdu Engine (Group) Co. Ltd.	AVIC II	Chengdu, Sichuan	Turbojets
Harbin Dongan Engine (Group) Co. Ltd.	AVIC II	Harbin, Heilongjiang	Turboprops
Shanghai Aero-Engine Manufacturing Plant	AVIC I	Shanghai	Turbofans
Changzhou Lanxiang Machinery Works	AVIC II	Changzhou, Jiangsu	Turboshafts

and J-8 fighters and the Q-5 attack aircraft, and is now developing the WS-10 turbofan; Xi'an, which makes the WP-8 engine for the H-6 medium bomber; Liyang, which currently makes turbojets for the J-7 and J-8 fighters; and China National South Aeroengine Company, which makes turboprops for the Y-8 medium transport and turboshafts for the Z-9 helicopter.

Chengdu, Harbin, Shanghai, and Changzhou do not appear to be currently involved in whole-engine production, but Chengdu and Shanghai produce components for foreign and domestic jet engines, Harbin produces transmissions, crankshafts, connecting rods, and reduction gears for helicopters, and Changzhou overhauls turboprops and turbine engines. In addition, as with China's airframe manufacturers, these companies are engaged in considerable production of nonaviation items, including industrial turbines, electric power generators, compressors, gasoline engines, pressure vessels, boilers, motorcycles, fiberglass boats, cement mixers, shock absorbers, pumps, welding equipment, corrugated pipe, cleaning equipment, drafting equipment, typewriters, pharmaceuticals, shoes, and paper.[45]

Efforts to Improve the Performance of China's Military-Aviation Sector

Although China is one of the few countries in the world with a military-aviation industry that produces almost all major types of military aircraft (fighters, bombers, transports, helicopters, etc.), many of the military aircraft produced in China are obsolete by Western standards. For example, many of the fixed-wing military aircraft currently manufactured in China are based on 1950s-era Soviet systems. Although the performance of these aircraft has improved over time with the introduction of new versions and models, the underlying designs are now over 40 years old. In addition, there are significant gaps in China's production capabilities, such as the inability to produce large bombers, jet transports, or purpose-built attack helicopters.[46]

---

[45] Information on Chengdu Fadongji Youxian Gongsi, Harbin Dongan Fadongji Youxian Gongsi, Changzhou Lanxiang Jixie Zongchang, and Shanghai Hangkong Fadongji Zhizaochang as taken from AVIC II website (available online at http://www.avic2.com.cn/ReadNews.asp?NewsID=170&BigClassName=企业风采&SmallClassName=发动机类&DispType=1&SpecialID=0; accessed May 20, 2004); AVIC II website (available online at http://www.avic2.com.cn/ReadNews.asp?NewsID=171&BigClassName=企业风采&SmallClassName=发动机类&DispType=1&SpecialID=0; accessed May 20, 2004);AVIC II website (available online at http://www.avic2.com.cn/ReadNews.asp?NewsID=168&BigClassName=企业风采&SmallClassName=发动机类&DispType=1&SpecialID=0; accessed May 20, 2004); AVIC I website (available online at http://www.avic1.com/cn/Chinese/qyzc/qyzc_zyqy_shhkfdjzzc.htm; accessed May 20, 2004).

[46] China did produce a prototype of a jet transport, the Y-10, based on reverse engineering the Boeing 707, and this aircraft apparently actually flew in 1980. The program was discontinued, however, "due to reasons of market and expenditure"—meaning, presumably, that with the opening up of China's economy beginning in 1978, it was far less expensive to simply purchase airliners from abroad. Thus, China appears to have demonstrated the capability to produce jet transports, but apparently at costs significantly higher than those of Western manufacturers. See Ye Weiping, "Challenges and Opportunities for Ordnance Industry Following China's Entry to WTO (Part 2 of 2)," 2000; Zhou Rixin, *Hangkong zhishi*, November 6, 2000, pp. 4–6, in *FBIS* as "PRC Aircraft Designer Cheng Bushi Profiled," November 6, 2000; Xiao Xu, *China Daily* (Internet

Chinese industry officials and analysts are clearly aware of the shortcomings of the military-aviation industry, and efforts are being made to improve its capabilities. One such effort was the 1999 reorganization of AVIC into AVIC I and AVIC II. An explicit goal of this restructuring was to break up monopolies and foster a "fair market economy mechanism"[47]: The president of AVIC stated prior to its division that the two new aviation groups would "both compete and co-operate."[48] Competition in military aircraft is still very limited, however, because there is minimal overlap between the AVIC I's and AVIC II's areas of production. The rough division of labor is this: Almost all combat aircraft are produced by AVIC I, and all helicopters are produced by AVIC II.

The most overt areas of competition in large aviation platforms are in transport aircraft and fighter trainers. Both AVIC I and AVIC II entities produce transports, although the different sizes of the aircraft they produce suggests that they may not compete directly against each other. Similarly, AVIC II's Hongdu Aviation Industry Group has produced the K-8 basic jet trainer and is developing, with assistance from Russia's Yakolev aircraft corporation, a "next generation advanced/lead-in fighter trainer" called the L-15; AVIC I's China National Guizhou Aviation Industry Group has been promoting its developmental FTC-2000 and LFC-16 advanced/lead-in trainers.[49]

---

version), January 11, 2002, in *FBIS* as "PRC Aviation Firm Says Emphasis on Development of Small Aircraft," January 11, 2002.

[47] Shen Bin, "AVIC to Be Split into 2 Groups," *China Daily (Business Weekly Supplement),* January 31–February 6, 1999, p. 1, in *FBIS* as "Aviation Industries of China to Split into 2 Groups," January 31, 1999.

[48] Shen Bin, "AVIC to Be Split into 2 Groups," 1999, p. 1.

[49] *China National Guizhou Aviation Industry (Group) Co., Ltd., Hongdu Aviation Industry Group,* and *L15 A Next Generation Advanced/Lead-In Fighter Trainer,* brochures acquired at Airshow China, Zhuhai, November 2002; *Moscow Interfax,* November 3, 2004, in *FBIS* as "Russian, Chinese Aircraft Builders to Cooperate"; *The Nation* (Islamabad), untitled article, June 8, 2000, pp. 1, 17, in *FBIS* as "Pakistan, China Jointly Build K8E Aircraft," June 8, 2000; Robert Karniol, "China Debuts L-15 Trainer Mock-Up," *Jane's Defence Weekly,* November 10, 2004; Robert Karniol, "New Variant of Chinese Fighter Planned,"

Although officially separate corporations, the extent to which AVIC I and AVIC II are truly independent entities is unclear, because they both still share the same headquarters compound at 67 Jiaodaokou Nandajie in Beijing.[50] It is possible, however, that a higher degree of competition between AVIC I and AVIC II (as well as among entities within both group corporations) exists at the levels of military-aviation subsystems (e.g., avionics, propulsion, or radars) or even at the level of components used in such subsystems. Given the government emphasis on breaking down monopolies (both within sectors as well as regional ones), competition among aviation industry entities to supply subsystems and components for major military platforms is a distinct possibility.

A second goal of the 1999 restructuring was to make individual aviation enterprises behave more as independent corporations and less as ministerial organs with soft budget constraints. After the reforms, AVIC I and AVIC II now function as holding companies whose primary role appears to be managing capital, coordinating activities among subsidiary companies, managing relations with government agencies such as COSTIND, and acting as an interface between the subsidiary companies and foreign business partners. Their role is no longer to manage the daily operations of the subsidiaries; in other words, individual industrial enterprises (although not research institutes) are now responsible for their own finances and management practices.[51]

The rationalization of its organization and workforce is a third measure being taken to improve the performance of China's military-aviation sector. In 1998, prior to its division, AVIC was reportedly

---

Jane's Defence Weekly, November 10, 2004. The L-15 is said to be due to enter serial production in 2007.

[50] Author's personal observation, September 2003. Moreover, within the compound, AVIC I offices are interspersed with AVIC II offices.

[51] To be sure, these enterprises do not choose their leaders. Selection is still done at the level of AVIC I and AVIC II. Li Jiamo, "Hangkong Zhuji Sheji Ying yu Zhizao Qiye Jinmi Jiehe," [Design and Manufacturing of Major Aviation Items Should Be Tightly Integrated]), *Guofang keji gongye* (*Defense Science and Technology Industry*), No. 5, 2002.

planning to reduce the number of subordinate enterprises from 250 to about 100 and to reduce the number of employees by 50,000 to 100,000 from the 500,000 employed at that time.[52] AVIC I and AVIC II now employ about 450,000 workers, and, as of 2002, AVIC I had 54 "large and medium-sized industrial enterprises" under it and AVIC II had 56 "industrial enterprises" under it.[53] Thus, the total number of enterprises and workers in the industry appear to have been significantly reduced.

A fourth strategy for improving the performance of China's military-aviation sector has been to leverage the capabilities of the civilian-aviation sector, such as using the fabrication of components for commercial aircraft to improve China's military-aircraft production capabilities. Articles in the Chinese media argue that the "military aviation industry must combine both military and civilian development," noting that "as a result of the open character of the civilian aviation industry, some of its technologies may prove to be more advanced, more reliable, and more economical, thus spurring progress in military aviation technology." These articles also note that there are economies of scale in producing parts and components that have both military and civilian use; and that civilian aircraft can be put to use as reconnaissance, early warning, electronic warfare, command, refueling, or transport aircraft.[54] In addition, some Chinese writings even state that the sales and service network for civilian aircraft can support the development of military aircraft.[55]

---

[52] Paul Beaver, "Business Focus: China Focuses on Core Aerospace Production," 1998.

[53] *China Aviation Industry Corporation I* and *China Aviation Industry Corporation II,* 2002. In 1998, 34,000 workers were laid off. Shen Bin, "AVIC to Be Split into 2 Groups," 1999, p. 1. It is unclear how many "small" enterprises are under AVIC I and whether they were included in the original estimate of 250.

[54] Huang Qiang, "Will China's Aviation Industry Be Able to Get Out of the Doldrums Soon?" *Keji ribao,* July 8, 1999, p. 8, in *FBIS* as "Current Situation of Aerospace Industry," August 11, 1999. Huang Qiang, the article's author, is director of Shaanxi's Number 603 Research Institute. Wang Xiaoqiang, "Whither China's Aviation Industry?" 1999.

[55] Wang, "Whither China's Aviation Industry?" 1999.

This civilian-military integration strategy has two other elements. The first consists of facilitating technology transfers from foreign aircraft producers by encouraging them to contract with Chinese industries for component and subassembly production, assemble aircraft in China, and collaborate with Chinese aviation companies in the development of new models of civilian aircraft. Aware that most foreign investors are not willing to fund aviation programs that have military applications, China's leaders have instead sought foreign investment in China's civil-aviation sector. Their belief is that doing so will result in improvements to China's capability to produce military aircraft as well.[56] As one article in a PRC-owned Hong Kong newspaper notes, the "technology, equipment, and technical force" used in the production of subcomponents or the assembly of passenger airplanes can also be used for military aircraft production, "after some readjustments."[57] As noted above, China is already engaged in significant production of parts and subassemblies for Western aircraft manufacturers, but Chinese aviation officials hope to continue to expand the scale of this work beyond subcomponent cooperation, which was valued at US$120 million in 2001.[58] In the area of collaborative development: engineers from the Chinese aviation industry have participated in the development and certification of the Airbus A318: AVIC II and Eurocopter are collaborating on the development of a medium-lift helicopter; and Ukraine's Antonov and "a number of Western suppliers" are said to be cooperating with the Shaanxi Aircraft Company in the development of the Y-8X, a new version of Shaanxi's venerable Y-8 transport. In addition, in 2002 COSTIND

---

[56] Paul Beaver, "Business Focus: China Focuses on Core Aerospace Production," 1998.

[57] Ye Weiping, "Challenges and Opportunities for Ordnance Industry Following China's Entry to WTO (Part 2 of 2)," 2000.

[58] Zhang Yi, "China Aviation Products to Make Key Breakthrough in '10th Five Year Plan'," *Xinhua Domestic Service,* January 18, 2000, in *FBIS* as "China Aviation Industry to Provide More High-Tech Weapons," February 10, 2000; Guo Aibing, *China Daily* (Internet version), June 13, 2000, in *FBIS* as "PRC Aviation Makers to Focus on Building Small Airplanes," June 13, 2000; *Xinhua,* March 19, 2002. One of the ways this expansion is done is by making localization of production an explicit or implicit condition for access to China's aviation market.

and Russia's Aircraft and Space Agency reportedly signed an agreement to jointly develop a new generation of civilian aircraft.[59]

The second element of this civil-military strategy is for China to develop its own jetliner. In the late 1990s, China was hoping to develop a 100-seat trunk liner and persuaded a European consortium that included Airbus and Singapore Technologies to join AVIC in the development of an aircraft dubbed the AE-100. This program was terminated in 1998, however, when Airbus pulled out because it felt that the project would not produce an adequate return on Airbus's investment.[60] Since that time, Chinese officials have reset their goal to producing "medium and small-size" "feeder" (smaller than trunkliner) turbofan airplanes with 50 to 70 seats, such as those turned out by Brazil's Embraer and Canada's Bombardier. The Chinese government hopes to then gradually work its way up to 100-seat (and, presumably, larger) aircraft.[61] AVIC I and four of its subsidiaries—Xi'an Aircraft Company, Chengdu Aircraft Industry Group, Shenyang Aircraft Corporation, and the Shanghai Aircraft Industrial Group[62]—have formed a consortium based in Shanghai to develop and produce a 70-seat short-range aircraft, known as the

[59] Xue Cheng, *China Daily* (Internet version), June 25, 1999; *Xinhua*, October 8, 1999; Liu Ting, "Design for 5.5 Ton Helicopter's Rotor Has Passed Evaluation," *Zhongguo hangkong bao*, December 7, 2001, p. 1, in *FBIS* as "PRC S&T: Design for Helicopter Rotor Has Passed Evaluation," January 16, 2002; Robert Sae-Liu, "China Advances Helicopter Projects," 2002; Robert Hewson, "China Unveils Future Y-8 Airlifter," 2002; *AFP,* April 18, 2002, in *FBIS* as "AFP: China, Russia Sign Pact to Develop New Generation of Civil Aircraft," April 18, 2002. The Y-8X may also be based on Antonov's new An-70, which is, in turn, based on the An-12, on which the Y-8 is modeled. Cassie Biggs, "China Looks Abroad to Tap Potential of Aviation Market," 2000; "Regional Overviews: China," Airbus website (accessed June 2004).

[60] Michael Mecham, "Staking a Claim in Civil Production," 2002.

[61] Huang Qiang, "Will China's Aviation Industry Be Able to Get Out of the Doldrums Soon?"1999; Wang Xiaoqiang, "Whither China's Aviation Industry?" 1999; *Xinhua,* November 8, 2000, in *FBIS* as "Foreign Manufacturers Show Interest in China's Feeder Aircraft Market," November 8, 2000.

[62] Shanghai Aircraft is a civilian-only aircraft company that assembled McDonnell Douglas MD-82 and MD-83 jetliners from 1985 to 1994.

ARJ-21.[63] Meanwhile, in December 2002, AVIC II formed a joint venture with Brazil's Embraer to produce, under license, Embraer's ERJ-135, ERJ-140, and ERJ-145 30–50-seat regional jetliners. Finally, Chengdu Aircraft Industry Group is said to be working on plans to cooperate with foreign partners in the development of business jets.[64]

A small number of foreign companies have been willing to collaborate on aviation programs that have military applications. The Shenyang Aircraft Corporation is currently coproducing Russia's Sukhoi Su-27 heavy fighters. Under this arrangement, Shenyang plans to eventually produce 200 Su-27s. The first 50 were to be assembled from knock-down kits (i.e., China just assembles the aircraft from kits; it does not actually fabricate any of the components), but by the end of the program, Chinese manufacturers hope to produce all of the components except for the engines and avionics. As of November 2004, reports had suggested that between 20 and 70 Su-27s had been completed under this program.[65] However, there were also reports that coproduction of the Su-27 might be halted after roughly 100 aircraft are completed, possibly in favor of the Su-30, which is

---

[63] Guo Aibing, *China Daily* (Internet version), June 13, 2000; Huo Yongzhe, Gong Zhengzheng, *China Daily* (Internet version), May 15, 2001, in *FBIS* as "Article on PRC Plan to Develop New Generation of Regional Passenger Planes," May 15, 2001; Bertrand Marotte, "Bombardier Rival Strikes Regional Jet Deal in China," 2002; "Shanghai to Assemble Feeder Turbo Jets," *China Daily*, December 20, 2002 (available online at www1.chinadaily.com.cn/news/cn/2002-12-20/98564.html; accessed December 20, 2002). That this program is considered to be of strategic importance is indicated by the fact that 98 percent of the funds—2 billion RMB—will be provided by the central government, whereas each of the participating enterprises will provide token investments. Gong Huo, *China Daily*, May 15, 2001.

[64] Xiao Xu, *China Daily*, January 11, 2002; Bertrand Marotte, "Bombardier Rival Strikes Regional Jet Deal in China," 2002; Gong Huo, *China Daily*, 2001.

[65] "Country Briefing—People's Republic of China, Air Force Frontliners to See New Fighter Breed," 1998; Yihong Zhang, "Industry Round-Up—Chinese Boost Fighter Production with Su-27 Assembly," *Jane's Defence Weekly*, December 13, 2000; Douglas Barrie, "Great Leap Forward . . . in Small Steps," 2004.

capable of performing in an air-to-ground role as well as in an air-to-air role.[66]

China has also received substantial assistance from Israel Aircraft Industries (IAI) in the development of the J-10 fighter. IAI is said to have provided the avionics, radar, and other technologies for the J-10.[67]

A final measure that is being taken to improve the financial and managerial performance of China's aviation industry is the listing of aviation firms on China's stock markets. In April 2003, AVIC II established an entity called AviChina Industry and Technology Co. Ltd. (*Zhongguo Hangkong Keji Gongye Gufen Youxian Gongsi* 中国航空科技工业股份有限公司), which consists of the group's "major non-military" enterprises. In October 2003, this company was listed on the Hong Kong Stock Exchange. This action caused AVIC II to become "the first of China's large defense groups to complete implementation of a joint stock system for its main business."[68] As a result of this listing, the European Aeronautic Defense and Space Company (EADS) now owns a 5-percent stake in AviChina.

Future Prospects for China's Aviation Industry

China's aviation industry appears to finally be acquiring the capability to design and produce fourth-generation fighters, modern fighter-bombers, multi-role helicopters, and turbofan engines, albeit with

---

[66] Richard Fisher, "Report on the 5th Airshow China," 2004; Robert Hewson, "China's Su-27s May Fall Short in Capability, *Jane's Defence Weekly*, November 17, 2004.

[67] "Country Briefing—People's Republic of China, Air Force Frontliners to See New Fighter Breed," 1998.

[68] Xu Dashan, "Military Firm Eyes Rosy Market Future," 2001; "Zhong Hang Han Er Jituan Wancheng Gufenzhi Gaizao Zhu Ying Feiji Qiche Deng" ("AVIC II Completes Stock System Transformation: Main Areas of Business Are Aircraft, Automobiles, Etc."), *People's Daily Online*, May 19, 2003 (available online at www.peopledaily.com.cn/GB/junshi/60/20030519/995654.html; accessed May 20, 2003); "Chinese Puzzle," *Jane's Defence Weekly*, January 21, 2004; *Guoji hangkong*, February 2004.

varying rates of production and degrees of foreign assistance. Yet, significant gaps in its R&D and production capabilities remain—at the same time that other countries, particularly the United States, are in the process of developing and fielding even more-advanced military-aviation systems. In the view of the director of the Defense Industry Department of Russia's Ministry of Industry and Energy, although China's production capabilities have improved significantly, "our Chinese colleagues have to negotiate quite a long road of formation of the scientific and design school. And, in our view, this process is still very far from completion."[69]

The ability of China's military-aviation industry to close the technological gap between it and the advanced military powers will depend on a number of factors: its existing manufacturing capability; the human and financial resources available for the effort; the economic environment of China's aviation industry; the degree of competition Chinese aviation firms face; the operation of the capital, labor, and technology markets; the nature of the ownership of firms in China's aviation industry; and the institutional infrastructure available to support technological progress. These factors are addressed below.

Manufacturing Technology

The manufacturing and design capabilities of China's aviation industry are modest but improving. The production of components and subassemblies for foreign commercial aircraft has required many of China's military-aircraft producers to build modern factories, purchase modern manufacturing equipment, provide better training for their personnel, and obtain financing for these activities.[70] The Chengdu Aircraft Industry Group, for example, now uses a computer-integrated manufacturing system and factory automation in the forms

---

[69] "What's the Reason Why We Are Reforming," *Vermya Novostey,* November 3, 2004, in *FBIS* as "Russian Official Sees China's Relations with Russia Helping PRC More Than with US, Europe."

[70] Wang Xiaoqiang, "Whither China's Aviation Industry?" 1999.

of computer-aided design, computer-aided process planning, computer-aided manufacturing, numerically controlled machine tools, and an integrated manufacturing planning information system.[71] According to Chinese media reports, the JH-7 was designed entirely using computer-assisted design management tools, and, in 1999, the Number 603 Research Institute in Xi'an began using Dassault Systemes's state-of-the-art CATIA three-dimensional design tool to create virtual prototypes. Similarly, by using digital design, manufacturing, and control systems, the designer of the FC-1 reportedly took less than six months from the initiation of design work to the construction of the first prototype.[72] Finally, a number of aviation enterprises have been certified as meeting the requirements for International Organization for Standardization (ISO) 9001 and 9002 certification (international quality-control standards).[73]

However, not all aircraft design and manufacturing in China is state of the art. As of 2002, for example, even the Chengdu Aircraft Industry Group, generally considered one of China's more-capable aircraft manufacturers, was still using "wire model" three-dimensional design tools, whereas three-dimensional solids are now the industry

[71] Wang Hanlin, "Chengdu Aircraft [Corp] Uses High Technology to Grab New Vitality," 1998; Xu Zeliang, "CAIG: Using the 'Dumbell-Shaped' Model to Enter the Market," 2002.

[72] "China's Flying Leopard Will Be Shown at the Great Celebration," 1999, p. A2; Lei Biao and Dang Chaohui, "No. 603 Research Institute's Three-Dimensional Design Reaches Advanced World Level," *Shaanxi ribao*, December 2, 2001, p. 1, in *FBIS* as "Shaanxi Institute's 3-Dimensional Aircraft Design Reaches World Advanced Level," December 15, 2001; Huang Tung, "Successful Test-Flight of New Flying Leopard Fighter Bomber JH-7A," *Kuang chiao ching*, November 16, 2002, p. 97, in *FBIS* as "PRC Flying Leopard Fighter Bomber JH-7A Profiled in Test Flight—PHOTO," November 16, 2002; Su Yen, "Undercover the Mysterious Veil of China's New-Type Fighter Plane," 2002. Computer-assisted design tools are 1980s technology, but the design of the JH-7 began in the early 1980s, so was state-of-the-art technology at the time.

[73] Wang Lianping, "Bravely Writing a New Tablet," *Zhongguo hangkong bao*, March 2, 2001, p. 1, in *FBIS* as "PRC Aeronautical Industry Institute Achievements Traced," March 2, 2001; *Beijing Aeronautical Manufacturing Technology Research Institute, Xi'an Aero-Engine Controls Co., China, Xi'an XR Aero Components Co. Ltd, Beijing Shuguang Electrical Machinery Factory, Pingyuan Hydraulic Filters,* and *Tianjin Aviation Electro Mechanical Co., Ltd.,* brochures acquired at Airshow China, Zhuhai, November 2002.

standard.[74] More significantly, Chinese observers admit that most enterprises are not operated according to modern management principles. Financial management and accounting need improvement; on-time production and fulfilling of all targets and missions are apparently rare; and quality control remains a serious problem.[75] Even the assembly of Su-27s from knock-down kits has proved challenging. The Kunlun engine was in development for 21 years before being accepted by the PLA Air Force, as compared with a mean development time of less than four years for new models of Western engines.[76] In the view of a China-based manager for BAE Systems, "in areas where there is high labor content, China could become an important and strategic partner for us—but we have to pump in technology and cultivate a management process."[77] Some Chinese analysts even feel that China's aviation industry is actually falling farther behind the rest of the world.[78]

Human Resources

The number of human resources in China's aviation industry are considerable. In 1999, AVIC I and AVIC II employed 100,000 engineers between them.[79] By comparison, Boeing and Lockheed Martin have

---

[74] Xu Zeliang, "CAIG: Using the 'Dumbell-Shaped' Model to Enter the Market," 2002.

[75] Huang Qiang, "Will China's Aviation Industry Be Able to Get Out of the Doldrums Soon?" 2001.

[76] "Country Briefing—People's Republic of China, Air Force Frontliners to See New Fighter Breed," 1998; *China Daily,* June 1, 2002; Obaid Younossi et al., *Military Jet Engine Acquisition,* 2002, p. 75. On the other hand, the reported development cost of 500 million RMB (US$60 million) for the Kunlun engine was much less than the $800–$900 million (in 2001 dollars) that is average for Western engines. See Obaid Younossi et al., *Military Jet Engine Acquisition,* 2002, p. 73.

[77] Cassie Biggs, "China Looks Abroad to Tap Potential of Aviation Market," 2000.

[78] Huang Qiang, "Will China's Aviation Industry Be Able to Get Out of the Doldrums Soon?" 1999; Li Jiamo, "Design and Manufacturing of Major Aviation Items Should Be Tightly Integrated," 2002.

[79] Shen Bin, "AVIC to Be Split into 2 Groups," 1999.

roughly 90,000 scientists and engineers.[80] Such a comparison is not exact, however. Only 20 percent or so of AVIC I and AVIC II's business consists of aviation-related products and services, probably a lower percentage than for Boeing and Lockheed Martin. Thus, while the total number of engineers employed by AVIC I and AVIC II may be comparable to that of Boeing and Lockheed Martin combined, the number involved in the development and production of aviation products is probably lower.

More important, the quality of the personnel employed by China's aviation industry is questionable. One Chinese analyst notes that, because compensation in China's aviation industry is too low, "large numbers of talented aviation industry personnel" are opting for "the superior working conditions and high wages of [China's] coastal cities and foreign-invested enterprises."[81] Similarly, the general manager of the Chengdu Aircraft Industry Group states that there is a need to raise the quality of product developers in China's aviation industry.[82] Some measures are being taken, however, to improve the treatment of scientific and technical personnel, including raising the salaries of newly hired college graduates, improving living conditions for professional employees, providing supplemental allowances for taking leadership in technical areas or assuming responsibility for scientific research and project development, and awarding prizes for

---

[80] Telephone interview with Ms. Megan Merriman of the Lockheed Martin Corporation and http://www.boeing.com/special/aboutus/overview/overview.htm. Lockheed Martin employs 40,000 scientists and engineers; no comparable numbers were available for Boeing. The number of scientists and engineers working at Boeing was estimated by assuming that they represented the same proportion of Boeing employees as they do of Lockheed Martin employees: 30 percent.

[81] Huang Qiang, "Will China's Aviation Industry Be Able to Get Out of the Doldrums Soon?" 2002. According to this article, in 1999 a new university graduate joining China's aviation industry would make no more than 500 RMB (about $60) a month.

[82] Li Jiamo, "Design and Manufacturing of Major Aviation Items Should Be Tightly Integrated," 2002.

technical personnel who make major contributions.[83] At least some firms now adjust salaries according to performance, and attempts are being made to rationalize the promotion system within enterprises so that managers and staff can be promoted or demoted according to their performance.[84]

Financial Resources

According to Chinese statistics, total expenditures on research and development by "large and medium enterprises" in the "aviation and aerospace equipment manufacturing industry" (*hangkong hangtian qi zhizao ye* 航空航天器制造业)—a category that includes companies that manufacture missiles and spacecraft in addition to aircraft—in 2000 were $199.6 million (at market exchange rates).[85] This amount is significantly lower than that expended by Western aviation manufacturers. Boeing and Lockheed Martin alone, for example, spend a combined total of about US$2.5 billion a year on R&D.[86] The lower wages earned by Chinese researchers make personnel costs somewhat less expensive in China than in the United States, but roughly half of the R&D expenditures in China's manufacturing sector is for equipment, much of which is imported and therefore at least as costly as in the United States.[87] At best, therefore, R&D in China may be half as expensive as in the United States; thus, on a comparable basis,

[83] Xu Zeliang, "CAIG: Using the 'Dumbell-Shaped' Model to Enter the Market," 2002; Huang Qiang, "Will China's Aviation Industry Be Able to Get Out of the Doldrums Soon?" 1999; *Zhongguo hangkong bao,* February 9, 2001, p. 2.

[84] Zhang Hongqing, "Ganwen Lu Zai Hefang: 609 Suo Gaige yu Tiaozheng Zhong de Tansuo yu Chuangxin" ("Dare to Seek a Path Ahead—Explorations and Innovations During the Reform and Adjustment of Institute 609"), *Guofang keji gongye,* No. 1, 2002; Xu Zeliang, "CAIG: Using the 'Dumbell-Shaped' Model to Enter the Market," 2002; *Zhongguo hangkong bao,* February 9, 2001, p. 2.

[85] National Bureau of Statistics, *China Statistical Yearbook 2002*, Beijing, China: China Statistics Press, 2002, pp. 612, 744–745. This figure, however, does not include expenditures by independent research and development institutes.

[86] Telephone interview with Ms. Megan Merriman of the Lockheed Martin Corporation and http://www.boeing.com/special/aboutus/overview/overview.htm. Some portion of this total undoubtedly consists of R&D on nonaerospace products.

[87] National Bureau of Statistics, *China Statistical Yearbook 2002,* 2002, pp. 726–727.

China's research and development expenditures for aerospace are the equivalent of, at most, US$400 million, less than 15 percent of those expenditures of Lockheed Martin and Boeing.

As with other developing countries, however, China has the "follower's" advantage of being able to benefit from the technological progress of other countries. First, Chinese scientists can take advantage of publicly available information about aviation technologies developed abroad. Second, foreign aviation companies are often willing to transfer technologies, particularly relatively mature technologies, to China for a fraction of the cost originally required to develop the technology. As noted above, China is engaged in a substantial number of subcontracting and codevelopment projects with foreign aircraft producers, and in most cases this participation requires the foreign partner to provide the Chinese partner with technology and management know-how. Most of these arrangements are related to civilian aircraft, but much of the equipment and technologies involved are applicable to combat aircraft. There is also direct assistance. The coproduction of Su-27 aircraft in Shenyang, which reportedly involves the presence of 40 Russian technical experts,[88] and the development of the J-10 in Chengdu with Israeli assistance, is transferring to China advanced technology for the development and production of combat aircraft. Nonetheless, technology acquired in this way is not a pure substitute for domestic technology-development efforts: Aviation enterprises still need to assimilate and absorb technologies developed abroad. The head of at least one aviation industry enterprise group in China has noted his company's difficulty in doing so.[89] The estimation of at least some Western observers is that, despite technology transfers from abroad, funding for R&D in China's aviation industry remains inadequate.[90]

---

[88] Yihong Zhang, "Industry Round-Up—Chinese Boost Fighter Production with Su-27 Assembly," 2000.

[89] Xu Zeliang, "CAIG: Using the 'Dumbell-Shaped' Model to Enter the Market," 2002.

[90] Paul Beaver, "Business Focus: China Focuses on Core Aerospace Production," 1998.

Economic Environment

In addition to needing adequate human and financial resources for technological progress to occur, the economic environment must also provide incentives for innovation. Some incentives for innovation and efficiency come from the macroeconomic environment. The civil aviation market in China (and, until recent years, the rest of the world) has been growing rapidly, as a result of which Chinese airlines have been purchasing large numbers of aircraft. This rapid growth has created a strong incentive for China's aviation manufacturers to develop products for China's domestic aviation market.

Most of the growth has been in the area of large passenger aircraft, a market with high barriers to entry that is currently monopolized by foreign manufacturers. But, through the intervention of the Chinese government, the growth of China's civil-aviation market has stimulated technological progress in China's aviation industry. The Chinese government has made the participation of Chinese manufacturers in the production of components for foreign passenger aircraft a condition for access to the Chinese aviation market. Production of components for foreign aircraft companies, in turn, has required (and financed investments in) upgrading the domestic industry's production technologies. In addition, also with government assistance, China's aviation manufacturers are attempting to acquire the capability to produce small regional passenger jets, such as the ARJ21 project, which aims to deliver an indigenously developed 70–90-seat aircraft by 2007, and the Embraer ERJ-series aircraft that Harbin Aircraft Industry will be coproducing. This is a market also currently dominated by foreign manufacturers, but with lower barriers to entry.

The market for military aircraft also appears to be growing in China. Since the late 1990s, and particularly since 1999, there have been signs of a renewed push for military modernization in China. According to the *Shaanxi Daily* (*Shaanxi ribao* 陕西日报), for example, "since the Spring Festival (Chinese New Year) of 1999, the No. 603 Research Institute [responsible for development of bombers, early warning, and transport aircraft] has been operating at full staff every day."[91] Similarly, according to a 2000 article in the Hong Kong magazine *Yazhou zhoukan* (亚洲周刊), "ordnance enterprises in Shaanxi, Sichuan, and Chongqing Municipality," which "had little production assignments several years ago," have "begun to accelerate their production."[92]

Thus, after shrinking dramatically in the early 1980s,[93] China's military-aviation market may now be enjoying a period of significant expansion. Such expansion will tend to stimulate technological development, because longer production runs frequently result in improvements in process engineering and because the potential returns on investment in technological progress will be higher in a rapidly expanding market than in a stagnant market.

Competition

According to most research on technological development, competition among enterprises stimulates technological innovation and efficiency in production. Without competition, firms have little incentive to innovate or to use resources wisely. In a highly competitive environment, by contrast, those firms that do not innovate will tend to be squeezed out. Competition in China's military-aircraft sector appears to be circumscribed. For example, each of the current three major combat aircraft manufacturers produces for a separate market segment. Xian produces bombers (H-6, JH-7), Chengdu produces single-engine light fighters (J-7, J-10, FC-1), and Shenyang produces

---

[91] Lei Biao and Dang Chaohui, "No. 603 Research Institute's Three-Dimensional Design Reaches Advanced World Level," 2001, p. 1.

[92] Wang Chien-min, "Ordnance Factories in Western China Work Overtime to Ensure Logistical Supply," *Yazhou zhoukan*, May 22, 2000, pp. 68–69, in *FBIS* as "PRC Ordnance Factories Creating Logistical Equipment," May 22, 2000.

[93] See Kenneth W. Allen, Glenn Krumel, and Jonathan D. Pollack, *China's Air Force Enters the 21st Century*, 1995, p. 162.

twin-engine heavy fighters (J-8, Su-27).[94] Whether this specialization reflects a bias by the Chinese military-industrial leaders toward particular companies for particular projects or whether it is simply the result of the different comparative advantages of the three manufacturers is unclear. In the past, for example, Shenyang also produced light fighters (the J-5/MiG-17 and J-6/MiG-19), and both Chengdu and Shenyang reportedly have put forward designs for twin-engine stealth fighter aircraft, although Shenyang has apparently been selected to produce this aircraft as well.[95] In any case, all three of these companies are owned by the same holding company, AVIC I, so competition among them is clearly not the same as it would be if they were truly independent companies in a free market.

Also unclear is the extent to which the Chinese military is able to make procurement decisions based purely on the objective merits of a system and not take into account the defense industry's interests. If the military does not have independent decisionmaking authority, then the existence of competing suppliers is irrelevant. The creation of the General Armaments Department in 1998 was clearly designed to increase the military's autonomy from the defense industries in its procurement decisions. One test is the fate of the FC-1: If the PLAAF is compelled to order it to to ensure that there is an export market for the aircraft, then this would indicate that its authority is not circumscribed by other national priorities.

Somewhat more competition exists in the area of noncombat aircraft. As noted above, for example, Harbin, Xi'an, and Shaanxi all produce turboprop transport aircraft, and both the ARJ-21 consortium and Harbin will be producing regional jets. The aircraft produced are of different sizes, however, so competition among these enterprises appears to be, at most, partial.

----

[94] In the past, Harbin and Nanchang also produced combat aircraft (the H-5 light bomber and J-6, respectively), and Nanchang may still be producing the obsolescent Q-5 attack aircraft.

[95] Shen Bin, "AVIC to Be Split into 2 Groups"; Huang Qiang, "Will China's Aviation Industry Be Able to Get Out of the Doldrums Soon?" 1999.

In addition to competition among domestic suppliers, a possible source of competition is from aviation imports. China has imported a number of military aircraft in recent years, including Il-76 jet transports and Su-27 and Su-30 twin-engine fighters from Russia. The Il-76s do not compete with any domestically produced aircraft, however, because China does not produce jet transports. Similarly, it is not clear that the importing of Su-27 and Su-30 fighters has resulted in a reduction of orders for China's indigenous twin-engine fighter, the J-8. Indeed, not only does the producer of the J-8, the Shenyang Aircraft Corporation, not appear to have suffered for the inadequacy of its product, but the producer was chosen as the Chinese company to participate in the coproduction of the competing product, the Su-27. This selection suggests that Shenyang has effectively been granted a monopoly on production of heavy fighters.

Capital Markets, Technology Markets, Labor Markets
Even in Western countries, capital expenditures for technological advances in military aviation do not operate as they do in the private sector. Aviation companies generally do not borrow money from banks or raise it on securities markets to invest in new technologies in the hopes of being able to sell new technologies to the military. Instead, technological development is typically funded by the government through contracts. Thus, competition for government contracts plays the role of capital markets in the development of military-aviation technology.

It is unclear how competition for development funds occurs in China's military-aviation sector. There are multiple aircraft and engine design institutes, for example, but the extent to which they compete for the same design contracts is not known. Traditionally, China's research institutes were completely funded by the state through annual budgetary allocations. Today the institutes apparently still receive partial support through annual budgetary outlays, but they depend on contracts for the remainder of their funding.[96] What is not clear is whether these contracts are awarded on a competitive basis or whether each institute is simply allocated contracts in its area of specialty. The aircraft design institutes tend to be associated with specific airframe manufacturers, for example, so it is possible that a division of labor exists between them that corresponds to the apparent division of labor in airframe manufacturers. If this is the case, then the significance of awarding funding through contracts would be diminished: The research institutes would not need to demonstrate their technological prowess relative to that of other research institutes in order to receive a contract. (The government would, in theory, have the option of withholding the contract entirely if a research institute were perceived as repeatedly underperforming.)

Markets for technologies in China's military-aviation sector appear to be largely nonexistent. After a design is completed, designers reportedly simply hand over the blueprints and design data to the manufacturing enterprise without compensation.[97] Thus, aircraft design institutes have limited financial incentives to develop innovative, practical, or cost-effective designs. As a result, they reportedly tend to focus purely on the completion of a design task, not on satisfying the requirements of the end-users.[98]

Labor markets in China's aviation sector are also problematic, although improving. Traditionally, employees were simply assigned to enterprises by the Ministry of Aviation Industry. Employment was generally for life, and security restrictions could be invoked to prevent employees of China's defense industry from leaving their

---

[96] Li Jiamo, "Design and Manufacturing of Major Aviation Items Should Be Tightly Integrated," 2002; Zhang Hongqing, "Dare to Seek a Path Ahead," 2002; Huang Qiang, "Will China's Aviation Industry Be Able to Get Out of the Doldrums Soon?" 1999.

[97] Huang Qiang, "Will China's Aviation Industry Be Able to Get Out of the Doldrums Soon?" 1999; conversation with senior manager of Western aviation manufacturer's China operations.

[98] Zhang Hongqing, "Dare to Seek a Path Ahead," 2002

employers to seek work elsewhere.[99] Today in China, however, state-owned enterprises are no longer assigned workers, and job seekers are free to find employment wherever they can.

At least some military-aviation companies and research institutes now allow employees to freely join or leave the enterprise, publicly recruit for job openings, consider more than one candidate for each opening, and adjust salaries according to performance.[100] Moreover, the incorporation of China's aviation sector into the social-security system is said to have allowed enterprises to lay off redundant staff; others are reducing staff through early retirements. Some enterprises claim to have been able to eliminate their worst-performing workers.[101] Nonetheless, Chinese observers note that further rationalization of the labor force in China's aviation sector is still needed.[102]

Ownership and Funding Sources

Another source of incentives for improved performance in China's military-aviation sector comes from the form of ownership of the enterprises and their funding sources. Since the survival of a state-owned enterprise depends on the government's continued willingness to fund its activities, which may not be related to its economic performance, such an enterprise generally has less incentive to provide innovative, high-quality, cost-effective products than would a private company. It would also typically be expected to support other agen-

---

[99] Job assignments were typically made in consultation with the enterprises, but the assignee had little say in his or her assignment, except through whatever influence he or she might have by way of personal relationships or other informal means with the individuals involved.

[100] Zhang Hongqing, "Dare to Seek a Path Ahead," 2002; *Zhongguo hangkong bao*, February 9, 2001.

[101] Li Jiamo, "Design and Manufacturing of Major Aviation Items Should Be Tightly Integrated," 2002; Zhang Hongqing, "Dare to Seek a Path Ahead," 2002.

[102] Xu Zeliang, "CAIG: Using the 'Dumbell-Shaped' Model to Enter the Market," 2002; Li Jiamo, "Design and Manufacturing of Major Aviation Items Should Be Tightly Integrated," 2002; Huang Qiang, "Will China's Aviation Industry Be Able to Get Out of the Doldrums Soon?" 1999.

das besides pure profitability, such as maintaining full employment and worker benefits, and managers tend to be appointed and promoted according to criteria other than simply their managerial abilities.

Aviation factories are reportedly now solely responsible for their own finances and no longer receive government subsidies. This situation at least gives them an incentive to maximize revenues.[103] However, because they remain state-owned enterprises, it is unclear who actually absorbs any profits or losses. Similarly, as noted above, AVIC II has created a number of publicly traded subsidiaries, although the government retains a controlling share in them. Some Chinese observers have argued that even after the corporatization of the Ministry of Aerospace Industry in 1993, aviation enterprises have still been run like governmental organizations, without accountability for success or failure.[104]

Similarly, China's aviation research institutes still receive annual funding from the government, but such funding is apparently insufficient to keep the staff fully employed. Thus, the institutes have incentives to compete for additional funding in the form of contracts, although it is unclear whether contracts for aviation products are solely dependent on performance. The reduction of government funding has also caused them to compete for technology-development contracts outside of the aviation sector,[105] but the contribution of these efforts to the development of their aviation-technology capabilities is questionable.

An additional problem associated with the ownership of the design institutes is that the manufacturing companies they ostensibly serve do not own them. Although the design institutes officially

---

[103] Li Jiamo, "Design and Manufacturing of Major Aviation Items Should Be Tightly Integrated," 2002.

[104] Li Jiamo, "Design and Manufacturing of Major Aviation Items Should Be Tightly Integrated," 2002; Huang Qiang, "Will China's Aviation Industry Be Able to Get Out of the Doldrums Soon?" 1999.

[105] Li Jiamo, "Design and Manufacturing of Major Aviation Items Should Be Tightly Integrated," 2002.

belong to the same local holding companies as the associated manufacturing enterprises, they are organizationally separate and have different organizational goals (even though they are often located within
the same compound).[106]

Institutional Infrastructure

In addition to resources and incentives, a supporting institutional
infrastructure is required for technological progress to occur.[107]
Although there are weaknesses in this aspect of China's aviation
sector, an extensive institutional infrastructure currently exists.
China's aviation sector, for example, has a variety of industrial
institutions that can facilitate the exchange of knowledge about the
existence of technologies and market opportunities and organize
industry-wide technology development efforts.

The two large holding companies, AVIC I and AVIC II, are the
most obvious such institutions. Their role includes establishing
industry-wide goals, coordinating activities of their subordinate companies, and managing competition among the subordinate companies.
They also apparently have the power to effect reorganizations among
their subsidiaries. In 2003, AVIC I created the First Aircraft Institute
by merging the Xi'an Aircraft Design and Research Institute with the
Shanghai Aircraft Design and Research Institute; it created the China
Aerial Rescue Equipment Company by merging the China Aviation
Life-Support Institute, Hanjiang Machinery Plant, Hongwei
Machinery Plant, and Hefei Jianghuai Aviation Instrument Factory.
In the same year, an Engine Business Department was created within
AVIC I to "reorganize all the existing engine scientific research and
manufacturing resources and implement professional operating

---

[106] The design institutes and manufacturing enterprises are said to belong to two
fundamentally different "systems" (*xitong*) within AVIC I and AVIC II: The design
institutes belong to the *shiye* system, and the manufacturing enterprises belong to the *qiye*
system. See Li Jiamo, "Design and Manufacturing of Major Aviation Items Should Be
Tightly Integrated," 2002.

[107] See Roger Cliff, *The Military Potential of China's Commercial Technology*, Santa Monica,
Calif.: RAND Corporation, MR-1292-AF, 2001, pp. 54–56.

scheme to develop both aviation engine and turbine engine business" within AVIC I.[108]

Similarly, AVIC I and AVIC II have been instrumental in creating multi-firm consortia for the pursuit of development projects that no one firm would have the capabilities to undertake, such as the ARJ21 regional jet project.[109] Similarly, over 400 enterprises (including some outside of AVIC I/II) reportedly participated in the development of the JH-7, and three organizations (the Number 601 Institute, China Air-to-Air Missile Research Institute, and Shenyang Aircraft Corporation) collaborated in the development of a new air-to-air missile.[110]

Another institution facilitated by the existence of these two holding companies is the "Jinhang Information Project," which includes an industry-wide secure intranet (AVICNET) linking the local area networks and computers of the headquarters, plants, research institutes, and other entities under AVIC I and AVIC II. Its main purpose is to: transmit management information on plans, statistics, scientific research, finance, personnel and labor, and administration; to support the designing and manufacturing of aircraft, engines, and airborne equipment; and to transmit commercial information.[111]

The links that AVIC I and AVIC II provide between their subordinate enterprises are reproduced on a smaller scale by each of the

---

[108] *Guoji hangkong,* February 2004.

[109] "Shanghai to Assemble Feeder Turbo Jets," 2002; *Xinhua,* March 25, 2000, in *FBIS* as "Xinhua Cites Liaowang on China's Aviation Industry," March 25, 2000; *Guoji hangkong,* February 2004.

[110] Guo Yuanfa, "The Painstaking Development of an Ace Aircraft—Report on the Birth of China's All Weather Supersonic Fighter-Bomber 'Flying Leopard'," 1999; "China's First-Ever Five Hits for Five Tries in Test of Air-to-Air Missile," *Qianlong xinwen wang,* September 4, 2002, in *FBIS* as "Qianlong: PRC Air-Air Missile Developed at 601 Institute Successfully Tested," September 4, 2002.

[111] Yang Kebin, "The Jinhang Information Project Comprehensive Information Network: Brief Introduction of AVIC's 'Golden Aviation' Information Network," *Guoji hangkong* (*International Aviation*), December 8, 1997, pp. 8–9, in *FBIS* as "Jinhang Navigation Information System Profiled," December 8, 1997.

major aviation-industry enterprises; the latter are themselves generally holding companies that combine airframe or engine-assembly plants with associated research institutes and local networks of suppliers. Although the fact that these networks are purely local implies a limited choice of suppliers and, thus, limited competition among suppliers, the interfirm links created by stable subcontracting networks can provide a mechanism between enterprises for communicating about technical requirements and capabilities, important for facilitating technological progress.[112] This mechanism works particularly well when all the firms belong to a single holding company, as they do in China.

Another industrial institution is the Chinese Society of Aeronautics and Astronautics (*Zhongguo Hangkong Xuehui* 中国航空学会), which publishes the monthly magazine *Aerospace Knowledge* (*Hangkong zhishi* 航空知识) and performs other functions, such as organizing seminars and conferences.[113] Such organs facilitate the exchange of knowledge within the aerospace sector. A similar institution is the China Aero-Information Center (*Zhongguo Hangkong Xinxi Zhongxin* 中国航空信息中心), which publishes, among other things, the trade journals *International Aviation* (*Guoji hangkong* 国际航), *Aviation News Weekly* (*Hangkong zhoukan* 航空周刊), and *Aviation Engineering and Maintenance* (*Hangkong gongcheng yu weixiu* 航空工程与维修), and undoubtedly provides other information-dissemination services as well. Trade and technical journals are themselves important institutions for the transmission and exchange of information about technologies, management methods, and markets. As of 2000, there were at least 100 such journals in the aerospace sector in China.[114]

---

[112] See, for example, Greg Felker, "Malaysia's Industrial Technology Development: Firms, Policies, and Political Economy," in K. S. Jomo, Greg Felker, Rajah Rasiah, eds., *Industrial Technology Development in Malaysia: Industry and Firm Studies,* New York: Routledge, 1998.

[113] See the Society's website at http://www.csaa.org.cn/.

[114] Dai Longji, Zhang Qisu, and Cai Ronghua, eds., *Index of Core Chinese Journals,* 2000, pp. 626–629.

A final type of industrial institution in China is high-technology-development zones, or "parks." Such zones, which can be funded privately or by a government, gather into a single location technology-development firms working in a number of related areas. They often provide a common infrastructure that no single firm would have the economies of scale to afford, and they sometimes offer consulting and marketing services to their residents as well. There are several hundred such high-technology parks in China. At least one, the Zhongguan Aeronautical Science and Technology Park, was established specifically for firms in the aviation sector.[115]

Research institutions are another part of the infrastructure important to technology development. China has a large number of research institutions involved in aviation-related research. Under AVIC I and AVIC II, 33 research and development institutes are currently engaged in various aspects of aviation-technology development. The results of this research are often published in the various technical journals mentioned above. In addition, many aviation manufacturers have established their own internal research and design institutes.[116] China's defense industries also jointly support seven institutions of higher education, which conduct research and development in aviation-related fields. Similarly, the Chinese Academy of Sciences in Beijing and the National Defense Science and Technology University in Changsha, Hunan, have subordinate institutes and departments involved in the development of aviation-related technologies. Aviation-related research also occurs in the engineering departments of other Chinese institutions of higher education, such as Tsinghua University. Finally, the "863" national technology-development program sponsors research in areas of significance to the aviation sector, such as composite materials.

---

[115] Jin Hang Shuma Keji Gongsi, "On the Establishment of Golden Aviation Digital Science and Technology Corporation," *Zhongguo hangkong bao,* December 29, 2000, p. 1, in *FBIS* as "PRC Information Technology Company Gains High-Level Support," December 29, 2000.

[116] Li Jiamo, "Design and Manufacturing of Major Aviation Items Should Be Tightly Integrated," 2002.

Training institutions are also vital to technological progress, because they represent a primary mechanism for the dissemination of scientific and technological knowledge. The seven institutions of higher education supported by China's defense industry, along with the science and engineering departments of National Defense Science and Technology University and other universities in China, provide scientists and engineers for the aviation sector. In addition, a number of other organizations are engaged in graduate-level training and education in aviation science and technology, including the research institutes under AVIC I and AVIC II and the Chinese Academy of Sciences.

What is unclear is whether a network of non-degree-granting industrial-training organizations exists that provides short-term training in specific applications and techniques or whether such training is provided strictly within individual enterprises. If such organizations do not exist, this would be disadvantageous for China's aviation sector, because independent training firms are able to much more easily keep up with and disseminate state-of-the-art technology than are individual manufacturing firms, which are focused on production.

China's aviation sector also appears to be developing a network of technology consulting and services companies. Such companies facilitate bringing new technologies to firms and supporting the technologies' implementation. In many industrial sectors in China, the reduction of government funding for industrial research institutes since the 1980s has caused these institutes to engage in such activities (on a contract basis) as a way of raising revenue. This phenomenon may be occurring in China's aviation sector, as well, as evidenced by the emergence of at least some technology consulting firms in the aviation sector.[117]

Government institutions involved in setting national technical standards, standardized research and development procedures, and

---

[117] One such firm is AVIC Information Technology Co. LTD (AVICIT). See its website at http://www.avicit.com/.

testing bureaus are also important supporting institutions for technological progress. China has aviation design regulations and a number of organizations that fulfill the role of government testing bureaus. These include the Number 623 Institute, which conducts "static intensity tests," and various flight-test institutes.[118]

Conclusions

China's military-aviation industry is undergoing important changes in structure, operations and capabilities. Prior to the late 1990s, all of the fixed-wing aircraft it produced, and their major subsystems, were essentially improved versions of 1950s Soviet technology. Since the late 1990s, China has begun producing progressively more-advanced aircraft and key aviation subsystems. The JH-7 fighter-bomber is comparable in performance to aircraft that entered service in the 1960s, 1970s, and 1980s in the United States, Russia, and Europe, and represents China's first completely indigenous airframe design. The Su-27s being assembled in Shenyang, although of Russian design and consisting largely of imported components, are highly capable fourth-generation aircraft. The Chengdu J-10, which may now be entering production, is also expected to be of fourth-generation performance and is primarily an indigenous development (albeit with Israeli guidance and design assistance).

A similar story holds for major subsystems, such as engines. China has gone from producing improved versions of Soviet turbojets to the indigenously designed Kunlun, and it may soon be producing an indigenously developed high-performance turbofan engine, the WS-10.

China's rate of improvement in the military-aviation sector is noteworthy. In the space of a decade, China's aviation industry has gone from producing second-generation fighters to being on the verge

---

[118] Huang Tung, "Successful Test-Flight of New Flying Leopard Fighter Bomber JH-7A," 2002; *Guoji hangkong*, February 2004.

of producing domestically developed fourth-generation aircraft. To be sure, this progress still leaves China a generation behind the United States, which is now beginning production of a fifth-generation fighter, the F-22.

Less dramatic but nonetheless significant have been China's improvements in rotary-wing aircraft. Since beginning license-production of the Dauphin 2 in the early 1980s, China's aviation industry can now domestically produce most or all of the components for the Dauphin 2 and two other Eurocopter designs. China's aviation industry has also begun producing indigenously developed variants of the Dauphin and licensed versions of the Arriel turboshaft engine. Thus, China's aviation industry now has the capability to produce relatively modern multi-role helicopters and their engines.

China has yet to produce an indigenously designed helicopter, but the Z-10 is under development and could enter production in the next few years. It will serve as a bellwether of the improvements in China's helicopter design and production capabilities.

Future Directions and Challenges

As in other defense-industrial sectors examined in this study, progress in China's military-aviation industry is mixed and limitations persist. There remain important gaps in China's military-aviation R&D and production capabilities that will not soon be filled. In particular, China produces no long-range heavy bombers, modern fighter-bombers (such as the F-15E or Su-30), jet transports, stealth aircraft, or purpose-built attack helicopters. Any programs under way to fill these gaps are only in their very formative stages.

Much of China's progress has been a result of the "latecomer's (or "follower's") advantage" and access to foreign aviation designs and technologies that have already been developed abroad. Consequently, China is able to acquire such advanced aviation technologies more rapidly and less expensively than through indigenous development. This approach is not without its challenges: China must still make efforts to master and assimilate these technologies—a step that has been problematic in the past. In addition, most foreign companies are unwilling to provide China with their most advanced "core" technologies, especially those with direct military applications. On the other hand, Russia and Israel have provided China with modern military-aviation technologies, and Western firms, such as Boeing, Airbus, GE, Pratt & Whitney, Rolls-Royce, and other Western aviation manufacturers are transferring increasingly more-sophisticated civilian-aviation manufacturing technologies to China.

Nonetheless, as the capabilities of China's aviation industry begin to approach those of the rest of the world, the latecomer's advantage will no longer obtain. In particular, it is unclear whether the capabilities of the Russian aviation industry will advance significantly over their current level in the foreseeable future. Similarly, in the absence of an indigenous combat-aircraft program, Israel is unlikely to be able to provide China with state-of-the-art aviation technologies outside of such key subsystems as avionics.[119] Thus, further improvements in the capabilities of China's aviation industry will increasingly depend on its indigenous capacity for technological innovation.

China's aviation sector continues to face a number of challenges. Much of its talent has left China's inland state-owned aviation companies for private or foreign-invested enterprises located in China's coastal regions, and recent college graduates are even more reluctant to accept low-paying jobs in remote regions. Competition in China's aviation sector, either among the major airframe and engine manufacturers or among component suppliers, still appears to be limited and managed by the state. Although some AVIC I and AVIC II subsidiaries are listed on the Hong Kong or Chinese stock markets, major military airframe and engine producers, which remain wholly state-owned, lack this advantage. The aviation industry's research and design institutes largely remain organizationally and fiscally separate

---

[119] Conversely, a number of European leaders and governments have indicated that they would like to resume weapon sales to China, a development that could compensate for China's loss of Russia as a technology source. See "EU May End China Arms Sales Ban," Associated Press, January 24, 2004; Craig S. Smith, "France Makes Headway in Push to Permit Arms Sales to China," *New York Times,* January 27, 2004; Philip P. Pan, "U.S. Pressing EU to Uphold Arms Embargo Against China," *Washington Post,* January 31, 2004.

from the production enterprises, limiting both knowledge flows between the two types of organization and whatever incentives the institutes have to develop practical, production-feasible designs.

None of these shortcomings is unique to China. Even in the United States competition in the military-aviation sector hardly resembles that of a free market. Political considerations and concerns about maintaining multiple engine and airframe suppliers result in contracts being awarded according to criteria other than purely performance and cost. Similarly, highly capable aviation companies in many countries are at least partially state-owned. The Soviet Union built a formidable military-aircraft industry even though its design institutes and production enterprises were also organizationally separate. And it too lacked a network of training and technology consulting and service companies. Nonetheless, the combination of these limitations for a developing country such as China represents a major challenge.

The government's resources devoted to military aviation have increased in recent years, but they in no way approach those of the United States or the level that the Soviet Union devoted to it during the Cold War. And, unlike other countries with fewer resources to devote to aviation, such as France or Britain, China lacks their highly developed economies and relatively unrestricted access to the military technologies of allies. Finally, more so than any of these countries, the aviation sector in China has to compete with far higher-paying, more-prestigious, and higher-quality-of-life industries for the most talented workers and managers.

Consequently, while the technological gap between China's military-aviation industry and that of the most advanced countries will likely continue to close in coming years, China will certainly continue to lag behind these countries. The capabilities of domestically produced military aircraft will not begin to rival those of the United States or other advanced military powers unless further fundamental reforms are implemented in the near future. One such reform would be the introduction of true competition in the form of open bidding for R&D and production contracts for major aviation platforms. A second would be the integration of design institutes with production enterprises.[120] A third would be the privatization of China's major airframe and component manufacturers. Any of these reforms would provide a boost to the capacity of China's military-aviation industry to design and produce more-capable aircraft in the future.

---

[120] As noted early in this chapter, this process is already occurring to a certain extent in China. Some design institutes have been absorbed by manufacturing enterprises, although many have resisted such integration; many manufacturing enterprises are establishing their own internal design institutes and test facilities; and some research institutes are expanding into production. See Li Jiamo, "Design and Manufacturing of Major Aviation Items Should Be Tightly Integrated," 2002.

CHAPTER FIVE

"The Digital Triangle": A New Defense-Industrial Paradigm?

The Chinese military is in the midst of a C^4ISR (command, control, communications, computers, and intelligence) revolution, characterized by the wholesale shift to digital, secure communications via fiber-optic cable, satellite, microwave, and encrypted high-frequency radio.

The pace and depth of these advances cannot be explained by traditional Chinese defense-industrial reforms. Instead, they originate in a paradigm shift that could be called the "digital triangle," the three vertices of which are (1) China's booming commercial information-technology companies, (2) the state R&D institute and funding infrastructure, and (3) the military. The links among these three vertices are of long standing, given that telecommunications and information technology in China were originally developed under the auspices of the military, and the commercial relationships with state and military research institutes remain important.

The digital triangle approach resembles a classic techno-nationalist strategy à la Japan, with high-level bureaucratic coordination and significant state funding. But it also has the attributes of market-based, dynamic, nimble, and internationally oriented private enterprises. The techno-nationalist strategy has been attempted by the defense-industrial system in China in the past; that it is currently successful in information technology and shipbuilding may be driven more by the integration of those sectors into the global R&D and production chain than by China's technological strengths per se.

The digital triangle represents an important evolution in the military's strategy for telecommunications development. Under the previous model, such companies as the PLA General Staff Department's China Electronic Systems Engineering Corporation (CESEC) built commercial networks and served as a front company for the acquisition of technology for the military. Private Chinese companies such as Huawei, by contrast, represent the new digital-triangle model, whereby the military, other state actors, and their numbered research institutes help fund and staff commercially oriented firms that are designated "national champions," receive lines of credit from state banks, supplement their R&D funding with directed 863 money, and actively seek to build global market share. The military, for its part, benefits as a favored customer and research partner. Companies such as CESEC continue to exist, but they now serve as systems integrators of technologies from multiple outside vendors.

Most of the major Chinese IT and electronics companies are genuinely commercial in orientation, seeking to capture domestic and eventually international market share. If we compare these firms with traditional defense industries, the new IT companies carry none of the oft-cited structural burdens of the large, inefficient state-owned entities in the defense sector, such as bloated workforces, antiquated plant infrastructure, and lack of capital and advanced-technology inputs. These IT enterprises enjoy (1) new facilities in dynamic locales, (2) a lean, high-tech workforce motivated by market-based incentives and stock options, and (3) infusions of near state-of-the-art foreign technology, thanks to the irresistible siren song of China's huge IT market, which encourages foreign companies to transfer cutting-edge technology for the promise of market access.

The strong foundation under these dynamic enterprises, however, is the state research institute and R&D funding system. For defense-related work, these units include numbered research institutes under the Ministry of Information Industry, the PLA General Staff Department, and other defense-industrial entities, funded with money from the Ministry of Science and Technology's 863 Program (described later in this chapter), as well as revenue from their own commercial ventures.

Through this system, the military supports the *civilianization*—the use of civilian entities to conduct military work because they are more capable than the military—of military technical research, becoming an R&D partner and privileged consumer of products. This civilianization is the real transformational mechanism at the heart of the digital triangle, because it introduces commercial and profit-seeking motives as engines of change to improve China's overall technological level, thereby indirectly benefiting the military's IT levels. This synergy is further facilitated by two critical technology trends: (1) the growing use of COTS (commercial-off-the-shelf) technology, such as computer network switches and routers, for military communications, which allows the PLA to directly benefit from the globally competitive output of China's commercial IT companies; and (2) the rise of China as a locus for global fabless integrated-circuit production,[1] which potentially permits the PLA access to the advanced microelectronics that lay at the heart of modern military sensors and weapon systems.

Of these two trends, COTS, particularly in telecommunications equipment, has provided the greatest early dividends to the PLA, as evidenced by the expansion of its fiber-optic computer networks. Microelectronics, by contrast, may be slower in advancement, since the component designs are generally more military-specific and, therefore, cannot directly benefit from global COTS technology developments. At the same time, the increasing sophistication of China's commercial semiconductor fabrication facilities ("fabs") provide the base production capacity necessary for the military to implement design ideas in a secure, domestic environment.

---

[1] A *fabless semiconductor company* specializes in the design and sale of hardware devices implemented on semiconductor chips. It achieves an advantage by outsourcing the fabrication of the devices to a specialized semiconductor manufacturer, called a *semiconductor foundry,* or *fab.* Fabless companies may concentrate their research and development resources on the end market, without being required to invest resources in staying current in semiconductor manufacturing technology. For this reason, they are also known as IP firms, because their primary product is intellectual property. See the definition at http://en.wikipedia.org/wiki/Fabless_semiconductor_company.

For the PLA, the digital triangle offers great gains in some crucial information-technology areas, but the operational impact is uncertain. The introduction of secure communications, for instance, has likely improved communications and operational security, but the influence of these systems on actual warfighting performance cannot be known with absolute certainty until there is a military conflict.

This chapter examines the relationship between China's IT sector broadly defined, the state R&D base, and the military, drawing macro-level implications of these new trends for overall Chinese defense modernization. It is presented in three sections. The first section introduces the relationship between information technology and defense modernization, outlines the structure of the IT sector, and compares the features of the Chinese information-technology sector with other defense-industrial sectors. The second section outlines the strategies, policies, and organizations that make up the "digital triangle," describing the salient aspects of its three vertices (commercial IT companies, state R&D institutes and funding programs, and the military). The third section assesses the implications of this phenomenon for military modernization and reform of the defense-industrial base as a whole.

The IT Sector and Chinese Defense Modernization: The New Paradigm

Relationship Between Information Technology and Defense Modernization

Information technology is now universally recognized as the core of future warfare, sometimes labeled the Revolution in Military Affairs (RMA). In both theoretical and practical terms, the Chinese military has shown a keen interest in the RMA, viewing the approach as an asymmetric strategy to deal with challenges posed by possible conflicts with Taiwan and the United States and its allies. On the theoretical side, PLA scholars have written extensively about the RMA and its implications for China, and these writings in recent years have become increasingly integrated with an ongoing doctrinal revolution and rapidly expanding technical research and development.

On the practical side, the first implementation of the RMA in China has been the PLA's wholesale modernization of its C⁴ISR infrastructure. The military's unexpectedly rapid and broad evolution from Morse code and high-frequency radio to fiber-optic cables, digital microwave, and satellite communications has reportedly improved operational and communications security in the armed forces, and it holds out the promise of achieving synergy with future generations of conventional weapons.[2]

The operating principles behind this transformation were outlined in a 1997 survey article in *Liberation Army Daily,* and they mirror the general information-technology revolution under way in China proper: (1) analog technology to digital technology, (2) electric cables to fiber-optic cables, (3) mechano-electrical switches to program-controlled switches, (4) single-function terminals to multi-function terminals, (5) single-tasking networks to multi-tasking networks, and (6) manual operation to automated and intelligent-network management.[3]

A 1993 *Liberation Army Daily* article was more specific, asserting that the PLA was moving toward a C⁴ISR system based mainly on fiber-optic cables, digital microwave, and satellite communications.[4] By 2000, some additional transformative principles had been added to the strategy, reflecting the growing maturity of China's information-technology sector: (1) stationary telecommunications technology to mobile telecommunications technology; (2) ground and air

---

[2] James C. Mulvenon, "Chinese C4I Modernization: An Experiment in Open Source Analysis," in James C. Mulvenon and Andrew N. D. Yang, eds., *A Poverty of Riches: New Challenges and Opportunities in PLA Research,* Santa Monica, Calif.: RAND Corporation, CF-189-NSRD, 2003.

[3] Cheng Gang and Li Xuanqing, "Military Telecommunications Building Advances Toward Modernization with Giant Strides," *Liberation Army Daily,* July 17, 1997, in *FBIS,* August 20, 1997; and Li Xuanqing and Ma Xiaochun, "Armed Forces' Communications Become 'Multidimensional'," *Xinhua Domestic Service,* July 16, 1997.

[4] *Liberation Army Daily,* August 9, 1993.

telecommunications technology to space telecommunications technology; (3) support telecommunications technology to command and control technology and information warfare technology; (4) narrowband telecommunications network to a wideband telecommunications network; (5) regional or trans-regional telecommunications network into a global telecommunications network; (6) specialized military telecommunications network into a telecommunications network formed by both specialized networks and public networks; and (7) military telecommunications network into a military information network.[5] The military information network envisions the fusion of traditional telecommunications networks with advanced computer networks.

Such an ambitious transformation could only be achieved with support from the highest levels of the political leadership and the dedicated efforts of the state industrial base and R&D infrastructure. On the political side, China's current leaders have consistently recognized the importance of modernizing the military's C[4]ISR systems. A former Minister of Electronics Industry, China's former Chinese Communist Party General-Secretary and current Central Military Commission Chairman, Jiang Zemin, has emphasized that "electronics is of crucial importance to economic construction and national defense communications."[6] In summarizing the experiences of the Gulf War after 1991, Jiang Zemin went further, asserting that "military electronics has a bearing on national security" and "must be given first place."[7] At the time of the Gulf War, however, the defense-industrial electronics sector was not yet producing state-of-the-art or even relatively modern equipment, compared with Western counterparts, and China's commercial information-technology sector was virtually nonexistent.

---

[5] Zhang Fuyou, "With Joint Efforts Made by Army and People, Military Telecommunications Makes Leap Forward," *Liberation Army Daily,* September 27, 2000, p. 9.

[6] Zhang Xiaojun, "Modern National Defense Needs Modern Signal Troops," *National Defense,* No.10, October 15, 1995, pp. 20–21.

[7] Zhang Xiaojun, "Modern National Defense Needs Modern Signal Troops," 1995, pp. 20–21.

As we shall see in the next section, the Chinese system was about to make a significant leap forward, thanks to a new alliance between state science and technology funding, state research and development institutes, and a nascent commercial information-technology apparatus.

The IT Sector as a Defense-Industrial Sector?

The PLA's C⁴ISR modernization is being facilitated by China's information-technology sector. Not always linked with military modernization, the IT sector is instead perceived by some outsiders as a primarily commercial sector affiliated with such non-defense-industrial ministries as the Ministry of Information Industry.

While it is true that the Chinese IT industry is commercially oriented, the research and financial apparatus underlying its success derives significantly from state research and development institutes, including those affiliated with the defense industry and military units. In this sense, the information-technology sector, particularly those firms supplying finished C⁴ISR and related products to the PLA, could be seen as a new defense-industrial sector in China, although differing significantly from its historical counterparts.

The traditional defense sectors in China are made up of former military-industrial ministries related to ordnance, aviation, space, shipbuilding, nuclear weapons, and electronics production. Following two and a half decades of defense-industrial reform (since the early 1980s), each of these ministries has been transformed into corporations, which concentrate on selling civilian and military-related output to both domestic and international markets. These corporations, whose constituent elements are known as "defense-industrial enterprises" operate within a chain of command that proceeds vertically from the enterprises, through the ministerial leadership, to the government's State Council, headed by the Premier. Unlike some countries in which the defense-industrial system is subordinate to or part of the military bureaucracy, however, it is important to note that Chinese defense-industrial corporations are completely distinct from the Chinese People's Liberation Army.

The Chinese military is composed of combat and support units, including the four General Departments (Staff, Political, Logistical, Armament), the Military Regions and Districts, and the active-duty and reserve forces of the Army, Navy, Air Force, and Strategic Rocket Forces. For many years, the Commission for Science, Technology, and Industry for National Defense (COSTIND) served as a military entity that coordinated R&D and procurement relationships between the PLA and China's defense-industrial enterprises. As noted in earlier chapters, much changed during the reforms initiated in 1998. COSTIND became a strictly civilian entity, functioning as the administrative and regulatory point of contact for the defense industry.

As discussed at great length in the literature, the Chinese defense-industrial system has long suffered from a wide-ranging set of structural problems that have impeded development of modern military equipment.[8] Among its impediments, the system is beset by antiquated plant infrastructure, a bloated workforce, lack of capital, and a dearth of advanced technology inputs. Some of the more-obvious remedies to these impediments—asset privatization, layoffs, relocation of plants from the remote Third Line to the coastal areas, or even bankruptcy—have been stymied by myriad political and economic obstacles, all subsumed under the rubric of maintaining "social stability."[9]

The more-limited strategies of gradual defense conversion have failed, as has the riskier method of steal, acquire, reverse engineer, and produce. In perhaps the most scathing indictment of all, the military, after years of waiting for the F-10 fighter and other systems,

---

[8] For an excellent historical survey of the literature on Chinese defense industries, see Bates Gill, "Chinese Military-Technical Development: The Record for Western Assessments, 1979–1999," in James C. Mulvenon and Andrew N. D. Yang, eds., *Seeking Truth from Facts: A Retrospective on Chinese Military Studies in the Post-Mao Era,* Santa Monica, Calif.: RAND Corporation, CF-160-CAPP, 2001.

[9] Barry Naughton, "The Third Front: Defense Industrialization in the Chinese Interior," *China Quarterly,* No. 115, September 1988, pp. 351–386.

filled short-term capability gaps in the 1990s with purchases of systems from Russia and other providers.

Dynamics of the IT Industry Structure

In analyzing the dynamics of the IT sector, it is first necessary to divide the defense portion of the IT sector into two related but distinct categories. The first includes those subsectors providing the PLA with commercial-off-the-shelf IT systems, such as routers, switches, and computers, which have become increasingly central to the digitization of the U.S. military. Key companies in this category include such "red chips" (the Chinese equivalent of U.S. blue-chip companies) as Huawei, Zhongxing, Datang, Julong, and the Wuhan Research Institute, all of which are private companies spun off from state research institutes that enjoy national-champion preferences within the system. They are marked by new facilities in dynamic locales, such as southern and eastern China, a high-tech workforce, and infusions of foreign technology. These firms are not obligated to provide a social safety net for thousands of unemployable workers and their families in rural areas. Instead, they hire and fire staff using market-based incentives and stock options.

In terms of strategies for success, these companies have adopted the winning formulas of the United States, Japan, and Taiwan, gaining market entry and market share from established multinationals through lower labor cost, better service, and rates of reinvestment of revenue into R&D unheard of in other Chinese industrial sectors. As a result, 22.9 percent (nearly US$108.5 billion) of China's $474 billion in foreign trade in 2000 was electronics-related, and this share is expected to increase to US$260–$270 billion in 2005.[10] In the first six months of 2001, production of switches was up 139.2 percent, to 40.8 million lines; production of mobile phones was up 70.5 percent, to 28.79 million handsets (including export of 8.821 million handsets); production of PCs was up 9.5 percent, to 2.54 million

---

[10] United States Information Technology Office, *Mid 2001 Report: China's International Trade and Information Technology Sector,* Beijing, China, July 2001. Available online at www.usito.org.

computers; and production of integrated circuits was up 59.3 percent, to 135 million chips.

Aside from hardware, China has more than 2,200 software companies, generating annual sales of nearly US$3.6 billion. Beijing's recent accession to the World Trade Organization (WTO) is expected to accelerate this pace of development even further, as more foreign companies, including powerhouse Taiwanese firms, transfer their information-technology production bases to the mainland.

The second category of IT-sector enterprises encompasses those subsectors with less-viable commercial orientation, including many of the developers of specialized defense electronics found in radars and specific weapon subsystems. The research institutes that form the backbone of this category, and the commercial front companies associated with them, tend to look more like traditional defense-industrial entities, with the same structural problems: They are not able to exploit market dynamics as easily as their commercial counterparts, since the defense-electronics sector cannot leverage market access to acquire commercial state-of-the-art know-how and technology. Nor is there an attractive export dynamic, such as that on the commercial side, since PRC defense electronics cannot compete with Western equivalents and also confront proliferation issues (e.g., illicit technology transfer abroad) not relevant to COTS. Instead, many times they were forced to fall back upon less-successful, slower, and riskier approaches, cobbling together internally funded research, espionage, and legally ambiguous spin-on from related technologies. More recently, the shift in global integrated-circuit (IC) production to China has enabled new access to near-state-of-the-art design and production technology, permitting the defense-electronics sector to benefit from some of the same dynamics as its telecommunications counterparts.

Ironically, both IT-sector categories trace their heritage to the defense industry and the PLA, providing the key bridge between commercial trends and military modernization. The Chinese information-technology base originated in such state ministries as the Ministry of Posts and Telecommunications and the Ministry of Electronics Industry, both of which trace their origins to the PLA.[11] In both cases, the links survive in the form of relationships between state R&D institutes under the Ministry of Information Industry, defense-industrial corporations, and the PLA's General Staff Department.

Using the irresistible siren song of China's IT market as a lure for cutting-edge foreign technology, China's IT companies, state R&D institutes and R&D funding programs, and the military form a potent digital triangle, combining the significant resources of the state with the market-driven dynamism of the commercial sector. In some sectors, particularly those centered on COTS, this arrangement has succeeded where other defense-industrial reform paradigms, including reverse engineering and conversion, have failed. The digital triangle is seen by the Chinese as an attractive model for reform of other defense-industrial sectors. Progress on the defense-electronics side has been less impressive and less comprehensive across all technologies, but still positive in key areas, such as semiconductors, which form the heart of modern defense electronics. The remainder of the chapter analyzes the strategy, structure, process, and implications of the digital triangle.

The Digital Triangle: A New Model of Defense Procurement

Strategy and Policy

In broad terms, the digital triangle is facilitated by a combination of a techno-nationalist development strategy, high-level bureaucratic coordination, and significant fiscal support from national five-year

---

[11] During the civil war (1940–1949), telecommunications was placed under military control. After liberation, the Ministry of Posts and Telecommunications was founded, but most of its senior leaders in the early years were former high-ranking military officers, including the father of Chinese telecommunications, General Wang Zheng. This link lasted until the Cultural Revolution in 1966, when the ministry collapsed.

plans and state science and technology (S&T) budget programs, such as the 863 Program.

The strategy underlying the triangle derives from Deng Xiaoping's 16-character guiding principles for defense-industrial change, summarized by Evan Feigenbaum as "integration of military and civilian-side activities in each plant, the need not to lose sight of latent military requirements as the focus of the sector shifted to the civilian side; attention to the maintenance of military capability during the transformation, and the use of the civilian to nurture the military."[12] Deng's rationale for this fundamental shift, according to the author, was to change the system in such a way that high-technology achievements would be judged not purely by their national defense benefits but "according to the ease with which they might be commercialized and industrialized."[13] While the implementation of this strategy in some traditional defense-industrial sectors, such as ordnance, resulted in the conversion of military-production capacity to civilian production (tanks to trucks or civilian explosives) with little hope of reversing the transition, the lack of a large, pre-existing industrial base in certain new technology realms (e.g., routers) allowed the information-technology sector to sidestep many of the structural pitfalls.

The digital triangle was also helped by later modifications of the strategy that focused on technology development rather than industrial production. In 1986, the military S&T apparatus was ordered to shift its focus to national economic construction, on the premise that it was "easier to build a military-technical base on the corpus of the national S&T base rather than the other way around."[14] By 1989, the previous focus on dual-use technology was supplemented by a call

---

[12] Evan Feigenbaum, "The Military Transforms China: The Politics of Strategic Technology from the Nuclear to the Information Age," Dissertation Manuscript, Palo Alto, Calif.: Stanford University, August 1997, p. 309.

[13] Evan Feigenbaum, "The Military Transforms China: The Politics of Strategic Technology from the Nuclear to the Information Age," 1997, p. 347.

[14] Evan Feigenbaum, "The Military Transforms China: The Politics of Strategic Technology from the Nuclear to the Information Age," 1997, p. 372.

for the explicit "civilianization of military technology itself," beginning with the commercialization of research and development institutes.[15] To this end, a State Council "Outline on Medium and Long-Term Science and Technology Development (1990-2000-2010)" recommended the implementation of all "necessary steps to remove the existing institutional barriers to facilitate the transfer process."[16] Because of the fungibility of the technology, the IT sector was uniquely placed to exploit this new trend by commercializing portions of the state R&D base for the benefit of both the civilian economy and military procurement. The resulting digital triangle is presented in Figure 5.1. Each of its vertices is described in the following subsections.

Vertex No. 1: Commercial IT Companies. The two most important categories of Chinese IT firms, particularly in dealings with foreign multinationals, are telecommunications equipment and electronics. Publicly, the major players in telecommunications—Huawei, Datang, Zhongxing, and Great Dragon (Julong)—appear to be independent, private-sector actors. By contrast, many of the electronics firms are grouped under ostensibly commercially oriented conglomerates, such as China Electronics Corporation. However, one does not need to dig too deeply to discover that many of these electronics companies are the public face for, sprang from, or are significantly engaged in joint research with state research institutes under the Ministry of Information Industry, defense-industrial corporations, or the military. Indeed, each of the "four tigers" of the Chinese telecommunications equipment market (Huawei, Zhongxing, Datang,

---

[15] Evan Feigenbaum, "The Military Transforms China: The Politics of Strategic Technology from the Nuclear to the Information Age," 1997, p. 349.

[16] Wang Shouyun, "Conversion, Dual Use, and Transfer of Technology," in Qian Haiyan, ed., *Restructuring the Military Industry: Conversion for the Development of the Civilian Economy,* Beijing: China Association for the Peaceful Use of Military Industrial Technology and the United Nations Department of Development Support and Management Services, 1993, pp. 105–107.

Figure 5.1
The Three Vertices of the Digital Triangle

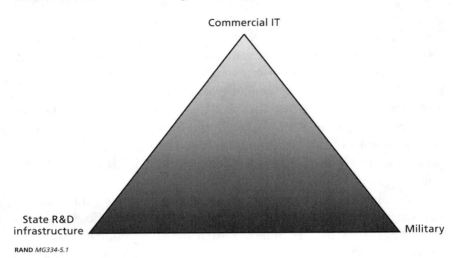

RAND *MG334-5.1*

and Julong) originated from a different part of the existing state tele-communications research and development infrastructure, often from the internal telecommunications apparatus of different ministries or the military. These connections provide channels for personnel transfers, commercialization of state-sponsored R&D ("spin-off"), and militarization of commercial R&D ("spin-on").

Huawei Shenzhen Technology Company. Huawei was founded in 1988 by Ren Zhengfei, a former director of the PLA General Staff Department's Information Engineering Academy, which is responsible for telecom research for the Chinese military. Huawei maintains deep ties with the Chinese military, which serves a multi-faceted role as an important customer, as well as Huawei's political patron and research and development partner. Both the government and the military tout Huawei as a national champion, and the company is currently China's largest, fastest-growing, and most impressive tele-communications-equipment manufacturer.

Huawei is the main supplier to telecommunication giants China Telecom and China Unicom, and one of the world's ten-largest producers, employing more than 22,000 people.[17] The company's sales have grown dramatically, increasing from US$350 million in 1996 to more than US$3 billion in 2002. Its main products include switching systems, intelligent networks, Synchronous Digital Hierarchy (SDH) transmission networks, wireless, datacoms, broadband integrated services (B-ISDN), power supplies, and free-space optical systems. Company sources claim that "only" 1 percent of sales involved military customers, although this likely deflated number still represents more than $30 million per year in equipment sales and service.[18]

Huawei has also become the most successful Chinese exporter of equipment, entering international markets in 1996. According to one source, "For the future, Huawei wants to be the Cisco of the PRC, but also is ambitious to become a global player."[19] The company is rapidly penetrating Africa, Russia, India, and many other areas ignored by Western telcos. While foreign sales still make up a relatively small percentage of its total sales, exports are its fastest-growing account. Out of total sales of US$1.5 billion in 1999, only US$100 million (7 percent) came from international markets. This amount increased to US$300 million in 2000, representing 12 percent of the total sales figure of US$2.5 billion. This number is expected to continue to rise, reaching 20 percent of sales in 2001 and 40 percent of sales by 2005.

Huawei's foreign strategy has been helped by its having sales offices in 45 countries. In Asia, Huawei has won major public contracts in countries such as Thailand and Pakistan. Huawei also enjoys extensive partnerships with U.S. companies in Alabama, Alaska, Arizona, California, Georgia, Hawaii, Illinois, Iowa, Kansas, Maryland,

---

[17] Bruce Gilley, "Huawei's Fixed Line to Beijing," *Far Eastern Economic Review*, December 28, 2000–January 4, 2001.

[18] Interviews in Beijing suggest that the real number is between 5 and 6 percent.

[19] Bruce Gilley, "Huawei's Fixed Line to Beijing," 2000–2001.

Massachusetts, Minnesota, Missouri, Nebraska, New Hampshire, New Jersey, New York, North Carolina, Ohio, Oklahoma, Oregon, Pennsylvania, Texas, and Wyoming.

Huawei's secret in the beginning years was very similar to the formula used by the Japanese in the 1960s and the Koreans in the 1970s: Obtain foreign technology at first, then sink significant amounts of money into original R&D to keep up with the competition. Huawei did reverse engineer some Lucent products in the beginning, but it currently reinvests at least 10 percent of revenue back into R&D each year, and it maintains an extensive domestic research base. It also attracts the top graduates of China's high-tech universities, even though the starting salary is 20 percent less than that of Cisco. Graduates are instead drawn by the nationalist call of an indigenous company, and the loss of salary is somewhat offset by the internal shareholding arrangements of an employee-owned company. Recent evidence suggests that these benefits are not sufficient to keep employees loyal for life: A large segment of Huawei's senior management defected from the company in early 2001, to start a new network equipment provider named Harbour Networks.

To increase its internal strength and expand its shares in developing foreign markets, Huawei is also rapidly expanding its relationships with foreign companies, a partial list of which includes Texas Instruments, Motorola, IBM, Intel, Agere, ALTERA, Sun, Microsoft, and NEC. According to an Indian IT headhunter, Huawei is particularly adept at poaching people from Cisco/India, paying the highest salaries in the region. Huawei is also the only telco joint venture (JV) in Russia, partnered with a company (Beto) that used to be involved in missile production. The company also maintains close sales and research relationships with countries in Eastern Europe, including Lithuania and Bulgaria. Recent interviews suggest that the company is having some financial difficulties, mainly as a result of expanding too quickly and pursuing a global array of product lines rather than specializing in niche areas.[20]

Zhongxing. Originating from the Number 691 electronics factory under the China Aerospace Industry Corporation, Zhongxing Telecom (ZTE) has grown to become one of China's top equipment producers. In 2000, ZTE generated revenue of 10.2 billion RMB. Headquartered in Shenzhen, Zhongxing is also staffed by a high percentage of employees with advanced degrees. In 2000, the company employed over 10,000 professionals, 86 percent of whom possessed a bachelor's degree or above; 300 of whom have a doctorate or post-doctorates, and 2,000 of whom hold master's degrees.

Zhongxing also conducts its own indigenous R&D, currently holding over 300 patents or pending patents. The company is also committed to a nationwide sales-and-support structure, maintaining 26 sales offices, 26 customer-service centers, and seven private network-engineering offices. The company has set up 11 research and development organizations in Beijing, Chongqing, Nanjing, Shanghai, Shenzhen, and Xi'an, as well as numerous foreign JV labs. Zhongxing has also developed a significant number of research-exchange institutions with both domestic and foreign partners, managing joint laboratories with Texas Instruments, Motorola, Beijing University of Post and Telecommunication, and the University of Electronic Science and Technology (also referred to as MII No. 29).

In terms of specific telecoms sectors, Zhongxing has expanded beyond its original focus on switching systems to manufacture access, transmission, and data-communication products. In 2000, it held a 30-percent share of the domestic communications market, including a 20-percent share of the switches and access-servers market. In terms of foreign sales, Zhongxing's seven regional offices extend its products and services to over 70 countries and regions. Its switches, GSM (Global System for Mobile Communication) devices, video-conferencing systems, intelligent network, and other products are running in over 30 Southeast Asian and West Asian, Latin and North

---

[20] Interviews with industry experts, Beijing, China, 2001–2003.

American, East European, and African countries. It has successfully built systems in developed countries and regions such as the United States, the Commonwealth of Independent States, and Hong Kong, as well as conducting high-profile projects in the developing world, including a joint venture in Congo, a US$95-million project to supply ZXJ10 switches in Pakistan, and an intelligent-network project in Cyprus. For the future, Zhongxing is focusing on mobile communications technology, developing both GSM900 and Code Division Multiple Access (CDMA) equipment.

Datang. Originally established in 1993 as Xi'an Datang Telephone Company, the company was renamed Datang Telecom Technology Co., Limited, in 1998, when it listed on the Shanghai Stock Exchange. The company is the commercial outgrowth of the former China Academy of Telecommunications Technology (CATT), one of China's leading telecommunications R&D institutions for more than 40 years. With over 4,600 employees, Datang has grown to include multiple research centers, five subsidiaries hold controlling stakes in four companies and two publicly listed companies, as well as a company that has direct ownership relations with other companies and institutions in the Ministry of Information Industry (MII).

As does Huawei, Datang invests heavily in indigenous research and development, and maintains partnerships with both domestic and foreign R&D partners. The company has research cooperation agreements with three domestic universities (Dongnan University, Qinghua University, and Xi'an Jiaotong University), and a joint-venture relationship with Siemens (Germany) to produce third-generation cellular systems with the Chinese Time Division Synchronous Code Division Multiple Access (TD-SCDMA) standard. Its foreign partners include Compaq, Nortel, and Siemens.

As did Zhongxing, Datang began as a switching supplier. It is now moving to develop products in the data-communications and data-transmission-equipment markets. Datang's flagship product is the SP30 backbone switch, which it has sold to 22 provincial Post and Telecommunications Administrations (PTAs). In the transmission market, the company's presence is still fairly minimal, although its SDH and Dense Wave Division Multiplexing (DWDM) products have been gaining market share domestically. Datang is also looking to foreign markets, opening offices in Brazil, Vietnam, and Kazakhstan. For the future, Datang is moving into the automated teller machine (ATM) market and adding information-processing (IP) functionality to its core switching products. The company is also very focused on its third-generation wireless business, in particular its TD-SCDMA project with Siemens. On April 11, 2001, Datang and Siemens of Germany jointly released TD-SCDMA, promising full development of the system for the China market.[21] At the same time, the company hedged its bets by producing equipment for both GSM and CDMA technology.

Great Dragon (Julong) Information Technology (Group) Co., Ltd. In an effort to centralize China's nine largest telephone-exchange manufacturers, Great Dragon Information Technology (Group) Co., Ltd., was established on March 2, 1995, by the National Engineering Technology Research Center and the China Post and Telecommunications Industry General Corporation.[22] In 2000, Julong had 1,000 R&D personnel, of which 85 percent possessed post-graduate degrees. Its registered capital was 550 million RMB, and it had 3 billion RMB in overall capital. As does Huawei, Great Dragon reinvests 10 percent of its profits back into R&D. It also enjoys foreign R&D cooperation with companies in the United States, Russia, Japan, Canada, Israel, and Colombia.

Great Dragon's flagship product, the HJD-04, was the first indigenously produced commercial phone switch. Its chief architect, Wu Jiaxing, is president of the company, as well as director of the State Digital Switching Systems Engineering Technology Research Center, located at the PLA Information Engineering Institute in

---

[21] "China's 3G Mobile Technology Debuts," *China Daily,* April 12, 2001.

[22] Of the nine core firms under Great Dragon Telecom, four are former Ministry of Posts and Telecommunications factories: Luoyang Telephone Equipment Factory, Chongqing Communications Equipment Factory, Hanzhou Communications Equipment Factory, and the Changchun Telephone Equipment Factory. The remaining five factories are former Ministry of Electronics Industry switch producers: Huilong Electronics Company, Beijing Wire Communications General Factory, Shenzhen Xinnuo Telecommunications Company, China Zhenhua Group, and Dongfeng Machinery Factory.

Luoyang, Henan Province. The PLA origins of this system suggest a deeper link between Julong and the PLA than was previously assumed.

Apart from the HJD-04 product line, Julong also manufactures routers, connectors, transmitters, and mobile, network, and digital communications devices, SDH and DWDM systems, wireless local loop systems, high-speed Ethernet switches, and telephone systems. Domestically, these products have been installed in every province or autonomous region in China, save for Tibet and Hainan Island. In recent years, Julong has begun targeting foreign markets, resulting in sales to Bangladesh, Pakistan, Vietnam, Cuba (a telecommunication network for Cuba's Youth Island and an additional US$300 million contract with Cuba for an undisclosed project), North Korea, Colombia, and Russia (digital routers for telecommunication networks owned by the Russia Telecommunications Company). For the future, Julong plans on developing ATM systems, as well as IP and broadband products, high-speed routers, integrated access servers, Private Branch Exchange (PBX) systems, wireless access products, intelligent-network-management systems, and optical exchanges. However, Julong is reportedly the financially weakest of the four tigers, because it has failed to develop a follow-on technology with the same appeal as the HJD-04.[23]

Overall Assessment. China's telecommunications equipment companies are no longer niche producers in the domestic market. Instead, they are poised to become regional and, in some cases, global competitors. The reasons for the success of these domestic telecommunications-equipment producers are complex. To their credit, the leaders of these companies have displayed a rare entrepreneurial spirit, recruiting the best talent from Chinese universities and offering them competitive packages of remuneration and advanced working facilities. The firms keep costs low, thus driving the prices for equipment as much as 30 percent below international levels, and they provide excellent native service to domestic operators. Yet, these

---

[23] Interviews with industry experts, Beijing, China, 2001–2003.

firms have also clearly benefited from significant assistance from the civilian government, state banking apparatus, foreign companies, defense-industrial base, and, most important for this study, the civilian and military information-technology research and development base.

Vertex No. 2: State R&D Infrastructure. Bureaucratically, China's dual-use R&D is coordinated by the Science and Technology Leading Group, led by the Politburo member with the portfolio for science and technology issues.[24] Beneath this group, the key organizations in the bureaucracy are the State Development and Reform Commission, the Ministry of Science and Technology (MoST), the Chinese Academy of Sciences, the PLA GAD, and the Commission on Science and Technology for National Defense (COSTIND). Military inputs to the R&D process are facilitated through a number of organs, including the GAD and the COSTIND S&T Committee (*keji weiyuanhui*), the latter of which was historically responsible for "setting long-range R&D agendas for military and dual-use technologies."[25] However, because so much of China's long-range science and technology research has military implications, the COSTIND S&T Committee also had a key role in planning a significant percentage of China's civilian high-technology development strategy. Area-specific committees under the MoST include nuclear weapons, shipbuilding, aircraft development, electronics (which includes computing and information technologies), and special groups that cover issues such as C3 (command, control, and communications) technology.[26]

In the information-technology realm, the State Informatization Leading Small Group, or SILSG, traditionally headed by the Politburo member with the portfolio for telecommunications and electronics, is the most powerful information-related organ in the

---

[24] Evan Feigenbaum, "The Military Transforms China: The Politics of Strategic Technology from the Nuclear to the Information Age," 1997, p. 439.

[25] Evan Feigenbaum, "The Military Transforms China: The Politics of Strategic Technology from the Nuclear to the Information Age," 1997, p. 388.

[26] Evan Feigenbaum, "The Military Transforms China: The Politics of Strategic Technology from the Nuclear to the Information Age," 1997, p. 390.

Chinese government. Officially billed as an interagency coordination body, the SILSG is charged with formulating macro-level policy and deconflicting jurisdictional disputes among government agencies.

The SILSG's mandates are usually carried out by the Ministry of Information Industry, China's premier government-oversight organization, which regulates telecommunications, computer hardware, and computer software. It was founded in 1998, combining the former Ministry of Electronics Industry, which oversaw the computer hardware and software industry, and the Ministry of Posts and Telecommunications, which oversaw postal and telecommunications services. The merged "super-agency" (www.mii.gov.cn) wields enormous regulatory power over China's information industries, shaping the PRC information market, technology standards, and many other critical policy areas, including telecommunications, multimedia, broadcasting, satellite communications, and the Internet.

One little-known but reportedly critical bureaucratic coordination organ for information technology and electronics-related research, particularly military research, is the Electronic Science Academy (*Dianzi kexue yuan* 电子科学院 or *Diankeyuan* 电科院 for short), or ESA.[27] Internet sources suggest that the ESA was originally located under the former Ministry of Electronics Industry[28] but is now in some way subordinate to the Ministry of Information Industry,[29] although the roles of its officials and subordinate units suggest that this subordination may be a formality covering a much more important systemic function. Officials in ESA perform significant leadership roles in expert groups and national professional associations,[30] and ESA is credited with "managing the results" of the

---

[27]   National Mobile Communications Engineering Research Center website, http://www.mc21st.com/techfield/expert/main.asp.

[28] Anhui Province, Bengbu City Government website, http://www.bengbu.gov.cn/zjzy/wxs.htm.

[29] Guilin University of Electronic Technology website, http://www2.gliet.edu.cn/dept2/yj.htm.

[30] For example, see http://www.etnet.com.cn/xhxh/semiconductor.htm.

IT and electronics portions of the 7th Five Year Plan,[31] suggesting that this management may be an ongoing function of the ESA to the present day.

In terms of defense electronics, at least one of ESA's departments, the Military Industry Basic Bureau (*jungong jichuju* 军工基础局), may coordinate IT and electronics research with the military industry,[32] whereas the MII's Electronic Products Bureau appears to be in charge of the lesser functions of establishing standards and facilitating foreign trade.[33] One other source lists the ESA's Preparatory Research Fund (*dianzi kexueyuan yuyan jijin* 电子科学院演基金) as one of eight important "national defense plans" (*guofang jihua* 国防计划).[34]

Beneath the MII structure are the former Ministry of Electronics Industry (MEI) and Ministry of Posts and Telecommunications (MPT) numbered research institutes, which have maintained long-standing ties with the Chinese military and its IT research organs (Figure 5.2) and which are commercially affiliated with the China Electronics Corporation (CEC) and its subordinate state import-export companies, China Electronics Import-Export Corporation (CEIEC), and China Electronics Trade Group Corporation (CETGC).

MII Institutes. Of the MII institutes, one of the most important for military-related research is the 54th Research Institute (www.cti.ac.cn), a long-established center for research on communications and monitoring technologies, including microwave relay communications, wireless communications, scatter communications, satellite communications, satellite broadcast access, remote sensing, telemetry, surveys, communications countermeasures, intelligence,

---

[31] Guilin University of Electronic Technology website, http://www.gliet.edu.cn/gaikuang/lishi86_90.htm.

[32] See mention of bureau at http://www.cesi.gov.cn/CQMAEI/dir/7.htm.

[33] See Ministry of Information Industry website, http://www.mii.gov.cn.

[34] Xidian University, Xian, http://202.117.114.54/page/chushijianjie/keyanbu.htm.

Figure 5.2
Partial List of Civilian and Military IT Research Institutes (RIs)

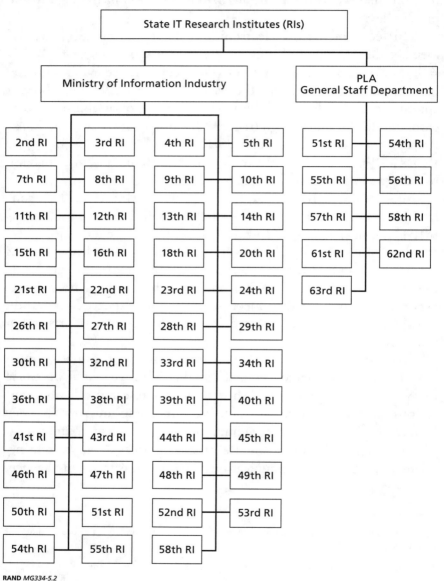

and reconnaissance. The institute produced China's first fully digital satellite-communications ground station, first large shipborne satellite-communications ground station, first area air-defense communications network, and first man-made satellite monitoring equipment.[35]

Each of the defense-industrial corporations has one or more information-technology or electronics research institutes, and these institutes collaborate with their military and civilian counterparts on everything from communications to microelectronics. AVIC institute Number 303 researches semiconductor-manufacturing equipment.[36] Norinco Institutes Numbers 203, 206, and 212 produce electronics systems ranging from computers to radars to software. Aerospace institute Numbers 504 and 506 conduct research on communications and data-management systems, and institute Number 771 is responsible for microelectronics. CSIC institute Number 709 focuses on computers and software; and Number 716 produces automation systems, and Number 724 deals with radars.

PLA Institutes. Among the PLA institutes, the 56th Research Institute develops computer systems. The 61st Research Institute reportedly develops command automation systems, as well as C3I (command, control, communications, and intelligence) systems, and it hosted the 1997 Defense Information Modernization Symposium.[37] The 62nd Research Institute performs research and development on communications equipment, computers, and command automation. The former 63rd Research Institute (now merged into the PLA Science and Engineering University) in Nanjing reportedly conducted research into microwaves and, possibly, encryption. One of these institutes was likely the subject of a 1999 article describing

---

[35] *China Electronic News,* September 22, 2000.

[36] The summaries of the research interests in this paragraph are based upon frequency analysis of thousands of articles in Chinese technical journals. See Garret Albert, "Research Priorities of China's Top Numbered Research Institutes," Santa Monica, Calif.: unpublished RAND Corporation research.

[37] Liang Zhenxing, "New Military Revolution: Information Warfare," *Zhongguo dianzi bao,* October 24, 1997, p. 8, in *FBIS,* January 12, 1998.

"a certain communications technology research institute under the General Staff Department" that had developed a phased-array antenna for satellite communications, thereby achieving "the goal of mobile communications and improving the rapid-reaction capability of its troops."[38] Analysis of Chinese technical IT journals, participant lists from conferences, and interviews in China over several years reveal significant levels of intercourse between these civilian and military institutes, ranging from shared chairing of expert committees (see below) to joint research.[39]

State R&D Funding Programs. The lubricant facilitating these cooperative relationships between the state R&D sector and the commercial IT sector is state-sponsored research and development funding from the national five-year plans and the 863 Program. For commercial companies, these state R&D monies permit economies of scale for expensive R&D and serve as a form of subsidy to allow them to divert monies to marketing or production.

Funding Source No. 1: Five Year Plans. The most significant government support is provided through national science and technology R&D funding programs. At the top of the S&T funding system are the key technology projects of the Tenth Five Year Plan (2001–2005). In July 2000, the State Council approved a Chinese Academy of Science proposal to carry out 12 important high-tech projects, including high-speed information networks and super-computers.[40] R&D targets include 20-percent annual growth in R&D funding, integrated circuits between 0.18 and 0.25 microns (m), output of 20 billion chips, third-generation mobile cellular systems, optical communications, and network-access technologies. Most important, these technologies must be developed indigenously,

---

[38] "PLA Develops Mobile Satellite Communications Antenna," *Xinhua,* December 14, 1999, in *FBIS.*

[39] Interviews in Beijing, China, 1999–2003, and RAND databases.

[40] *Xinhua,* July 27, 2000.

with Chinese intellectual-property rights (IPR).[41] More recently, the focus on IPR has expanded to include an emphasis on the creation of home-grown Chinese IT standards, including 3G mobile (TD-SCDMA), digital video discs (EVD), and wireless local area network (LAN) encryption (WAPI), among others.

Funding Source No. 2: National Defense Funding Programs. On the defense-funding side, at least eight national defense funding programs are active, including the National Defense 863 Program (*Guofang 863 Jihua* 国防863计划), National Defense 973 (Space Research) Program (*Guofang 973 Jihua* 国防科73 计划), Military Model Projects (*Junshi Xinghao Xiangmu* 军事型号项目), National Defense Science and Technology Preparatory Research Fund (*Guofang Keji Yuyan Jijin* 国防科技预演基金), National Defense Key Laboratory Opening Task Fund (*Guofang Zhongdian Shiyanshi Kaifang Keti Jijin* 国防重点实验室开放课题基金), National Defense Science and Technology Advance Research Plan Projects (*Guofang Keji Yuxian Yanjiu Jihua Xiangmu* 国防科技预先研究计划项目), Equipment Technology Basic Projects (*Zhuangbei Jishu Jichu Xiangmu* 装备技术基础项目), and the Electronic Science Academy Preparatory Research Fund (*Dianzi Kexueyuan Yuyan Jijin* 电子科学院预演基金).[42]

Perhaps the most critical national defense S&T funding effort is the 863 Program. The program's name derives from the date (March 1986) of a letter by four of China's most senior scientists to the country's leaders that stressed the need for a national commitment to supporting research and development. Their letter contained four main points:

- Technology is the key to rapid economic development.
- China's quest to become a world power required that it build its own high technology base.

---

[41] *Guangming Daily,* July 20, 2000.

[42] Xidian University, Xian, http://202.117.114.54/page/chushijianjie/keyanbu.htm.

- The essential nature of technology had changed during the 1970s and China had missed the change.
- China must quickly adjust its technology base to conform to these changed realities or risk permanent second-rate status behind Japan and the West.[43]

To remedy this situation, the scientists strongly argued that "the Central state, in close partnership with some of the country's most renowned scientists and engineers, must bear the burden to funding and concentrating policy attention on critical R&D areas of long-range strategic value to China's economic development and national security."[44] However, operationalizing this strategy required that the state change its view of directed S&T research.[45] The four operative principles of the new approach are as follows:

- A solely military-oriented S&T base could not sustain China's modernization efforts into the 21st century.

---

[43] Quoted in Evan Feigenbaum, "The Military Transforms China: The Politics of Strategic Technology from the Nuclear to the Information Age," 1997, p. 378.

[44] Evan Feigenbaum, "The Military Transforms China: The Politics of Strategic Technology from the Nuclear to the Information Age," 1997, p. 378.

[45] The organizational structure of Program 863 is outlined in Evan Feigenbaum, "The Military Transforms China: The Politics of Strategic Technology from the Nuclear to the Information Age," 1997. Program 863 was historically administered by SSTC in cooperation with COSTIND and the State Planning Commission (SPC), but it is currently housed in the Ministry of Science and Technology. The 863 Leading Group is a formal, intersectoral coordination structure linking the military and civilian bureaucracies. It rarely meets, so day-to-day authority rests with the 863 Coordination Group, consisting of three members and an SPC liaison. The Chinese Academy of Sciences provides the experts for the management and planning apparatus, as well as the task forces. The SPC manages much of the cross-agency coordination that precedes project evaluation and decision phases, through functionally oriented departments and bureaus under the day-to-day control of the various vice-ministers of the commission. The focal field management committees are empowered to select task groups in charge of subareas or topics of narrower focus. To manage each topic, the focal field committees are authorized to appoint topic group members, who then set agendas and targets, and select the institutes or enterprises to receive 863 disbursements. These expert groups became so powerful that the 863 leadership instituted competitive bidding in the 1990s.

- The distinction between "purely" military and civilian technologies was artificial and irrelevant.
- Product-oriented sectors, such as missiles, could not progress without process-oriented modernization.
- China's successful strategic weapons program provided a model for state-led R&D.[46]

The ultimate goal, according to a leading expert on the subject, was twofold: (1) Close the technology gap with the West and (2) pursue strategic technologies with implications for China's long-range industrial competitiveness and national power.[47] Program 863 thus sought to plug gaps in the national R&D infrastructure by guaranteeing that "strategic" sectors would not lag behind those sectors driven by exclusively commercial imperatives, whose investment and R&D choices would be automatically and directly tested by the rigors of the marketplace.[48] As a result, 863 became the "primary vehicle for S&T agenda control in China."[49]

The creation of the 863 process did not seek to eliminate military R&D, but it changed the orientation of the work to focus on commercial applications rather than pure military applications for critical technologies. Through Program 863, the state sought to intensify government-university partnerships in particular, as well as to link centrally directed money with smaller-scale, commercially driven innovation by public-sector spin-off firms at the local level.[50]

---

[46] Evan Feigenbaum, "The Military Transforms China: The Politics of Strategic Technology from the Nuclear to the Information Age," 1997, p. 448.

[47] Evan Feigenbaum, "The Military Transforms China: The Politics of Strategic Technology from the Nuclear to the Information Age," 1997, p. 448.

[48] Evan Feigenbaum, "The Military Transforms China: The Politics of Strategic Technology from the Nuclear to the Information Age," 1997, p. 459.

[49] Evan Feigenbaum, "The Military Transforms China: The Politics of Strategic Technology from the Nuclear to the Information Age," 1997, p. 484.

[50] Francis Corinna-Barbara, "Commercialization Without Privatization: Government Spin-Offs in China's High Technology Sector," in Judith B. Sedaitis, ed., *Commercializing High Technology: East and West: Selected Conference Papers,* Stanford, Calif.: Center for International Security and Arms Control, 1997, pp. 259–284.

This intensification was facilitated by the fact that 863 money is often funneled through ministries or other state organs. Universities, for example, receive their 863 money through the State Education Commission.

Yet, it is important to note that Program 863 was not focused on privatization but, instead, on "fostering competition among state and (especially) collective firms, exposing them to some market discipline and potentially spurring innovation."[51] Thus, the "two poles" of the Chinese R&D system—centrally directed "Big Science" and market-driven "Small Science"—were brought together to form the "backbone of the country's 21st century technology infrastructure,"[52] fundamentally altering the way that Chinese elites "think about the building blocks of technological modernization and the pattern of exchange between civilian and military-oriented R&D."[53]

Operationally, the central government began with the advantage that "virtually the entire advanced industrial, R&D, and research university systems involve some form of state ownership."[54] The 863 Leading Group sits atop this vast system and enjoys wide-ranging "proprietary and coordination powers." A smaller 863 program office based in the headquarters of the State Science and Technology Commission historically coordinated efforts across China's many stovepiped hierarchies, especially the allocation of resources across bureaucratic boundaries, and this function may have moved to the MoST.

At the strategic level, the 863 Program is focused on seven main research fields: biotechnology, aerospace, information technology, lasers, automation technology, energy technology, and new materials.

---

[51] Evan Feigenbaum, "The Military Transforms China: The Politics of Strategic Technology from the Nuclear to the Information Age," 1997, p. 459.

[52] Evan Feigenbaum, "The Military Transforms China: The Politics of Strategic Technology from the Nuclear to the Information Age," 1997, p. 379.

[53] Evan Feigenbaum, "The Military Transforms China: The Politics of Strategic Technology from the Nuclear to the Information Age," 1997, p. 449.

[54] Evan Feigenbaum, "The Military Transforms China: The Politics of Strategic Technology from the Nuclear to the Information Age," 1997, p. 379.

Each of these fields is headed by a managerial group, and the entire program is run under an "expert responsibility system" (*zhuanjia fuzezhi* 专家负责制).[55] Each of the seven fields is overseen by a "field expert committee" (*lingyu zhuanjia weiyuanhui* 领域专家委员会).[56] Under each of these managerial groups is a set of first-tier "expert groups" (*zhuanjiazu* 专家组), focused on a significant research subarea, which is itself divided even further into more narrowly specialized second-tier expert groups. The field expert committee is responsible for supervising these expert groups. The first-tier expert groups are charged with planning and management, and are vested not only with planning power but decisionmaking authority, including patronage opportunities at the core of the Chinese power game: the right to choose contractors, to arbitrate among winners and losers in the ranks of competing contractors, and thus to parcel out ultimate R&D responsibility under the auspices of the program. The money itself comes from the state science and technology budget, but it is a special and separately listed item that does not fall under the state's five-year S&T budget.

By contrast, COSTIND dispenses money for basic and applied research to defense-industrial enterprises, the General Armaments Department allocates money to PLA institutes, and civilian units receive their money from the MoST through their super-ordinate ministries and commissions. The technical expert committees are also charged with evaluating bids and proposals, monitoring the use of 863 money, and assessing the progress of various efforts.

From the beginning, information technology was singled out as one of the most important of the key fields chosen as the research core of Program 863. China was judged to be deficient in IT, which was deemed crucial to China's long-range competitiveness. In the

---

[55] Ministry of Science and Technology, Center for High-Tech Research & Development, 1998–2005 863 Program Combined Research Office website, http://www.863.gov.cn/863_105/863briefing/briefing/200210150012.html.

[56] Ministry of Science and Technology, Center for High-Tech Research & Development, 1998–2005 863 Program Combined Research Office website, http://www.863.gov.cn/863_105/863briefing/briefing/200210150012.html.

10th Five Year Plan for Program 863, this focus became even more explicit: Information technology was identified as the most important "focal point" (*zhongdian* 重点).[57] The stress on IT in Program 863 is suggested by funding levels, although data are scarce. In 1988, for instance, IT received 23.68 percent of the 863 pie, third out of eight behind biotech (32.95 percent) and new materials (26.95 percent).[58] To manage information technology research under 863, the IT Managerial Committee set up a first tier of specialized topic groups, including "steering" committees in telecommunications, optical electronics, information superhighway–related issues, artificial intelligence, and information technology–related automation systems.[59]

Vertex No. 3: The People's Liberation Army and Information Technologies. The PLA dominated the early history of information technology and telecommunications in China. During the 1945–1949 civil war, telecommunications was placed under military control. After liberation, the Ministry of Posts and Telecommunications was founded, but most of its senior leaders in the early years were former high-ranking military officers, including the "father" of Chinese telecommunications, General Wang Zheng.[60] This link lasted until the Cultural Revolution, when the ministry collapsed. To this day, however, the PLA's involvement in these areas is sustained by its military IT research institutes; privileged ownership of telecommunications infrastructure, bandwidth and frequencies; and relationships with commercial IT companies, ranging from outright ownership to elite customer status.

The PLA's relationship with information technologies and electronics in the post-Mao period has gone through two phases. The

---

[57] Ministry of Science and Technology, Center for High-Tech Research & Development, 1998–2005 863 Program Combined Research Office website, http://www.863.gov.cn/863_105/863briefing/briefing/200210150012.html.

[58] Evan Feigenbaum, "The Military Transforms China: The Politics of Strategic Technology from the Nuclear to the Information Age," 1997, p. 435.

[59] Evan Feigenbaum, "The Military Transforms China: The Politics of Strategic Technology from the Nuclear to the Information Age," 1997, p. 427.

[60] *Tongxinbingshi*, Beijing, China: PLA Press, n.d.

first phase was essentially driven by the commercialization of the Chinese military, mainly in telecommunications networks and services.[61] Not only was the PLA able to build military networks with commercial technology and generate revenue from building and operating these networks, but the construction itself attracted foreign companies seeking to participate in joint ventures and willing to transfer technology. The military's integrator companies, such as the GSD's CESEC, maintained working relations with both civilian and military numbered research institutes, permitting diffusion of these technologies in military-related research and development projects. Since divestiture of the PLA's enterprises in 1998, the military has entered a second, more advanced phase. While some commercial telecommunications construction still occurs through affiliated companies, the PLA has more openly embraced the digital-triangle model, providing capital and R&D support to globally oriented firms in exchange for privileged-customer status.

Phase One: Telecommunications Buildout. The most dynamic sector of PLA business activities before divestiture of military businesses in 1998 was telecommunications. The military's participation in this sector was facilitated by two critical structural privileges (relating to access and special rights of the military in Chinese society). Beginning in 1988, the armed forces began to commercially exploit limited portions of its dedicated internal telecommunications networks to provide service to civilian customers. Initially, the army leased telephone lines and connected its exchanges for use by nearby individuals and businesses, but, over time, it increasingly used its spare capacity in landline and analog Advanced Mobile Phone System (AMPS; the original standard for cellular products prior to GSM and CDMA) cellular networks for commercial gain.

At the same time, the PLA exploited its exclusive control (mainly for reasons of national security) over large sections of China's bandwidth spectrum. Among the sections of bandwidth dominated

---

[61] James C. Mulvenon, *Soldiers of Fortune: The Rise and Fall of the Chinese Military-Business Complex, 1978–1998,* Armonck, N.Y.: M. E. Sharpe, 2001; Tai Ming Cheung, *China's Entrepreneurial Army,* Studies on Contemporary China, Oxford University Press, 2002.

by the PLA is the important 800-MHz section, which is ideal for mobile cellular communications. To generate profits from the military's broadcast bandwidth that otherwise would have been left in unproductive static, a joint venture was forged in late 1995 between the former MPT's China Telecom and General Staff Department Communications Department's China Electronic System and Engineering Corporation (CESEC).

CESEC is the key to PLA telecommunications. Its interests range from mobile communications to secure telephone lines, computer networks, encryption, microwaves, computer applications, and dedicated military C^{4}ISR systems. CESEC is largely responsible for designing, integrating, and operating the PLA's telecommunications and computer networks. It develops software applications, and it is closely affiliated with the aforementioned critical General Staff Department research institutes that specialize in C^{4}ISR, microwave, and encryption.

A second and equally profitable spin-off from the PLA bandwidth monopoly was mobile radio paging. In Guangzhou, for example, of the ten largest pager companies, three were owned by the PLA Air Force, the Guangdong Military District, and a COSTIND subsidiary.[62] The Air Force company, known as the Guangzhou Bayi Telecommunications Group, ran a commercial radio-paging service that claimed 100,000 subscribers in 1994.[63] These paging companies were significantly aided by foreign equipment and investment. One joint venture was established in 1995 between GTE and a PLA company called Guangtong, which controlled the relevant military frequencies. Known as Guangzhou Guangtong GTE, the joint-venture company invested in the company, known as Tianwei, that actually ran the paging operation. Another set of paging deals involved Hong Kong businessman Paul Kan and his company Champion Technol-

---

[62] Guangzhou Enterprise Evaluation Association, *Zhongguo Guangzhou daxing qiye paixu* (*Ranking of Guangzhou's Large-Sized Enterprises*), Guangzhou, China: Zhongshan University Publishing House, 1994, pp. 115–117.

[63] Kathy Chen, "Soldiers of Fortune: Chinese Army Fashions Major Role for Itself as a Business Empire," *Wall Street Journal*, May 24, 1994, pp. A1, A9.

ogy, which also partnered with PLA companies in Guangdong to develop radio-paging markets.[64] This business expanded to include paging franchises in dozens of Chinese cities, mainly through partnerships with firms controlled by local PLA units. At its height, Kan estimated that PLA units had enrolled about 25 percent of China's 36 million paging subscribers, with the market continuing to expand by 1 million new customers a month.

A third area of PLA investment and commercial interest was fiber-optic cables. PLA units were used as labor to lay most of China's national fiber-optic trunk lines, in exchange for financial remuneration and a percentage of the fibers in the trunks (for their own communications uses). But the PLA also laid its own dedicated fiber lines, some of which were designed for commercial purposes. One example is a nationwide fiber-optic network that was constructed by the Office of Telecom Support for Economic Construction, an office under the General Staff Department's Communications Department that has branch offices in each of China's seven military regions.[65] The fiber project was started in late 1997, when the PLA took on construction for a Chinese client who originally intended to enter a joint venture with a British-based telecom firm. As long as they were digging trenches and installing fiber for the client, the PLA inserted their own strands. The deal between the foreign telecom firm and the client eventually fell apart, and state spin-off telecom operator China Unicom became a replacement for the original client. The PLA fiber remained unused throughout most of the network, except in Guangdong, where there was considerable building activity in anticipation of serving local cable companies and trunk service for long-awaited CDMA traffic.

Phase Two: From Producer to Digital-Triangle Consumer. The PLA's direct involvement in the construction of commercial telecommunications networks came to an end in the late 1990s. On July 22, 1998, at an enlarged session of the Central Military Commission,

---

[64] Andrew Tanzer, "The People's Liberation Army, Inc.," *Forbes,* March 24, 1997, p. 46.

[65] Tai Ming Cheung, *China's Entrepreneurial Army,* 2002.

Chairman Jiang Zemin gave a speech in which he called for the dissolution of the military-business complex. Since then, the PLA has effectively removed the commercial components of the military economy while retaining production elements essential to the maintenance of the standard of living of the rank-and-file, such as farms and small-scale factories.

Initially, some sectors of the military economy, including telecommunications, were exempted from divestiture on the grounds that they were too important to the military's mission. Interviews in Beijing strongly suggest that PLA telecoms in general were given a "get-out-of-jail-free" card from the central leadership, because the resulting information-technology acquisition was seen as an essential contributor to the C4I revolution currently under way in the PLA.

To manage the post-divestiture operations, the PLA created two communications groups. Reportedly, the first is dedicated exclusively to internal military traffic at high levels of security. The second leases capacity of existing networks to civilian operators. In the second case, the PLA was considered to be delinked if it did not directly enroll individual subscribers (i.e., deal directly with "the public"), yet it could lease to operators who did enroll customers (i.e., cable companies). Although radio paging was abandoned (e.g., CITIC/Pacific bought the Bayi radio paging business in Guangzhou) and many companies had to break their high-profile links with foreign companies, the CESEC, in particular, was not only allowed to retain its Great Wall CDMA cellular network (provided it found a new partner to deal with the customer base) but, in some cases expanded its operations. Providers of CDMA handsets and base stations, such as Huawei and Zhongxing, stood to gain from any expansion of the system.

In 2001, CESEC was forced to transfer the CDMA networks to China Unicom, which has expressed a sometimes-shaky commitment to building a nationwide CDMA network alongside its existing GSM network rollout. For Huawei and Zhongxing, the loss of CESEC as a potential customer was more than offset by the prospect of supplying equipment to Unicom's national network. This circumstance highlights an important evolution in the military's strategy for telecommunications development. Under the old model, such companies as CESEC built commercial networks and served as a front company for the acquisition of technology for the military. Such companies as Huawei, by contrast, represent the new digital-triangle model, whereby the military, other state actors, and their numbered research institutes help fund and staff commercially oriented firms that are designated national champions, receive lines of credit from state banks, supplement their R&D funding with directed 863 money, and actively seek to build global market share. The military, for its part, benefits as a favored customer and research partner. Companies like CESEC continue to exist, but they now serve as systems integrators of technologies from multiple outside vendors.

Role of Foreign Companies, Capital, and Technology

Foreign companies have aided the efforts of the digital triangle through infusions of technology, capital, and know-how to important commercial companies linked to the Chinese IT sector, mainly as an attempt for securing market access. These interactions have begun to occur between Chinese subsidiaries in the United States and other U.S. companies, but the majority of them occur in China, between Chinese companies and foreign subsidiaries. This latter dynamic is the more serious of the two from an export-control and export-proliferation perspective, because the nature of the regulatory and commercial environment in China places enormous pressure on American companies to transfer technology.

For U.S. information-technology companies, simply breaking into the China market has proven to be difficult. Although the state-owned infrastructure providers have proven willing to buy large amounts of equipment, the regulatory environment before WTO entry sought to limit foreign operation or ownership of services, and the commercial playing field has increasingly tilted toward domestic companies. As a result, foreign companies worked to build technology partnerships with their domestic counterparts. Foreign companies tried to buy market access by investing heavily in domestic R&D and joint-venture labs with Chinese competitors. Huawei, for example, has established technology-cooperation agreements or labs with

Lucent, Motorola, Intel, IBM, AT&T, Texas Instruments, and Sun Microsystems. Some multinationals even agreed to transfer core technologies, such as source code, in order to secure market position. Ericsson, for example, agreed to turn over the source code to its CDMA cellular technology to its Chinese partner, as did Microsoft with the source code to Windows. In some cases, companies have even agreed to relinquish R&D data. Network Solutions, in an effort to speed along the certification of an anti-virus product by the Ministry of Public Security's lab, handed over 300 computer viruses to the security apparatus.

In July 2003, the link between foreign technology and defense IT modernization became more overt and explicit with the formation of a Chinese military IT alliance. The Chinese government news agency announced that more than 50 information-technology firms, including at least three U.S. firms (Network Associates, Sybase, and Luxeon), were forming an alliance to "strengthen their hand in the lucrative defense market, as the Chinese military is reforming its purchase system by adopting the practice of government procurement."[66] These companies are listed in Table 5.1.

Li Jinnai, a member of the Central Military Commission and director of the General Armament Department of the Chinese People's Liberation Army, attended the ceremony to mark the launch of the coalition. Twelve of the firms donated IT products to the army, including servers, personal computers, exchanges, and routers. Company representatives pledged to help train IT personnel for the military and create greater awareness about the industry among the forces. The establishment of the alliance was sponsored by the Information Institute of Electronics Science and Technology under the Chinese Ministry of Information and the Computer World Media Group, and was approved jointly by the PLA General Armament Department, the Ministry of Information Industry, and the China Electronics Science and Technology Group Corporation (CESTGC).

---

[66] "Li Jinnai Attends Ceremony of Launch of IT Firm Alliance for Military Procurement," *Xinhua,* July 30, 2003.

Table 5.1
Foreign Companies Participating in Chinese Military IT Alliance

---

上海博达通信公司
Shanghai Baud Data Communication Co., Ltd.[a]

方正科技股份集团公司
Founder Technology Group Corporation[a]

联想集团有限公司
Legend Group Limited[a]

凝思科技有限公司总经理
Linx Technology Co., Ltd.[a]

中国电子科技集团公司第十五研究所
MII 15[a]

清华紫光比威网络技术有限公司
Tsinghua Unisplendour Bitway Networking Technology Co., Ltd.[a]

北京方正数码有限公司总裁时西忠
Beijing EC-Founder Co., Ltd.'s Head Examiner Shi Xizhong [a]

北京华旗资讯数码科技有限公司总经理冯军
Beijing Huaqi Information Digital Technology Co. Ltd.'s President Ping Jun[a]

上海浙大网新易得科技发展有限公司
Shanghai Joint-Harvest Technology-Science Co., Ltd.[a]

星盈科技（深圳）有限公司
Galactic Computer Corporation[a]

北京同华顺达贸易有限公司
Vindaway Trading Co., Ltd[a]

艾美加太平洋私人有限公司[a]
Iomega Pacific Private Ltd

BEA系统中国有限公司
BEA System (China) Telecom

安奈特（中国）网络有限公司
Allied Telesis (China) Ltd.

宝利通中国POLYCOM
Polycom Inc.

北京晨拓联达科贸有限责任公司
Beijing Center Electronic Technology Co., Ltd

北京城市热点资讯有限公司
Beijing City Hotspot Information Co., Ltd

北京飞天诚信科技有限公司
Beijing Feitian Technologies Co., Ltd

北京合力共创网络技术有限公司
Beijing Co-Founding Network Technology Co., Ltd

北京捷德智能卡系统有限公司
Beijing G&D Card Systems Co.,Ltd

北京金山软件股份有限公司
Jinshan Software Limited

Table 5.1—Continued

北京巨龙数码科技有限责任公司
　　Beijing Julong Digital S&T Co., Ltd

北京朗新公司
　　Beijing New Company

北京理工光河科技发展有限公司
　　Beijing Science and Engineering Guanghe S&T Development Co. Ltd

北京隆振元科贸有限公司
　　Beijing Longzhen Yuanke Technology Co., Ltd

北京赛门铁克信息技术有限公司
　　Beijing Symantec Information Technology Co., Ltd.

北京网新易尚科技有限公司
　　Yishang Innovation Technology Co., Ltd

北京唯美星计算机安全保护技术有限公司
　　Well Star Co., Ltd

北京亿美软通科技有限公司
　　Beijing Emay Softcom Technology Ltd.

北京用友安易软件技术有限公司
　　Anyi Software Technology Co. Ltd

大唐电信科技产业集团
　　Datang Telecom Technology and Industry Group

港湾网络有限公司
　　Harbour Networks Ltd.

湖南福莱特信息技术有限公司
　　Hunan Fulaite Technology Company Co., Ltd

迈普（四川）通信技术有限公司
　　Maipu (Sichuan) Communication Technology Co., Ltd

美国丽讯科技
　　Luxeon Corporation (USA)

美国网络联盟公司
　　Network Associates (USA)

清华同方计算机系统本部
　　Qinghua Tongfang Computer System Business Group

赛贝斯软件(中国)有限公司
　　Sybase Software (China) Co., Ltd

上海思波通讯科技有限公司
　　Shanghai Sibo Telecom Co., Ltd

上海中晶科技有限公司
　　Microtek Co., Ltd

深圳达讯科技有限公司
　　Shenzhen Daxun S&T Co. Ltd

深圳市中兴通讯股份有限公司
　　Shenzhen ZTE Co. Ltd

神州数码（中国）有限公司
　　Digital China Co., Ltd

Table 5.1—Continued

实达电脑科技有限公司	Start Computer Science & Technology Co., Ltd
实达电脑设备有限公司	Start Computer Equipment Co.,Ltd
实达网络科技有限公司	Start Network Technology Co., Ltd
速联通讯股份有限公司	Fast Communication Co., Ltd
太极计算机股份有限公司	Taiji Computer Co., Ltd
西南应用磁学研究所	Southwest Institute of Applied Magnetics (also known as MII 9)
系统软件联合全球科技(中国)有限公司	SSA Global Technologies
香港天星机电有限公司	Star Micronics Asia Ltd
新趋网络科技（上海）有限公司	Trend Micro (Shanghai) Incorporated
中宝运通（无锡）有限公司	China Bridge Ltd
中国电子科技集团公司第二十二研究所	MII 22
中国电子科技集团公司第五十八研究所	MII 58
中国电子科技集团公司第五十五研究所	MII 55
中国电子科技集团公司信息化工程总体研究中心	MII Informationized Engineering Research Center
中科红旗软件技术有限公司	Red Flag Software Co., Ltd

ªMade a donation to the S&T Alliance.

Over time, Chinese sources assert that technology transfers from abroad have made the government ministries and companies less dependent on foreign money and technology. This dynamic is what Chinese interlocutors and outside analysts refer to as the "new model," or path to development: cooperation, learning, mastering, independent development, replacement, indigenous innovation, global competitiveness. In the IT and telecoms subsectors, this self-sustaining path has effectively replaced the old, risky, defense-industrial model of "steal, acquire, reverse engineer, and produce."

Interviews in Beijing suggest that foreign market entrants are fully aware that these technology codevelopment relationships with Chinese companies are aiding domestic partners at their expense, but they feel that they have no other choice, given the structural asymmetries in the market. Ruey-bin Kao, Motorola's chief of network solutions in China, even told a Western reporter that he has no doubt that Huawei plans to use its partnership on GSM technology to replace Motorola's base stations with its own one day.[67] Even China's WTO entry will probably not reverse this trend, since domestic companies in key sectors (e.g., Legend in PCs) have already grabbed dominant market share in areas that used to be controlled by foreign technology suppliers and now continue to offer near-state-of-the-art innovation to compete with foreign products. The situation is less rosy in the defense-electronics sector, given the lack of a domestic market to lure multinational corporations and leverage technology transfer, but some subsectors, particularly semiconductors, have begun to exploit this dynamic with considerable success.

Overall Implications of the Digital Triangle

Implications for Other Defense-Industrial Sectors

The evidence clearly shows that the telecommunications and micro-electronic sub-sectors have found a successful formula for mixing state direction with commercial dynamism to improve both China's civilian and military information-technology infrastructure. Yet the success of the IT sector in becoming a new model of defense-industrial production immediately raises the question: Could the model be applied to China's other, less-successful defense-industrial sectors?

According to interviews, the experience of procuring military-related IT equipment from Chinese companies has taught the Gen-

---

[67] See Bruce Gilley, "Huawei's Fixed Line to Beijing," 2000–2001.

eral Armaments Department a great deal about contracting, competition, and bidding, and it has emboldened procurement officials to apply the lessons to the traditional defense-industrial producers.[68] Indeed, there is evidence that similar transfers of manufacturing technology and know-how to the Chinese commercial shipbuilding industry (see Chapter Three), combined with the important 1998 defense-industry reforms, have had a demonstrably positive effect upon the pace and quality of naval production. Yet, officials are also quick to point to the limits or constraints of wholesale transfer of these lessons, given the unique advantages of the IT sector over its far less nimble and dynamic counterparts in traditional defense-industrial sectors, especially the laggard aviation sector.

For the time being, most interlocutors agreed that the top state goal of maintaining "social stability" would impede the implementation of the most significant defense-industrial reforms across the entire defense-industrial base, since these changes would undoubtedly involve painful consolidations, layoffs, or even bankruptcies. As a result, analysts of the Chinese defense industry, who once could discuss similar structural obstacles across sectors, must now confront the more difficult task of analyzing sectors progressing at different rates, with the digital triangle as an exemplar of rapid success.

Implications for Chinese Military Modernization

Throughout its history, the PLA has suffered from inadequate and outdated information technology, characterized by limited capacity and lack of security. In the past, these weaknesses have severely limited the military's ability to transmit and process large amounts of information or coordinate activities among the various military regions, thereby reducing military effectiveness. For example, a number of observers believe that inadequate communications were a major factor in the heavy losses suffered by the PLA during China's

---

[68] Interviews with General Armaments Department officials, September 2000–September 2001.

invasion of Vietnam in 1979.[69] In stark contrast, the PLA is very much aware of the critical role played by information-based C[4]ISR (command, control, communications, computers, intelligence, surveillance, and reconnaissance) technologies in the 1991 Gulf War, and the importance of these technologies in securing the eventual Allied victory against a force made up of largely Soviet and Chinese equipment.[70]

To overcome these deficits, the PLA has embarked on a well-financed effort to modernize its C[4]ISR infrastructure. In the beginning, an important goal of this modernization was the acquisition of advanced telecommunications equipment from abroad, based on the premise that the technologies of the information revolution provided China with the opportunity to vastly improve capabilities by "leapfrogging." The transfer of these technologies to China in general and the PLA in particular was facilitated by two mutually supporting trends. First, there was enormous competition among Western telecommunications firms to get a share of the relatively backward but rapidly expanding Chinese telecommunications market, which is the largest market in the world. Naturally, the lure of potential billions has attracted every major player— Lucent, Nokia, Ericsson, Nortel—and countless others. From these companies, China bought between US$15 and $20 billion worth of telecom equipment a year.

However, as this chapter argues, the Chinese IT sector, backed by state R&D funding and national labs, has moved beyond merely importing Western technology to codeveloping technology with foreign firms, and even to developing indigenously near-state-of-the-art technology. Significant players in the Chinese telecoms market, such as Huawei and Datang, maintain deep codevelopment relationships with the world's top information-technology powerhouses, but they

[69] See James C. Mulvenon, "The Limits of Coercive Diplomacy: The 1979 Sino-Vietnamese Border War," *Journal of Northeast Asian Studies,* Fall 1995.

[70] For an example of PLA writings on this point, see Li Qingshan, ed., *Xin junshi geming yu gaoshuji zhanzheng* (*The New Military Revolution and High-Tech Warfare*), Beijing, China: Military Science Press, 1995, especially pp. 122–125.

also have clear ties to the Chinese military, which has now become both a research partner and a valued customer for their IT products. In microelectronics, China is quickly becoming an important design and production base in the global semiconductor industry, providing the PLA with potential access to a secure supply of advanced integrated circuits for use in sensors and weapon systems. The result is significant levels of military access to cutting-edge information technology, fueling a C^4ISR revolution in the armed forces.

But what are the specific military benefits of these information technologies? Thanks to the introduction of an advanced, secure telecommunications infrastructure, the PLA has reportedly achieved significant improvement in its communications and operational security,[71] as well as in its capacity to transmit information:

> The use of advanced optical fiber communications facilities, satellites, long-distance automated switches and computer-controlled telephone systems has significantly accelerated the Chinese armed forces' digitization process and the rapid transmission and processing of military information. The speedy development of strategic communications networks has shortened the distance between command headquarters and grassroots units, and between inland areas and border and coastal areas. Currently the armed forces' networks for data exchange have already linked up units garrisoned in all medium-sized and large cities in the country as well as in border and coastal areas. As a result of the automated exchange and transmission of data, graphics and pictures within the armed forces, military information can now be shared by all military units.[72]

On the sensor front, China has also made significant advances, as evidenced by the deployment of new constellations of navigation

---

[71] For a more detailed examination of this topic, see James C. Mulvenon, "Chinese C4I Modernization: An Experiment in Open Source Exploitation," 2003.

[72] Li Xuanqing and Ma Xiaochun, "Armed Forces' Communications Become 'Multidimensional'," *Xinhua Domestic Service,* July 16, 1997.

satellites (*Beidou*),[73] communications satellites (*Dongfanghong-4, Fenghuo*),[74] and phased-array radars.[75]

Yet the real question is: Will this increasingly advanced information-technology system in the military only improve the handling of information, or will it perform the much larger function of bootstrapping the PLA's much more primitive, much less informationized conventional forces? For the time being, the benefits seem restricted to the communications and information security arenas, and problems remain in "practical operation" (i.e., the practical application of these technologies to actual warfighting capabilities) in battle.[76] Yet the recent debate in Chinese military writings about "informationization" (*xinxihua* 信息化) provides some clues about their strategy, which appears to involve upgrading existing mechanized systems with information-technology systems rather than waiting to deploy next-generation high-tech platforms.[77] This is not the Revolution in Military Affairs or "network-centric warfare" as defined in the West, but a realistic use of China's growing IT capabilities to achieve short-term military capability gains. In an environment in which the United States and China continue to face the real possibility of military conflict over the Taiwan Strait, the accumulated contributions of the digital triangle could have a direct impact

---

[73] Geoffrey Forden, "Strategic Uses for China's Bei Dou Satellite System," *Jane's Intelligence Review,* October 1, 2003.

[74] Mark A. Stokes, *China's Strategic Modernization: Implications for the United States,* 1999; and Bill Gertz, "China's Military Links Forces to Boost Power," 2000, p. 1.

[75] "China's New Missile Destroyer: The 'Magic Shield of China'," *People's Daily,* May 29, 2003.

[76] Yan Yong, "Improving Capability to Handle Information," *Jiefangjun bao,* December 11, 2003.

[77] Many theoretical articles discuss this concept, which was first introduced by Jiang Zemin. For a typical theoretical treatment, see Su Kejia, "Thoughts on Promoting Military Changes with Chinese Characteristics" *Zhongguo guofang bao,* September 18, 2003, p. 3. Examples abound of the application of IT to existing equipment. For example, see He Kuangyang, Liu Jihua, Yuan Zhongchi, Jiao Weibo, and Pan Jinxin, "Adding Informatized Wings," *Jiefangjun huabao,* October 1, 2003, pp. 10–11.

on U.S. military operations, national security, and the defense of allies in the region.

To blunt or counter these trends, it is tempting to consider placing export controls on information technologies to China. The inherently dual-use nature of most information technology makes nonproliferation efforts difficult, if not mostly impossible. Moreover, the global nature of the IT industry renders most unilateral controls by the United States irrelevant. For example, even if the U.S. government can find a way to prevent Cisco from selling a system to a Chinese unit, a representative from Alcatel or Siemens will pick up the contract before it hits the ground. There are, of course, exceptions to this generalization. In some cases, the U.S. government may indeed have some leverage over international transfers of these technologies on a global level, and all appropriate measures should be taken. One suboptimal case is U.S. total dominance of a market, where export-control concerns need to be balanced against the possibility of giving aid and comfort to potential international competitors. A better case is the former sanctions regime in Iraq, where the UN mechanism provided a forum for preventing suspicious transfers.

Rather than focusing on stemming the tide of technology, it would be more productive to recognize the global proliferation of these technologies, then seek ways to exploit the proliferation to further U.S. interests. Doing so requires a two-step policy. The first goal should be the effective tracking of these technologies, which includes a range of activities from sophisticated information collection to simply reaching out to corporate representatives in a systematic way. Indeed, most of this information can be found easily in open sources. Second, the key to the power of these technologies is their integration, which requires a greater understanding by analysts of the technologies themselves, their limitations, and their possibilities.

CHAPTER SIX

Conclusions: Future Prospects of China's Defense Industry

China's defense industry has made gradual progress in improving the efficiency of its operations and the technological sophistication of its products. As measured by improvements in design and production processes and the quality of defense-enterprise output, defense-industrial reform and modernization are taking hold and appear to have accelerated in the past five years. These trends suggest that certain defense sectors are emerging from the doldrums of two and a half decades of systemic inefficiency, corruption, and neglect. At the same time, the improvements in China's defense-production capabilities have been decidedly mixed within sectors and uneven across them.

Current R&D and Production Activities Must Be Examined Sector by Sector

In examining improvements in China's defense industry, we have found that the progress curve is neither steep nor linear and that it is no longer possible to make broad generalizations about the Chinese defense-industrial base as a whole. While sweeping conclusions about the backwardness of the defense-industrial complex are no longer accurate, similar claims about *systemic* reform are equally unwarranted. Rather, this study argues that the current R&D and production activities of China's defense industry must now be examined sector by sector—an analytic approach that reveals more textured and nuanced conclusions about the ability of the various defense-industrial sectors to meet the needs of China's modernizing military, as well as highlighting new and innovative pathways for weapon procurement in China.

China's emerging IT sector, for example, is at the forefront of such trends; yet, it is atypical in many ways. Although not an officially designated part of China's defense-industrial complex, it is the most innovative and economically dynamic producer of equipment for China's military. China's IT enterprises do not suffer from many of the structural weaknesses and burdens that have hindered development of modern military equipment in China's traditional defense sectors. Rather, they are situated in dynamic locales with privileged access to pools of high-tech labor, capital, and foreign technology. And although they are primarily (and exclusively, in most instances) oriented toward domestic and international commercial markets, the PLA has been able to effectively leverage certain production capabilities to improve the military's C4I capabilities—a critical element of the PLA's modernization efforts. As China reaps the benefits of being the fastest-growing large market for IT equipment and consolidates its position as the global IT workshop, the Chinese military will continue to be an important, if indirect, beneficiary.

Unlike the IT industry, China's shipbuilding industry has been burdened with many of the trappings of the centrally planned economy of the past. Nonetheless, the industry has gradually flourished since Deng's reform and openness policies were introduced. It has rapidly expanded exports and has gained increasing access to foreign shipbuilding equipment and technical expertise as a consequence. As its commercial shipbuilding capabilities have expanded and improved, naval production has benefited, as well. China's shipbuilding industry now produces a wide range of increasingly sophisticated naval platforms, using modern design methods, production techniques, and management practices—as reflected in the serial production of several new platforms in the past five years. These improvements are likely to continue in the future. Yet, Chinese defense enterprises (both inside and outside the shipbuilding sector) still lack the ability to build some critical naval subsystems, limiting the overall warfighting capabilities of Chinese-produced naval vessels.

China's missile sector has historically been one of the brightest stars in China's defense industry. The technological progress that had been slow and steady since the 1980s appears to have accelerated in the past five years. Missile-production enterprises continued to produce new and increasingly advanced ballistic and cruise missiles— including serial production of new types of SRBMs. China may soon begin fielding land attack cruise missiles, modern long-range surface-to-air missiles, fire-and-forget air-to-air missiles, and anti-radiation missiles. China's ability to produce and deploy such systems in a timely manner will serve as an indicator of continued reform of the missile sector.

Until recently, the relative progress of the IT, shipbuilding, and missile sectors could be contrasted sharply with the failures of China's aviation industry. For years, this sector suffered under the weight of a large, bloated, technologically unsophisticated, and highly inefficient collection of R&D institutes and factories that failed to produce modern military aircraft in a timely manner. Those military fixed-wing aircraft that were produced were mainly improved versions of 1950s-era technology. In recent years, limited signs of progress have begun to emerge in this industry. China's first indigenously designed and produced combat aircraft (JH-7) recently entered service, and China is on the verge of producing a domestically developed fourth-generation aircraft (J-10/F-10), albeit with substantial foreign design assistance. China is also expected to begin producing its first operational turbofan engines, possibly ending its dependence on imported engines to power the modern combat aircraft it produces.

Important gaps in China's aviation design and production capabilities remain, however. China has not yet mastered serial production of complex aviation platforms, such as fourth-generation fighters. In addition, China is still unable to produce heavy bombers or large transport aircraft, and it has yet to field an indigenously designed helicopter. Although China has begun production of fourth-generation fighter aircraft, the United States has begun fielding fifth-generation fighters. Most importantly, critical structural weaknesses remain in China's aviation sector, inhibiting R&D advances. Thus, although China's aviation industry may be narrowing the gap with the world's most-advanced nations, it is unlikely to achieve parity with those nations in the foreseeable future.

Overall, relative to other countries, the Chinese defense industry's most acute weaknesses are *not* its lack of basic capabilities or institutions, which take years or even decades to build from scratch. Rather, many of the most severe shortcomings are in the incentives presented to the sectors and their component enterprises. These could shift in the medium term as the sectors become exposed to market-based pressures and/or the central government increases pressures for greater efficiency and quality.

In other words, China's defense industry now has the *potential* to become more competitive in some technologies with the defense industries of the world's advanced military powers in the next two decades. Indeed, our analysis of various indicators suggests that key defense sectors are already overcoming long-standing weaknesses. To be sure, the prevailing data set on defense-industry operations is still limited, and current progress has been mixed within defense sectors and uneven across them.

Four Factors Explain Progress in China's Defense Industry

As Chapters Two through Four have argued, the *recent* successes of the Chinese defense industry have been facilitated by four factors.

First, the gradual increases in government defense procurement have undoubtedly positively affected the output of defense enterprises. Such funds have been used to boost research and development and to facilitate new production practices, such as serial production of complex weapon platforms. The Chinese government has also rapidly increased expenditures devoted to raising the quality of physical capital in the industry. However, there are real limits to what more funding can buy in terms of technological innovation.

Second, defense enterprises have matured and commercialized gradually as China's economy has grown and modernized, and the spin-off-related benefits of commercial business operations have been particularly important in some defense sectors. Those Chinese enterprises with robust and rational commercial activities, especially those linked to international markets, have shown the greatest improvements in R&D and production capabilities (e.g., shipbuilding).

Third, many Chinese defense enterprises have consistently benefited from access to weapon technologies and technical expertise from foreign suppliers, such as Russia and Israel. Such access provided opportunities for copy-production, as well as the improvement of the design and production capabilities of China's engineers.

Fourth, recent organizational and policy reforms in the defense industry (at the government level and at the enterprise level of operations) have created incentives for managers to boost efficiency and improve their R&D and production capabilities. This factor will have an increasingly significant and enduring effect on facilitating defense-industrial modernization in the coming years.

Determining the relative importance of each one of these factors in creating a successful industry is beyond the currently available data. A key, unknown consideration is the extent to which the defense industry's increased and qualitatively improved output in the past few years is a result of growing government defense procurement and increased attention from the PLA or of genuine reform of defense-enterprise operations. Such knowledge would help in assessing the efficiency and innovative capacity of China's defense enterprises, thereby allowing a better evaluation of its future capabilities and output.

Many of the weaknesses of China's defense industry could be ameliorated in the medium term, assuming China does not deviate from its present course of reform of the defense-industrial system and government investment in defense R&D and production. Similarly, by breaking defense-industry corporations into semi-autonomous enterprises able to compete and participate in open bidding for contracts, China appears to be introducing limited competition into its defense-procurement process. If the government continues to push for open contracting and takes a tough line on cost overruns, the rate of innovation and quality of weapon systems should continue to improve. China is also beginning to encourage enterprises to improve the quality of their labor forces by freely hiring and firing employees, although this transformation will take time. China possesses a large and growing pool of technical talent that could be convinced to work for the defense sector if it is provided with the proper incentives. However, even though such reform could be accelerated, it will not happen overnight. Time is needed to train new employees into skilled defense-industry engineers and technicians. It will also take time to change management behavior and stimulate innovation, even after new management-incentive systems are implemented.

Thus, China's defense industry is currently on a course that will increasingly be able to provide China's military with highly capable weapons and equipment on a par with all but the world's most advanced militaries.

There Are Indicators of Future Improvements in Defense-Industry Operations

Traditional analyses of China's defense-industrial capabilities rely on observations of operational performance, engineering assessments of Chinese-produced items, and anecdotal accounts of industry operations. These will remain the most reliable means of evaluating the ability of China's defense industry to produce more-sophisticated weapon systems for the military. However, these measurements come after the fact and reveal little about enterprise-level reforms and how such weapon systems were actually designed and constructed.

We offer a number of leading indicators that will help analysts evaluate whether China's defense sectors are continuing the current path of improving their ability to produce sophisticated, quality weapon platforms and related subsystems. The indicators are

- Reports of traditional producers losing major contracts through a competitive bidding process and evidence that production has been transferred to the winning bidder
- Credible reports of substantial rewards or penalties for producing superior or inferior products
- Closure of poorly performing plants, while better performing plants continue to operate
- Significant contract awards to nontraditional suppliers, including nonstate enterprises
- Divestures and acquisitions driven by decisions taken by enterprise management, not ministries
- Privatization of defense manufacturers
- Substitution of domestic production for imports.

These indicators function as crucial benchmarks for evaluating both the willingness and ability of Chinese policymakers and defense-industry leaders to embrace the meaningful but painful policy changes that are needed to improve their innovative capacity and bolster their efficiency—the key challenges for them in the future. The extent to which some or all of these indicators are apparent in key sectors of China's defense economy in the future will also serve as important markers for evaluating the pace and scope of defense-industrial reform. The defense industry's implementation of such reforms, furthermore, will heavily influence the Chinese government's ability to translate its expanding resource base (in particular, the fraction devoted to military spending) toward PLA modernization. In this sense, assessing the current and future direction of China's defense-industrial capabilities is an important indicator of the future direction of the Chinese military, which is rapidly emerging as a central player in the future security and stability of the Asia-Pacific region in the 21st century.

Bibliography

NOTE ON ALPHABETIZATION OF NAMES: In keeping with the Chinese convention of stating last names first, we include last names of authors from China first and without a comma. All other names begin with the last name, then the first name, separated by a comma.

Aerospace Times Instrument Corporation, company brochure, 2002.

AFP, April 18, 2002, in *FBIS* as "AFP: China, Russia Sign Pact to Develop New Generation of Civil Aircraft," April 18, 2002.

Ai Min, "China Ordnance Moves Toward High-Tech Internationalization," *Liaowang,* April 12, 2004, pp. 32–33, as translated in *FBIS,* April 12, 2004.

Albert, Garret, "Research Priorities of China's Top Numbered Research Institutes," Santa Monica, Calif.: unpublished RAND Corporation research, 2004.

Allen, Kenneth W., Glenn Krumel, and Jonathan D. Pollack, *China's Air Force Enters the 21st Century,* Santa Monica, Calif.: RAND Corporation, MR-580-AF, 1995.

Almquist, Peter, "Chinese and Russian Defense Industries: Problems and Prospects," Washington, D.C.: unpublished manuscript, 2003.

An Weiping, "Thoughts on Developing Armaments by Leaps and Bounds," *Jiefangjun bao,* April 6, 1999, in *FBIS,* April 6, 1999.

Anhui Province, Bengbu City Government website, http://www.bengbu .gov.cn/zjzy/wxs.htm.

"ARJ-21 Will Be the Centerpiece of Airshow China 2004," *Aviation Week and Space Technology*, September 13, 2004.

Arnett, Eric, "Military Technology: The Case of China," *SIPRI Yearbook 1995: Armaments, Disarmament and International Security*, New York: Oxford University Press, 1995.

AVIC I website, http://www.avic1.com.cn/Chinese/qyzc/qyzc_zyqy_shhkfdjzzc.htm; accessed May 20, 2004.

"AVIC II Completes Stock System Transformation: Main Areas of Business Are Aircraft, Automobiles, Etc.," *People's Daily Online*, May 19, 2003. Available online at www.peopledaily.com.cn/|GB/junshi/60/20030519/995654.html; accessed May 20, 2003.

AVIC II website, http://www.avic2.com.cn/ReadNews.asp?NewsID=170 &BigClassName=企业风采&SmallClassName=发动机类&DispType= 1&SpecialID=0 (accessed May 20, 2004); http://www.avic2.com.cn/ ReadNews.asp?NewsID=171&BigClassName=企业风采&SmallClassNa me=发动机类 &DispType=1&SpecialID=0 (accessed May 20, 2004. 常州兰翔机械总厂.

AVIC IT website, http://www.avicit.com/.

Baark, Erik, "Fragmented Innovation: China's Science and Technology Policy Reforms in Retrospect," in Joint Economic Committee, ed., *China's Economic Dilemmas in the 1990s: The Problems of Reforms, Modernization, and Interdependence*, Washington, D.C.: U.S. Government Printing Office, 1991.

———, "Military Technology and Absorptive Capacity in China and India: Implications for Modernization," in Eric Arnett, ed., *Military Capacity and the Risk of War: China, India, Pakistan and Iran*, Oxford, England: Oxford University Press, 1997.

Barrie, Douglas, "Chinese Fireworks," *Aviation Week and Space Technology*, November 8, 2004.

———, "Great Leap Forward . . . in Small Steps," *Aviation Week and Space Technology*, November 8, 2004.

Barrie, Douglas, and Jason Sherman, "China Seeks British Engine," *Defense News*, July 2–8, 2001.

Beaver, Paul, "Business Focus: China Focuses on Core Aerospace Production," *Jane's Defence Weekly*, March 11, 1998.

Beijing Aeronautical Manufacturing Technology Research Institute, Xi'an Aero-Engine Controls Co., China, Xi'an XR Aero Components Co. Ltd, Beijing Shuguang Electrical Machinery Factory, Pingyuan Hydraulic Filters, and *Tianjin Aviation Electro Mechanical Co., Ltd.,* brochures acquired at Airshow China, Zhuhai, November 2002.

Beijing Avic Property Management Co., established by No. 1 and No. 2 China Aviation Industry Groups and BEIJING RUISI http://www.avic2. com.cn/ReadNews.asp?NewsID=168&BigClassName=企业风采&Small ClassName=发动机类&DispType=1&SpecialID=0; accessed May 20, 2004.

Bie Yixun and Xu Dianlong, *Xinhua Domestic Service,* January 7, 1998, in *FBIS* as "Wu Bangguo Greets Opening of Ordnance Industry Meeting," January 12, 1998.

Biggs, Cassie, "China Looks Abroad to Tap Potential of Aviation Market," *AFP in English,* November 6, 2000, in *FBIS* as "AFP: China Hoping Foreign Alliances Will Boost Aviation Industry," November 6, 2000.

Bingqi zhishi, March 2004, in *FBIS* as "PRC Anti-Tank Missile HJ-9A Features Advanced Guidance System."

Bitzinger, Richard, "Arms to Go: Chinese Arms Sales to the Third World," *International Security,* Fall 1992.

———, "Just the Facts, Ma'am: The Challenge of Analysing and Assessing Chinese Military Expenditures," *China Quarterly,* No. 173, 2003, pp. 164–175.

Boeing website, http://www.boeing.com/special/aboutus/overview/overview.htm.

Brömmelhörster, Jorn, and John Frankenstein, eds., *Mixed Motives, Uncertain Outcomes: Defense Conversion in China,* Boulder, Colo.: Lynne Rienner Publishers, 1997.

Burles, Mark, *Chinese Policy Toward Russia and the Central Asian Republics,* Santa Monica, Calif.: RAND Corporation, MR-1045-AF, 1999.

Burles, Mark, and Abram N. Shulsky, *Patterns in China's Use of Force: Evidence from History and Doctrinal Writings,* Santa Monica, Calif.: RAND Corporation, MR-1160-AF, 2000.

Byman, Daniel, and Roger Cliff, *China's Arms Sales: Motivations and Implications,* Santa Monica, Calif.: RAND Corporation, MR-1119-AF, 1999.

Cao Zhi, Tian Zhaoyun, and Xu Zhuangzhi, "Launch of 'Shenzhou' Space-craft," *Xinhua,* December 29, 2002, in *FBIS,* December 29, 2002.

"CASC's Solid Rocket Motor Research Institute Celebrates 40 Years," *Shaanxi ribao,* July 1, 2002, in *FBIS*, July 1, 2002.

"CASIC Displays New Aerospace Products," *Zhongguo hangtian,* October 1, 2002, in *FBIS*, October 1, 2002.

CASIC website, www.casic.com.cn/docc/qiye/content.asp?id-114; accessed December 29, 2003.

CASIC website, www.casic.com.cn/docc/qiye/content.asp?id-113; accessed December 29, 2003.

CASIC website, www.casic.com.cn/docc/qiye/content.asp?id=60; accessed December 29, 2003.

CASIC website, www.casic.com.cn/docc/qiye/content.asp?id=59; accessed December 29, 2003.

"Central Military Commission Chairman Jiang Zemin Signs Order Promulgating and Implementing Chinese People's Liberation Army Equipment Procurement Regulations," *Xinhua,* November 1, 2002, as noted in *FBIS*, November 1, 2002.

Central Television Program One Network, July 1, 1999, in *FBIS* as "Zhu at Defense Ceremony," July 1, 1999.

Chen, Kathy, "Soldiers of Fortune: Chinese Army Fashions Major Role for Itself as a Business Empire," *Wall Street Journal,* May 24, 1994.

Chen Lan, "Xie Shijie, Zhang Zhongwei Address, Huang Yinki Presides, at Seminar Held by Provincial Party Committee and Provincial Government for Some of the War Industry Enterprises and Institutions: Have a Clear Understanding of the Situation, Change Concept, and Seize Opportunity to Speed Up Development," *Sichuan ribao,* December 4, 1999, in *FBIS* as "Provincial Party Holds Seminar for War Industry Firms," December 4, 1999.

Chen Song, *Bingqi zhishi,* November 2003.

Chen Wanjun and Chen Guofang, "Birth of China's First Defense Mobilization Vessel," *Jianchuan zhishi* (*Naval and Merchant Ships*), February 6, 1997, in *FBIS*, February 6, 1997.

Chen Zengjun, "Ordnance Industry Turns into Vital New National Economic Force," *Jingji ribao,* November 20, 1998, in *FBIS* as "Ordnance Industry Becomes 'Vital' Economic Force," December 12, 1998.

Cheng Gang and Li Xuanqing, "Military Telecommunications Building Advances Toward Modernization with Giant Strides," *Liberation Army Daily,* July 17, 1997, in *FBIS*, August 20, 1997.

Cheung, Tai Ming, *China's Entrepreneurial Army,* Studies in Contemporary China, Oxford University Press, 2002.

China Aerospace Science & Technology Corporation website, http://www.spacechina.com/index.asp?modelname=htzz_gd; accessed December 30, 2003.

"China Aerospace Science and Technology Corporation," *Zhongguo hangtian (China Aerospace),* October 1, 2002, in *FBIS*, October 2002.

China Aviation Industry Corporation I and *China Aviation Industry Corporation II,* brochures obtained at Airshow China, Zhuhai, November 2002.

"China Company to Export 200 Planes in Next 5 Years," *Xinhua,* January 10, 2000, in *FBIS*, January 10, 2000.

China Daily, September 1, 1999.

China Daily (Internet version), June 1, 2002, in *FBIS* as "China's 'Kunlun' Engine Ready Soon to Power Nation's Military Planes," June 1, 2002.

China Electronic News, September 22, 2000.

China Enterprise Federation/China Enterprise Directors Association website, http://www.cec-ceda.org.cn/news/?id=288.

"China Launches a Powerful Super Warship," *Jane's Defence Weekly,* February 3, 1999.

China National Guizhou Aviation Industry (Group) Co., Ltd., Hongdu Aviation Industry Group, and *L15 A Next Generation Advanced/Lead-In Fighter Trainer,* brochures acquired at Airshow China, Zhuhai, November 2002.

China Sanjiang Space Industry Group website, www.cssg.com.cn; accessed December 29, 2003.

"China Sets New Record in Shipbuilding in 2003," *People's Daily Online,* January 6, 2004.

China Ship News, December 1995.

China Space News, July 16, 2003.

"China Tests New Land-Attack Cruise Missile," *Jane's Missiles and Rockets,* October 1, 2004.

"China's First-Ever Five Hits for Five Tries in Test of Air-to-Air Missile," *Qianlong xinwen wang,* September 4, 2002, in *FBIS* as "Qianlong: PRC Air-Air Missile Developed at 601 Institute Successfully Tested," September 4, 2002.

"China's Flying Leopard Will Be Shown at the Great Celebration," *Ta kung pao,* September 21, 1999, in *FBIS* as "New Generation of Jets to Appear at National Day," September 21, 1999.

China Shipbuilding Info-Tech Co., Ltd. website, www.shipbuilding. com.cn.

"China's Largest Shipbuilding Company Receives 6 Million Tons of New Orders in 2004," *Xinhua,* January 24, 2005.

China's National Defense in 2002, Beijing, China: Information Office of the State Council, October 2002.

China's National Defense in 2002, December 9, 2002, in *FBIS* as "Xinhua: 'Full Text' of White Paper on China's National Defense in 2002," December 9, 2002.

China's National Defense in 2004, Beijing, China: Information Office of the State Council, December 2004. Available at http://www.china.org.cn/ ewhite/20041227/index.htm

"China's New Missile Destroyer: The 'Magic Shield of China'," *People's Daily,* May 29, 2003.

"China's Ordnance Industry Achieves Marked Successes in Reform and Reorganization to Streamline and Improve Core Business," *Xinhua Domestic Service,* January 19, 2000, in *FBIS* as "PRC Ordnance Industry Reform Results," February 10, 2000.

"China's Shipbuilding Capacity Remains Third in World," *Xinhua,* January 24, 2005.

"China's Shipbuilding Giant Consolidates Bases," *Xinhua,* November 26, 2002.

China's Shipbuilding Trading Company Ltd. website, www.chinaships .com/co/xuke.htm.

China's Shipyards: Capacity, Competition and Challenges, London, UK: Drewery Shipping Consultants Ltd., July 2003.

"China's 3G Mobile Technology Debuts," *China Daily,* April 12, 2001.

Chinese Defence Today website, www.sinodefence.com. (Chinese Defence Today is an unofficial website. Opinions and comments in this website do not reflect the views or positions of the Chinese or any other government or military authority.)

"Chinese Defence Industry: Chinese Puzzle," *Jane's Defence Weekly,* January 21, 2004.

Chinese Military Aviation website, http://www.concentric.net/~Jetfight/index.htm.

"Chinese Premier Underlines Science, Technology for National Defense," *People's Daily* (English edition), July 2, 1999.

"Chinese Puzzle," *Jane's Defence Weekly,* January 21, 2004.

Ci Shihai, *Budui zhuangbei guanli gailun* (*Army Equipment Management Theory*), Beijing, China: Junshi Kexue Chubanshe, 2001.

Cliff, Roger, *The Military Potential of China's Commercial Technology,* Santa Monica, Calif.: RAND Corporation, MR-1292-AF, 2001.

Commission of the European Communities, *Second Report from the Commission to the Council on the Situation in World Shipbuilding,* Brussels, May 2000. Available online at http://europa.eu.int/comm/enterprise/maritime/shipbuilding_market/doc/com2000-263_en.pdf.

"Company Introduction," CASIC website, http://www.casic.com.cn/docc/jieshao/jianjie.asp; accessed December 31, 2003.

Conroy Richard, *Technological Change in China,* Paris: Development Centre of the Organization for Economic Co-operation and Development, 1992.

Corinna-Barbara, Francis, "Commercialization Without Privatization: Government Spin-Offs in China's High Technology Sector," in Judith B. Sedaitis, ed., *Commercializing High Technology: East and West: Selected Conference Papers,* Stanford, Calif.: Center for International Security and Arms Control, 1997.

"Country Briefing—People's Republic of China, Air Force Frontliners to See New Fighter Breed," *Jane's Defence Weekly,* December 16, 1998.

"CPMIEC Hongqi-1 Medium- to High-Altitude Surface-to-Air Missile System," *Jane's Land-Based Air Defence 1996–1997,* April 12, 1996. Available online at http://online.janes.com/; accessed November 25, 2003.

CSIS website, www.csic.com.cn.

CSSC website, www.cssc.net.cn.

CSTC website, www.cstc.com.cn.

Dai Longji, Zhang Qisu, and Cai Ronghua, eds., *Index of Core Chinese Journals,* Beijing, China: Peking University Press, 2000, pp. 626–629.

"Defense Commission Minister Sets Targets for 2002," *Zhongguo xinwen she,* January 7, 2002, in *FBIS,* January 7, 2002.

"Defense Industry Breaks Even in 2002," *China Daily* (Internet version), January 9, 2002.

Ding, Arthur S., "Economic Reform and Defence Industries in China," in Gerald Segal and Richard S. Yang, eds., *Chinese Economic Reform,* New York: Routledge, 1996.

Downs, Erica Strecker, *China's Quest for Energy Security,* Santa Monica, Calif.: RAND Corporation, MR-1244-AF, 2000.

DSTI Digest, December 1995.

Eikenberry, Karl W., *Explaining and Influencing Chinese Arms Transfers,* Washington, D.C.: National Defense University, McNair Papers 36, February 1995.

Electronic Science Academy (ESA) website, http://www.etnet.com.cn/xhxh/semiconductor.htm.

"EU May End China Arms Sales Ban," Associated Press, January 24, 2004.

Fan Juwei, "Quality of Our Large-Sized Complicated Armaments Is Steadily Improving," *Jiefangjun bao,* July 19, 2001, translated in *FBIS,* July 19, 2001.

Fan Rixuan, "The Profound Impact of China's WTO Accession on People's Lives and Thinking, as Well as on National Defense and Military Modernization Drive—Thoughts on China's WTO Admission and National Defense Building," *Jiefangjun bao* (Internet version), April 30, 2002, in *FBIS* as "Article Discusses Impact of China's WTO Admission on National Defense Building," May 2, 2002.

FBIS (Foreign Broadcast Information Service), "Highlights: PRC Central Leaders' Activities 3 Jun–1 Jul 03," July 1, 2003.

———, "Report on PRC Central Leaders' Activities 26 Aug–6 Sep," September 7, 2001.

———, "*Xinhua:* 'Full Text' of White Paper on China's National Defense in 2002," December 9, 2002.

Feigenbaum, Evan, "The Military Transforms China: The Politics of Strategic Technology from the Nuclear to the Information Age," Dissertation Manuscript, Palo Alto, Calif.: Stanford University, August 1997.

Felker, Greg, "Malaysia's Industrial Technology Development: Firms, Policies, and Political Economy," in K. S. Jomo, Greg Felker, and Rajah Rasiah, eds., *Industrial Technology Development in Malaysia: Industry and Firm Studies,* New York: Routledge, 1998.

Fisher, Richard, "Report on the 5th Airshow China," China Brief, Washington, D.C.: Jamestown Foundation, December 13, 2004.

Forden, Geoffrey, "Strategic Uses for China's Bei Dou Satellite System," *Jane's Intelligence Review,* October 1, 2003.

Foss, Christopher F., "China Markets Improved Red Arrow 9 Missile," *Jane's Defence Weekly,* November 10, 2004.

———, "China Markets Upgraded Anti-Tank Weapon, *Jane's Defence Weekly,* July 23, 2003.

"Fourteen Pilots with Right Stuff Ready for Liftoff," *South China Morning Post,* May 22, 2002, in *FBIS* as "China Prepares Fourteen Pilots as Astronauts," May 22, 2002.

Frankenstein, John, "China's Defense Industries: A New Course?" in James C. Mulvenon and Richard H. Yang, eds., *The People's Liberation Army in the Information Age,* Santa Monica, Calif.: RAND Corporation, CF-145-CAPP/AF, 1999.

———, "The People's Republic of China: Arms Production, Industrial Strategy and Problems of History," in Herbert Wulf, *Arms Industry Limited,* New York: Oxford University Press for SIPRI, 1993.

Frankenstein, John, and Bates Gill, "Current and Future Challenges Facing Chinese Defense Industries," *China Quarterly,* June 1996, pp. 394–427.

Frieman, Wendy, "Arms Procurement in China: Poorly Understood Processes and Unclear Results," in Eric Arnett, ed., *Military Capacity and the Risk of War: China, India, Pakistan and Iran,* Oxford, England: Oxford University Press, 1997.

————, "China's Defence Industries," *Pacific Review,* Vol. 6, No. 1, 1993.

————, "China's Military R&D System: Reform and Reorientation," in Denis Fred Simon and Merle Goldman, eds., *Science and Technology in Post-Mao China,* Cambridge, Mass.: Harvard University Press, 1989.

Fu Jing, "Defense Industry Eyes Foreign Cash," *China Daily,* July 4, 2001, in *FBIS* as "Chinese Defense Industry Eyes More Foreign Investment," July 4, 2001.

Fu Zhenguo, "Go, Go, Flying Leopard, Flying Leopard," *Renmin ribao* (Overseas Edition), October 4, 1999, in *FBIS* as "PLA Air Force Displays 'Flying Leopard,' Aerial Refueling," October 8, 1999.

Gallagher, Joseph P., "China's Military Industrial Complex," *Asian Survey,* Vol. XXVII, No. 9, September 1987.

Gao Jiquan, "Shoulder Heavy Responsibilities, Accept New Challenges— Interviewing Liu Jibin, Newly Appointed State Commission of Science, Technology, and Industry for National Defense Minister," *Jiefangjun bao,* April 9, 1998, in *FBIS* as "New COSTIND Minister Interviewed," April 9, 1998.

Gertz, Bill, "China's Military Links Forces to Boost Power," *Washington Times,* March 16, 2000.

Gill, Bates, *Chinese Arms Transfers: Purposes, Patterns and Prospects in the New World Order,* Westport, Conn.: Praeger Publishers, 1992.

————, "Chinese Military-Technical Development: The Record for Western Assessments, 1979–1999," in James C. Mulvenon and Andrew N. D. Yang, eds., *Seeking Truth from Facts: A Retrospective on Chinese Military Studies in the Post-Mao Era,* Santa Monica, Calif.: RAND Corporation, CF-160-CAPP, 2001.

————, "The Impact of Economic Reform on Chinese Defense Production," in C. Dennison Lane, ed., *Chinese Military Modernization,* London, United Kingdom: Paul Kegan International, 1996.

Gill, Bates, and Lonnie Henley, *China and the Revolution in Military Affairs,* Carlisle, Pa.: U.S. Army War College, Strategic Studies Institute, 1996.

Gilley, Bruce, "Flying Start: Europeans Offer China Aircraft-Carrier Systems," *Far Eastern Economic Review,* March 11, 1999.

———, "Huawei's Fixed Line to Beijing," *Far Eastern Economic Review,* December 28, 2000–January 4, 2001.

Goldstein, Lyle, and William Murray, "China Emerges as a Maritime Power," *Jane's Intelligence Review,* October 2004.

Gong Fangling, "There Should Be New Ideas in Defense Economic Building," *Jiefangjun bao,* September 14, 1999, in *FBIS* as "Article on 'Defense Economic Building'," September 23, 1999.

Gong Huo, *China Daily,* May 15, 2001.

Government Accountabililty Office, *Export Controls: Sale of Telecommunications Equipment to China,* Washington, D.C., GAO/NSIAD-97-5, November 1996.

———, *Export Controls: Sensitive Machine Tool Exports to China,* Washington, D.C., GAO/NSIAD-97-4, November 1996.

"Government Procurement Again Recommended at NPC," *Xinhua,* March 8, 1999, in *FBIS* as "Government Procurement Again Recommended at NPC," March 8, 1999.

Gu Ti, *Zhongguo hangtian bao,* November 20, 2002, in *FBIS* as "PRC S&T: Kaituozhe New Choice for Small Satellite Launches," November 20, 2002.

Guangming Daily, July 20, 2000.

Guangming ribao, June 6, 2002.

———, August 27, 2002.

Guangzhou Enterprise Evaluation Association, *Zhongguo Guangzhou daxing qiye paixu (Ranking of Guangzhou's Large-Sized Enterprises),* Guangzhou, China: Zhongshan University Publishing House, 1994.

Guilin University of Electronic Technology websites, http://www.gliet.edu.cn/gaikuang/lishi86_90.htm and http://www2.gliet.edu.cn/dept2/yj.htm.

Guizhou Aviation Corporation brochure, 2002.

Gunston, Bill, and Mike Spick, *Modern Air Combat: The Aircraft, Tactics, and Weapons Employed in Aerial Warfare Today,* New York: Crescent Books, 1983.

Guo Aibing, *China Daily* (Internet version), June 13, 2000, in *FBIS* as "PRC Aviation Makers to Focus on Building Small Airplanes," June 13, 2000.

Guo Yuanfa, "The Painstaking Development of an Ace Aircraft—Report on the Birth of China's All Weather Supersonic Fighter-Bomber 'Flying Leopard'," *Liaowang*, October 4, 1999, in *FBIS* as "Development of 'Flying Leopard' Recounted," October 4, 1999.

"Guofang Keji Gongye Jinyibu Canyu Xibu Dakaifa he Dongbei Zhenxing de Zhidao Yijian," *Kegongwei Tongzhi* (*COSTIND Notification*), No. 815, July 17, 2004. Available online at www.costind.gov.cn; accessed January 2005.

Guoji hangkong, February 2004, pp. 10–15, in *FBIS* as "PRC S&T: Focusing on China's Aviation Industry in 2004."

Hangtian (*China Aerospace*), June 28, 1996, in *FBIS* as "Chinese Perigee Kick Motor Developed, Used for AsiaSat, Echostar Satellite Launches," June 28, 1996.

He Kuangyang, Liu Jihua, Yuan Zhongchi, Jiao Weibo, and Pan Jinxin, "Adding Informatized Wings," *Jiefangjun huabao*, October 1, 2003.

Hewson, Robert, "AS-17 'Krypton' (Kh-31A, Kh-31P), YJ-91/KR-1," *Jane's Air-Launched Weapons*, Vol. 43, September 19, 2003. Available online at http://online.janes.com/; accessed November 25, 2003.

————, "C-701 (YJ-7)," *Jane's Air-Launched Weapons*, Vol. 42, July 16, 2003. Available online at http://online.janes.com/; accessed November 25, 2003.

————, "China, Iran Share Missile Know-How," *Jane's Defence Weekly*, December 4, 2002.

————, "China's New Air-to-Air Missile Operational This Year," *Jane's Defence Weekly*, January 7, 2004.

————, "China's Su-27s May Fall Short in Capability," *Jane's Defence Weekly*, November 17, 2004.

————, "China Unveils Future Y-8 Airlifter," *Jane's Defence Weekly*, December 4, 2002.

————, "500 kg Laser-Guided Bomb (LGB)," *Jane's Air-Launched Weapon Systems*, Vol. 43, October 7, 2003. Available online at http://online.janes.com/; accessed November 25, 2003.

————, "HJ-8 (HONGJIAN 8)," *Jane's Air-Launched Weapons,* Vol. 41, September 12, 2002. Available online at http://online.janes.com; accessed November 25, 2003.

————, "HY-4 (C-201)," *Jane's Air-Launched Weapons,* Vol. 40, July 9, 2002. Available online at http://online.janes.com/; accessed November 25, 2003.

————, "LY-60 Air-Launched Variant," *Jane's Air-Launched Weapons,* Vol. 42, April 30, 2003. Available online at http://online.janes.com; accessed November 25, 2003.

————, "PL-2/PL-3," *Jane's Air-Launched Weapons,* Vol. 40, May 30, 2002. Available online at http://online.janes.com/; accessed November 25, 2003.

————, "PL-5," *Jane's Air-Launched Weapons,* Vol. 43, September 19, 2003. Available online at http://online.janes.com; accessed November 25, 2003.

————, "PL-7," *Jane's Air-Launched Weapons,* Vol. 42, April 30, 2003. Available online at http://online.janes.com/; accessed November 25, 2003.

————, "PL-8," *Jane's Air-Launched Weapons,* Vol. 42, April 30, 2003. Available online at http://online.janes.com/; accessed November 25, 2003.

————, "PL-9," *Jane's Air-Launched Weapons,* Vol. 42, July 23, 2003. Available online at http://online.janes.com/; accessed November 25, 2003.

————, "PL-10/PL-11," *Jane's Air-Launched Weapons,* Vol. 42, April 30, 2003. Available online at http://online.janes.com; accessed November 25, 2003.

————, "PL-11 (PL-10) and FD-60, AMR-1," *Jane's Air-Launched Weapon Systems,* Vol 43, November 26, 2004. Available online at http://online.janes.com; accessed January 21, 2005.

————, "SD-10 (PL-12)," *Jane's Air-Launched Weapons,* Vol. 42, July 16, 2003. Available online at http://online.janes.com/; accessed November 25, 2003.

————, "TY-90," *Jane's Air-Launched Weapons,* Vol. 41, January 17, 2003. Available online at http://online.janes.com/; accessed November 25, 2003.

————, "YJ-6/C-601 (CAS-1 'Kraken')," *Jane's Air-Launched Weapons,* Vol. 40, July 9, 2002. Available online at http://online.janes.com/; accessed November 25, 2003.

————, "YJ-6/C-601 (CAS-1 'Kraken')," *Jane's Air-Launched Weapons,* Vol. 40, July 9, 2002. Available online at http://online.janes.com/; accessed November 25, 2003.

————, "YJ-91, KR-1 (Kh-31P)," *Jane's Air-Launched Weapons,* Vol. 43, September 19, 2003. Available online at http://online.janes.com/; accessed November 25, 2003.

Hooten, E. R., "C-701," *Jane's Naval Weapon Systems,* Vol. 38, December 20, 2002. Available online at http://online.janes.com/; accessed November 25, 2003.

————, "CSS-N-1 'Scrubbrush' (SY-1/HY-1); CSS-N-2 'Silkworm'; CSS-N-3 'Seersucker' (HY-2/FL-1/FL-3A)," *Jane's Naval Weapon Systems,* Vol. 39, September 11, 2003. Available online at http://online.janes.com/; accessed November 25, 2003.

————, "CSS-N-4 'Sardine' (YJ-1/C-801); CSS-N-8 'Saccade' (YJ-2/C-802); CY-1/C-803)," *Jane's Naval Weapon Systems,* Vol. 39, August 28, 2003. Available online at http://online.janes.com/; accessed November 25, 2003.

————, "SD-1 (CSA-N-2)," *Jane's Naval Weapon Systems,* Vol. 39, May 6, 2003. Available online at http://online.janes.com/; accessed November 25, 2003.

Hsiao Cheng-chin, "Liu Jibin, Minister in Charge of the State Commission of Science, Technology, and Industry for National Defense and a Veteran Who Has Rejoined His Original Unit," *Hsin pao,* June 3, 1998, in *FBIS* as "Article on New Minister Liu Jibin," June 12, 1998.

Huang Jianding and Zhang Fenglin, *Hangtian,* May 1995, in *FBIS* as "Solid Rocket Motors for Launch Vehicles, Tactical Missiles Detailed," May 1, 1995.

Huang Pingtao, "Strengthen International Cooperation to Promote the Conversion to Civilian Shipbuilding Production," paper presented at the

International Conference on the Conversion of China's Military Industries, Beijing, June 1995.

Huang Qiang, "Will China's Aviation Industry Be Able to Get Out of the Doldrums Soon?" *Keji ribao,* July 8, 1999, in *FBIS* as "Current Situation of Aerospace Industry," August 11, 1999.

Huang Tung, "China's 'New Flying Leopard' Short-Range Air Defense Missile System," *Kuang chiao ching,* No. 365, February 16, 2003, p. 61, in *FBIS* as "China's New 'Flying Leopard' Short-Range Air-Defense Missile System," February 16, 2003.

———, "Successful Test-Flight of New Flying Leopard Fighter Bomber JH-7A," *Kuang chiao ching,* November 16, 2002, in *FBIS* as "PRC Flying Leopard Fighter Bomber JH-7A Profiled in Test Flight—PHOTO," November 16, 2002.

Hunter, Jamie, "Boeing (McDonnell Douglas) F-4 Phantom II," *Jane's All the World's Aircraft,* January 26, 2004. Available online at http://online.janes.com; accessed May 18, 2004.

———, "Nanchang Q-5," *Jane's All the World's Aircraft,* February 10, 2004. Available online at http://online.janes.com; accessed May 18, 2004.

———, "Panavia Tornado IDS," *Jane's All the World's Aircraft,* April 15, 2004. Available online at http://online.janes.com; accessed May 18, 2004.

———, "Sukhoi Su-24," *Jane's All the World's Aircraft,* April 28, 2004. Available online at http://online.janes.com; accessed May 18, 2004.

———, "Xian (Antonov) Y-7," *Jane's Aircraft Upgrades 2004–2005,* February 10, 2004. Available online at http://online.janes.com; accessed March 8, 2004.

Huo Yongzhe and Gong Zhengzheng, *China Daily* (Internet version), May 15, 2001, in *FBIS* as "Article on PRC Plan to Develop New Generation of Regional Passenger Planes," May 15, 2001.

"Interview by Central People's Radio Network Reporter Zhao Lianju: Work Earnestly to Usher in the Spring of Science and Industry for National Defense—Interviewing Liu Jibin, Minister in Charge of the Commission of Science, Technology, and Industry for National

Defense," March 30, 1998, in *FBIS* as "PRC Minister on Future Projects for Defense Commission," March 30, 1998.

Ion, Edward, "China Mounts Renewed Challenge," *Shipbuilding and Shiprepair,* Summer 1992.

———, "Guangzhou Provides Beacon for Mainland," *Shipbuilding and Shiprepair,* Winter 1995.

Jackson, Paul, "Sukhoi Su-27," *Jane's All the World's Aircraft,* October 16, 2003. Available online at http://online.janes.com; accessed May 18, 2004.

Jacobs, Gordon, "Chinese Naval Developments Post Gulf War," *Jane's Intelligence Review,* February 1993.

———, "Chinese Navy Destroyer Dalian," *Navy International,* September/October 1992.

———, "PLAN's ASW Frigate Siping," *Navy International,* March/April 1993.

Jane's Land-Based Air Defence, 2003.

Jane's Strategic Weapon Systems, Vol. 39, 2003.

Jencks, Harlan, "The General Armaments Department," in James C. Mulvenon and Andrew N. D. Yang, eds., *The People's Liberation Army as Organization: Reference Volume v1.0,* Santa Monica, Calif.: RAND Corporation, CF-182-NSRD, 2002. Available only online at http://www.rand.org/publications/CF/CF182/.

Ji Xiang, "China's Shipbuilding Industry Moving to World's Top Ranks," *Ta kung pao (Da gong bao),* October 27, 2004.

Jia Xiping and Xu Dianlong, "China's Ordnance Industry Achieves Marked Successes in Reform and Reorganization to Streamline and Improve Core Business," *Xinhua Domestic Service,* January 19, 2000, in *FBIS* as "PRC Ordnance Industry Reform Results," February 10, 2000.

Jian Yun, "'Hongqi' Dares to Compare Itself with 'Sidewinder'—Interview with Zhong Shan, Academician at Chinese Academy of Engineering and Chief Designer of Hongqi Low-Altitude Missile Series," *Qingnian cankao,* February 20, 2002, in *FBIS,* February 20, 2002.

Jiang Huai and Fu Cheng, "Beijing Military Representatives Bureau Cooperates with Five Provinces and Cities in North China in Building

Regional Cooperation with Various Layers and Professions," *Jiefangjun bao,* September 18, 2000, as translated in *FBIS,* September 18, 2000.

Jiang Zemin et al., in *FBIS* as "Report on PRC Central Leaders' Activities 26 Aug–6 Sep," September 7, 2001.

Jiangnan Shipyard website, www.jnshipyard.com.cn.

Jiangnan Space Group website, www.cjspace.com.cn; accessed December 31, 2003.

Jiefangjun bao, November 14, 2001, translated in *FBIS* as "PRC: Article on PLA Plant Manufacturing Special Military Vehicles," November 14, 2001.

Jin Hang Shuma Keji Gongsi, "On the Establishment of Golden Aviation Digital Science and Technology Corporation," *Zhongguo hangkong bao,* December 29, 2000, in *FBIS* as "PRC Information Technology Company Gains High-Level Support," December 29, 2000.

"Jungong Shangshi Qiye 2001 Nian Pandian," *Zhongguo junzhuanmin* (*China Defense Conversion*), July 2002.

Kaplan, Brad (USN), "China's Navy Today: Storm Clouds on the Horizon . . . or Paper Tiger?" *Seapower,* December 1999.

Karniol, Robert, "Air Defence Systems Unveiled," *Jane's Defence Weekly,* November 17, 2004.

———, "Airshow China 2002—China's New Turbojet Engine," *Jane's Defence Weekly,* November 13, 2002.

———, "Beijing Displays New Tactical Surface-to-Surface System," *Jane's Defence Weekly,* November 10, 2004.

———, "China Debuts L-15 Trainer Mock-Up," *Jane's Defence Weekly,* November 10, 2004.

———, "New Variant of Chinese Fighter Planned," *Jane's Defence Weekly,* November 10, 2004.

———, "Turbofan Engine Boasts Greater Thrust Capability," *Jane's Defence Weekly,* November 17, 2004.

Ke Wen, "Advantages and Disadvantages of WTO Accession to China's Military Industry, Science and Technology—Interviewing Liu Jibin, Minister in Charge of Commission of Science, Technology, and Industry for National Defense," *Chiao ching,* June 16, 2000, in *FBIS* as "Minister

Liu Jibin on Pros, Cons of WTO Accession to PRC Defense Industry," June 20, 2000.

Khalilzad, Zalmay, Abram N. Shulsky, Daniel Byman, Roger Cliff, David T. Orletsky, David A. Shlapak, and Ashley J. Tellis, *The United States and a Rising China: Strategic and Military Implications,* Santa Monica, Calif.: RAND Corporation, MR-1082-AF, 1999.

Koenig, Philip C., *Report on SNAME's Technical Delegation to China,* December 29, 2000. Available online at http://www.onrglobal .navy.mil/reports/2000/sname.htm; accessed June 2004.

Kuan Cha-chia, "Jiang Zemin Sets Up General Equipment Department, Zhu Rongji Advances Military Reform," *Kuang chiao ching,* April 16, 1998, in *FBIS* as "Establishment of Military Department Noted," May 6, 1998.

Lardier, Christian, "Chinese Space Industry's Ambition," *Air & Cosmos/ Aviation International,* October 25, 1996, pp. 36–37, in *FBIS* as "Ambitions of Nation's Space Industry Outlined at IAF 96 World Space Congress," October 25, 1996.

Laur, Timothy M., and Steven L. Llanso, *Encyclopedia of Modern U.S. Military Weapons,* New York: Berkley Books, 1995.

Lei Biao and Dang Chaohui, "No. 603 Research Institute's Three-Dimensional Design Reaches Advanced World Level," *Shaanxi ribao,* December 2, 2001, in *FBIS* as "Shaanxi Institute's 3-Dimensional Aircraft Design Reaches World Advanced Level," December 15, 2001.

Lennox, Duncan, "AGM/RGM/UGM-84 Harpoon/SLAM/SLAM-ER," *Jane's Strategic Weapon Systems,* Vol. 40, October 27, 2003. Available online at http://online.janes.com/; accessed November 30, 2003.

———, "AMR-1," *Jane's Air-Launched Weapons,* Vol. 37, January 16, 2001. Available online at http://online.janes.com; accessed November 25, 2003.

———, "C-701," *Jane's Air-Launched Weapons,* Vol. 36, May 13, 2000. Available online at http://online.janes.com/; accessed November 25, 2003.

———, "CAS-1 'Kraken' (YJ-6/YJ-62/YJ-63/C-601/C-611)," *Jane's Strategic Weapon Systems,* Vol. 40, July 31, 2003. Available online at http://online.janes.com/; accessed November 25, 2003.

————, "CSA-1/HQ-2," *Jane's Strategic Weapon Systems,* Vol. 39, January 6, 2003. Available online at http://online.janes.com/; accessed November 25, 2003.

————, "CSA-4/-5, HQ-7/RF-7, FM-80/-90," *Jane's Strategic Weapon Systems,* Vol. 39, January 6, 2003. Available online at http://online.janes.com/; accessed November 25, 2003.

————, "CSA-N-2 (HQ-61/RF-61/SD-1)," *Jane's Strategic Weapon Systems,* Vol. 39, January 6, 2003. Available online at http://online.janes.com/; accessed November 25, 2003.

————, "CSS-1 (DF-2)," *Jane's Strategic Weapon Systems,* Vol. 40, June 3, 2003. Available online at http://online.janes.com; accessed November 25, 2003.

————, "CSS-2 (DF-3)," *Jane's Strategic Weapon Systems.* Vol. 40, June 3, 2003. Available online at http://online.janes.com; accessed November 25, 2003.

————, "CSS-3 (DF-4)," *Jane's Strategic Weapon Systems,* Vol. 40, June 3, 2003. Available online at http://online.janes.com; accessed November 25, 2003.

————, "CSS-4 (DF-5)," *Jane's Strategic Weapon Systems,* Vol. 40, June 3, 2003. Available online at http://online.janes.com; accessed November 25, 2003.

————, "CSS-5 (DF-21)," *Jane's Strategic Weapon Systems,* Vol. 40, June 3, 2003. Available online at http://online.janes.com; accessed November 25, 2003.

————, "CSS-6 (DF-15/M-9)," *Jane's Strategic Weapon Systems,* Vol. 40, June 3, 2003. Available online at http://online.janes.com; accessed November 25, 2003.

————, "CSS-7 (DF-11/M-11)," *Jane's Strategic Weapon Systems,* Vol. 40, June 3, 2003. Available online at http://online.janes.com; accessed November 25, 2003.

————, "CSS-8 (M-7/Project 8610)," *Jane's Strategic Weapon Systems,* June 4, 2004. Available online at http://online.janes.com/; accessed January 4, 2004.

————, "CSSC-5 'Saples' (YJ-16/C-101)," *Jane's Strategic Weapon Systems,* Vol. 40, July 31, 2003. Available online at http://online.janes.com/; accessed November 25, 2003.

————, "CSSC-6 'Sawhorse' (HY-3/C-301)," *Jane's Strategic Weapon Systems,* Vol. 40, July 31, 2003. Available online at http://online.janes.com/; accessed November 25, 2003.

————, "CSS-N-1 'Scrubbrush Mod 2' (FL-1), CSS-NX-5 'Sabbot' (FL-2), FL-7, and FL-10," *Jane's Strategic Weapon Systems,* Vol. 40, July 31, 2003. Available online at http://online.janes.com; accessed November 25, 2003.

————, "CSS-N-1 'Scrubbrush' (SY-1), CSS-N-2 'Safflower' (HY-1), CSSC-2 'Silkworm' (HY-1), CSSC-3 'Seersucker' (HY-2/C-201)," *Jane's Strategic Weapon Systems,* Vol. 40, July 31, 2003. Available online at http://online.janes.com/; accessed November 25, 2003.

————, "CSS-N-3 (JL-1/-21)," *Jane's Strategic Weapon Systems,* Vol. 40, June 3, 2003. Available online at http://online.janes.com; accessed November 25, 2003.

————, "CSS-N-4 'Sardine' (YJ-1/-12/-82 and C-801) and CSSC-8 'Saccade' (YJ-2/-21/-22/-83 and C-802/803)," *Jane's Strategic Weapon Systems,* Vol. 40, July 31, 2003. Available online at http://online.janes.com/; accessed November 25, 2003.

————, "HN-5 (SA-7 'Grail') and TY-90," *Jane's Air-Launched Weapons,* Vol. 37, January 16, 2001. Available online at http://online.janes.com; accessed November 25, 2003.

————, "HQ-12, FT-2000," Jane's Strategic Weapon Systems, Vol. 39, January 6, 2003. Available online at http://online.janes.com/; accessed November 25, 2003.

————, "HQ-9/-15, HHQ-9A, RF-9," *Jane's Strategic Weapon Systems,* Vol. 39, January 6, 2003. Available online at http://online.janes.com/; accessed November 25, 2003.

————, "KS-1/-2/HQ-8/FT-2100," *Jane's Strategic Weapon Systems,* Vol. 39, January 6, 2003. Available online at http://online.janes.com/; accessed November 25, 2003.

————, "LGM-30F Minuteman II," *Jane's Strategic Weapon Systems*, Vol. 40, October 27, 2003. Available online at http://online.janes.com/; accessed November 30, 2003.

————, "LY-60/HQ-11/RF-11," *Jane's Strategic Weapon Systems*, Vol. 39, January 6, 2003. Available online at http://online.janes.com/; accessed November 25, 2003.

————, "MGM-31A Pershing I," *Jane's Strategic Weapon Systems*, Vol. 40, June 3, 2003. Available online at http://online.janes.com/; accessed November 29, 2003.

————, "MGM-31B Pershing II," *Jane's Strategic Weapon Systems*, Vol. 40, June 3, 2003. Available online at http://online.janes.com/; accessed November 29, 2003.

————, "MGM-140 ATACMS (M39) Pershing I," *Jane's Strategic Weapon Systems*, Vol. 40, October 27, 2003. Available online at http://online.janes.com/; accessed December 31, 2003.

————, "MM 38/40, AM 39 and SM 39 Exocet," *Jane's Strategic Weapon Systems*, Vol. 40, July 31, 2003. Available online at http://online.janes.com/; accessed November 30, 2003.

————, "PL-1," *Jane's Air-Launched Weapons*, Vol. 37, January 16, 2001. Available online at http://online.janes.com; accessed November 25, 2003.

————, "QW-1/-2 Vanguard," *Jane's Air-Launched Weapons*, Vol. 37, January 16, 2001. Available online at http://online.janes.com; accessed November 25, 2003.

————, "SA-10/20 'Grumble' (S-300, S-300 PMU, Buk/Favorit/5V55/48N6)," *Jane's Strategic Weapon Systems*, February 21, 2003. Available online at http://online.janes.com; accessed December 1, 2003.

————, "SS-N-22 'Sunburn' (P-80/-270/3M-80/3M82 Zubr/Moskit)," *Jane's Strategic Weapon Systems*, Vol. 40, September 25, 2003. Available online at http://online.janes.com/; accessed November 30, 2003.

————, "UGM-27 Polaris (A-1/-2/-3)," *Jane's Strategic Weapon Systems*, Vol. 40, June 3, 2003. Available online at http://online.janes.com/; accessed November 30, 2003.

————, "UGM-96 Trident C-4," *Jane's Strategic Weapon Systems,* Vol. 40, October 27, 2003. Available online at http://online.janes.com/; accessed November 30, 2003.

————, "YJ-1 (C-801) and YJ-2 (C-802)," *Jane's Air-Launched Weapons,* Vol. 38, November 9, 2001. Available online at http://online.janes.com/; accessed November 25, 2003.

————, "YJ-16/C-101," *Jane's Air-Launched Weapons,* Vol. 38, November 9, 2001. Available online at http://online.janes.com/; accessed November 25, 2003.

Li Jiamo, "Design and Manufacturing of Major Aviation Items Should Be Tightly Integrated," *Defense Science and Technology Industry,* No. 5, 2002.

"Li Jinnai Attends Ceremony of Launch of IT Firm Alliance for Military Procurement," *Xinhua,* July 30, 2003.

Li Ming and Mao Jingli, eds., *Zhuangbei caigou lilun yu shijian* (*The Theory and Practice of Military Equipment Procurement*), Beijing, China: Guofang Gongye Chubanshe, August 2003.

Li Qingshan, ed., *Xin junshi geming yu gaoshuji zhanzheng* (*The New Military Revolution and High-Tech Warfare*), Beijing, China: Military Science Press, 1995.

Li Xinliang, General, "Hi-Tech Local Wars' Basic Requirements for Army Building," *Zhongguo junshi kexue,* November 20, 1998, in *FBIS* as "Li Xinliang on High-Tech Local War," May 17, 1999.

Li Xiuwei, "Applying Technology to National Defense," *China Space News,* May 26, 1999, p. 1, in *FBIS* as "Applying Technology to National Defense," May 26, 1999.

Li Xuanqing and Ma Xiaochun, "Armed Forces' Communications Become 'Multidimensional'," *Xinhua Domestic Service,* July 16, 1997.

Li Xuanqing, Fan Juwei, and Fu Mingyi, "All-Army Weaponry Work Conference Convened in Beijing," *Jiefangjun bao,* November 4, 1999, in *FBIS* as "Army Weaponry Work Conference Opens," November 10, 1999.

Li Xuanqing, Fan Juwei, and Su Kuoshan, "Defense Science and Technology Forges Sharp Sword for National Defense—Second Roundup on Achievements of Army Building Over Past 50 Years," *Jiefangjun bao,*

September 7, 1999, in *FBIS* as "Overview of PLA Defense S&T Modernization," September 21, 1999.

Liang Zhenxing, "New Military Revolution: Information Warfare," *Zhongguo dianzi bao,* October 24, 1997, in *FBIS*, January 12, 1998.

Liao Wengen and Xi Qixin, "Our Country's Third Beidou Navigation and Positioning Satellite Launched into Space," *Xinhua,* May 24, 2003, in *FBIS*, May 24, 2003.

Liberation Army Daily, August 9, 1993.

Lieberthal, Kenneth, and Michel Oksenberg, *Policy Making in China: Leaders, Structures, and Processes,* Princeton, N.J.: Princeton University Press, 1988.

Liu Cheng, "Creating a New Situation in Weapons and Equipment Modernization Effort," *Jiefangjun bao,* October 14, 2002 as translated in *FBIS*, October 14, 2002.

Liu Cheng and Tian Zhaoyun, "China Launches First Marine Satellite," *Xinhua,* May 15, 2002, in *FBIS* as "Xinhua: China Launches Weather, Marine Satellites 15 May," May 15, 2002.

Liu Cheng, Jiang Hongyan, and Liu Xiaojun, "Talented Personnel to Support Leapfrog Developments of Weaponry," *Keji ribao,* October 31, 2001, Internet version (www.stdaily.com.cn) as translated in *FBIS*, October 31, 2001.

Liu Jibin, "Implementing Thinking on 'Three Represents,' Reinvigorate National Defense Science, Technology, and Industry," *Renmin ribao* (Internet version), September 29, 2001, in *FBIS* as "Renmin Ribao on Implementing 'Three Represents' to Reinvigorate National Defense," September 29, 2001.

———, "Implement the Guideline of Military-Civilian Integration, Rejuvenate the National Defense Science and Technology Industry," *Renmin ribao,* February 2, 1999, in *FBIS* as "Military-Civilian Integration in Industry," February 2, 1999.

Liu Ting, "Design for 5.5 Ton Helicopter's Rotor Has Passed Evaluation," *Zhongguo hangkong bao,* December 7, 2001, in *FBIS* as "PRC S&T: Design for Helicopter Rotor Has Passed Evaluation," January 16, 2002.

Liu Xiaoxing et al., "The Development Strategy of China's Shipbuilding Industry," *Chuanbo gongcheng (Ship Engineering)*, Vol. 25, No. 4, August 2003.

Liu Zhenying and Sun Jie, *Xinhua Domestic Service,* July 1, 1999, in *FBIS* as "More on Zhu at Defense Group Ceremony," July 1, 1999.

"Living Condition and Wage of China's Aerospace Scientists Are Much Improved and Sci-Tech Talents Are Returning to Their Original Units," *Zhongguo xinwen wang,* December 2, 2002, in *FBIS*, December 2, 2002.

Lloyds' Register, *World Shipbuilding Statistics,* London, UK, 2004.

Lok, Joris Janssen, and Robert Karnoil, "Spain Offers Carrier Designs to Chinese," *Jane's Defence Weekly,* February 18, 1995.

Lu Yi, "China's Antiship Missiles Draws Attention of World's Military Circles," *Kuang chiao ching,* August 16, 2001, in *FBIS* as "Article on China's Development of Antiship Missiles," August 16, 2001.

Ma Dongpo, "China's Twinstar Positioning System and Its Uses," *Xiandai bingqi,* January 1, 2002, in *FBIS*, January 1, 2002.

Ma Xiaojun, "While Inspecting Guizhou Province, Zeng Qinghong Stresses That a Modern Distance Education Project Should Be Built to Let Cadres Be Educated Regularly and Let Peasants Get Real Benefits for a Long Time," *Guizhou ribao,* April 16, 2003, in *FBIS* as "PRC Vice President Zeng Qinghong Inspects Guizhou, Promotes Distance Education," April 16, 2003.

"Maritime Ambition: China's Naval Modernization," *Jane's Navy International,* April 1998.

Marotte, Bertrand, "Bombardier Rival Strikes Regional Jet Deal in China," *The Globe and Mail* (Internet version), September 13, 2002, in *FBIS* as "Canada's Bombardier, Brazil's Embraer Compete for PRC Regional Jet Market," September 13, 2002.

Mecham, Michael, "Staking a Claim in Civil Production," *Aviation Week and Space Technology,* November 4, 2002.

Medeiros, Evan S., "Revisiting Chinese Defense Conversion: Some Evidence from China's Shipbuilding Industry," *Issues and Studies,* May 1998.

Medeiros, Evan S., and Bates Gill, *Chinese Arms Exports: Policy, Players, and Process,* Carlisle, Pa.: U.S. Army War College, Strategic Studies Institute, 2000.

"Military Representatives of Engineering Corps Work Hard to Ensure Assault Boats['] Quality," *Jiefangjun bao,* July 17, 2002, p. 10, as translated in *FBIS,* 2004.

Miller, David, *The Cold War: A Military History,* New York: St. Martin's Press, 1999.

Ministry of Information Industry (MII) website, http://www.mii.gov.cn/.

Ministry of Information Industry, 54th Research Institute (Zhongguo Dianzi Keji Jituan Gongsi Diwushisi Yanjiu Suo) website, www.cti.ac.cn.

Ministry of Information Industry website, http://202.117.114.54/page/chushijianjie/keyanbu.htm.

Ministry of Science and Technology, Center for High-Tech Research & Development 1998–2005 863 Program Combined Research Office website, http://www.863.gov.cn/863_105/863briefing/briefing/200210150012.html.

Moore, Thomas G., *China in the World Market,* Cambridge, UK: Cambridge University Press, 2002.

Moscow Interfax, November 3, 2004, in *FBIS* as "Russian, Chinese Aircraft Builders to Cooperate."

Muller, David, *China as a Maritime Power,* Boulder, Colo.: Westview Press, 1983.

Mulvenon, James C., "Chinese C4I Modernization: An Experiment in Open Source Exploitation," in James C. Mulvenon and Andrew N. D. Yang, eds., *A Poverty of Riches: New Challenges and Opportunities in PLA Research,* Santa Monica, Calif.: RAND Corporation, CF-189-NSRD, 2003.

———, "Chinese Military Commerce and U.S. National Security," Santa Monica, Calif.: unpublished RAND research, 1997.

———, "The Limits of Coercive Diplomacy: The 1979 Sino-Vietnamese Border War," *Journal of Northeast Asian Studies,* Fall 1995.

———, *Soldiers of Fortune: The Rise and Fall of the Chinese Military-Business Complex, 1978–1998,* Armonck, N.Y.: M. E. Sharpe, 2001.

Mulvenon, James C., and Andrew N. D. Yang, *The People's Liberation Army as Organization: Reference Volume v1.0,* Santa Monica, Calif.: RAND Corporation, CR-182-NSRD, 2002. Available only online at http://www.rand.org/publications/CF/CF182/.

Mulvenon, James C., and Andrew N. D. Yang, eds., *A Poverty of Riches: New Challenges and Opportunities in PLA Research,* Santa Monica, Calif.: RAND Corporation, CF-189-NSRD, 2003.

————, *Seeking Truth from Facts: A Retrospective on Chinese Military Studies in the Post-Mao Era,* Santa Monica, Calif.: RAND Corporation, CF-160-CAPP, 2001.

Mulvenon, James C., and Richard H. Yang, *The People's Liberation Army in the Information Age,* Santa Monica, Calif.: RAND Corporation, CF-145-CAPP/AF, 1999.

Munson, Kenneth, "CAC FC-1 Xiaolong," *Jane's All the World's Aircraft,* January 15, 2003. Available online at http://online.janes.com; accessed March 8, 2004.

————, "CAC J-10," *Jane's All the World's Aircraft,* April 22, 2004. Available online at http://online.janes.com; accessed May 18, 2004.

————, "CAC J-7," *Jane's All the World's Aircraft,* April 22, 2004. Available online at http://online.janes.com; accessed May 18, 2004.

————, "CHAIG Z-8," *Jane's All the World's Aircraft,* June 17, 2003. Available online at http://online.janes.com; accessed March 8, 2004.

————, "CHAIG Z-11," *Jane's All the World's Aircraft,* June 17, 2003. Available online at http://online.janes.com; accessed March 8, 2004.

————, "CHRDI Z-10," *Jane's All the World's Aircraft,* April 22, 2004. Available online at http://online.janes.com; accessed May 19, 2004.

————, "HAI (Eurocopter) Z-9 Haitun," *Jane's All the World's Aircraft,* November 24, 2003. Available online at http://online.janes.com; accessed March 8, 2004.

————, "SAC J-8 II," *Jane's All the World's Aircraft,* November 24, 2004. Available online at http://online.janes.com; accessed May 18, 2004.

————, "SAC Y-8," Jane's All the World's Aircraft, June 17, 2003. Available online at http://online.janes.com; accessed March 8, 2004.

————, "XAC JH-7," *Jane's All the World's Aircraft*, April 22, 2004. Available online at http://online.janes.com; accessed May 18, 2004.

Nation, The (Islamabad), untitled article, June 8, 2000, in *FBIS* as "Pakistan, China Jointly Build K8E Aircraft," June 8, 2000.

National Bureau of Statistics, *China Statistical Yearbook 2002*, Beijing, China: China Statistics Press, 2002.

National Mobile Communications Engineering Research Center website, http://www.mc21st.com/techfield/expert/main.asp.

"National News Hookup," *China Central Television One*, April 21, 1998, in *FBIS* as "Interview with Minister of National Defense Science," April 21, 1998.

Naughton, Barry, "The Third Front: Defense Industrialization in the Chinese Interior," *China Quarterly*, No. 115, September 1988.

————, *Growing Out of the Plan*, Cambridge, UK: Cambridge University Press, 1996.

Novichkov, Nikolai, "China Buys Fighter Aircraft Engines from Russia," *Jane's Defence Weekly*, January 12, 2005.

Office of Naval Intelligence, *Worldwide Submarine Challenges*, Suitland, Md.: U.S. Navy, 1996.

Office of the Secretary of Defense, *Proliferation: Threat and Response*, Washington, D.C.: U.S. Government Printing Office, January 2001.

O'Halloran, James C., "Chinese Self-Propelled Surface-to-Air Missile System Programmes," *Jane's Land-Based Air Defence*, January 27, 2003. Available online at http://online.janes.com/; accessed November 25, 2003.

————, "CNPMIEC FM-90 Surface-to-Air Missile System," *Jane's Land-Based Air Defence*, January 27, 2003. Available online at http://online.janes.com/; accessed November 25, 2003.

————, "CNPMIEC FN-6 Low-Altitude Surface-to-Air Missile System," *Jane's Land-Based Air Defence*, November 11, 2003. Available online at http://online.janes.com/; accessed November 25, 2003.

————, "CNPMIEC FT-2000 Surface-to-Air Anti-Radiation Missile System," *Jane's Land-Based Air Defence*, January 27, 2003. Available online at http://online.janes.com/; accessed November 25, 2003.

———, "CNPMIEC Hong Nu-5 Series Man-Portable Anti-Aircraft Missile System," *Jane's Land-Based Air Defence*, November 11, 2003. Available online at http://online.janes.com/; accessed November 25, 2003.

———, "CNPMIEC Hongqi-2 Low- to High-Altitude Surface-to-Air Missile System," *Jane's Land-Based Air Defence*, September 4, 2003. Available online at http://online.janes.com/; accessed November 25, 2003.

———, "CNPMIEC Hongqi-61A Low- to Medium-Altitude Surface-to-Air Missile System," *Jane's Land-Based Air Defence*, May 28, 2003. Available online at http://online.janes.com/; accessed November 25, 2003.

———, "CNPMIEC HQ-7 (FM-80) Shelter-Mounted Surface-to-Air Missile System," *Jane's Land-Based Air Defence*, September 4, 2003. Available online at http://online.janes.com/; accessed November 25, 2003.

———, "CNPMIEC KS-1/KS-1A Low- to High-Altitude Surface-to-Air Missile System," *Jane's Land-Based Air Defence*, May 28, 2003. Available online at http://online.janes.com/; accessed November 25, 2003.

———, "CNPMIEC Lieying-60 (LY-60) Low- to Medium-Altitude Surface-to-Air Missile System," *Jane's Land-Based Air Defence*, September 4, 2003. Available online at http://online.janes.com/; accessed November 25, 2003.

———, "CNPMIEC QW-1 Vanguard Low-Altitude Surface-to-Air Missile System," *Jane's Land-Based Air Defence*, November 11, 2003. Available online at http://online.janes.com/; accessed November 25, 2003.

———, "FT-2000 Missile System," *Jane's Land-Based Air Defence*, February 20, 2003. Available online at http://online.janes.com/; accessed November 25, 2003.

———, "Kolomna KBM Strela-2/Strela-2M—Low-Altitude Surface-to-Air Missile System," *Jane's Land-Based Air Defence*, September 4, 2003. Available online at http://online.janes.com/; accessed December 1, 2003.

———, "Liuzhou Changhong Machinery Manufacturing's QW-2—Low-Altitude Surface-to-Air Missile System," *Jane's Land-Based Air Defence*, November 11, 2003. Available online at http://online.janes.com/; accessed November 25, 2003.

————, "NORINCO PL-9C Low-Altitude Surface-to-Air Missile System," *Jane's Land-Based Air Defence,* January 27, 2003. Available online at http://online.janes.com/; accessed November 25, 2003.

————, "Thales Defence Systems Crotale Low-Altitude Surface-to-Air Missile System," *Jane's Land-Based Air Defence,* January 27, 2003. Available online at http://online.janes.com/; accessed January 2, 2004.

Ostrov, Benjamin A., *Conquering Resources: The Growth and Decline of the PLA's Science and Technology Commission for National Defense,* Armonk, N.Y.: M. E. Sharpe, 1991.

Pai Chuan, "Command System of the Chinese Army," *Ching pao,* December 1, 1998, in *FBIS* as "Overview of PLA Structure," December 12, 1998.

Pan, Philip P., "U.S. Pressing EU to Uphold Arms Embargo Against China," *Washington Post,* January 31, 2004.

Park, Yong, S., Office of Naval Research, U.S. Navy, Asia Office, Tokyo, Japan, March 21, 1996, http://www.onr.navy.mil/onrasia/systems/1996/032196s.html.

————, "China's Shipbuilding Leaping Forward, Improvement in Repair Technology and Increased Export Volume," September 27, 1996. Available online at http://www.onr.navy.mil/onrasia/systems/1996/092796S.html; accessed March 1997.

Peacock, Lindsay, "Lockheed Martin F-16 Fighting Falcon," *Jane's All the World's Aircraft,* February 27, 2004. Available online at http://online.janes.com/; accessed May 17, 2004.

Peng Kai-lei, "Five Major Military Industry Corporations Formally Reorganized," *Wen wei po,* July 1, 1999, in *FBIS* as "Military Industry Reorganization Planned," July 6, 1999.

"PLA Develops Mobile Satellite Communications Antenna," *Xinhua,* December 14, 1999, in *FBIS.*

"PLA Refits Merchant Ships in Reserve," *Ming pao,* November 2, 1999, in *FBIS,* November 2, 1999.

Porter, Michael, *Competitive Strategy: Techniques for Analyzing Industries and Competitors,* New York: Free Press, 1980.

"PRC Armed Forces Adopt Government Procurement System to Meet Demands of Economic Reforms," *Xinhua,* January 9, 2002, as translated in *FBIS,* January 9, 2002.

"PRC Plans Reform of Army Purchasing System," *Xinhua,* January 9, 2002, as translated in *FBIS,* January 9, 2002.

Qian Xiaohu, "Crossing Frontier Passes and Mountains with Golden Spears and Armored Horses—Interviewing Ma Zhigeng, President of China Ordnance Group Corporation," *Jiefangjun bao* (Internet version), April 17, 2000, in *FBIS* as "China Ordnance Group Chief Interviewed," April 17, 2000.

Raytheon website, http://www.raytheon.com/about/; accessed December 29, 2003.

"Regional Overviews: China," Airbus website. Available at http://www.airbus.com/media/china.asp; accessed January 18, 2005.

Sae-Liu, Robert, "Beijing Seeks More Engines from Ukraine," *Jane's Defence Weekly,* October 6, 2004.

———, "China Advances Helicopter Projects," *Jane's Defence Weekly,* May 3, 2002.

Schloss, Glenn, "Arms Dealer Norinco Out in Open in Hong Kong," *South China Morning Post,* June 14, 1998, in *FBIS* as "Mainland's Military Links Run Deep," June 14, 1998.

Shaanxi ribao, July 1, 2002, in *FBIS* as "CASC's Solid Rocket Motor Research Institute Celebrates 40 Years," July 1, 2002.

Shambaugh, David, *Modernizing China's Military: Progress, Problems, and Prospects,* Berkeley, Calif.: University of California Press, 2003.

Shanghai Ship Design and Research Institute website, www.sdari.com.cn/.

"Shanghai to Assemble Feeder Turbo Jets," *China Daily,* December 20, 2002. Available online at www1.chinadaily.com.cn/news/cn/2002-12-20/98564.html; accessed December 20, 2002.

Shanghai Waigaoqiao Shipbuilding Company Ltd website, www.chinasws.com.

Sharpe, Richard, *Jane's Fighting Ships 1996–1997,* Surrey, UK: Jane's Information Group, 1996.

Sharpe, Richard, *Jane's Fighting Ships 1995–1996,* Surrey, UK: Jane's Information Group, 1995.

Shen Bin, "AVIC to Be Split into 2 Groups," *China Daily* (Business Weekly Supplement), January 31–February 6, 1999, in *FBIS* as "Aviation Industries of China to Split into 2 Groups," January 31, 1999.

Shi Hua, *China Daily,* September 1, 1999, in *FBIS* as "PRC Challenges U.S. Satellite Design," September 1, 1999.

Shi Lei et al., "Tingzhi de Jiliang—Zhongguo Hangtian Kegong Jituan Gongsi Liu Yuan Fazhan Jishi," *Guofang keji gongye,* No. 10, 2001, pp. 8–12

Shipbuilding in the PRC, Hong Kong: Asian Strategies Limited, 1995, unpublished consultants report. For a summary of the report, see www.asiaonline.net.hk/asl/s_ship.htm.

Shipbuilding Market in 2001, The, consultant report, Paris, France: Barry Rogliano Salles Shipbrokers, 2002. Available online at http://www.brs -paris.com/research/index.html.

Si Yanwen and Chen Wanjun, *Xinhua Domestic Service,* June 9, 1999, in *FBIS* as "General Armaments Director on Developing Weapons," June 9, 1999.

Siddiqa, Ayesha, "Sino-Pakistani Fighter Deliveries to Start in 2006," *Jane's Defence Weekly,* April 28, 2004.

Singh, Ravinder Pal, ed., *Arms Procurement Decision Making: China, India, Israel, Japan, South Korea and Thailand,* Stockholm International Peace Research Institute, Oxford, UK: Oxford University Press, 1998.

6th Academy website, www.zghx.com.cn.gaikuang.htm; accessed December 31, 2003.

Smith, Craig S., "France Makes Headway in Push to Permit Arms Sales to China," *New York Times,* January 27, 2004.

Society of Aeronautics and Astronautics website, http://www.csaa.org.cn/.

Sokolsky, Richard, Angel Rabasa, and C. R. Neu, *The Role of Southeast Asia in U.S. Strategy Toward China,* Santa Monica, Calif.: RAND Corporation, MR-1170-AF, 2000.

Space China website, http://www.spacechina.com/index.asp?modelname= htzz_gd; accessed December 30, 2003.

"Speech of Liu Jibin at COSTIND Working Meeting," *Zhongguo hangkong bao* (*China Aviation News*), April 30, 1999, as translated in *FBIS*, April 30, 1999.

"Standardizing Our Military Armament Procurement Work According to Law," *Jiefangjun bao,* November 2, 2002, as translated in *FBIS*, November 2, 2002.

State Statistical Bureau, *China Statistical Yearbook 1996,* Beijing, China: China Statistical Publishing House, 1996.

Stokes, Mark A., *China's Strategic Modernization: Implications for the United States,* Carlisle, PA: U.S. Army Strategic Studies Institute, September 1999.

Su Hongyu, "How to Cross the Taiwan Strait," *Jianchuan zhishi* (*Naval and Merchant Ships*), July 19, 1999, in *FBIS*, July 24, 1999.

Su Hui, "The Development of Scientific and Technological Industry for National Defense in Shaanxi," *Shaanxi ribao,* March 28, 2001, in *FBIS* as "Report on Development of Shaanxi's Military Industry," March 28, 2001.

Su Kejia, "Thoughts on Promoting Military Changes with Chinese Characteristics," *Zhongguo guofang bao,* September 18, 2003, p. 3.

Su Yen, "Undercover the Mysterious Veil of China's New-Type Fighter Plane," *Zhongguo tongxun she,* September 20, 2002, in *FBIS* as "HK ZTS Describes PRC-Made Super-7 Combat Plane for Export Market," September 20, 2002.

Sun Hongjin and Sun Zifa, "Research and Manufacturing System of China's Space Technology Has Realized a Major Change," *Zhongguo xinwen she,* December 28, 2001, in *FBIS* as "PRC S&T: Major Change in Space Research and Manufacturing Systems," December 28, 2001.

Sun Zhifan, *Zhongguo xinwen she,* November 28, 2002, in *FBIS* as "ZXS: China Aerospace Second Academy Strives to Become First-Class Institution," November 28, 2002.

Sun Zifa, "China Forms Aerospace Instrument Company," *Zhongguo xinwen she,* July 28, 2001, in *FBIS*, July 28, 2001.

Suttmeier, Richard P., "China's High Technology: Programs, Problems, and Prospects," in Joint Economic Committee, ed., *China's Economic Dilemmas in the 1990s: The Problems of Reforms, Modernization, and*

Interdependence, Washington, D.C.: U.S. Government Printing Office, 1991.

_____, "Emerging Innovation Networks and Changing Strategies for Industrial Technology in China: Some Observations," *Technology in Society,* Vol. 19, Nos. 3 & 4, 1997.

Tang Hua, "Science, Technology, and Industry for National Defense Increases Intensity of Innovation," *Liaowang,* July 26, 1999, in *FBIS* as "Report on Innovation in Defense Industry," August 16, 1999.

Tanzer, Andrew, "The People's Liberation Army, Inc.," *Forbes,* March 24, 1997.

Taverna, Michael A., and Pierre Sparaco, "Courting China," *Aviation Week and Space Technology,* October 18, 2004.

"Ten Military Industry Corporations Are Founded," *Zhongguo hangtian* (*China Aerospace*), August 1999, as translated in *FBIS*, August 1, 1999.

Tongxinbingshi, Beijing, China: PLA Press, n.d.

"TRIBON Dominant in Asia," *Japan Maritime Daily,* October 9–23, 1998.

Tribon Solutions (owned by The Sixth Swedish National Pension Fund) website, http://www.tribon.com/corporate/pressRelease020418.asp.

Tseng Hai-tao, "Jiang Zemin Pushes Forward Restructuring of Military Industry—Developments of State Commission of Science, Technology, and Industry for National Defense and Five Major Ordnance Corporations," *Kuang chiao ching,* July 16, 1998, in *FBIS* as "Journal on PRC Military-Industrial Reform," July 28, 1998.

Tseng Shu-wan, "Special Dispatch," *Wen wei po,* October 31, 2000, in *FBIS*, October 31, 2000.

Tung Yi and Sing Tao, *Jih pao,* September 6, 2000, in *FBIS* as "Russian Experts Said Helping PRC Make High-Tech Weaponry," September 6, 2000.

"Ukraine Highly Optimistic About Prospects for Defense Ties with China," *Moscow Interfax,* November 18, 2002.

U.S. Department of Defense, *Annual Report on the Military Power of the People's Republic of China,* annual report to Congress pursuant to FY2000 National Defense Authorization Act, Washington, D.C., 2002.

U.S. Department of Defense, *Annual Report on the Military Power of the People's Republic of China,* FY04 Report to Congress on PRC Military Power Pursuant to the FY2000 National Defense Authorization Act, Washington, D.C., May 2004.

U.S. Department of Defense, *Annual Report on the Military Power of the People's Republic of China,* Washington, D.C., July 28, 2003.

United States Information Technology Office, *Mid 2001 Report: China's International Trade and Information Technology Sector,* Beijing, China, July 2001. Available online at www.usito.org.

U.S. Navy, *Worldwide Submarine Challenges,* Suitland, Md.: Office of Naval Intelligence, 1996.

Wang Chien-min, "Ordnance Factories in Western China Work Overtime to Ensure Logistical Supply," *Yazhou zhoukan,* May 22, 2000, in *FBIS* as "PRC Ordnance Factories Creating Logistical Equipment," May 22, 2000.

Wang Congbiao, "Implement the Strategy of Strengthening the Military Through Science and Technology to Improve the Defensive Combat Capabilities of China's Military—Studying Jiang Zemin's 'On Science and Technology'," *Jiefangjun bao* (Internet version), February 13, 2001, in *FBIS* as "Review of Jiang Zemin's Views on High-Tech Military," February 13, 2001.

Wang Fan and Zhang Jie, "A Qualitative Leap in the Overall Strength of National Defense Over Past 50 Years," *Liaowang,* July 26, 1999, in *FBIS* as "Xinhua Journal Reviews PRC Defense Growth," August 4, 1999.

Wang Hanlin, "Chengdu Aircraft [Corp] Uses High Technology to Grab New Vitality," *Keji ribao* (*Science and Technology Daily*), May 28, 1998, in *FBIS* as "Chengdu Aircraft Industry Corp Profiled," June 15, 1998.

Wang Jianhua, "Thoughts on 'WTO Entry' and Development of Armament," *Jiefangjun bao* (Internet version), March 14, 2000, in *FBIS* as "Impact of WTO on PRC Armament Development," March 15, 2000.

Wang Jianmin and Zhang Zuocheng, "Speed Up the Progress of Basic Model, Then Serialization, and Work Hard to Develop China's Cruise Missile Industry," *Zhongguo hangtian,* September 1996, in *FBIS* as "President of CASC's Third Academy Details Contribution of HY-2, C601, C801 Cruise Missile Series," September 1, 1996.

Wang Li, *Xinhua,* July 3, 2000, in *FBIS* as "PRC Aerospace Technology Achievements Viewed," July 3, 2000.

Wang Lianping, "Bravely Writing a New Tablet," *Zhongguo hangkong bao,* March 2, 2001, in *FBIS* as "PRC Aeronautical Industry Institute Achievements Traced," March 2, 2001.

Wang Shouyun, "Conversion, Dual Use, and Transfer of Technology," in Qian Haiyan, ed., *Restructuring the Military Industry: Conversion for the Development of the Civilian Economy,* Beijing: China Association for the Peaceful Use of Military Industrial Technology and the United Nations Department of Development Support and Management Services, 1993.

Wang Ti, *Xinhua,* July 3, 2000, in *FBIS* as "PRC Aerospace Technology Achievements Viewed," July 3, 2000.

Wang Wenjie, "Delegate Li Jinai Emphasizes: Grasp Tightly the Important Strategic Opportunity, Accelerate the Development by Leaps of Our Army's Weapons and Equipment," *Jiefangjun bao,* March 8, 2003, translated in *FBIS,* March 8, 2003.

Wang Xiaoqiang, "Whither China's Aviation Industry?" *Ta kung pao,* August 25, 1999, in *FBIS* as "Article Views Civil Aviation Industry," September 21, 1999.

Wang Yawei, "New Military Aircraft Displayed at the National-Day Grand Military Parade," *Liaowang,* November 8, 1999, in *FBIS* as "Article on New Fighters Displayed on 1 Oct," December 20, 1999.

Wang Zhigang, Li Qing, Chen Shilu, and Li Renhou, *Yuhang xuebao,* November 1, 2001, pp. 35–39, in *FBIS* as "PRC S&T: Orbit Transfer of Three-Satellite Constellation," November 1, 2001.

Wen Yangyang, "Beijing Changfeng Shiji Satellite Science and Technology Corporation Pushes Forward the Field of Satellite Application," October 11, 2002, in *FBIS* as "PRC S&T: Changfeng Century Develops Mobile Communications System," October 11, 2002.

"What's the Reason Why We Are Reforming," *Vermya Novostey,* November 3, 2004, in *FBIS* as "Russian Offical Sees China's Relations with Russia Helping PRC More Than with US, Europe."

"White Paper on National Defense Published," China Internet Information Center. Available online at http://www.china.org.cn/english/2004/Dec/116032.htm; accessed December 30, 2004.

Wikipedia website, http://en.wikipedia.org/wiki/.

Wu Jinning and Wang Guoxin, "Introduction to Deploying Civilian Vessels in Landing Operations," *Guofang,* October 2004.

Wu Ruihu, "Navy Military Representative Hard at Work in Supervising Armament Development," *Jiefangjun bao,* April 10, 2002, as translated in *FBIS*, April 10, 2004.

Xi Qixin, "PRC Successfully Launches 'China Resources-II' Satellite," *Xinhua,* October 27, 2002, in *FBIS*, October 27, 2002.

Xi Qixin and Liu Siyang, "Jiang Zemin Watches the Launch of a Spacecraft from the Manned Spacecraft Launch Center," March 25, 2002, in *FBIS* as "PRC President Jiang Zemin Observes Launch of Shenzhou-3 Spacecraft," March 25, 2002.

Xia Guohong, You Zheng, Meng Bo, and Xin Peihua, *Zhongguo hangtian,* August 1, 2002, in *FBIS* as "PRC S&T: Aerospace Qinghua Satellite Technology Company," August 1, 2002.

Xiao Xu, *China Daily* (Internet version), January 11, 2002, in *FBIS* as "PRC Aviation Firm Says Emphasis on Development of Small Aircraft," January 11, 2002.

Xiao Yusheng, "Building a Strong People's Army," *Liaowang,* July 29, 2002, in *FBIS* as "PRC Article on PLA Military Buildup over Last 10 Years, Preparations for Future," August 8, 2002.

Xiao Yusheng and Chen Yu, "Historic Leaps in China's Military Scientific Study," *Renmin ribao,* February 25, 1999, p. 9, in *FBIS* as "Military Scientific Studies Take Leap," March 2, 1999.

Xie Dajun, "The Procurement and Supervision of the Manufacture of Foreign Armaments," *Xiandai junshi,* August 15, 1999, as translated in *FBIS*, August 15, 1999.

Xinhua, October 16, 1995, in *FBIS* as "Hubei Becomes French Market Foothold," October 16, 1995.

———, January 7, 1998, in *FBIS* as "PRC National Ordnance Industry Conference Opens," January 7, 1998.

———, January 23, 1998, in *FBIS* as "Chengdu Plant Delivers Aircraft to Boeing," January 23, 1998.

————, March 10, 1998, in *FBIS* as "NPC Adopts Institutional Restructuring Plan," March 10, 1998.

————, April 9, 1998, in *FBIS* as "Beijing Plans to Develop 500-Meter Radio Telescope," April 9, 1998.

————, April 26, 1998, in *FBIS* as "Belarus to Cooperate with China to Build Trucks," April 26, 1998.

————, April 16, 1999, in *FBIS* as "China Aviation, Rolls-Royce Agree on Compensation Trade."

————, July 1, 1999, in *FBIS* as "Zhu Rongji Urges Sci-Tech Work for National Defense," July 1, 1999.

————, September 3, 1999, in *FBIS* as "Missile Experts Refute Li's Splittist Remarks," September 3, 1999.

————, October 8, 1999, in *FBIS* as "Airbus Expands Partnership with Chinese Aviation Industry," October 8, 1999.

————, December 21, 1999, in *FBIS* as "Xian Aircraft Group Produces Boeing 737 Vertical Tails," December 21, 1999.

————, March 25, 2000, in *FBIS* as "Xinhua Cites Liaowang on China's Aviation Industry," March 25, 2000.

————, April 11, 2000, in *FBIS* as "PRC's PLA 'Speeds Up' Training for Armament Officers," April 11, 2000.

————, July 27, 2000.

————, November 8, 2000, in *FBIS* as "Foreign Manufacturers Show Interest in China's Feeder Aircraft Market," November 8, 2000.

————, November 10, 2000, in *FBIS* as "China Sets Targets for Aviation Industry," November 10, 2000.

————, July 18, 2001, in *FBIS* as "PRC: MOFTEC Says PRC-Belarus Economic Cooperation Increased by 366.7% in '00," July 18, 2001.

————, March 19, 2002, in *FBIS* as "Chinese, French Firms Sign Aircraft Fuselage Subcontract," March 19, 2002.

————, February 3, 2003, in *FBIS* as "Xinhua Cites Chinese Scientists on Columbia Tragedy, PRC Space Flight," February 3, 2003.

Xinhua Domestic Service, in *FBIS* as "Wu Bangguo Speaks at Defense Industry Conference," April 27, 1999.

————, July 1, 1999, in *FBIS* as "Jiang Congratulates Defense Enterprise Restructuring," July 2, 1999.

————, October 27, 1999, in *FBIS* as "Official Urges Major Defense Industry Shakeup," November 3, 1999.

————, "China's Military Industrial Industry Last Year Decreased Losses by a Large Margin," January 5, 2001, in *FBIS* as "PRC Says Military Industry Reduces Losses," January 5, 2001.

Xinhua (Hong Kong), April 23, 1998, in *FBIS* as "Xian Aircraft Company Wins Europe Subcontract Market," April 23, 1998.

Xinhua Net Chongqing Channel website, http://www.cq.xinhuanet.com/subject/2004/500qiang.

Xu Dashan, *China Daily* (Internet version), August 19, 2000, in *FBIS* as "PRC: Prospects for Joint EC120 Helicopter Project Noted," August 19, 2000.

————, *China Daily* (Internet version), August 16, 2001, in *FBIS* as "Experts Say Helicopter Sector 'Important' for Increasing PRC's Military Hardware," August 16, 2001.

————, *China Daily* (Internet version), September 13, 2001, in *FBIS* as "China Daily: Helicopter Sector to Be Promoted," September 13, 2001.

————, *China Daily* (Internet version), July 11, 2002, in *FBIS* as "PRC's New H410A Helicopter Model Receives Certification; CAAC Says 'Huge Achievement'," July 11, 2002.

————, "Military Firm Eyes Rosy Market Future," *China Daily* (Internet version), January 11, 2001, in *FBIS*, January 11, 2001.

Xu Penghang, "Give Play to the Strength of Military Industries to Participate in Development of China's West," *Renmin Ribao Overseas Edition* (Internet version), March 24, 2000, in *FBIS* as "RMRB on Utilizing Military Industries to Develop China's West," March 24, 2000.

Xu Sailu, Gu Xianguang, and Xu Xiangmin, *Zhongguo junshi kexue,* June 20, 2000, in *FBIS* as "Article on Effects of WTO Membership on PRC Military Economy," July 27, 2000.

Xu Tong, "China's C701 Small-Scale Multifunctional Missile," *Bingqi zhishi,* March 2000, pp. 2–3, in *FBIS* as "PRC Missile C701 Able 'To Target Patrol Boat Threats'."

Xu Yunxin, "Shipborne Meteorological Satellite Tracking System Displays Invincible Might," *Keji ribao,* April 27, 1998, in *FBIS* as "Shipborne Weather Satellite Tracking System," April 27, 1998.

Xu Zeliang, "CAIG: Using the 'Dumbell-Shaped' Model to Enter the Market," *Defense Science and Technology Industry,* No. 1, 2002.

———, *Zhongguo hangkong bao,* February 9, 2001.

Xue Cheng, *China Daily* (Internet version), June 25, 1999, in *FBIS* as "Further on AVIC-Airbus Agreements," June 25, 1999.

Xun Zhenjiang, Maj. Gen., and Captain Geng Haijun, "Exploring the Chinese Way to Develop Military Weaponry," *Zhongguo junshi kexue,* June 20, 2002, in *FBIS* as "Chinese General Recommends R&D Strategy for Weapons and Equipment," June 20, 2002.

Yan Yan, "Paradigm for Small Satellite Development," *Keji ribao,* June 17, 1999, in *FBIS* as "Paradigm for Small Satellite Development," June 17, 1999.

Yan Yong, "Improving Capability to Handle Information," *Jiefangjun bao,* December 11, 2003.

Yang Jian, "Li Peng Sends Letter to the China Aerospace Science and Industry Corporation on Its Important Progress," *Zhongguo hangtian bao,* January 15, 2000, in *FBIS* as "PRC CAMEC Development Strategies 2000–2010," January 15, 2000.

Yang Kebin, "The Jinhang Information Project Comprehensive Information Network: Brief Introduction of AVIC's 'Golden Aviation' Information Network," *Guoji hangkong* (*International Aviation*), December 8, 1997, in *FBIS* as "Jinhang Navigation Information System Profiled," December 8, 1997.

Ye Dingyou and Zhang Dexiong, "Challenges and Opportunities for Ordnance Industry Following China's Entry to WTO (Part 2 of 2)," *Xinhua,* October 24, 2000, in *FBIS* as "China Produces 100 Tails for Boeing-737s," October 24, 2000.

———, *Zhongguo hangtian,* December 1, 2002, in *FBIS* as "PRC S&T: Progress in Solid Rocket Propellant Technology," December 1, 2002.

Ye Weiping, "Challenges and Opportunities for Ordnance Industry Following China's Entry to WTO (Part 2 of 2)," *Ta kung pao* (Internet version), April 26, 2000, in *FBIS* as "Part 2: Ta Kung Pao on WTO Impact on Ordnance Industries," May 3, 2000.

Yi Jan, "Jiang-Zhu Relationship as Viewed from Army Structural Adjustment," *Ching pao,* March 1, 1999, in *FBIS* as "Jiang-Zhu Relations in Army Reform Viewed," March 9, 1999.

Yihong Chang, "China Launches FC-1 Fighter Production," *Jane's Defence Weekly,* January 22, 2003.

———, "China Launches New Stealth Fighter Project," *Jane's Defence Weekly,* December 11, 2002.

Yihong Zhang, "Beijing Develops New Radar-Absorbing Materials," *Jane's Defence Weekly,* February 24, 1999.

———, "Industry Round-Up—Chinese Boost Fighter Production with Su-27 Assembly," *Jane's Defence Weekly,* December 13, 2000.

Yi-min Lin and Tian Zhi, "Ownership Restructuring in Chinese State Industry: An Analysis of Evidence on Initial Organizational Changes," *China Quarterly,* September 2001.

Young, Philip, *Chinese Military Digest,* http://www.gsprint.com/cmd/navy.

Younossi, Obaid, Mark V. Arena, Richard M. Moore, Mark A. Lorell, Joanna Mason, and John C. Graser, *Military Jet Engine Acquisition: Technology Basics and Cost-Estimating Methodology,* Santa Monica, Calif.: RAND Corporation, MR-1596-AF, 2002.

Yu Bin and Hao Dan, "Qualitative Changes in National Defense Modernization Standard, Overall Strength," *Liaowang,* No. 39, September 27, 1999, pp. 52–54, in *FBIS* as "Changes in National Defense, Power," October 18, 1999.

Yun Shan, "General Equipment Department—Fourth PLA General Department," *Liaowang,* May 25, 1998, in *FBIS* as "China: New PLA General Equipment Department," June 12, 1998.

Yung, Christopher D., *People's War at Sea: Chinese Naval Power in the Twenty-First Century,* Alexandria, Va.: CNA Corporation (CNAC), CRM 95-214, March 1996.

Zeng Min, *China Daily,* February 3, 2001, in *FBIS* as "China to Launch More Meteorological Satellites in 'Fengyun' Series," February 3, 2001, in

FBIS as "China to Launch More Meteorological Satellites in 'Fengun' Series," February 3, 2001.

Zhang Fuyou, "With Joint Efforts Made by Army and People, Military Telecommunications Makes Leap Forward," *Liberation Army Daily,* September 27, 2000.

Zhang Hongqing, "Dare to Seek a Path Ahead—Explorations and Innovations During the Reform and Adjustment of Institute 609," *Guofang keji gongye,* No. 1, 2002.

Zhang Huiting, *Hangtian,* May/June 1997, in *FBIS* as "HQ-61 SAM Weapon System Described," September 29, 1997.

Zhang Jinfu, "CAS Reveals Past Role in China WMD Programs," *Kexue shibao,* May 6, 1999, in *FBIS,* May 6, 1999.

Zhang Qingwei, "China Explores Path for Diversified Space Development," *Liaowang,* June 2, 2003, in *FBIS,* June 2, 2003.

Zhang Xiaojun, "Modern National Defense Needs Modern Signal Troops," *National Defense,* No.10, October 15, 1995.

Zhang Xinyu et al., "Infrared Detector Array with Quartz Microlens," *Hongwai yu haomibo xuebao,* April 1998, in *FBIS* as "IR Detector Array with Quartz Microlens," April 1, 1998.

Zhang Yi, "China Aviation Products to Make Key Breakthrough in '10th Five Year Plan'," *Xinhua Domestic Service,* January 18, 2000, in *FBIS* as "China Aviation Industry to Provide More High-Tech Weapons," February 10, 2000.

———, "It Is Estimated That China's Military Industrial Enterprises Covered by the Budget Reduce Losses by More Than 30 Percent," *Xinhua* (Hong Kong Service), January 7, 2002, in *FBIS* as "PRC Military Industry Reports 30 Percent Decrease in Losses for 2001," January 7, 2002.

———, "Li Peng Sends Letter to Congratulate the China Aerospace Science and Industry Corporation on Its Important Progress in Developing New and High Technology, Weapons and Equipment," *Xinhua,* January 23, 2003, in *FBIS* as "Li Peng Congratulates China Aerospace Industry Corporation on Its Achievements," January 23, 2003.

———, "Liu Jibin, Minister of Commission of Science, Technology, and Industry for National Defense, 27 October Says in a Meeting That

China's High-Tech Industry for National Defense Will Be Restructured on a Large Scale," *Xinhua Domestic Service,* October 27, 1999, in *FBIS* as "Official Urges Major Defense Industry Shakeup," November 3, 1999.

——, "The State Adopts Effective Measures for Improving Quality of National Defense-Related Products," *Xinhua,* March 23, 2000, as translated in *FBIS,* March 23, 2000.

Zhang Yi and Zhang Xiaosong, "Wu Bangguo Calls on China Aerospace Science and Technology Corporation to Make New Contributions to China's Aerospace Undertaking," *Xinhua,* August 13, 2002, in *FBIS* as "Wu Bangguo Sends Letter to China Aerospace Science, Technology Corp. on Occasion of Its 2nd Work Meeting," August 13, 2002.

Zhang Yi and Zhang Yusheng, "Continue to Maintain PRC Aerospace Industry's Leading Position—an Interview with Wang Liheng, President of the China Aerospace Science and Technology Corporation," *Xinhua,* November 11, 2000, in *FBIS,* November 11, 2000.

——, "Speed Up Marketing of High-Tech Aerospace Products— Interview with General Manager Xia Guohong of China Aerospace Machinery and Electric Equipment Group," *Xinhua,* November 12, 2000, in *FBIS,* November 12, 2000.

Zhang Yihao and Zhou Zongkui, "China's Science, Technology, and Industry for National Defense Face Up to WTO—an Interview with Liu Jibin, Minister in Charge of the Commission of Science, Technology, and Industry for National Defense," *Jiefangjun bao* (Internet version) March 13, 2000, in *FBIS* as "WTO Impact on PRC Defense Industry," March 14, 2000.

Zhang Zhaozhong, "Master New Development Trends of Military Equipment," *Jiefangjun bao,* April 14, 1998.

Zhang Zhiqian and Wang Shibin, "Creating the World's Top-Class Aerospace Corporation—Interview with Wang Liheng, President of China Aerospace Science and Technology Group," *Jiefangjun bao,* May 1, 2000, in *FBIS,* May 1, 2000.

Zhao Huanxin, *China Daily* (Internet version), December 19, 2000, in *FBIS* as "China Daily: Military Technology Transfer to Spur Growth in Civilian Sector," December 19, 2000.

Zheng Wei, "Fengyun-4: Gaze Upon the Earth After 10 Years," *Wen hui bao,* September 6, 2002, in *FBIS* as "PRC S&T: Fengyun-4 Meteorological Satellite to Launch in 10 Years," September 6, 2002.

Zheng Wei and Zhang Jie, "Long March Rockets, Developed by Shanghai Aerospace Bureau, Achieve 20 Successful Consecutive Launches; 'Long March' Rockets Never Miss Target," *Wen hui bao,* October 21, 1999, in *FBIS* as "Shanghai Space Unit Sets Record in Long March Launches," October 21, 1999.

Zhong Aihua, "New Weapons Compete for Attention at International Defense Electronics Exhibition," *Xinhua,* April 1, 2002, in *FBIS* as "Defense Electronics Exhibition Presents New PRC Air Defense Equipment," April 3, 2002.

Zhongguo hangkong bao, February 9, 2001.

Zhongguo hangtian, No. 7, July 1997, pp. 3–4, in *FBIS* as "Additional Details on Launch of FY-II Geo-stationary Meteorological Satellite," July 1, 1997.

———, October 1, 2002, in *FBIS* as "PRC S&T: CASIC Displays New Aerospace Products," October 1, 2002.

Zhongguo Wen She, "China's Military Science and Technology Develop by Leaps and Bounds," *Renmin ribao* (Internet version), July 27, 2000, in *FBIS* as "PRC Claims Military Science, Technology Becoming More 'Dependable'," July 27, 2000.

Zhou Chengqiang, "Hoisting the Sails While the Wind Is Fair— Interviewing Huang Pingtao, President of the CSIC," *Jiefangjun bao,* April 3, 2000, as translated in *FBIS*, April 3, 2000.

Zhou Jiahe, "Zeng Qinghong Inspects No. 061 Base, Encouraging the Base to Make Greater Contributions to the Modernization of National Defense," *Zhongguo hangtian bao,* April 18, 2003, in *FBIS* as "PRC S&T: Zeng Qinghong Inspects 061 Aerospace Plant," April 18, 2003.

Zhou Jiahe and Zhu Shide, "Jiangnan Aerospace Group Revived Through Great Efforts," *Guizhou ribao,* September 14, 2000, in *FBIS*, September 14, 2000.

Zhou Rixin, *Hangkong zhishi,* November 6, 2000, in *FBIS* as "PRC Aircraft Designer Cheng Bushi Profiled," November 6, 2000.

Zhou Yuan, "Reform and Restructuring of China's Science and Technology System," in Denis Fred Simon, ed., *The Emerging Technological Trajectory of the Pacific Rim,* Armonk, N.Y.: M. E. Sharpe, 1995.

Zhu Qinglin, *Zhongguo Caijun yu Guofang Zirenmimbi Peizhi Yanjiu,* Beijing, China: National Defense University Press, 1999.

Zhu Zhaowu, "Pushing Forward Reform of Administrative Logistics, Promoting Development of Aerospace Industry," *Jingji ribao,* February 19, 1999, in *FBIS* as "Aerospace Administrative Logistics Reform," February 19, 1999.

"Zhuyao Zhize" ("Primary Responsibilities"). Available at COSTIND website, http://www.costind.gov.cn/htm/jgjj/zyzz.asp; accessed July 19, 2004.

Zou Fanggen and Fan Juwei, "Chinese Army's Armament, Scientific Research, and Procurement System Insists on Simultaneously Promoting Development of Scientific Research and Cultivation of Skilled Personnel," *Jiefangjun bao* (Internet version), February 19, 2002, in *FBIS* as "PRC: PLA Implements Measures to Simultaneously Train Personnel, Develop New Weaponry," February 19, 2002.